THE NYÂYA SÛTRAS OF GOTAMA

THE
NYÂYA SÛTRAS OF GOTAMA

Translated by
M.M. SATISA CHANDRA VIDYÂBHÛṢANA

Revised & Edited by
NANDALAL SINHA

MOTILAL BANARSIDASS PUBLISHERS
PRIVATE LIMITED • DELHI

First Edition: *Allahabad, 1930*
Reprinted: Delhi, 1990

ISBN: 81-208-0748-0

Also available at:
MOTILAL BANARSIDASS
41 U.A., Bungalow Road, Jawahar Nagar, Delhi 110 007
120 Royapettah High Road, Mylapore, Madras 600 004
24 Race Course Road, Bangalore 560 001
Ashok Rajpath, Patna 800 004
Chowk, Varanasi 221 001

PRINTED IN INDIA
BY JAINENDRA PRAKASH JAIN AT SHRI JAINENDRA PRESS, A-45 NARAINA INDUSTRIAL AREA, PHASE I, NEW DELHI 110 028 AND PUBLISHED BY NARENDRA PRAKASH JAIN FOR MOTILAL BANARSIDASS PUBLISHERS PVT. LTD., BUNGALOW ROAD, JAWAHAR NAGAR, DELHI 110 007.

IN MEMORIAM

Major Vâmanadâsa Vasu,

I. M. S. (Retired),

Scholar, Saint and Philosopher,

the versatile Editor of

The Sacred Books of the Hindus,

the Author of

The Indian Medicinal Plants,

The Historian of India,

this work

is humbly dedicated

as a mark of

Everlasting Love and Reverence.

TABLE OF CONTENTS.

Page.

INTRODUCTION I

BOOK I, CHAPTER I.

The Sixteen categories 1
Release (अपवर्ग) 2
Means of knowledge (प्रमाण) 3
Perception (प्रत्यक्ष) 3
Inference (अनुमान) 4
Comparison (उपमान) 4
Word or verbal testimony (शब्द) defined 5
Objects of knowledge (प्रमेय) 5
Soul (आत्मन्) defined 6
Body (शरीर) defined 6
Sense (इन्द्रिय) defined 6
Element (भूत) defined 7
Qualities (गुण) of earth, etc. 7
Intellect (बुद्धि) defined 7
Mind (मनः) defined 7
Activity (प्रवृत्ति) defined and explained 8
Fault (दोष) defined 8
Transmigration (प्रेत्यभाव) defined 9
Fruit (फल) defined 9
Pain (दुःख) defined 9
Release (अपवर्ग) defined 9
Doubt (संशय) defined and explained 10
Purpose (प्रयोजन) defined 11
Example or familiar instance (दृष्टान्त) 11
Tenet (सिद्धान्त) defined 11
A dogma of all the Schools (सर्व्वतन्त्रसिद्धान्त) 12
A dogma peculiar to some School (प्रतितन्त्रसिद्धान्त) ... 12
A hypothetical dogma (अधिकरणसिद्धान्त) 12
An implied dogma (अभ्युपगमसिद्धान्त) 13

Page.

Members of a syllogism (अवयव) 13
Proposition (प्रतिज्ञा) .. .. — .. 14
Reason (हेतु) 14
Homogeneous or affirmative reason (साधर्म्यहेतु) 14
Heterogeneous or negative reason(वैधर्म्यहेतु) 15
Example (उदाहरण) 15
Homogeneous or affirmative example (साधर्म्योदाहरण) ... 15
Heterogeneous or negative example (वैधर्म्योदाहरण)... ... 15
Application, affirmative and negative (उपनय) 16
Conclusion (निगमन) 17
Confutation (तर्क) 17
Ascertainment (निर्णय) 17

BOOK I, CHAPTER II.

Discussion (वाद) 19
Wrangling (जल्प) 20
Cavil (वितण्डा) 20
Fallacies of reason (हेत्वाभास) 21
The erratic (सव्यभिचार) 21
The contradictory (विरुद्ध) 21
The controversial or equal to the question (प्रकरणसम) ... 22
The reciprocal or unproved (साध्यसम) 22
The mistimed (कालातीत) 23
Quibble (छल) 23
Quibble in respect of a term (वाक्छल) 24
Quibble in respect of a genus (सामान्यछल) 24
Quibble in respect of a metaphor (उपचारछल) 25
Futility (जाति) 26
An occasion for rebuke (निग्रहस्थान) 27

BOOK II, CHAPTFR I.

Doubt (संशय) examined 29
The means and objects of knowledge (प्रमाण-प्रमेय) examined... 32
Perception (प्रत्यक्ष) examined 38
Special kinds of knowledge (ज्ञानविशेष) 40
The relation of perception and inference (प्रत्यक्षमनुमानम्) ... 41
The whole (अवयविन्) and its parts (अवयव) 42

Page.
Inference (अनुमान) examined 43
The time present, past and future (वर्तमान, अतीत, अनागत) examined44
Comparison (उपमान) exmined 46
Word or verbal testimony (शब्द) examined 48
The Veda (वेद) examined 50
Injunction (विधि) 52
Persuasion (अर्थवाद) 53
Praise (स्तुति) 53
Blame (निन्दा) 53
Warning (परकृति) 53
Prescription (पुराकल्प) 53
Reinculcation (अनुवाद) 53
Tautology (पुनरुक्त) 54
The Medical Science (आयुर्वेद) 54

BOOK II, CHAPTER II.

Means of knowledge (प्रमाण) examined 55
Rumour (ऐतिह्य) 55
Presumption (अर्थापत्ति) 55
Probability (सम्भव) 55
Non-existence (अभाव) 55
The nature of sound (शब्द) examined 59
Otherness (अन्यत्व) 65
Letters, their modifications and substitutes (वर्णविकार) ... 69
Word (पद) 75
Individual (व्यक्ति) 75
Form (आकृति) 75
Genus (जाति) 75

BOOK III, CHAPTER I.

Sense (इन्द्रिय) is not soul(आत्मन्) 80
Body (शरीर) is not soul (आत्मन्) 81
Duality of the eye (चक्षु:) 82
Remembrance (स्मृति) 84
Mind (मन:) is not soul (आत्मन्) 85
The soul (आत्मन्) established 86
The body (शरीर) is earthy 88

Page.
The eye-ball (कृष्णसार) is material 90
The senses (इन्द्रिय) are material (भौतिक) 92
The eye (चक्षुः) and its ray (रश्मिः) 92
The senses (इन्द्रिय) are more than one 96
Touch (त्वक्) 97
The senses are five (पञ्चेन्द्रिय) 98
The qualities of the elements (भूतगुण) 100

BOOK III, CHAPTER II.

Intellect or knowledge (बुद्धि) is not eternal 105
Knowledge is not momentary 108
The nature of knowledge (ज्ञान)... 111
Recollection (स्मृति) 115
Desire and aversion (इच्छाद्वेष) 117
The mind (मनः) is not the seat of knowledge 119
Memory (स्मरण) and its causes 120
Knowledge (ज्ञान) is not a natural quality of the body ... 124
Non-simultaneousness of knowledge (ज्ञानायौगपद्य) 127
The mind (मनः) is atomic (अणु) 128
Desert (पूर्व्वकृतफल) producing the body 128

BOOK IV, CHAPTER I.

Activity (प्रवृत्ति) 133
Faults (दोष) 133
Stupidity (मोह) 134
Transmigration (प्रेत्यभाव) 135
Entity does not arise from non-entity (न अभावाद् भावोत्पत्तिः) ... 136
God (ईश्वरः) 138
Production from no-cause (अनिमित्ततो भावोत्पत्तिः) 139
All are not non-eternal (न सर्व्वमनित्यम्) 140
All are not eternal (न सर्व्वं नित्यम्) 141
All are not distinct (न सर्व्वं पृथक्)... 142
Self-existence (स्वभावसिद्धि) and relative non-existence (इतरेतराभाव)144
No fixity of number (संख्यैकान्तासिद्धि) 146
Fruit (फल) examined 147
Pain (दुःख) examined 151

Page.
Release (अपवर्ग) examined 152
Debts and troubles (ऋण क्लेश) 152

BOOK IV, CHAPTER II.

The rise of true knowledge (तत्त्वज्ञानोत्पत्ति) 157
The whole and its parts (अवयवावयविन्) 157
Atom (अणु) 162
The non-reality of things (भावानां याथात्म्यानुपलब्धिः) ... 165
False apprehension (मिथ्योपलब्धिः) 168
Meditation (समाधिः) 170
Discussion, wrangling and cavil (वादजल्पवितण्डाः) 173

BOOK V, CHAPTER I.

Futility (जाति) 174
Balancing the homogeneity (साधर्म्यसमा)... 174
Balancing the heterogeneity (वैधर्म्यसमा) 174
Balancing an addition (उत्कर्षसमा) 176
Balancing a subtraction (अपकर्षसमा) 176
Balancing the questionable (वर्ण्यसमा) 176
Balancing the unquestionable (अवर्ण्यसमा) 176
Balancing the alternative (विकल्पसमा) 176
Balancing the reciprocity (साध्यसमा) 176
Balancing the co-presence (प्राप्तिसमा) 182
Balancing the mutual absence (अप्राप्तिसमा) 182
Balancing the infinite regression (प्रसङ्गसमा) 184
Balancing the counter-example (प्रतिदृष्टान्तसमा) 184
Balancing the non-produced (अनुत्पत्तिसमा) 186
Balancing the doubt (संशयसमा) 187
Balancing the controversy (प्रकरणसमा) 189
Balancing the non-reason (अहेतुसमा) 190
Balancing the presumption (अर्थापत्तिसमा)... 192
Balancing the non-difference (अविशेषसमा) 193
Balancing the demonstration (उपपत्तिसमा) 195
Balancing the perception (उपलब्धिसमा) 196
Balancing the non-perception (अनुपलब्धिसमा) 197
Balancing the non-eternal (अनित्यसमा) 198
Balancing the eternal (नित्यसमा) 200

Page.
Balancing the effect (कार्य्यसमा) 201
Admission of an opinion (मतानुज्ञा) 203
Six-winged disputation (षट्पक्षी कथा) 204

BOOK V, CHAPTER II.

Occasions for rebuke (निग्रहस्थान) 207
Hurting the proposition (प्रतिज्ञाहानि) 208
Shifting the proposition (प्रतिज्ञान्तर) 209
Opposing the proposition (प्रतिज्ञाविरोध) 209
Renouncing the proposition (प्रतिज्ञासंन्यास) 210
Shifting the reason (हेत्वन्तरम्) 210
Shifting the topic (अर्थान्तरम्) 211
The meaningless (निरर्थक) 212
The unintelligible (अविज्ञातार्थ) 212
The incoherent (अपार्थक) 212
The inopportune (अप्राप्तकाल) 213
Saying too little (न्यून) 213
Saying too much (अधिक) 214
Repetition (पुनरुक्तम्) 214
Silence (अननुभाषण) 215
Ignorance (अज्ञान) 216
Non-ingenuity (अप्रतिभा) 216
Evasion (विक्षेप) 216
Admission of an opinion (मतानुज्ञा) 216
Overlooking the censurable (पर्य्यनुयोज्योपेक्षण) 217
Censuring the non-censurable (निरनुयोज्यानुयोग) 217
Deviating from a tenet (अपसिद्धान्त) 218
Fallacies of a reason (हेत्वाभास) 218

FOREWORD.

I

Differences of opinion prevail as to the precise number of the original aphorisms of the Nyâya-Sûtra of Gotama. Mahâmahopâdhyâya Dr. Satîs'a-chandra Vidyâbhûṣaṇa* is inclined to take the extreme view that it is only the first book of the Nyâya-Sûtra containing a brief explanation of the sixteen categories that we are justified in ascribing to Gotama, while the remaining four books bear marks of different hands and ages, the last and most considerable additions having been made by Vâtsyâyana who sought to harmonise the different, and at times conflicting, additions and interpolations by the ingenious introduction of Sûtras of his own making fathered upon Gotama. We are unable to subscribe to this view. The Nyâya-Sûtra is admittedly a *system* of philosophy, and its method, like that of the Vais'eṣika, consists in the enumeration, definition and examination of the categories. You cannot retain the first book, and reject the others, without mutilating the system. As regards the so-called references in the second, third and fourth books to the tenets of the Vais'eṣika, Yoga, Mîmâṃsâ, Vedânta and Buddhist philosophy, it should not be forgotten that every system of thought which has flourished on the soil of India has its source in a common fund of national philosophy, "a large Mânasa lake of philosophical thought and language, far away in the distant North, and in the distant past, from which each thinker was allowed to draw for his own purposes". Similarity of words and ideas here and there is therefore not a safe guide in the determination of the originality or otherwise of one system in relation to another. Moreover, isolated similarity of thought and expression is no ground for the rejection of whole books as spurious. The parallelism between the wording of some of the aphorisms and certain passages in the Lankâvatâra Sûtra, Mâdhyamika Sûtra, and the Śataka is also misleading. For instnace, as observed by Dr. Keith**, on the authority of Winternitz, Gesch. d. ind. Litt., II. i. 243, the Lankâvatâra Sûtra in its present form is not earlier than the sixth century A. D., that is, is later than even Vâtsyâyana.

The Nyâya-Bhâṣya of Vâtsyâyana also presents a most formidable obstacle to the acceptance of the theory propounded by Dr. Vidyâbhûṣaṇa. For it is not confined to the first book alone but covers the other books as well. The difficulty can be overcome only by denying the authentic character of the Bhâṣya in its present form. And this is exactly what Dr. Vidyâbhûṣaṇa has done. We are not aware of any good reason for doubting the genuineness of the Bhâṣya as it has come down to us. Let us examine

* Introduction, page X.

** Indian Logic and Atomism, by A. B. Keith, 1921, page 23.

Dr. Vidyâbhûṣaṇa's reasons. He translates aphorism II. i. 29 (II .i. 28 of the Bibliotheca Indica series edition) as follows : "It may be objected that the contact of a sense with its object is not the cause of perception, as it is inefficient in some instances", and then proceeds :

"An objector may say that the contact of a sense with its object is not the cause of perception, as we find that a person listening to a song may not see colour, though it comes in contact with his eye.

"Vâtsyâyana interprets the aphorism as follows :—If the conjunction of soul with mind is not accepted as the cause of perception a well-known conclusion will be debarred, viz., the mark of the mind is that only one act of knowledge is possible at a time. This interpretation, here inappropriate, is based on the Bhâṣya-commentary published by the Asiatic Society of Bengal in 1865. I fully agree with those who hold that the real Bhâṣya-commentary of Vâtsyâyana is not yet available to us."

Similarly he translates the next aphorism as follows : "It is not so, because there is pre-eminence of some particular object", and proceeds :

"It is admitted that a person while listening to a song may not see colour, though it comes in contact with his eye. Yet the instance does not prove that the contact of a sense with its object is not the cause of perception, for it is to be understood that his intent listening prevents him from seeing the colour. In other words, the auditory perception supersedes the visual perception, because the song is more attractive than the colour.

"Vâtsyâyana interprets the aphorism thus :—The conjunction of the soul with mind is not rendered useless, even if there is predominance of the senses and their objects. If perception is produced when a person is asleep or inattentive, it is because there is then the predominance of his sense and its object, though even then there is a faint conjunction of soul with mind. This interpretation is based on the Bhâṣya-commentary as available to us. It is ingenious but out of place here."

With due respect to the memory of the distinguished critic we submit that he has not been quite fair in his representation of the Nyâya-Bhâṣya on these two aphorisms. In the translation and explanation which we have felt constrained to substitute in the text in place of the above we have tried to show what Vâtsyâyana exactly means. It will be seen that Vâtsyâyana's interpretation of the two aphorisms is not necessarily inappropriate or out of place. It also goes without saying that for a pseudo-Vâtsyâyana who could produce a Bhâṣya which has commanded universal respect through all the ages, it would not have been difficult to avoid such inappropriateness as is alleged, or to grasp the more obvious interpretation which he is supposed to have missed. Moreover, it is well-known that uncertainties as to the correct reading of the Nyâya-Sûtra and the Nyâya-Bhâṣya have given rise to two different schools of interpretation from very early times. One of these schools is represented by Tâtparya-París'uddhi and Nyâya-Parisi'ṣṭa of Udayanâchârya and Paris'uddhi-Prakâs'a and Anvîkṣâ-Naya-Tattvabodha of Vardhamâna Upâdhyâya ; the other school, by Tâtparya-Tîkâ and Nyâya-Sûchî-Nibandha of Vâchaspati Mis'ra. Mere difference of opinion as to the appropriateness of the Bhâṣya here and there cannot, therefore, be accepted as a sufficient reason for questioning the authenticity of the Bhâṣya in its present form. On the other hand, the Bhâṣya has been accepted as genuine in all the seats of Sanskrit learning in India, and, among modern researchers in the field, by Mahâmahopâdhyâyas Chandrakânta Tarkâlankâra, Bhîmâchârya Jhalkikar, Gangâdhara Śâstrî Tailanga, and Dr. Ganganâtha Jhâ. Even amongst European orientalists Dr. Herrman Jacobi does not doubt that the author of the complete Nyâya-Bhâṣya is one and the same person. Dr. Keith also is convinced that there is no evidence of any corruption of the text of the Nyâya-Bhâṣya, and that the suggestion that Vâtsyâyana is responsible for remodelling the Nyâya-Sûtra is wholly unsupported by evidence.*

Vâtsyâyana is an ancient Ṛiṣi. By tradition he is regarded as "Bhagavân", "Muni", "Mahâmuni", and "Maharṣi". His date cannot be very far removed from the time when the aphorisms of Gotama were first reduced to writing. Mahâmahopâdhyâya Vâsudeva Śâstri Abhyankar assigns *circa* 300 A. D. to him.** It is therefore reasonable to conclude that all the original aphorisms of Gotama have been preserved in the Nyâya-Bhâṣya of Vâtsyâyana. Difficulties have been experienced from very early times in picking out the Sûtra from the Bhâṣya, particularly in those places where the Bhâṣya does not clearly indicate the Sûtra. These difficulties have been considerably enhanced by the privilege enjoyed by Bhâṣya-writers and undoubtedly exercised by Vâtsyâyana of raising issues and solving them in the course of the Bhâṣya in the form of aphorisms.*** This has misled many scholars in attributing the aphorisms of Vâtsyâyana to Gotama and *vice versa.* The results of such diverse readings are shown below in a tabular form :

1. Reading referred to by M.-M. Chandrakânta Tarkâlankâra in Śrîgopâla Vasumallik Fellowship Lectures on Hindu Philosophy, 1898 ... ... 547 aphorisms.

---

*Indian Logic and Atomism, by A. B. Keith, 1921, pages 25 and 27.

**Sarva-Dars'ana-Sangraha, Government Oriental (Hindu) Series No. 1, Poona, 1924.

***Cf. "The knowers of Bhâṣyas know that to be a Bhâṣya by which is explained the meaning of aphorisms by means of words appropriate to the aphorisms as well as texts of the commentator himself."

2. Publication by the Asiatic Society of Bengal in the Bibliotheca Indica series, 1865 ... 540 aphorisms.
3. According to Nyâyakoṣa by M. M Bhîmâchârya Jhâlkikar, second edition, 1893 (Bombay Sanskrit Series No. XLIX) ... 537 „
4. According to M. M. Dr. Gangânâtha Jhâ in the Nyâya-Dars'ana, Chowkhamba Sanskrit Series, 1920—25 ... ... 532 „
5. According to M. M. Gangâdhara Śâstrî Tailan'ga in the Vizianagram Sanskrit Series, volume IX, 1896 ... ... 531 „
6. According to Nyâyasûchînibandha of Vâchaspati Mis'ra, *circa*. 841 ... 528 „

The diversity of readings, again, is not confined only to the number of the aphorisms, but extends also to the aphorisms themselves; for in regard to particular aphorisms commentators and compilers differ as to whether they are aphorisms or are the assertions of the author of the Bhâṣya. The statement below will explain the position from this point of view. Thus:

Book.	Chapter.	Number of aphorisms according to the edition of the Asiatic Society of Bengal, 1865.	Number rejected by Vâchaspati.	Number added by Vâchaspati.	Number of aphorisms according to Nyâya-Sûchî-Nibandha of Vâchaspati Mis'ra.
I	i	41	*	*	41
	ii	20	*	*	20
II	i	69	2	1	68
	ii	71	3	1	69
III	i	75	6	4	73
	ii	78	6	*	72
IV	i	68	2	1	67
	ii	50	*	1	51
V	i	43	*	*	43
	ii	25	1	*	24
I-V	i-x	540	20	8	528

Since the publication of the Nyâya-Bhâṣya by the Asiatic Society of Bengal a fairly large number of valuable manuscripts have come to light, and the results of recent investigations go to confirm the correctness of the Index to the Aphorisms of Nyâya (Nyâya-Sûchî-Nibandha) by Vâchaspati Mis'ra. We have therefore revised the work of Dr. Vidyâbhûṣaṇa according to, and on the authority of, Vâchaspati. The twenty rejected aphorisms are however retained in appendix B. The eight additional aphorisms bear serial numbers 81, 172, 226, 227, 228, 261, 404 and 461 of the present edition.

M. M. Dr. Gangânâtha Jhâ and Pandit Dhuṇḍirâja Śâstrî have also followed the Nyâya-Sûchî-Nibandha in their edition of the "The Sûtras of Gautama and Bhâṣya of Vâtsyâyana with two Commentaries" published in the Chowkhamba Sanskrit Series, Benares, 1925. They have, however, retained four aphorisms which have been omitted from the Nyâya-Sûchî-Nibandha. The total number of aphorisms according to them is therefore 532 instead of 528. The learned editors have not assigned any specific reasons for treating these four aphoristic statements as aphorisms of Gotama. They merely state that they "feel constrained to deviate from it (*i. e.*, the Nyâya-Sûchî-Nibandha) on the clear authority of either the Bhâṣya or the Vârtika." With due respect for the authority of Dr. Jhâ we are unable to persuade ourselves to be of the same view. The absence of these so-called aphorisms leaves no extraordinary or unsual gap in the line of thought in the aphorisms of Gotama. We are therefore content to follow the lead of M. M. Chandrakânta Tarkâlankâra in accepting Vâchaspati Mis'ra as a reliable guide to the aphorisms of Gotama.

II

In his posthumous work entitled "History of Indian Logic", published by the University of Calcutta in the year 1921, Dr. Vidyâbhûṣaṇa has completely changed his opinions as to the authorship and the date of the composition or compilation of the Nyâya-Sûtras. We give below a resume of the results of his later researches with our comments thereon.

"The word *nyâya* popularly signifies 'right' or 'justice'. The *Nyâya-s'âstra* is therefore the science of right judgment or true reasoning."[1] "Technically the word *nyâya* signifies a syllogism (or a speech of five parts), and the Ânvîkṣikî was called *Nyâya-s'âstra*, when *nyâya* constituted its special topic."[1] "The term 'Nyâya' in the sense of Logic does not appear to have been used in literature before the first century A. D. Pâṇini (about 350 B. C.) did not know the word 'Nyâya' in the sense of Logic."[2] "There is no doubt that Pâṇini derives the word *nyâya* (evidently in the sense of justice) from

1. History of Indian Logic, 1921, page 40.
2. *Ibid.*, page 41.

the root *nî* in his Aṣṭâdhyâyî, 3—3—122, as follows :—अध्याय न्यायोद्यावसंहाराश्च His Aṣṭâdhyâyî, 4—2—60, क्रतुकथादि सूत्रान्ताट्ठक्, does not, however, presuppose *nyâya* in the sense of 'Logic'."[3]

"Medhâtithi Gautama (was) the founder of Ânvîkṣikî *par excellence* (circa 550 B. C.)".[4] He "was quite different from Akṣapâda. While one lived in Mithilâ, the other flourished at Prabhâsa in Kathiawar. The Brahmâṇḍa-purâṇa describes Akṣapâda and Kaṇâda as the sons of a Brâhmaṇa named Soma-Śarmâ who was Śiva incarnate, and well-known for his practice of austerities at the shrine of Prabhâsa during the time of Jâtûkarṇya Vyâsa."[5] "It is by no means easy to determine who was the real author of the Nyâya-sûtra. Gautama and Akṣapâda seem both to have contributed to the production of the work."[6]

The Nyâya-Sûtra "treats of four distinct subjects, viz. (1) the art of debate (*tarka*) (2) the means of valid knowledge *(pramâṇa)*, (3) the doctrine of syllogism *(avayava)*, and (4) the examination of contemporaneous philosophical doctrines (*anyamata-parîksâ*)".[7] The first two subjects, " combined together, constitute the Tarka-s'âstra (the philosophy of reasoning), popularly known as Gautamî-vidyâ (the Gotamide learning)."[7] "The third subject, the doctrine of the Syllogism, does not appear to have been known in India a considerable time before the Christian era. The fourth subject refers to numerous philosophical doctrines that were propounded from time to time upto the second century A. D. Gotama's Tarka-s'âstra, after these two subjects had been introduced into it, became, about the second century A. D., designated as the Nyâya-sûtra, the aphorisms on logic."[7]

" Ananta-yajvan, in his commentary on the Pitṛmedha-sûtra, observes that Gautama and Akṣapâda were the same person, while the Nyâya-koṣa mentions a legend to account for the name as applied, according to it, to Gautama. As no credible evidence has been adduced in either case, I consider the identification as fanciful, and maintain that Gotama or Gautama was quite different from Akṣapâda, but that both of them contributed to the production of the Nyâya-sûtra, one at its early stage and the other in its final form."[8]

---

3. *Ibid*., page 41, footnote 4.
4. *Ibid*., page 17.
5. *Ibid*., page 49.
6. *Ibid*., p. 49.
7. *Ibid*., p. 497.
8. *Ibid*., p. 498.

"Though Akṣapâda introduced into the Nyâya-sûtra the doctrine of the syllogism, he was by no means the first promulgator of the doctrine—nay, not even its first disseminator. The doctrine was carried to great perfection in Greece by Aristotle in the fourth century B. C. (384—322 B. C.). That it was known even in India prior to Akṣapâda is apparent from a notice of the same in the Charaka-saṃhitâ, about 78 A. D."[9]

" Some philosophical doctrines of the third and fourth centuries A. D. were incorporated into the Nyâya-sûtra of Akṣapâda by Vâtsyâyana the first commentator (about 400 A. D.), through the introduction of certain sûtras of his own making fathered upon Akṣapâda."[10]

Thus, according to Dr. Vidyâbhûṣaṇa, " Ancient logic was called *Anvîksiki*, or the science of debate, but with the introduction of syllogism or proper reasoning it came to be called Nyâya from the first century A. D.",[11] and that "The Ancient School, which reached the height of its development at the hands of Akṣapâda about 150 A. D., extended over a period of one thousand years, beginning with Gautama about 550 B.C. and ending with Vâtsyâyâna about 400 A. D."[12]

III

It is gratifying to find that Dr. Vidyâbhûṣaṇa has discarded his former opinion that only the first book of the Nyâya-sûtra is the work of Gotama, while the remaining four books bear marks of different hands and ages. His opinion now is that Gotama's "work on Ânvîkṣikî has not come down to us in its original form,"[13] and that Akṣapâda is " the real author of the Nyâya-sûtra which derived a considerable part of its materials from the Ânvîkṣikî-vidyâ of Gautama."[14]. We have already explained why the charge against Vâtsayâyana, viz., that he interpolated into the Nyâya-sûtra aphorisms of his own making fathered upon Akṣapâda, must be rejected. The theory, again, that Gotama and Akṣapâda are two different persons is equally unsound. Dr. Vidyâbhûṣaṇa is wrong in supposing that Akṣapâda and Kaṇâda were sons of Soma-s'armâ. The word 'sons' in the text of the Brahmâṇḍa Purâṇa means disciples. There is also no inconsistency in Gotama, born in Mithilâ, proceeding to Prabhâsa for education. The identity of Gotama and Akṣapâda does not admit of doubt. Dr. Vidyâbhûṣaṇa himself has fully established it in the Introduction. We shall only point out that the commentators on Amara-koṣa : Naiyâyikaḥ tu akṣapâdaḥ", explain that Akṣapâda, Âkṣapâda—

---

[9] *Ibid.*, pp. 498—499.

[10] *Ibid.*, p. 497, foot note 3.

[11] *Ibid.*, Introduction, p. xvi.

[12] *Ibid.*, p. 157.

[13] *Ibid.*, p. 20.

[14] *Ibid.*, p. 50.

these two are the names of Gotama who holds that the number of Predicables is sixteen, viz., Pramâṇa, Prameya, Saṃs'aya, etc.

Dr. Vidyâbhuṣaṇa seems to us to have been induced to change his opinion as to the authorship and the date of the composition or compliation of the Nyâya-Sûtra by the idea that the doctrine of the syllogism was imported into India from Greece. We propose, therefore, to discuss this point, not fully, but in some detail. Dr. Vidyâbhûṣaṇa's reference to Páṇini is incomplete. Pânini does not use the word " Nyâya" in the sense of justice only. In Aṣṭâdhyâyî, I. 3.36 सम्माननोत् सञ्जना चार्य करण ज्ञानभृति विगणन व्ययेषु नियः the root nî is said to take the âtmanepada form of conjugation when it is used in one or other of the seven senses mentioned therein. One of these senses is Jñâna, knowledge. The commentators explain Jñâna as Prameyanis'chaya, ascertainment of the object of right knowledge. They also illustrate the use of the verb in this sense thus : Tattvam nayate, demonstrates or verifies the truth. It is therefore idle to argue that Pâṇini did not know the word "Nyâya" in the sense of Logic. And Pâṇini is as old as "Most probably the seventh century B. C. in my opinion, for which good authority might be cited" (Ancient and Hindu India by V. A. Smith, second edition, 1923, page 57, footnote 1).

Again, according to Dr. Vidyâbhûṣaṇa, the old Ânvîkṣikî was called Nyâya-Śâstra when Nyâya in the technical sense of the syllogism came to constitute its special topic, *i.e.*, about the second century A. D. This argument is demolished by Bhâsa's reference to "Medhâtitheḥ Nyâyas'âstram", the Nyâya-Śâstra of Medhâtithi, in his drama *Pratimâ*. Dr. Vidyâbhûṣaṇa seeks to get out of the difficulty by observing that by "Nyâya-s'âstra" Bhâsa "really meant its prototype the Ânvîkṣikî." But the question is not what Bhâsa really meant, but that the term Nyâya-Śâstra in the sense of Logic was prevalent in the days of Bhâsa whereas, according to Dr. Vidyâbhûṣaṇa, it came into use about the second century A. D. And Bhâsa, in the opinion of M.-M. Pandit Gaṇapati Śâstrî, is even older than Pâṇini (vide his introduction to *Pratimâ* nâṭaka).

Dr. Keith shows a more correct appreciation of the position of Indian Logic *vis a vis* the Logic of Greece. He says : "Of logical doctrine in its early stages there is no reason whatever to suspect a Greek origin : the syllogism of Gautama and Kaṇâda alike is obviously of natural growth, but of stunted development. It is with Dignâga only that the full doctrine of invariable concomitance as the basis of inference in lieu of reasoning by analogy appears, and it is not unreasonable to hazard the suggestion that in this case again Greek influence may have been at work. But the possibility of a natural development is not excluded......"[15]

---

15. Indian Logic and Atomism, 1921, p. 18.

But we do not agree with the learned Doctor that the doctrine of invariable concomitance was unknown to Indian Logic before the time of Dignâga. We apprehend that he has missed the full significance and the true function of the *example* in the syllogism. The reasoning of Kaṇâda and Gotama was not merely from particular to particular and their *example* was not a mere particular experience. Generally, as Welton points out, "even in cases where the inference at first sight seems to be founded on one or more particular experiences, it is really based on the recognition of the universal element in which they agree ; and this may be expressed in a general proposition which forms the major premise of a syllogism"[16]. The need for the universal was fully recognised by Kaṇâda and Gotama. They do not draw their conclusion from the *example* alone, but from the *reason* as well. The function of the *example* and the *reason* have also been distinguished by Kaṇâda. According to him inference is based on the relation of "It is its' between the *subject* and the *reason*, and this relation can be grasped by the intellect and not by the sense. He has also explained (Vais'eṣika-Sûtra, III. i. 14) that the mark of inference must be preceded by the recollection of its universal relation *(prasiddhi)* to that of which it is a mark. The Vais'eṣika-Sûtra is older than the Nyâya-Sûtra. It is clear therefore that the doctrine of the universal relation was not borrowed from Greece.

N. S.

---

16. Intermediate Logic by J. Welton and A. J. Monahan, 1911, p. 271.

INTRODUCTION.

I.—GOTAMA THE FOUNDER OF NYAYA PHILOSOPHY.

The word "Nyâya explained.

Pâṇini, the celebrated Sanskrit grammarian, who is supposed to have flourished about 350 B. C.,* derives the word "Nyâya"† from the root "i" which conveys the same meaning as "gam"—to go. "Nyâya" as signifying logic is therefore etymologically identical with "nigama" the conclusion of a syllogism. Logic is designated in Sanskrit not only by the word "Nyâya" but also by various other words which indicate diverse aspects of the science. For instance, it is called "Hetu-vidyâ"‡ or "Hetu-Śâstra" the science of causes, "Ânvîkṣikî"§ the science of inquiry, "Pramâṇa-Śâstra" the science of correct knowledge, "Tattva-Śâstra" the science of categories, "Tarka-vidyâ" the science of reasoning, "Vâdârtha" the science of discussion and "Phakkikâ-

---

*Paṇini is said to have been a disciple of Upavarṣa, minister of a King of the Nanda dynasty, about 350 B. C., as is evident from the following :—

अथ कालेन वर्षस्य शिष्यवर्गो महानभूत् ।
तत्र एकः पाणिनिर्नाम जडबुद्धितरोऽभवत् ॥

(Kathâsarit-sâgara, Chapter IV., verse 20).

Dr. Otto Bœhtlingk observes :—

"We need therefore only make a space of fifty years between each couple of them, in order to arrive at the year 350, into the neighbourhood of which date our grammarian is to be placed, according to the Kathâsarit-sâgara."—Goldstucker's Pâṇini, p. 85.

† अध्यायन्यायोद्यावसंहाराश्च ।

(Paṇini's Aṣṭâdhyâyî 3-3-122.)

‡ निर्घण्टौ निगमे पुराणे इतिहासे वेदे व्याकरणे निरुक्ते शिक्षायां छन्दसि यज्ञकल्पे ज्योतिषि सांख्ये योगे क्रियाकल्पे वैशेषिके वैशिके अर्थविद्यायां बार्हस्पत्ये आश्चर्ये आसुरे मृगपक्षिरुते हेतुविद्यायां जतुयन्त्रे........सर्वत्र बोधिसत्त्व एव विशिष्यते स्म ॥

(Lalitavistara, Chapter XII., p. 179, Dr. Rajendra Lal Mitra's edition).

§ आन्वीक्षिकी दण्डनीतिस्तर्कविद्यार्थशास्त्रयोः ।

(Amarakoṣa, svargavarga, verse 155).

Śâstra" the science of sophism. Nyâya-sûtra is the earliest work extant on Nyâya Philosophy.

The founder of Nyâya called Gotama, Gautama, Akṣapâda or Dîrghatapas.

The Nyâya or logic is said to have been founded by a sage named Gotama.* He is also known as Gautama, Akṣapâda† and Dîrghatapas.‡ The names Gotama and Gautama point to the family to which he belonged while the names Akṣapâda and Dîrghatapas refer respectively to his meditative habit and practice of long penance.

The family of Gotama.

In the Ṛigveda-saṃhitâ as well as the Śathapatha-Brâhmaṇa of the white Yajurveda we find mention of one Gotama who was son of Rahûgaṇa § and priest of the Royal family of Kuru-sṛiñjaya for whose victory in battle he

---

*मुक्तये यः शिलात्वाय शास्त्रमूचे महामुनिः ।
गोतमं तमवेतैव यथा वित्थ तथैव सः ॥

(Naiṣadhacharitam 17-75.)

कणादेन तु सम्प्रोक्तं शास्त्रं वैशेषिकं महत् ।
गोतमेन तथा न्यायं सांख्यं तु कपिलेन वै ॥

(Padmapurâṇa, Uttarakhaṇḍa, Chapter 263.)

गोतमः स्वेन तर्केण खण्डयन् तत्र तत्र हि ।

(Skanda-purâṇa, Kâlikâ Khaṇḍa, Chapter XVII.)

†यदक्षपादः प्रवरो मुनीनाम् शमाय शास्त्रं जगतो जगाद ।
कुतार्किकाज्ञाननिवृत्तिहेतुः करिष्यते तत्र मया निबन्धः ॥

(Udyotakâra's Nyâyavârtika, opening lines.)

In the Sarvadars'ana-saṃgraha Nyâya philosophy is called the Akṣapâda system.

‡Kâlidâsa's Raghuvaṃs'am 11-33.

§ अत्रेदमाख्यानम् । रहूगणपुत्रो गोतमः कुरु सृंजयानां राज्ञां पुरोहित आसीत् । तेषां राज्ञां परैः सह युद्धे सति स ऋषिरनेन सूक्तेनेन्द्रं स्तुत्वा स्वकीयानां जयं प्रार्थयामासेति । तस्य च तत्पुरोहितत्वं वाजसनेयिभिराम्नातम् । गोतम ह वै राहूगण उभयेषां कुरु सृंजयानां पुरोहित आसीत् ।

(Ṛigveda-saṃhitâ, Maṇḍala 1, Sûkta 81, Mantra 3, Sâyaṇa's commentary).

विदेघो ह माथवोऽग्निं वैश्वानरं मुखे बभार ।
तस्य गोतमो राहूगण ऋषिः पुरोहित आस ॥

(Śatapatha Brâhmaṇa of the white Yajurveda, Kâṇḍa 1, Adhyâya 4 Mâdhyandinîya recension.)

prayed to Indra. Nodhâḥ, * son of Gotama, was also called Gotama who composed several new hymns in honour of Indra. The sages sprung from the family of Gotama are designated Gotamâsaḥ † who were very intelligent ; and Agni, pleased with their adoration, gave them cattle and rice in abundance. It is related that Gotama, once pinched with thirst, prayed for water of the Marut-Gods, who out of mercy, placed a well‡ before him transplanted from elsewhere. The water gushing out copiously from the well not only quenched his thirst but formed itself into a river, the source of which was the seat of the original well.

The teachers called Gautama.

In the Ṛigveda-saṃhitâ the descendants of Gotama as already noticed are also called Gotama while in later Vedic literature they are called Gautama. The Vaṃsa-Brâhmaṇa of the Sâmaveda mentions four members of the Gotama family§ among the teachers who transmitted that

---

*सनायते गोतम इन्द्र नव्यमतक्षद्ब्रह्म हरियोजनाय ।
सुनीथाय नः शवसान नोधाः प्रातर्मक्षू धिया वसुर्जगम्यात् ॥
(Ṛigveda-saṃhitâ, Maṇḍala 1, Sûkta 63, Mantra 13.)

†एवा ते हरियोजना सुवृक्तीन्द्र ब्रह्माणि गोतमासो अक्रन् ।
(Ṛigveda-saṃhitâ, Maṇḍala 1, Sûkta 61, Mantra 16).

एवाग्निर्गोतमेभिर्ऋतावा विप्रेभिरस्तोष्ट जातवेदाः ।
स एषु द्युम्नं पीपयत् स वाजं स पुष्टिं याति जोषमाचिकित्वान् ॥
(Ṛigeda-saṃhitá, Maṇḍala 77, Sûkta 77, Mantra 5).

‡जिह्मं नुनुद्रेऽवतं तया दिशासिंचन्नुत्सं गोतमाय तृष्णजे ।
आगच्छंतीमवसा चित्रभानवः कामं विप्रस्य तर्पयंत धामभिः ॥
(Ṛigveda-saṃhitá, Maṇḍala 1, Sûkta 85, Mantra 11.)

Sâyaṇa in commenting on Ṛigveda saṃhitâ, Maṇḍala 1, Sûkta 77, Mantra 10, observes :—

अत्रेयमाख्यायिका । गोतम ऋषिः पिपासया पीड़ितः सन् मरुत उदकं ययाचे । तदनंतरं मरुतोऽदूरस्थं कूपमुद्धृत्य यत्र स गोतम ऋषिस्तिष्ठति तां दिशं नीत्वा ऋषिसमीपे कूपमवस्थाप्य तत्पार्श्वं आहावं च कृत्वा तस्मिन्नाहावे कूपमुत्सिच्य तमृषिं तेनोदकेन तर्पयांचक्रुः । अयमर्थोऽनया उत्तरया च प्रतिपद्यते ।

The well (utsadhi) is alluded to in the Ṛigveda, Maṇḍala 1, Sûkta 88, Mantra 4, thus :—

अहानि गृध्राः पर्या व आगुरिमां धियं वार्कार्यां च देवीं ।
ब्रह्म कृण्वंतो गोतमासो अर्कैरूर्ध्वं नुनुद्र उत्सधिं पिबध्यै ॥

§ राधाच्च गौतमाद्राधो गौतमो गातुर्गौतमात् पितुर्गाता गौतमः ।
Sâmavedîya Vaṃs'a-Brâhmaṇa, Khaṇḍa 2, Satyavrata Sâmâs'rami's edition, p. 7.)

Veda to posterity, *viz.*, the Râdha-Gautama, Gâtṛi-Gautama, Sumantabâbhrava-Gautama and Saṃkara-Gautama, and the Chhândogya Upaniṣad of the same Veda mentions another teacher named Hâridrumata-Gautama* who was approached by Satya-Kâma Jâvâla to be his teacher. The Gobhila Gṛihya Sûtra of the Sâmaveda cites the opinion of a Gautama † who held that during the winter season there should be three oblations offered to the dead ancestors. Another Gautama was the author of the Pitṛimedha Sûtra‡ which perhaps belongs to the Sâmaveda. The Bṛihadâraṇyaka § of the white Yajurveda mentions a teacher named Gautama, while in the Kaṭhopaniṣad of the Black Yajurveda the sage Nâchiketas|| who conversed with Yama on the mystery of life, is called Gautama which evidently is a generic name as his father is also called Gautama in the same work. A Gautama ¶ is mentioned as a teacher in the Kauśika sûtra

---

सुमन्ताद् बाभ्रवाद् गौतमात् सुमन्तो बाभ्रवो गौतमः ।

(Sâmavedîya Vaṃs'a-Brâhmaṇa, Khaṇḍa 2).

संकराद् गौतमात् संकरो गौतमः ।

(Sâmavedîya Vaṃs'a-Brâhmaṇa, Khaṇḍa 3.)

* स ह हारिद्रुमतं गौतममेत्योवाच ब्रह्मचर्यं भगवति वत्स्याम्युपेयां भगवन्तमिति ॥ ३ ॥

(Chhândogya Upaniṣad, Adhyâya 4, Khaṇḍa 4).

† चतुरष्टको हेमन्तः ॥ ४ ॥

त्र्यष्टक इत्यौद्गाहमानिः ॥ ७ ॥

तथा गौतमवार्कखण्डी ॥ ८ ॥

(Gobhila Gṛihya Sûtra, 3-10.)

‡ An incomplete manuscript of the Pitṛimedha Sûtra is contained in the Library of the Calcutta Sanskrit College, but the work was printed in America several years ago.

§गौतमाद् गौतमः ॥ १ । २ । ३ ॥

(Bṛihadáraṇyaka, Adhyâya 4.)

|| हन्त त इदं प्रवक्ष्यामि गुह्यं ब्रह्म सनातनम् ।

यथा च मरणं प्राप्य आत्मा भवति गौतम ॥ ६ ॥

(Kaṭhopaniṣad, Valli 5.)

शान्तसंकल्पः सुमना यथा स्याद्वीतमन्युर्गौतमो माभिमृत्यो ।

त्वत् प्रसृष्टं माभिवदेत् प्रतीत एतत् त्रयाणां प्रथमं वरं वृणे ।

(Kaṭhopaniṣad, Valli 5.)

¶ Vide Weber's History of Indian Literature, p. 153.

of the Atharvaveda while to another Gautama is attributed the authorship of the Gautama Dharma sûtra* an authoritative work on the sacred law.

We need not take any notice of one Gautama† who, at the bidding of his mother, as stated in the Mahábhárata, cast into the Ganges his old and blind father Dîrghatamas who was however miraculously saved.

Gautama, husband of Ahalyâ.

The Râmâyaṇa mentions a Gautama‡ who had his hermitage in a grove at the outskirts of the city of Mithilâ where he lived with his wife Ahalyâ. It is well-known how Ahalyâ, for her seduction by Indra, was cursed by her lord to undergo penace and mortification until her emancipation at the happy advent of Râma. The Adhyâtma Râmâyaṇa, while repeating the same account, places the hermitage of Gautama§ on the banks of the Ganges ; and our great poet Kâlidâsa follows the Râmâyaṇic legend describing Gautama‖ as Dîrghatapas, a sage who practised long penance.

---

* The text of the Gautama Dharma-sûtra has been printed several times in India while an English translation of it by Dr. G. Bûhler has appeared in the Sacred Books of the East Series.

† स वै दीर्घतमा नाम शापादृषिरजायत ॥ २२ ॥
जात्यन्धो वेदवित् प्राज्ञः पत्नीं लेभे स विद्यया ॥ २३ ॥
तरुणीं रूप सम्पन्नां प्रद्वेषीं नाम ब्राह्मणीम् ।
स पुत्रान् जनयामास गौतमादीन् महायशाः ॥ २४ ॥
(Mahâbhârata, Âdiparva Adhyâya 104).

‡ मिथिलोपवने तत्र आश्रमं दृश्य राघवः ।
पुराणं निर्जनं रम्यं पप्रच्छ मुनिपुङ्गवम् ॥ ११ ॥
इदमाश्रमसंकाशं किं न्विदं मुनिवर्जितम् ।
श्रोतुमिच्छामि भगवन् कस्यायम्पूर्व आश्रमः ॥ १२ ॥
गौतमस्य नरश्रेष्ठ पूर्वमासीन्महात्मनः ।
आश्रमो दिव्यसंकाशः सुरैरपि सुपूजितः ॥ १५ ॥
Râmáyaṇa, Âdikâṇḍa, Sarga 48).

§ इत्युक्त्वा मुनिभिस्ताभ्यां ययौ गङ्गासमीपगम् ।
गौतमस्याश्रमं पुण्यं यत्राहल्या शिलामयी ॥ १४ ॥
(Adhyâtma Râmâyaṇa, âdikâṇḍa, adhyâya 6)

‖ तैः शिवेषु वसतिर्गताध्वभिः ।
सायमाश्रमतरुष्वगृह्यत ।

The Vâyupurâṇa describes a sage named Akṣapâda* as the disciple of a Brâhmaṇa named Soma Śarmâ who was Śiva incarnate and well-known for his practice of austerities at the shrine of Prabhâsa during the time of Jâtûkarṇya Vyâsa. This Akṣapâda mentioned along with Kaṇâda is evidently no other person than Gotama or Gautama who founded the Nyâya philosophy. As to the origin of the name Akṣapâda ("having eyes in the feet") as applied to Gautama, legend has it that Gautama was so deeply absorbed in philosophical contemplation that one day during his walks he fell unwittingly into a well out of which he was rescued with great difficulty. God therefore mercifully provided him with a second pair of eyes in his feet to protect the sage from further mishaps. Another legend† which represents Vyâsa, a disciple of Gautama, lying prostrate before his master until the latter condescended to look upon him, not with his natural eyes, but with a new pair of eyes in his feet, may be dismissed with scanty ceremony as being the invention of a later generation of logicians, anxious to humiliate Vyâsa for vilification of the Nyâya system in his Mahâbhârata and Vedânta sûtra.

Akṣapâda.

येषु दीर्घतपसः परिग्रहो
वासवक्षणकलत्रतां ययौ ॥ ३३ ॥
प्रत्यपद्यत चिराय यत् पुन·
श्चारुगौतमबधूः शिलामयी ।
स्वं वपुः स किल किल्विषच्छिदां
रामपादरजसामनुग्रहः ॥ ३४ ॥
(Raghuvaṃs'a, Sarga 11).

* सप्तविंशति मे प्राप्ते परिवर्त्ते क्रमागते ।
जातुकर्ण्यो·यदा ब्यासो भविष्यति तपोधनः ॥ २०१ ॥
तदाहं संभविष्यामि सोमशर्म्मा द्विजोत्तमः ।
प्रभासतीर्थमासाद्य योगात्मा लोकविश्रुतः ॥ २०३ ॥
तत्रापि मम ते पुत्रा भविष्यन्ति तपोधनाः ।
अक्षपादः कणादश्च उलूको वत्स एव च ॥ २०३ ॥
(Vâyupurâṇa, Adhyâya 23).

† गौतमो हि स्वमतदूषकस्य ब्यासस्य मुखदर्शनं चक्षुषा न कर्त्तब्यमिति प्रतिज्ञाय पश्चात् ब्यासेन प्रसादितः पादे नेत्रं प्रकाश्य तं दृष्टवान् इवि पौराणिकी कथा ।
(Nyâyakoṣa, 2nd edition, by M. M. Bhimâcârya Jhâlakikara, Bombay).

The people of Mithilâ (modern Darbhanga in North Behar) ascribe the foundation of Nyâya philosophy to Gautama, husband of Ahalyâ, and point out as the place of his birth a village named Gautamasthâna where a fair is held every year on the 9th day of the lunar month of Chaitra (March-April). It is situated 28 miles north-east of Darbhanga and has a mud-hill of considerable height (supposed to be the hermitage of Gautama) at the base of which lies the celebrated "Gautama-kuṇḍa" or Gautama's well the water whereof is like milk to the taste and feeds a perennial rivulet called on this account Kṣîrodadhi or Khiroi (literally the sea of milk). Two miles to the east of the village there is another village named Ahalyâsthâna where between a pair of trees lies a slab of stone identified with Ahalyâ in her accursed state. In its vicinity there is a temple which commemorates the emancipation of Ahalyâ by Râma Chandra. The Gautama-kuṇḍa and the Kṣīrodadhi river, which are still extant at Gautama-sthâna, verify the account of Gotama given above from the Ṛigveda while the stone slab and the temple of Râma at Ahalyâsthâna are evidence corroborative of the story of Ahalyâ as given in the Râmâyaṇa. There is another tradition prevalent in the town of Chapra that Gautama, husband of Ahalyâ and founder of the Nyâya philosophy, resided in a village now called Godnâ at the confluence of the rivers Ganges and Sarayû where a Sanskrit academy called Gautama Thomson Pâthasâlâ has been established to commemorate the great sage.

Local tradition.

It seems to me that Gautama, son of Rahûgaṇa, as mentioned in the Ṛigveda, was the founder of the Gautama family from which sprang Gautama, husband of Ahalyâ, as narrated in the Râmâyaṇa. It is interesting to note that Śatânanda*, son of Gautama by Ahalyâ, is a priest in the royal family of Janaka much in the same way as Gautama,

The founder of Nyâya philosophy identified.

---

*शतानन्दं पुरस्कृत्य पुरोहितमनिन्दितः।
प्रतिगृह्य तु तां पूजां जनकस्य महात्मनः।

(Râmâyaṇa, âdikâṇḍa, Sarga 50).

गौतमश्च शतानन्दो जनकानां पुरोहितः।

(Uttara Râma charitam).

son of Rahûgaṇa, is a priest in the royal family of Kurusṛiñjaya. The fields waving with paddy plants which greet the eyes of a modern traveller near and round Gautama-sthâna bear testimony to Agni's gift of rice and cattle in abundance to the family of Gautama. The Nyâya philosophy was, on the authority of the tradition prevalent in Mithilâ, founded by Gautama, husband of Ahalyâ. The same Gautama has been designated as Akṣapâda in the Vâyu Purâṇa already referred to. Akṣapâda has been identified by Anantayajvan* with the author of the Pitṛimedha Sûtra as well as with that of the Gautama Dharma sûtra, and it is possible that he is not other than the Gautama referred to in the Kauśika sûtra of the Atharva Veda. The other Gautamas mentioned in the Brâhmaṇas, Upaniṣads, etc., appear to be the kinsmen of their illustrious name-sake.

His residence.

The Rámáyaṇa, as we have found, places the hermitage of Gautama, husband of Ahalyâ, at Gautama-sthâna twenty-eight miles north-east of Darbhâṅgâ while the Adhyâtma Râmâyaṇa places it on the banks of the Ganges at its confluence with the Sarayû off the town of Châprâ. The Vâyu-purâṇa fixes the residence of Akṣapâda, supposed to be identical with Gautama, at Prabhâsa† beyond Girnar in Kathiawar on the

---

*To the Gṛihya Sûtras of the Sâmaveda probably belong also Gautama's Pitṛimedhasûtra (Cf. Burnell, p. 57; the commentator Anantayajvan identifies the author with Akṣapâda the author of the Nyâya-sûtra), and the Gautama-dharma-sûtra.—Weber's History of Indian Literature, p. 85.

† Prabhâsa washed on its western side by the river Sarasvati and reputed as the residence of Kṛiṣṇa, is mentioned in the Śrîmad Bhâgavata thus :—

न वस्तव्यमिहास्माभिर्जिजीविषुभिरार्य्यकाः ।
प्रभासं सुमहत्पुण्यं यास्यामोऽद्यैव माचिरम् ॥ ३५ ॥

(Bhâgavata, Skandha II, adhyâya 6.)

स्त्रियो बालाश्च वृद्धाश्च शंखोद्धारं व्रजन्त्वितः ।
वयं प्रभासं यास्यामो यत्र प्रत्यक् सरस्वती ॥ ६ ॥

(Bhâgavata, Skandha II, adhyâya 30.)

Prabhâsa was situated beyond the rock of Girnar in Kathiawar where we come across all the edicts of As'oka as well as as an inscription of Rudradâma supposed to be the first inscription in Sanskrit dated about 100 A. D. which mentions Chandra Gupta and As'oka by names. There are also some inscriptions in Gupta characters, and there is no doubt that Prabhâsa situated on the Sarasvati acquired celebrity in very old times.

sea-coast. To reconcile these conflicting statements it has been suggested that Akṣapâda otherwise known as Gotama or Gautama was the founder of the Nyâya philosophy, that he was born at Gautama-sthâna in Mithilâ on the river Kṣîrodadhi, lived for some years at the village now called Godnâ at the confluence of the Ganges and Sarayû until his retirement to Prabhâsa the well-known sacred place of pilgrimage in Kathiawar on the sea-coast.

His age about 550 B. C.

The Śatapatha Brâhmaṇa mentions Gautama along with Âsurâyaṇa and the Vâyupurâṇa (already quoted) states that Akṣapâda, *alias* Gotama or Gautama, flourished during the time of Jâtûkarṇya Vyâsa. Now Jâtûkarṇya according to the Madhukâṇḍa and Yâjñavalkya Kâṇḍa of the Śatapatha Brâhmaṇa * (Kâṇva recension), was a pupil of Âsurâyaṇa and Yâska who are supposed to have lived about 550 B. C. This date tallies well with the time of another Gautama who, together with Araṇemi, is described in the Divyâvadâna†, a Buddhist Sanskrit work translated into Chinese in the 2nd century A. D., as having transmitted the Vedas to posterity before they were classified by Vyâsa. It does not conflict with the view that Akṣapâda is identical

---

This Prabhâsa is not to be confounded with another town called Prabhâsa in Kausámbi near Allahabad on the Jumna where there is an inscription, dated about the 2nd century B. C., of Aṣadasena, a descendant of Sonakâyana of Adhicchatra, (vide Dr. Fuhrer's Pabhosa inscriptions in Epigraphia Indica, Vol. II, pp. 242-243.)

* *Vide* Weber's History of Indian Literature, p. 140.

In the Mâdhyandinîya recension of the Śatapatha Brâhmaṇa a teacher intervenes between Yâska and Jâtûkarṇya, *viz.* Bhâradvâja. Cf.

जातुकर्ण्याज्जातुकर्ण्यो भारद्वाजाद् भारद्वाजो भारद्वाजाच्चासुरायणाच्च गौतमाच्च गौतमो............पाराशर्य्यात् पाराशर्य्यो जातुकर्ण्याज्जातुकर्ण्यो भारद्वाजाद् भारद्वाजो भारद्वाजाच्चासुरायणाच्च यास्काच्चासुरायणः ।

(Śatapatha Brâhmaṇa, Mâdhyandinîya recension, Kâṇḍa 14, adhyâya 5.)

† The 33rd chapter of the Divyâvadâna called Mâtaṅga Sûtra, in Chinese Mo-tan-nu-cin, was translated into Chinese by An-shi-kao-cie of the Eastern Han dynasty in A. D. 148-170. (*Vide* Bunjiu Nanjio's Catalogue of the Chinese Tripiṭaka). In it we read :—

ब्रह्मा देवानां परमतापसः इन्द्रस्य कौशिकस्य वेदार्थान् वाचयति स्म । इन्द्रः कौशिकोऽरणेमीगौतमे वेदान् वाचयति । अरणेमीगौतमौ श्वेतकेतुं वेदान् वाचयतः श्वेतकेतुः शुकं पण्डितं वेदान् वाचयति । शुकः पंडितश्चतुर्धा वेदान् विभजति स्म ।

(Divyâvadâna, Chap. XXXIII).

with Gautama, author of the Gautama Dharma-Sûtra which is "declared to be the oldest of the existing works on the sacred law*." Akṣapâda-Gautama, founder of the Nyâya Philosophy, was almost a contemporary of Buddha-Gautama who founded Buddhism and Indrabhûti Gautama who was a disciple of Mahâvîra, the reputed founder of Jainism.

The fourfold division of the means of knowledge (Pramâṇa) into perception, inference, comparison and word found in the Jaina Prâkrita scriptures such as the Nandî-Sûtra, Sthânâṅga-Sûtra† and Bhagavatî Sûtra compiled by Indrabhûti-Gautama finds its parallel in the Nyâya-Sûtra of Akṣapâda-Gautama leading to the conclusion that this particular doctrine was either borrowed by Indrabhûti from Akṣapâda or was the common property of both. In the Pâli and Prâkṛita scriptures Gautama is called Gotama, and a Pâli Sutta mentions a sect called "Gotamakâ,"‡ who were followers of Gautama, identified perhaps with the founder of the Nyâya Philosophy. The Pâli Canonical scriptures such as the Brahmajâla Sutta, §

---

* Buhler observes :—These arguments which allow us to place Gautama before both Baudhâyana and Vâs'iṣṭha are that both these authors quote Gautama as an authority on law............ These facts will, I think, suffice to show that the Gautama Dharma Sûtra may be safely declared to be the oldest of the existing works on the sacred law." (Buhler's Gautama, Introduction, pp. XLIX and LIV, S. B. E. series).

† अथवा हेऊ चउव्विहे पन्नत्ते तं जहा
पच्चक्खे अनुमाणे उवमे आगमे ।

(Sthânâṅga-Sûtra, Page 309, published by Dhanapat Singh).

‡ *Vide* Prof. T. W. Rhys David's Introduction to the Kassapa-Sihanâda Sutta, pp. 220-222. It is observed :—

"The only alternative is that some Brâhmaṇa, belonging to the Gotama Gotra, is here referred to as having had a community of Bhikṣus named after him."

§ इध, भिक्खवे, एकच्चो समणो वा ब्राह्मणो व तक्की होति वीमंसी । सो तक्कपरियाहतं वीमंसानुचरितं सयं पटिभानं एवं आह "अधिच्चसमुप्पन्नो अत्ता च लोको चाति" ।

(Brahmajâla Sutta 1-32, edited by Rhys Davids and Carpenter).

याव सम्मासम्बुद्धा लोके नुप्पज्जन्ति, न तक्किका सुज्झन्ति न चापि सावका दुद्दिट्ठी न दुक्खा पमुच्चरेति ।

(Udâna, p. 10, edited by Paul Steinthal, P. T. S. edition).

Udâna, etc., which embody the teachings of Buddha, mention a class of Śramaṇas and Brâhmaṇas who were "takkî" or "takkika" (logicians) and "vîmamsî" (casuists) and indulged in "takka" (logic) and vîmamsâ (casuistry), alluding perhaps to the followers of Akṣapâda-Gautama described as "Gotamakâ."

The Kathâvatthuppakaraṇa *, a Pâli work of the Abhidhamma-piṭaka, composed by Moggaliputta Tissa at the third Buddhist Council during the reign of Aśoka about 255 B.C., mentions "patiññâ" (in Sanskrit: "pratijña," proposition), "Upanaya" (application of reasons), "Niggaha" (in Sanskrit: "Nigraha," humiliation or defeat) etc., which are the technical terms of Nyâya philosophy or Logic. Though Moggaliputta Tissa has not made any actual reference to Logic or Nyâya, his mention of some of its technical terms warrants us to suppose that that philosophy existed in some shape in India in his time about 255 B. C. These facts lead us to conclude that Gotama, Gautama or Akṣapâda, the founder of Nyâya Philosophy, lived about the year 550 B. C.

II. NYÂYASÛTRA THE FIRST WORK ON NYÂYA PHILOSOPHY.

The earliest contribution to the Sûtra literature.

To Gotama, Gautama or Akṣapâda, of whom a short account has been given above, is attributed the authorship of the Nyâya-Sûtra, the earliest work on Nyâya Philosophy. Sanskrit literature in the Sûtra or aphoristic style was presumably inaugurated at about 550 B. C. and the Nyâya-Sûtra the author of which lived, as already stated, at about that time, must have been the first† contribution to that literature. The "Sutta" or Sûtra section of the Pâli literature reads very

---

* The terms "Paṭiññâ" (pratijñâ, proposition) and "niggaha" (nigraha, defeat) occur in the following passages :—

न च मय तया तत्थ हेताय पटिज्जाय हेवं पटिजानन्ता हेवं निग्गहेतब्बो ।

(Kathâvatthuppakaraṇa, Siamese edition, p. 3).

"Niggaha-Catukkam" is the name of a section of the first chapter of the Kathâvatthuppakaraṇa while "Upanaya-Catukkam" is the name of another section of that work.

†Kapila is stated in the Sâmkhye-Kârikâ, verse 70, to have taught his philosophy to Âsuri who is mentioned in the S'atapatha Brâhmaṇa as a teacher, Âsurâyaṇa and Yâska who followed Âsuri were the teachers of Jâtûkarṇya, a contemporary of Akṣapâda-Gautama. Kapila therefore

much like a body of sermons bearing no affinity with the Sûtra works of the Brâhmanas.

The gradual development of the Nyâya-Sûtra.

The Nyâya-Sûtra is divided into five books, each containing two chapters called âhnikas or Diurnal portions. It is believed that Aksapâda finished his work on Nyâya in ten lectures corresponding to the âhnikas referred to above. We do not know whether the whole of the Nyâya-Sûtra, as it exists at present, was the work of Aksapâda, nor do we know for certain whether his teachings were committed to writing by himself or transmitted by oral tradition only. It seems to me that it is only the first book of the Nyâya-Sûtra containing a brief explanation of the 16 categories that we are justified in ascribing to Aksapâda, while the second, third and fourth books which discuss particular doctrines of the Vaiśesika, Yoga, Mîmâmsâ, Vedânta and Buddhist Philosophy bear marks of different hands and ages. In these books there are passages quoted almost *verbatim* from the Laṅkâvatâra-Sûtra *, a Sanskrit work of the Yogâchâra Buddhist Philosophy, from the Mâdhyamika Sûtra of Nâgârjuna† and from the Sataka‡ of Ârya Deva—works which were composed in the early centuries of Christ. The fifth book treating of the varieties of futile rejoinders and occasions for rebuke was evidently not the production of Aksapâda who dismissed those topics without entering into their details. The last and most considerable additions were made by Vâtsyâyana, otherwise known as Paksila Svâmi, who about 450 A. D. wrote the first regular commentary, "Bhâṣya", on the Nyâya Sûtra, and harmonised the different, and at times conflicting, additions and interpolations by the ingenious introduction of Sûtras of his own making fathered upon Akṣapâda.

---

preceded Akṣapâda by at least three generations. Kapila's Philosophy is believed to have come down by oral traditions and was not perhaps committed to writing in his life-time. Hence the Nyâya-Sûtra has been stated to be the first work of the Sûtra period.

* *Vide* Nyâya Sûtra 4-2-26, which quotes the Laṅkâvatâra Sûtra (dated about 300 A.D.)

† *Vide* Nyâya-Sûtra 2-1-39. 4-1-39, and 4-1-48, which criticise the Mâdhyamika Sûtra.

‡ *Vide* Nyâya-Sûtra 4-1-48 which criticises S ataka of Âryaveda.

Commentaries on the Nyâya-Sûtra.

The Nyâya-Sûtra has, since its composition, enjoyed a very great popularity as is evident from the numerous commentaries that have from time to time centred round it. A few of the commentaries are mentioned below :—

TEXT.

1. Nyâya-Sûtra by Gotama or Akṣapâda (550 B. C.)

Commentaries.

2. Nyâya-Bhâṣya by Vâtsyâyana (450 A D.)
3. Nyâya-Vârtika by Udyotakâra.
4. Nyâya-Vârtika-tâtparya-tîkâ by Vâchaspati Mis'ra.
5. Nyâya-Vârtika-tâtparyatîkâ-paris'uddhi by Udayana.
6. Paris'uddiprakâ sâ by Vardhamâna.
7. Vardhamânendu by Padmanâbha Mis'ra.
8. Nyâyâlaṅkâra by Śrîkaṇṭha.
9. Nyâyâlaṇkâra Vṛitti by Jayanta.
10. Nyâya-mañjarî by Jayanta.
11. Nyâya-Vṛitti by Abhayatilakopâdhyâya.
12. Nyâya-Vṛitti by Vis'vanâtha.
13. Mitabhâṣiṇî Vṛitti by Mahâdeva Vedântî.
14. Nyâyaprakâs'a by Kes'ava Mis'ra.
15. Nyâyabodhinî by Govardhana.
16. Nyâya Sûtra Vyâkhyâ by Mathurânâtha.

III. RECEPTION ACCORDED TO THE NYÂYA PHILOSOPHY.

Philosophy inaugurated by members of the military caste.

It appears from the Chhândogya-upanisad, Bṛihadâranyaka-upanisad and Kausîtakî Brâhmana* that Philosophy (Adhyâtma-Vidyâ) received its first impetus from the Kṣatriyas (members of the military caste) who carried it to great perfection. King Ajâtaśatru in an assembly of the Kuru-Pañchâlas consoled a Brâhmana named Svetaketu, son of Âruni of the Gautama family, that

---

* Kauṣitakî-Brâhmaṇa 2-1, 2; 16, 4.
Bṛihadâraṇyaka 2-1-20, 2-3-6.

Chhândogya 3-14-1 ; 5-11, 24 ; 1-8-9 ; 1-9-3, 7-1-3 and 5-11.

मा त्वं गौतमावदो यथेयं न प्राक् त्वत्तः पुरा विद्या ब्राह्मणान् गच्छति तस्मादु सर्व्वेषु लोकेषु क्षत्रस्यैव प्रशासनमभूदिति तस्मै होवाच ॥ ७ ॥

(Chhândogya-upanisad 5-3).

he had no cause of being sorry for his inability to explain certain doctrines of Adhyâtma-Vidyâ which were known only to the Kṣatriyas. It may be observed that Mahâvîra and Buddha who founded respectively Jainism and Buddhism—two universal religions based on poilosophy or Adhyâtma-Vidyâ—were also Kṣatriyas. Kapila is reputed to be the first Brâhmaṇa who propounded a system of philosophy called Sâṃkhya, but his work on the subject not having come down to us in its original form we are not in a position to ascertain what relation it bore to the Vedas or what kind of reception was given to it by the orthodox Brâhmaṇas. We know for certain that the most powerful Brahmaṇa who undertook to study and teach philosophy openly was Gotama, Gautama or Akṣapâda, the renowned author of the Nyâya-Sûtra He founded a rational system of philosophy called "Nyâya" which at its inception had no relation with the topics of the Vedic Saṃhita and Brâhmaṇa. At this stage the Nyâya was pure Logic unconnected with the scriptural dogmas. Akṣapâda recognised four means of valid knowledge, *viz.*, perception inference, comparison and word of which the last signified knowledge derived through any reliable assertion.

Nyâya (Logic) not ·eceived with favour.

This being the nature of Nyâya or Logic at its early stage it was not received with favour by the orthodox community of Brâhmaṇas who were anxious to establish an organised society, paid their sole attention to the Saṃhitâs and Brâhmaṇas which treated of rituals, ignoring

---

Professor P. Deussen observes :—

In this narrative, preserved by two different Vedic schools, it is expressly declared that the knowledge of the Brahman as âtman, the centrale doctrine of the entire Vedânta, is possessed by the King ; but, on the contrary, is not possessed by the Brâhmaṇa "famed as a Vedic scholar."—Philosophy of the Upanishads, pp. 17—18.

Again he remarks :—We are forced to conclude, if not with absolute certainty, yet with a very high degree of probability, that as a matter of fact the doctrine of the âtman standing as it did in such sharp contrast to all the principles of the Vedic ritual, though the original conception may have been due to Brâhmaṇas, was taken up and cultivated primarily not in Brâhmana but in Kṣatriya circles, and was first adopted by the farmer in later times. Philosophy of the Upanishads, p. 19.

सत्यं ज्ञानमनन्तं ब्रह्म। विज्ञानमानन्दं ब्रह्म। तत्त्वमसि श्वेतकेतो। सोऽहं ब्रह्म।

altogether the portions which had nothing to do with them. The sage Jaimini* in his Mîmâṃsa-Sûtra distinctly says that the Veda having for its sole purpose the prescription of actions, those parts of it which do not serve that purpose are useless We are therefore not surprised to find Manu † enjoining excommunication upon those members of the twice-born caste who disregarded the Vedas and Dharma-Sûtra relying upon the support of Hetu-Śâstra or Logic. Similarly Vâlmîki in his Râmâyaṇa ‡ discredits those persons of perverse intellect who indulge in the frivolities of Ânvîkṣikî, the science of Logic, regardless of the works of sacred law (Dharma-śâstra) which they should follow as their guide. Vyâsa in the Mahâbhârata,§ Sântiparva, relates the doleful story of a repentant Brâhmaṇa who, addicted to Tarkavidyâ (Logic), carried

These four pregnant expressions (Mahâvâkya) originated from the Brâhmaṇas, whence it may be concluded Nirguṇa-Brahma-Vidyâ or knowledge of absolute Brahman was confined among them. It was the Saguṇa-Brahma Vidyâ or knowledge of Brahman limited by form and attributes that is said to have been introduced by the Kṣatriyas.

* आम्नायस्य क्रियार्थकत्वात् आनर्थक्यम् अतदर्थानाम् । १ । २ । १ ।

(Mîmâṃsâ-Sûtra).

† योऽवमन्येत ते मूले हेतुशास्त्राश्रयाद्द्विजः ।
स साधुभिर्बहिष्कार्य्यो नास्तिको वेदनिन्दकः ॥

(Manu, adhyâya 2, verse II).

‡ धर्मशास्त्रेषु मुख्येषु विद्यमानेषु दुर्बुधाः ।
बुद्धिमान्वीक्षिकीं प्राप्य निरर्थं प्रवदन्ति ते ॥ ३६ ॥

(Râmâyaṇa Ayodhyâ Kâṇḍa, Sarga 100).

§ अहमासं पण्डितको हैतुको वेदनिन्दकः ।
आन्वीक्षिकीं तर्कविद्यामनुरक्तो निरर्थकाम् ॥ ४७ ॥
हेतुवादान् प्रवदिता वक्ता संसत्सु हेतुमत् ।
आक्रोष्टा चाभिवक्ता च ब्रह्मवाक्येषु च द्विजान् ॥ ४८ ॥
नास्तिकः सर्वशङ्की च मूर्खः पण्डितमानिकः ।
तस्येयं फलनिर्वृत्तिः शृगालत्वं मम द्विज ॥ ४९ ॥

(Mahâbhârata, S'ântiparva, adhyâya 180.)

In the Gandharva tantra we find :—

गोतमप्रोक्तशास्त्रार्थनिरताः सर्व एव हि ।
शार्गालीं योनिमापन्नाः सन्दिग्धाः सर्वकर्मसु ॥

(Quoted in Prâṇatoṣiṇîtantra).

on debates divorced from all faith in the Vedas and was on that account, turned into a jackal in his next birth as a penalty. In another passage of the Śântiparva,* Vyâsa warns the followers of the Vedânta Philosophy against communicating their doctrines to a Naiyâyika or Logician. Vyâsa† does not care even to review the Nyâya system in the Brahma-sûtra seeing that it has not been recognised by any worthy sage. Stories of infliction of penalties on those given to the study of Nyâya are related in the Śkanda Purâṇa,‡ and other works ; and in the Naiṣadha-charita§ we find Kali satirising the founder of Nyâya Philosophy as "Gotama" the "most bovine" among sages.

Nyâya reconciled with scriptural dogmas.

Gradually however this system of philosophy instead of relying entirely upon reasoning came to attach due weight to the authority of the Vedas, and later on, after its reconciliation with them, the principles of Nyâya were assimilated in other systems of philosophy such as the Vaiśeṣika,|| Yoga, Mîmâṃsâ,¶ Sâṃkhya**, etc.

---

* स्नातकानामिदं शास्त्रं वाच्यं पुत्रानुशासनम् ।
× × × × ×
न तर्कशास्त्रदग्धाय तथैव पिशुनाय च ॥ १८ ॥
(Mahâbhârata, S'ântiparva, adhyâya 246).

† अपरिग्रहाच्चात्यन्तमनपेक्षा ॥ १७ ॥
(Vedânta-sûtra 2-2).

‡ गोतमः स्वेन तर्केण खण्डयन् तत्र तत्र हि ।
शप्तोऽथ मुनिभिस्तत्र शार्गालीं योनिमृच्छति ।
पुनश्चानुगृहीतोऽसौ श्रुतिसिद्धान्ततर्कतः ।
सर्वलोकोपकाराय तव शास्त्रं भविष्यति ॥
(Skanda Purâṇa, Kâlikâkhaṇḍa, adhyâya 17).

§ मुक्तये यः शिलात्वाय शास्त्रमूचे महामुनिः ।
गोतमं तमवेतैव यथा वित्थ तथैव सः ॥

|| Vais'eṣika-sûtra 1-1-4, 2-1-15, 1-1-16, 2-1-17, 2-2-17, 2-2-32, 3-1-15, 9-2-3, 9-2-4.
(Jayanârâyaṇa Tarkapañchânanas edition).

¶ Mîmâṃsâ-sûtra 1-1-4, 1-3-1, 1-3-2, 1-3-3, 1-4-14, 1-4-35, 1-5-8, 3-1-17, 3-1-20, 4-3-18, 5-1-6, 10-3-35.

** Sâṃkhyâ-sûtra 1-60, 1-101, 1-106, 5-10, 5-11, 5-12.

Yoga-sûtra 1-5, 6.

Nyâya as an approved branch of knowledge.

Henceforth the Nyâya was regarded as an approved branch of learning. Thus the Gautama-Dharma-sûtra* prescribes a course of training in Logic (Nyâya) for the King and acknowledges the utility of *Tarka* or Logic in the administration of justice though in the case of conclusions proving incompatible ultimate decision is directed to be made by reference to persons versed in the Vedas. Manu† says that *dharma* or duty is to be ascertained by logical reasoning not opposed to the injunctions of the Vedas. He recommends Logic (Nyâya) as a necessary study for a King and a logician to be an indispensable member of a legal assembly. Yâjña-valkya‡ counts "Nyâya" or Logic among the fourteen principal sciences while Vyâsa§ admits that he was able to arrange and classify the Upaniṣads with the help of the Ânvîkṣiki or Logic. In the Padma-purâṇa|| Logic is included among the fourteen

---

* राजा सर्वस्येष्टे ब्राह्मणवर्जं, साधुकारी स्यात् साधुवादी, त्रय्याम् आन्वीक्षिक्याञ्चाभिविनीतः। ....न्यायाधिगमे तर्कोऽभ्युपायः। तेनाभ्युह्य यथास्थानं गमयेत्। विप्रतिपत्तौ त्रैविद्यवृद्धेभ्यः प्रत्यवहृत्य निष्ठां गमयेत्।

(Gautamadharma-sûtra, adhyâya 11)

† आर्षं धर्मोपदेशं च वेदशास्त्राविरोधिना।
यस्तर्केणानुसंधत्ते स धर्मं वेद नेतरः॥

(Manu, adhyâya 12, verse 106).

त्रैविद्येभ्यस्त्रयीं विद्याद् दण्डनीतिञ्च शाश्वतीम्।
आन्वीक्षिकीञ्चात्मविद्यां वार्त्तारम्भांश्च लोकतः।

(Manu, adhyâya 7, verse 43).

त्रैविद्यो हैतुकस्तर्की नैरुक्तो धर्म्मपाठकः।
त्रयश्चाश्रमिणः पूर्व्वे परिषत् स्याद्दशावरा॥

(Manu, adhyâya 12, verse 111).

‡ पुराणन्यायमीमांसा धर्म्मशास्त्राङ्गमिश्रिताः।
वेदाः स्थानानि विद्यानां धर्म्मस्य च चतुर्द्दश॥

(Yâjnavalkya saṃhitâ, adhyâya 1, verse 3).

§ तत्रोपनिषदं तात परिशेषं तु पार्थिव।
मथ्नामि मनसा तात दृष्ट्वा चान्वीक्षिकीं पराम्॥

(Mahâbhârata quoted by Vis'vanâtha in his Vṛitti on Nyâya-sûtra 1-1-1).

|| अङ्गानि चतुरो वेदान् पुराणन्यायविस्तरान्।
मीमांसां धर्म्मशास्त्रञ्च परिगृह्याथ साम्प्रतम्॥
मत्स्यरूपेण च पुनः कल्पादावुदकान्तरे।

(Padma-purâṇa, *vide* Muir's Sanskrit text Vol, III, p. 27).

principal branches of learning promulgated by God Viṣṇu, while in the Matsya-purâṇa,* Nyâya-vidyâ, together with the Vedas, is said to have emanated from the mouth of Brahmâ himself. In fact so wide-spread was the study of Nyâya that the Mahâbhârata is full of references to that science.

In the Âdiparva of the Mahbâhârata Nyâya† or Logic is mentioned along with the Veda and Chikitsâ (the science of medicine), and the hermitage of Kâśyapa is described as being filled with sages who were versed in the Nyâya-tattva (logical truths) and knew the true meaning of a proposition, objection and conclusion. The Sânti-parva‡ refers to numerous tenets of Nyâya supported by reason and scripture while the Aśvamedha-parva§ describes the sacrificial ground as being resounded by logicians (Hetu vâdin) who employed arguments and counter-arguments to vanquish one another. In the Sabhâ-parva|| the sage Nârada is described as being versed in Logic

---

* अनन्तरञ्च वक्त्रेभ्यो वेदास्तस्य विनिःसृताः ।
मीमांसा न्यायविद्या च प्रमाणाष्टकसंयुता ॥

(Matsya-purâṇa 3-2).

† न्यायशिक्षा चिकित्सा च दानं पाशुपतं तथा ।
हेतुनैव समं जन्म दिव्यमानुषसंज्ञितम् ॥ ६७ ॥

(Mahâbhârata, Âdiparva, adhyâya 1).

न्यायतत्त्वात्मविज्ञानसम्पन्नैर्वेदपारगैः ॥ ४२ ॥
नानावाक्यसमाहारसमवायविशारदैः ।
विशेषकार्य्यविद्भिश्च मोक्षधर्म्मपरायणैः ॥ ४३ ॥
स्थापनाक्षेपसिद्धान्त परमार्थज्ञतां गतैः ।
शब्दच्छन्दोनिरुक्तज्ञैः कालज्ञानविशारदैः ॥ ४४ ॥
द्रव्यकर्म्मगुणज्ञैश्च कार्य्यकारणवेदिभिः ॥

(Mahâbhârata, Âdiparva, adhyâya 70).

‡ न्यायतन्त्राण्यनेकानि तैस्तैरुक्तानि वादिभिः ।
हेत्वागमसमाचारैर्यदुक्तं तदुपास्यताम् ॥ २२ ॥

(Mahâbhârata, Śântiparva, adhyâya 210).

§ तस्मिन् यज्ञे प्रवृत्ते तु वाग्मिनो हेतुवादिनः ।
हेतुवादान् बहूनाहुः परस्परजिगीषवः ॥ २७ ॥

(Mahâbhârata, A'svamedhaparva, adhyâya, 85).

|| न्यायविद् धर्म्मतत्वज्ञः षड़ङ्गविदनुत्तमः ।
ऐक्यसंयोगनानात्व समवायविशारदः ॥ ३ ॥

(Nyâyavid) and skilful in distinguishing unity and plurality ("aikya" and "nânâtva"), conjunction and co-existence ("saṃyoga' and "samavâya"), genus and species ("parâpara"), etc, capable of deciding questions by evidences (Pramâṇa) and ascertaining the validity and invalidity of a five-membered syllogism (Pañchâvayava-vâkya).

The course of Nyâya.

In fact the Nyâya (Logic) was in course of time deservedly held in very high esteem. If it were allowed to follow its original course unimpeded by religious dogmas it would have risen to the very height of perfection. Nevertheless the principles of Nyâya entering into the different systems of phi'osophy gave them each its proper compactness and cogency just as Bacon's Inductive Method shaped the sciences and philosophies of a later age in a different country. It is however to be regretted that during the last five hundred years the Nyâya has been mixed up with Law (smṛiti, Rhetoric (alaṅkâra), Vedânta, etc., and thereby has hampered the growth of those branches of knowledge upon which it has grown up as a sort of parasite.

SANSKRIT COLLEGE, CALCUTTA.
The 7th November, 1913.

SATIS CHANDRA VIDYABHUSANA.

वक्ता प्रगल्भो मेधावी स्मृतिमान्नयवित् कविः ।
परापरविभागज्ञः प्रमाणकृतनिश्चयः ॥ ४ ॥
पञ्चावयवयुक्तस्य वाक्यस्य गुणदोषवित् ।
उत्तरोत्तरवक्ता च वदतोऽपि बृहस्पतेः ॥ ५ ॥

(Mahàbhârata, Sabhâparva, adhyàya 5).

THE NYÂYA-SÛTRAS.

Book I.—Chapter I.

प्रमाण प्रमेय संशय प्रयोजन दृष्टान्त सिद्धान्ता वयव तर्क निर्णय वाद जल्प वितण्डा हेत्वाभास च्छल जाति निग्रहस्थानानां तत्त्वज्ञानान्निःश्रेयसाधिगमः ॥ १।१।१॥

प्रमाण pramâṇa, proof ; प्रमेय prameya, provable, knowable, object of proof ; संशय saṃśaya, doubt, uncertainty ; प्रयोजन Prayojana, aim, purpose; दृष्टान्त driṣṭânta, example, familiar instance ; सिद्धान्त siddhânta, conclusion; अवयव avayava, members of the syllogism ; तर्क tarka, hypothetical reasoning, confutation ; निर्णय nirṇaya, ascertainment; वाद vâda, discussion; जल्प jalpa, sophistry ; वितण्डा vitaṇḍâ, cavil, wrangling ; हेत्वाभास hetvâbhâsa, pseudo-mark, fallacy ; छल chhala, quibbling ; जाति jâti, futility ; निग्रहस्थान nigraha-sthâna, occasion for rebuke, opponent's errors ; तत्त्वज्ञानात् Tattva-jñânât, from knowledge of the true nature ; निःश्रेयसाधिगमः niḥśreyasa-adhigamaḥ, attainment of the supreme good.

1. **Supreme felicity** is attained by the knowledge about the true nature of the sixteen categories, *viz.*, means of right knowledge (pramana), object of right knowledge (prameya), doubt (samsaya), purpose (prayojana), familiar instance (dristanta) established tenet (siddhanta), members (avayava), confutation (tarka*), ascertain-

* The English equivalent for "tarka" is variously given as "confutation," "argumentation," "reductio ad absurdum," "hypothetical reasoning," etc.

ment (nirnaya), discussion (vada), wrangling (jalpa), cavil (vitanda), fallacy (hetvabhasa), quibble (chhala), futility (jati), and occasion for rebuke (nigrahasthana).

*Knowledge about the true nature of the sixteen categories** means true knowledge by the "enunciation," "definition" and "critical examination" of the categories. Book I (of the Nyâya Sûtra) treats of "enunciation" and "definition," while the remainning four Books are reserved for "critical examination." The attainment of supreme felicity is preceded by the knowledge of four things *viz*, (1) that which is fit to be abandoned *viz.*, (pain), (2) that which produces what is fit to be abandoned (*viz*, misapprehension, etc), (3) complete destruction of what is fit to be abandoned and (4) the means of destroying what is fit to be abandoned (*viz*, true knowledge†).

दुःख जन्म प्रवृत्ति दोष मिथ्याज्ञानाना मुत्तरोत्तरापाये तदनन्तरापायादपवर्गः ॥१।१।२॥

दुःख duḥkha, pain ; जन्म janma, birth ; प्रवृत्ति pravṛitti, activity ; दोष doṣa, fault ; मिथ्याज्ञान mithyâ-jñâna, false knowledge ; उत्तरोत्तरापाये uttara-uttara-apâye, on the disappearance of one after another in the reverse order ; तदनन्तरापायात् tat anantara apâyât, owing to the absence of each successive one ; अपवर्गः apavargaḥ, final release, attainment of the end.

2. Pain, birth, activity, faults and misapprehension—on the successive annihilation of these in the reverse order, there follows **release.**

Misapprehension, faults, activity, birth and pain—these in their uninterrupted course constitute the " world. " Release, which consists in the soul's getting rid of the world, is the condition of supreme felicity marked by perfect tranquillity and not tainted by any defilement. A person, by the true knowledge of the sixteen categories, is able to remove his misapprehensions. When this is done, his faults, *viz.*, affection,

* Vâtsyâyana observes :—

त्रिविधा चास्य शास्त्रस्य प्रवृत्तिः । उद्देशो लक्षणं परीक्षा चेति ।

—(Nyâyadarśana, p. 9, Bibliotheca Indica Series).

† हेयं तस्य निवर्त्तकं हानमात्यन्तिकं तस्योपायोऽधिगन्तव्य इत्येतानि चत्वारि अर्थपदानि सम्यक् बुद्ध्वा निःश्रेयसमधिगच्छति ।

—(Nyâyadarśana, p. 2)

aversion and stupidity, disappear. He is then no longer subject to any activity and is consequently freed from transmigration and pains. This is the way in which his release is effected and supreme felicity secured.

प्रत्यक्षानुमानोपमानशब्दाः "प्रमाणानि" ॥१।१।३॥

प्रत्यक्ष pratyakṣa, perception ; अनुमान anumâna, inference ; उपमान upamâna, comparison ; शब्द śabda, word ; प्रमाणानि pramâṇâni ; proofs, means of right knowledge.

3. Perception, inference, comparison and word (verbal testimony)—these are the **means of right knowledge.**

[The Chârvâkas admit only one means of right knowledge, *viz.*, perception (pratyakṣa) ; the Vaiśeṣikas and Bauddhas admit two *viz.*, perception and inference (anumâna) ; the Sâṅkhyas admit three, *viz.*, perception, inference and verbal testimony (âgama or śabda) ; while the Naiyâyikas, whose fundamental work is the Nyâya-sûtra, admit four, *viz.*, perception, inference, verbal testimony and comparison (upamâna). The Prâbhâkaras admit a fifth means of right knowledge called presumption (arthâpatti), the Bhâṭṭas and Vedantins admit a sixth, *viz.*, non-existence (abhâva), and the Paurâṇikas recognise a seventh and eighth means of right knowledge, named probability (sambhava) and rumour (aitihya)].

इन्द्रियार्थसन्निकर्षोत्पन्नं ज्ञानमव्यपदेश्यमव्यभिचारि व्यवसायात्मकं "प्रत्यक्षम्" ॥१।१।४॥

इन्द्रियार्थसन्निकर्षोत्पन्नम् indriya-artha-sannikarṣa-utpannam, produced from the contact of the sense with the object ; ज्ञानम् jñânam, knowledge ; अव्यपदेश्यम् a-vyapadeśyam, without naming ; अव्यभिचारि a-vyabhichâri, unerring ; व्यवसायात्मकं vyavasâya-âtmakam, certain in nature ; प्रत्यक्षं pratyakṣam, perception.

4. **Perception** is that knowledge which arises from the contact of a sense with its object, and which is determinate, unnameable and non-erratic.

Determinate.—This epithet distinguishes perception from indeterminate knowledge ; as, for instance, a man looking from a distance cannot ascertain whether there is smoke or dust.

Unnameable.—Signifies that the knowledge of a thing derived through perception has no connection with the name which the thing bears.

Non erratic—In summer the sun's rays coming in contact with earthly heat quiver and appear to the eyes of men as water. The knowledge of water derived in this way is not perception. To eliminate such cases the epithet non-erratic has been used.

[This aphorism may also be translated as follows:—**Perception** is knowledge and which arises from the contact of a sense with its object and which is non-erratic being either, indeterminate (nirvikalpaka, as "this is something") or determinate (savikalpaka, as "this is a Brâhmaṇa")]

अथ तत्पूर्व्वकं "त्रिविधमनुमानं" पूर्ववच्छेषवत्सामान्यतो दृष्टं च ॥१।१।५॥

अथ atha, then ; तत्पूर्वकं tat-pûrvakam, preceded by perception ; त्रिविधं tri-vidham, threefold ; अनुमानं anumânam, inference ; पूर्ववत् pûrva-vat, from cause to effect ; शेषवत् śesa-vat, from effect to cause ; सामान्यतो दृष्टं sâmânyto-dristam, commonly seen ; च cha, and.

5. **Inference** is knowledge which is preceded by perception, and is of three kinds, *viz.*, â priori, â posteriori and 'commonly seen.'

Â priori is the knowledge of effect derived from the perception of its cause. *e.g*, one seeing clouds infers that there will be rain.

Â posteriori is the knowledge of cause derived from the perception of its effects, *e.g.*, one seeing a river swollen infers that there was rain.

'Commonly seen' is the knowledge of one thing derived from the perception of another thing with which it is commonly seen, *e.g.*, one seeing a beast possessing horns, infers that it possesses also a tail, or one seeing smoke on a hill infers that there is fire on it.

प्रसिद्धसाधर्म्यात्साध्यसाधनम् "उपमानम्" ॥१।१।६॥

प्रसिद्धसाधर्म्यात् prasiddha-sâdharmyât, through similarity to a known object ; साध्यसाधनं sâdhya-sâdhanam, the making known of the thing posited ; उपमानं upamânam, comparison, analogy.

6. **Comparison** is the knowledge of a thing through its similarity to another thing previously well known.

A man, hearing from a forester that a *bos gavaeus* is like a cow, resorts to a forest where he sees an animal like a cow. Having recollected what he heard he institutes a comparison, by which he arrives at the conviction that the animal which he sees is *bos gavaeus*. This is knowledge derived through comparison Some hold that comparison is not a separate means of knowledge, for when one notices the likeness of a cow in a strange animal one really performs an act of perception In reply, it is urged that we cannot deny comparison as a separate means of knowledge, for how does otherwise the name *bos gavaeus* signify the general notion of the animal called *bos gavaeus*? That the name *bos gavaeus* signifies one and all members of the *bos gavaeus* class is not a result of perception, but the consequence of a distinct knowledge, called comparison.

आप्तोपदेशः "शब्दः" ॥१।१।७॥

आप्तोपदेशः âpta-upadeśaḥ, the direction or instruction of a reliable person ; शब्दः śabdaḥ, word, testimony.

7. **Word (verbal testimony)** is the instructive assertion of a reliable person.

A reliable person is one—may be a risi, ârya or mlechha,—who as an expert in a certain matter is willing to communicate his experiences of it.

[Suppose a young man coming to the side of a river cannot ascertain whether the river is fordable or not, and immediately an old experienced man of the locality, who has no enmity against him, comes and tells him that the river is easily fordable : the word of the old man is to be accepted as a means of right knowledge, called verbal testimony].

"स द्विविधो" दृष्टादृष्टार्थत्वात ॥१।१।८॥

सः saḥ, it, word ; द्विविधः dvi-vidhah twofold ; दृष्टादृष्टार्थत्वात् drista-adrista-artha-tvât, because its object may be seen or not seen.

8. It is of two kinds, *viz.*, that which refers to *matter which is seen*, and that which refers to *matter which is not seen*.

The first kind involves matter which can be actually verified. Though we are incapable of verifying the matter involved in the second kind, we can somehow ascertain it by means of inference.

[*Matter which is seen e.g*, a physician's assertion that physical strength is gained by taking butter].

[*Matter which is not seen, e g.*, a religious teacher's assertion that one conquers heaven by performing horse-sacrifices].

आत्मशरीरेन्द्रियार्थबुद्धिमनःप्रवृत्तिदोषप्रेत्यभावफल-
दुःखापवर्गास्तु "प्रमेयम्" ॥१।१।९॥

आत्मा âtmâ, soul ; शरीर śarîra, body ; इन्द्रिय indriya, sense ; अर्थ artha, object ; बुद्धि buddhi consciousness, intellect, reason, understanding ; मनः manas, mind, sensorium ; प्रवृत्ति pravṛitti ; दोष doṣa ; fault ; प्रेत्यभाव pretya-bhâva, rebirth ; फल phala, fruit ; दुःख duḥkha, pain ; अपवर्ग apavarga, release, salvation ; तु tu, excludes other provables ; प्रमेयम् prameyam, the object of proof.

9. Soul, body, senses, objects of sense, intellect, mind, activity, fault, transmigration, fruit, pain and release—are the **objects of right knowledge.**

The objects of right knowledge are also enumerated as substance, quality, action, generality, particularity, intimate relation [and non-existence which are the technicalities of the Vaiśeṣika philosophy]

इच्छा द्वेष प्रयत्न सुख दुःख ज्ञानानि "आत्मनो लिङ्गम्" इति ॥१।१।१०॥

इच्छा ichchhâ, desire ; द्वेष dveṣa, aversion ; प्रयत्न prayatna, effort ; सुख sukha, pleasure ; दुःख duḥkha, pain ; ज्ञान jñâna, cognition ; आत्मनः âtma-naḥ, of the soul ; लिङ्ग lingam, mark.

10. Desire, aversion, volition, pleasure, pain and intelligence are the marks of the soul.

[These abide in the soul, or rather are the qualities of the substance called soul]

चेष्टेन्द्रियार्थाश्रयः "शरीरम्" ॥१।१।११ ॥

चेष्टेन्द्रियार्थाश्रयः cheṣṭâ indriya-artha âśrayaḥ, site or locus of volition, or striving, senses, and objects, *viz.*, pleasure and pain ; शरीरम् śarîram body.

11. **Body** is the site of gesture, senses and sentiments.

Body is the site of *gesture*, inasmuch as it strives to reach what is desirable and to avoid what is hateful. It is also the site of *senses*, for the latter act well or ill, according as the former is in good or bad order. *Sentiments* which comprise pleasure and pain are also located in the body which experiences them.

घ्राण रसन चक्षु स्त्वक्श्रोत्राणि "इन्द्रियाणि" भूतेभ्यः॥१।१।१२॥

घ्राण रसन चक्षुस्त्वक् श्रोत्राणि ghrâṇa-rasana-chakṣus-tvak-śrotrâṇi, nose, tongue, eye, skin and ear ; इन्द्रियाणि indriyâṇi, organs of sense ; भूतेभ्यः bhûtebhyaḥ, from the elements.

12. Nose, tongue, eye, skin and ear are the senses produced from elements.

Nose is of the same nature as earth, tongue as water, eye as light, skin as air and ear as ether

पृथिव्यापस्तेजो वायुराकाशमिति "भूतानि" ॥१।१।१३॥

पृथिवी Prithivî, earth ; आप âpaḥ, water ; तेजस् tejas, fire ; वायु: vâyuḥ, air; आकाशं âkâśam, ether ; इति iti, these ; भूतानि bhûtâni, elements.

13. Earth, water, light, air and ether—these are the **elements.**

गन्धरसरूपस्पर्शशब्दा: "पृथिव्यादिगुणा:" तदर्था: ॥१।१।१४॥

गन्ध रस रूप स्पर्श शब्दा: Gandha-rasa rûpa-sparśa śabdâḥ, smell, taste, colour, touch and sound ; पृथिव्यादिगुणा: prithivî-âdi-guṇâḥ, attributes of earth, etc., तदर्था: Tat-arthâḥ, objects of them, the senses,

14. Smell, taste, colour, touch and sound are **objects of the senses** and qualities of the earth, etc.

Smell is the object of nose and the prominent quality of earth, taste is the object of tongue and quality of water, colour is the object of eye and quality of fire, touch is the object of skin and quality of air, and sound is the object of ear and quality of ether.

"बुद्धि:" उपलब्धिर्ज्ञानमित्यनर्थान्तरम् ॥१।१।१५॥

बुद्धि: buddhiḥ consciousness, understanding ; उपलब्धि: Upalabdhiḥ, apprehension, intuition ; ज्ञानं jñânam, cognition. ; इति iti, this. अनर्थान्तरं an-artha-antaram, statement of synonyms.

15. **Intellect,** apprehension and knowledge—these are not different from one another.

[The term apprehension (*upalabdhi*) is generally used in the sense of perception (*pratyakṣa*). According to the Sânkhya philosophy, intellect (*buddhi*), which is the first thing evolved out of primordial matter (*prakriti*), is altogether different from knowledge (*jñâna*), which consists in the reflection of external objects on the soul (*puruṣa*), the abode of transparent consciousness].

युगपज्ज्ञानानुत्पत्ति: "मनसो लिङ्गम्" ॥१।१।१६॥

युगपत् yugapat, simulaneous ; ज्ञानानुत्पत्तिः Jñâna-anutpattiḥ, non-apre-arance of cognitions ; मनसः manasaḥ, of manas, mind, लिङ्गम् liṅgam, mark.

16. The mark of the **mind** is that there do not arise (in the soul) more acts of knowledge than one at a time.

It is impossible to perceive two things simultaneously. Perception does not arise merely from the contact of a sense-organ with its object, but it requires also a conjunction of the mind Now, the mind, which is an atomic substance, cannot be conjoined with more than one sense-organ at a time, hence there cannot occur mere acts of perception than one at one time.

"प्रवृत्तिः" वाग्बुद्धिशरीरारम्भ इति ॥१।१।१७॥

प्रवृत्तिः Pravṛittiḥ, activity ; वाग्बुद्धिशरीरारम्भः Vâk-buddhi-śarîra-ârambhaḥ the start made by speech, manas and body.

17. **Activity** is that which makes the voice, mind and body begin their action.

There are three kinds of action, *viz.*, *vocal*, *mental* and *bodily*, each of which may be sub divided as good or bad.

Bodily actions which are *bad* are :—(1) killing, (2) stealing, and (3) committing adultery.

Bodily actions which are *good* are :—(1) giving, (2) protecting, and (3) serving.

Vocal actions which are *bad* are :—(1) telling a lie, (2) using harsh language, (3) slandering, and (4) indulging in frivolous talk.

Vocal actions which are *good* are :—(1) speaking the truth, (2) speaking what is useful, (3) speaking what is pleasant, and (4) reading sacred books.

Mental actions which are *bad* are :—(1)malice, (2) covetousness, and (3) scepticism.

Mental actions which are *good* are :—(1) compassion, (2) refraining from covetousness, and (3) devotion.

प्रवर्त्तनालक्षणा "दोषाः" ॥१।१।१८॥

प्रवर्त्तना लक्षणाः pravartanâ lakṣaṇâḥ, of which the characteristic is to move to activity ; दोषाः doṣâḥ, faults.

18. **Faults** have the characteristic of causing activity.

The faults are affection, aversion and stupidity.

पुनरुत्पत्तिः "प्रेत्यभावः" ॥ १ । १ । १९ ॥

पुनरुत्पत्तिः punar-utpattiḥ, re-appearance, re-birth ; प्रेत्यभावः pretya-bhâvaḥ, existence after passing away.

19. **Transmigration** means re-births.

Transmigration is the series of births and deaths. Birth is the connection of soul with body, sense-organs, mind, intellect, and sentiments, while death is the soul's separation from them.

प्रवृत्तिदोषजनितोऽर्थः "फलम्" ॥ १ । १ । २० ॥

प्रवृत्तिदोष जनितः pravṛitti-doṣa-janitaḥ, produced by activity and fault ; अर्थः arthaḥ, object ; फलम् phalam, fruit.

20. **Fruit** is the thing produced by activity and faults.

Fruit consists in the enjoyment of pleasure or suffering of pain. All activity and faults end in producing pleasure which is acceptable, and pain which is fit only to be avoided.

बाधनालक्षणं "दुःखम्" इति ॥ १ । १ । २१ ॥

बाधनालक्षणं bâdhanâ-lakṣaṇam, of which the characteristic is restraint or irritation ; दुःखम् ; duḥkham, pain.

21. **Pain** has the characteristic of causing uneasiness.

Pain is affliction which every one desires to avoid The aphorism may also be translated as follows :—

Pain is the mark of hindrance to the soul.

तदत्यन्तविमोक्षः "अपवर्गः" ॥ १ । १ । २२ ॥

तदत्यन्तविमोक्षः tat-atyanta-vimokṣaḥ, absolute deliverance from this ; अपवर्गः apavargaḥ, attainment of the goal, final release, salvation.

22. **Release** is the absolute deliverance from pain.

A soul which is no longer subject to transmigration is freed from all pains. Transmigration, which consists in the soul's leaving one body and taking another, is the cause of its undergoing pleasure and pain. The soul attains release as soon as there is an end of the body, and, consequently, of pleasure and pain. Those are mistaken who maintain that release enables the soul, not only to get rid of all pains, but also to attain eternal pleasure; for pleasure is as impermanent as pain and the body.

समानानेकधर्म्मोपपत्तेर्विप्रतिपत्तेरुपलब्ध्यनुपलब्ध्यव्यवस्थातश्च विशेषापेक्षो विमर्शः "संशयः" ॥१।१।२३॥

समानानेकधर्मोपपत्तेः samâna-aneka-dharma-upapatteḥ, from the appearance of several common properties ; विप्रतिपत्तेः vipratipatteḥ, from contradiction ; उपलब्ध्यनुपलब्ध्यव्यवस्थातः upalabdhi-anupalabdhi-avyavasthâtaḥ, from absence of uniformity of apprehension and from that of non-apprehension ; विशेषापेक्षः viśeṣa-apekṣaḥ, in which there is need of the distinguishing mark ; विमर्शः vimarśaḥ, consideration, judgment ; संशयः saṃśayaḥ, doubt.

23. **Doubt,** which is a conflicting judgment about the precise character of an object, arises from the recognition of properties common to many objects, or of properties not common to any of the objects, from conflicting testimony, and from irregularity of perception and non-perception.

Doubt is of five kinds, according as it arises from—

(1) *Recognition of common properties, e.g.*, seeing in the twilight a tall object we cannot decide whether it is a man or a post, for the property of tallness belongs to both.

(2) *Recognition of properties not common, e.g.*, hearing a sound, one questions whether it is eternal or not, for the property of soundnees abides neither in man, beast, etc., that are non-eternal, nor in atoms which are eternal.

(3) *Conflicting testimony, e.g.*, merely by study one cannot decide whether the soul exists, for one system of philosophy affirms that it does, while another system states that it does not.

(4) *Irregularity of perception, e.g.*, we perceive water in the tank where it really exists, but water appears also to exist in the mirage where it really does not exist.

A question arises whether water is perceived only when it actually exists, or even when it does not exist.

(5) *Irregularity of non-perception, e.g.*, we do not perceive water in the radish where it really exists, and also on dry land where it does not exist.

A question arises whether water is not perceived only when it does not exist, or also when it does exist.

यमर्थमधिकृत्य प्रवर्त्तते तत "प्रयोजनम्" ॥१।१।२४॥

यम् yam, which ; अर्थम् artham, object ; अधिकृत्य adhikṛitya, intending; प्रवर्त्तते pravartate, acts ; तत् tat, that प्रयोजनम् prayojanam, purpose.

24. **Purpose** is that with an eye to which one proceeds to act. Purpose refers to the thing which one endeavours to attain or avoid. [A man collects fuel for the purpose of cooking his food].

लौकिकपरीक्षकाणां यस्मिन्नर्थे बुद्धिसाम्यं स "दृष्टान्तः"

॥ १ । १ । २५ ॥

लौकिकपरीक्षकाणां laukika-parîkṣakâṇâm, of average men and of men possessing discrimination either by nature or as a result of education ; यस्मिन् अर्थे yasmin arthe, in which object ; बुद्धिसाम्यं buddhi-sâmyam, community of idea ; सः saḥ, that ; दृष्टान्तः dṛiṣṭântaḥ, example, familiar instance.

25. **A familiar instance** is the thing about which an ordinary man and an expert entertain the same opinion.

[With regard to the general proposition, "wherever there is smoke there is fire," the Samiliar instance is a kitchen in which fire and smoke abide together, to the satisfaction of an ordinary man as well as an acute investigator].

तन्त्राधिकरणाभ्युपगमसंस्थितिः "सिद्धान्तः" ॥ १ । १ । २६॥

तन्त्राधिकरणाभ्युपगमसंस्थितिः tantra-adhikaraṇa-abhyupagama-saṃsthitiḥ, established truth about the subject matter of a tantra or course of teaching about a number of interrelated subjects, or of an adhikarana or topic of discussion or of an abhyupagama or admission without proof ; सिद्धान्तः siddhântaḥ, conclusion, established tenet.

26. **An established tenet** is a dogma resting on the authority of a certain school, hypothesis, or implication.

सर्वतन्त्रप्रतितन्त्राधिकरणाभ्युपगमसंस्थित्यर्थान्तरभा-

वात् ॥१।१।२७॥

सर्वतन्त्र प्रतितन्त्राधिकरणाभ्युपगम संस्थित्यर्थान्तरभावात् sarva-tantra-prati-tantra-adhi-karaṇa-abhyupagama-saṃsthiti-artha-antara-bhâvât, owing to differences as tenets of all the tantras, of a particular tantra, of a topic or of an admission.

27. The tenet is of four kinds owing to the distinction between

a dogma of all the schools, a dogma peculiar to some school, a hypothetical dogma and *an implied dogma.*

सर्वतन्त्राविरुद्धस्तन्त्रेऽधिकृतोऽर्थः "सर्वतन्त्रसिद्धान्तः" ॥ १ । १ । २८ ॥

सर्वतन्त्राविरुद्धः sarva-tantra-aviruddhaḥ, unopposed in all tantras or systems ; तन्त्रे tantre, in the particular tantra or system ; अधिकृतः adhikṛitaḥ, included, intended, dealt with, treated ; सर्वतन्त्र सिद्धान्तः sarva-tantra-siddhântaḥ, established tenet of all the systems, universal tenet.

28. **A dogma of all the schools** is a tenet which is not opposed by any school and is claimed by at least one school.

The five elements (*viz.*, earth, water, light, air and ether), the five objects of sense (*viz.*, smell, taste, colour, touch and sound), etc., are tenets which are accepted by all the schools.

समानतन्त्रसिद्धः परतन्त्रासिद्धः "प्रतितन्त्रसिद्धान्तः" ॥ १ । १ । २९ ॥

समानतन्त्रसिद्धः samâna-tantra-siddhaḥ, accepted in identical or allied systems ; परतन्त्रासिद्धः para-tantra-asiddhaḥ, not accepted in different systems ; प्रतितन्त्र सिद्धान्तः prati-tantra-siddhântaḥ. established tenet of a particuler system, particular tenet.

29. **A dogma peculair to some school** is a tenet which is accepted by similar schools, but rejected by opposite schools.

" A thing cannot come into existence out of nothing"—this is a peculiar dogma of the Sâṅkhyas. [The eternity of sound is a peculiar dogma of the Mîmâṃsakas].

यत्सिद्धावन्यप्रकरणसिद्धिस्स "अधिकरणसिद्धान्तः" ॥ १ । १ । ३० ॥

यत्सिद्धौ yat-siddhau, on and in the proof of which. ; अन्यप्रकरणसिद्धिः anya-prakaraṇa-siddhiḥ, another sub-topic is proved and needed ; सः saḥ, that ; अधिकरण सिद्धान्तः adhikaraṇa-siddhântaḥ, established tenet of a topic of discussion.

30. **An hypothetical dogma** is a tenet which, if accepted, leads to the acceptance of another tenet.

"There is a soul apart from the senses, because it can recognise one and the same object by seeing and touching." If you accept this tenet you must also have accepted the following :—(1) That the senses are more than one, (2) that each of the senses has its particular object, (3) that the soul derives its knowledge through the channels of the senses, (4) that a substance which is distinct from its qualities is the abode of them, etc.

अपरीक्षिताभ्युपगमात्तद्विशेषपरीक्षणम् "अभ्युपगमसिद्धान्तः"

॥ १ । १ । ३१ ॥

अपरीक्षिताभ्युपगमात् a-parîkṣita-abhyupagamât, after admission of a tenet without proof or examination ; तद्विशेष परीक्षणं tat-viśeṣa-parîkṣaṇam, examination of particulars concerning it ; अभ्युपगम सिद्धान्तः abhyupagama-siddhântaḥ, established tenet of an admission without proof or of a concession.

31. **An implied dogma** is a tenet which is not explicitly declared as such, but which follows from the examination of particulars concerning it.

The discussion, whether sound is eternal or non-eternal, pre-supposes that it is a substance. "That sound is a substance" is here an implied dogma. [The mind has nowhere been stated in the Nyâya-sûtra to be a sense-organ, but it follows from the particulars examined concerning it that it is so].

प्रतिज्ञाहेतूदाहरणोपनयनिगमनानि "अवयवाः" ॥१।१।३२॥

प्रतिज्ञाहेतूदाहरणोपनयनिगमनानि pratijñâ-hetu-udâharaṇa-upanaya-nigamanâni, proposition, mark, instance, ratiocination and inference ; अवयवाः avayavâḥ, members of a syllogism.

32. The **members** (of a syllogism) are proposition, reason, example, application, and conclusion.

[1. Proposition.—This hill is fiery,

2. Reason.—Because it is smoky,

3. Example.—Whatever is smoky is fiery, as a kitchen,

4. Application.—So is this hill (smoky),

5. Conclusion.—Therefore this hill is fiery.]

Some lay down *five more members* as follows :—

1 (*a*) Inquiry as to the proposition (jijñâsâ).—Is this hill fiery in all its parts, or in a particular part ?

2 (*a*) Questioning the reason (saṃśaya).—That which you call smoke may be nothing but vapour.

3 (*a*) Capacity of the example to warrant the conclusion (śakyaprâpti) —Is it true that smoke is always a concomitant of fire ? In a kitchen there are of course both smoke and fire, but in a red-hot iron-ball there is no smoke.

4 (*a*) Purpose for drawing the conclusion (prayojana) —Purpose consists in the determination of the true conditions of the hill, in order to ascertain whether it is such that one can approach it, or such that one should avoid it, or such that one should maintain an att tude of indifference towards it.

4 (*b*) Dispelling all questions (saṃśayavyudâsa).—It is beyond all question that the hill is smoky, and that smoke is an invariable concomitant of fire.

साध्यनिर्देशः "प्रतिज्ञा" ॥ १ । १ । ३३ ॥

साध्यनिर्देशः sâdhya-nirdeśaḥ, declaration of what is to be established; प्रतिज्ञा pratijñâ, proposition.

33. **A proposition** is the declaration of what is to be established.

Sound is non-eternal—this is a proposition.

उदाहरणसाधर्म्यात्साध्यसाधनं "हेतुः" ॥१।१।३४॥

उदाहरणसाधर्म्यात् udâharaṇa-sâdharmyât, through similarity to instance; साध्य साधनं sâdhya-sadhanam, statement of the means of establishing what is to be established ; हेतुः hetuḥ, mark.

34. **The reason** is the means for establishing what is to be established through the *homogeneous* or affirmative character of the example.

Proposition.—Sound is non-eternal,

Reason.—Because it is produced,

Example (homogeneous).—Whatever is produced is non-eternal, as a pot.

The example " pot " possesses the same character as is implied in the reason, *viz.*, "being produced," inasmuch as both are non-eternal.

"तथा" वैधर्म्यात् ॥ १ । १ । ३५ ॥

तथा tathâ, likewise ; वैधर्म्यात् vaidharmyât, through dissimilarity to instance.

35. Likewise through *heterogeneous* or *negative* character.

Proposition.—Sound is non-eternal,

Reason.—Because it is produced,

Example (heterogeneous).—Whatever is not non-eternal is not produced, as the soul.

The example " soul " possesses a character heterogeneous to that which is implied in the reason, *viz*, "being produced," inasmuch as one is eternal and the other non-eternal.

साध्यसाधर्म्यात्तद्धर्मभावी दृष्टान्त "उदाहरणम्" ॥१।१।३६॥

साध्यसाधर्म्यात् sâdhya-sâdharmyât, through similarity to what is to be established ; तद्धर्मभावी tat-dharma-bhâvî, in which the property of what is to be established exists ; दृष्टान्तः dṛiṣṭântaḥ, example ; उदाहरणम्, udâharaṇam, instance.

36. **A homogeneous (or affirmative example** is a familiar instance which is known to possess the property to be established, and which implies that this property is invariably c ntained in the reason given.

Proposition.—Sound is non-eternal,

Reason.—Because it is produced,

Homogeneous example.—Whatever is produced is non-eternal, as a pot.

Here " pot " is a familiar instance which possesses the property of non-eternality and implies that whatever is "produced" is attended by the same property (non-eternality).

तद्विपर्ययाद्वा "विपरीतम्" ॥१।१।३७॥

तद्विपर्ययात् tat-viparyayât, through dissimilarity to what is to be established ; वा vâ, or ; विपरीतम् viparîtam, contrary, opposite.

37. **A heterogeneous (or negative) example** is a familiar instance which is known to be devoid of the property to be established

and which implies that the absence of this property is invariably rejected in the reason given.

Proposition.—Sound is non-eternal,

Reason.—Because it is produced,

Heterogeneous example.—Whatever is not non-eternal is not produced, as the soul.

Here the "soul" is a familiar instance which is known to be devoid of the property of non-eternality and implies that if anything were produced, it would necessarily be deprived of the quality of eternality, *i.e.* 'being produced' and 'eternal' are imcompatible epithets.

उदाहरणापेक्षस्तथेत्युपसंहारो न तथेति वा साध्यस्य "उपनयः" ॥ १ । १ । ३८ ॥

उदाहरणापेक्षः udâharaṇa-apekṣaḥ dependent upon instance ; तथा tathâ, so. उपसंहारः upasamhârah winding up, conluding. न तथा इति na tathâ iti, not so ; वा vâ, or ; साध्यस्य sâdhyasya, of what is to be established ; उपनयः upanayaḥ. ratiocination.

38. **Application** is a winding up, with reference to the example, of what is to be established as being so or not so.

Application is of two kinds : (1) *Affirmative* and (2) *Negative.* The affirmative application, which is expressed by the word "so," occurs when the example is of an affirmative character. The negative, which is expressed by the phrase "not so," occurs when the example is of a negative character.

Proposition —Sound is non-eternal,

Reason.—Because it is produced,

Example.—Whatever is produced is non-eternal, as a pot,

Affirmative application.—So is sound (produced),

Conclusion.—Therefore sound is non-eternal.

Or :

Proposition.—Sound is non-eternal,

Reason.—Because it is produced,

Example.—Whatever is eternal is not produced, as the soul,

Negative application.—Sound is not so (*i.e.*, sound is not not-produced),

Conclusion.—Therefore sound is not eternal.

हेत्वपदेशात्प्रतिज्ञायाः पुनर्वचनं "निगमनम्" ॥१।१।३९॥

हेत्वपदेशात् hetu-apadeśât, after statement of the mark ; प्रतिज्ञायाः pratijñâyâḥ, of proposition ; पुनर्वचनं punaḥ-vachanam, re-statement ; निगमनम् nigamanam, inference.

39. **Conclusion** is the re-stating of the proposition, after the reason has been mentioned.

Conclusion is the confirmation of the proposition, after the reason and the example have been mentioned.

Proposition.—Sound is non-eternal,

Reason.—Because it is produced,

Example.—Whatever is produced is non-eternal, as a pot,

Applicatian.—So is sound (produced).

Conclusion —Therefore sound is non-eternal.

अविज्ञाततत्त्वेऽर्थे कारणोपपत्तितस्तत्त्वज्ञानार्थमूहः "तर्कः" ॥ १ । १ । ४० ॥

अविज्ञाततत्त्वे a-vijñâta-tattve, true nature of which is not known, अर्थे arthe, in the case of an object ; कारणोपपत्तितः kâraṇa-upapatti-taḥ, by showing the appropriateness of the desired causes ; तत्त्वज्ञानार्थम् tattva-jñâna-artham, for the purpose of knowledge of true nature , ऊहः ûhaḥ, reasoning; तर्कः tarkaḥ, confutation, reductio ad absurdum.

40. **Confutation,** which is carried on for ascertaining the real character of a thing of which the character is not known, is reasoning which reveals the character by showing the absurdity of all contrary characters.

Is the soul eternal or non-eternal ? Here the real character of the soul, *viz.*, whether it is eternal, or non-eternal, is not known. In ascertaining the character, we reason as follows :—If the soul were non-eternal, it would be impossible for it to enjoy the fruits of its own actions, to undergo transmigration, and to attain final release But such a conclusion is absurd : such possibilities are known to belong to the soul : therefore, we must admit that the soul is eternal.

विमृश्य पक्षप्रतिपक्षाभ्यामर्थावधारणं "निर्णयः" ॥१।१।४१॥

विमृश्य vimṛiśya, arguing ; पक्षप्रतिपक्षाभ्यां pakṣa-pratipakṣâbhyâm, from opposite positions. ; अर्थावधारणं artha-avadhâraṇam, determination of object ; निर्णयः nirṇayaḥ, ascertainment.

41. **Ascertainment** is the removal of doubt, and the determination of a question, by hearing two opposite sides.

A person wavers and doubts if certain statements are advanced to him by one of two parties, but opposed by the other party. His doubt is not removed until by the application of reason he can vindicate either of the parties. The process by which the vindication is effected is called ascertainment. Ascertainment is not, however, in all cases preceded by doubt ; for instance, in the case of perception things are ascertained directly. So also we ascertain things directly by the authority of scriptures, or through discussion. But in the case of investigation, doubt must precede ascertainment.

इति श्रीगौतममहर्षिप्रणीते न्यायदर्शने प्रथमस्याध्यायस्य प्रथममाह्निकम् ॥ १ । १ ॥

BOOK I.—CHAPTER II.

प्रमाणतर्कसाधनोपालम्भस्सिद्धान्ताविरुद्धः पञ्चावयवोपपन्नः पक्षप्रतिपक्षपरिग्रहो "वादः" ॥ १ । २ । १ ॥

प्रमाणतर्कसाधनोपालम्भः pramâṇa-tarka-sâdhana-upâlambhaḥ, proof and disproof, affirmation and negation, by means of pramâṇas or proofs or instruments of right knowledge and tarka or confutation ; सिद्धान्ताविरुद्धः siddhânta-a-viruddhaḥ, not opposed to the established tenets ; पञ्चावयवोपपन्नः pañcha-avayava-upapannaḥ, presenting the five members of the syllogism ; पक्षप्रतिपक्षपरिग्रहः pakṣa-pratipakṣa-parigrahaḥ, admission of opposite views on the same subject ; वादः vâdaḥ, discussion.

42. **Discussion** is the adoption of one of two opposing sides. What is adopted is analysed in the form of five members, and defended by the aid of any of the means of right knowledge, while its opposite is assailed by confutation, without deviation from the established tenets —1.

[*A dialogue* or *disputation* (kathâ) is the adoption of a side by a disputant and its opposite by his opponent. It is of three kinds, *viz, discussion* which aims at ascertaining the truth, *wrangling* which aims at gaining victory, and *cavil* which aims at finding mere faults. A *discutient* is one who engages himself in a disputation as a means of seeking the truth].

An instance of discussion is given below :—

Discutient—There is soul.

Opponent—There is no soul.

Discutient—Soul is existent (proposition).

Because it is an abode of consciousness (reason).

Whatever is not existent, is not an abode of consciousness, as a hare's horn (negative example).

Soul is not so, that is, soul is an abode of consciousness (negative application).

Therefore soul is existent (conclusion).

Opponent—Soul is non-existent (proposition).

Because, etc.

Discutient—The scripture which is a verbal testimony declares the existence of soul.

Opponent ... ...

Discutient—If there were no soul, it would not be possible to apprehend one and the same object, through sight and touch.

Opponent ... ...

Discutient—The doctrine of soul harmonises well with the various tenets which we hold. *viz*, that there are eternal things, that everybody enjoys pleasure or suffers pain, according to his own actions, etc. Therefore, there is soul.

[The discussion will be considerably lengthened if the opponent happens to be a Buddhist, who does not admit the authority of scripture and holds that there are no eternal things, etc.]

यथोक्तोपपन्नश्छलजातिनिग्रहस्थानसाधनोपालम्भो "जल्पः" ॥ १ । २ । २ ।

यथोक्तोपपन्नः yathâ-ukta-upapannaḥ, presented as stated i. e. possessing all the characteristics of a discussion ; छलजातिनिग्रहस्थानसाधनोपालम्भः chhala-jâti-nigrahasthâna sâdhana-upâlambhaḥ, affirmation and negation by means of quibbling, futility, and opponent's errors ; जल्पः jalpaḥ, sophistry.

43. **Wrangling,** which aims at gaining victory, is the defence or attack of a proposition in the manner aforesaid, by quibbles, futilities, and other processes which deserve rebuke—2.

A wrangler is one who, engaged in a disputation, aims only at victory, being indifferent whether the arguments which he employs support his own contention or that of his opponent, provided that he can make out a pretext for bragging that he has taken an active part in the disputation.

स प्रतिपक्षस्थापनाहीनो "वितण्डा" ॥ १ । २ । ३ ॥

सः saḥ, that, i. e. sophistry ; प्रतिपक्षस्थापनाहीनः pratipakṣa sthâpanâhînaḥ, without the demonstration of one of the opposite views ; वितण्डा vitaṇḍâ, cavil.

44. **Cavil** is a kind of wrangling, which consists in mere attacks on the opposite side—3.

A *caviller* does not endeavour to establish anything, but confines himself to mere carping at the arguments of his opponent.

सव्यभिचारविरुद्धप्रकरणसमसाध्यसमकालातीता "हेत्वाभासाः" ॥ १ । २ । ४ ॥

सव्यभिचारविरुद्धप्रकरणसमसाध्यसमकालातीताः savyabhichâra-viruddha-prakaraṇasama sâdhyasama-kâlâtîtâḥ, erratic or multifarious, contradictory, synonymous with the prakaraṇa or subject under discussion, synonymous with what is to be established, and time-expired ; हेत्वाभासाः hetu-âbhâsâḥ, pseudo-marks.

45. **Fallacies of a reason** are the erratic, the contradictory, the equal to the question, the un roved, and the mistimed.—4.

अनैकान्तिकः "सव्यभिचारः" ॥ १ । २ । ५ ॥

अनैकान्तिकः ana eka-antikaḥ, not-one-pointed ; सव्यभिचारः sa-vyabhichâraḥ, erratic.

46. The **erratic** is the reason which leads to more conclusions than one—5.

An instance of the *erratic* is given below :—

Proposition.—Sound is eternal,

Erratic reason.—Because it is intangible,

Example—Whatever is intangible is eternal, as atoms,

Application.—So is sound (intangible),

Conclusion.—Therefore sonnd is eternal.

Again :

Proposition.—Sound is non-eternal,

Erratic reason.—Because it is intangible,

Example.—Whatever is intangible, is non-eternal, as intellect,

Application.—So is sound (intangible).

Conclusion.—Therefore sound is non-eternal.

Here from the reason there have been drawn two opposite conclusions, *viz.* : that sound is eternal, and that sound is non-eternal. The reason or middle term is erratic when it is not pervaded by the major term, that is, when there is no universal connection between the major term and the middle term, as pervader and pervaded. "Intangible" is pervaded neither by 'eternal' nor by 'non eternal.' In fact, there is no universal connection between 'intangible' and 'eternal' or 'non-eternal.'

सिद्धान्तमभ्युपेत्य तद्विरोधी "विरुद्धः" ॥१।२।६॥

सिद्धान्तम् siddhântam, established tenet ; अभ्युपेत्य abhyupetya, admitting or depending upon , तद्विरोधी tat-virodhî, contradictory thereof ; विरुद्धः viruddhaḥ, contradictory.

47. The **contradictory** is the reason which opposes what is to be established—6.

Proposition.—A pot is produced,

Contradictory reason.—Because it is eternal.

Here the reason is contradictory, because that which is eternal is never produced.

यस्मात्प्रकरणचिन्ता स निर्णयार्थमपदिष्टः "प्रकरणसमः" ॥ १ । २ । ७ ॥

यस्मात् yasmât, whence ; प्रकरणचिन्ता prakaraṇa-chintâ, discussion of the subject ; सः saḥ, that ; निर्णयार्थम् nirṇaya-artham, for the purpose of the inference ; अपदिष्टः apadiṣṭaḥ, assigned ; प्रकरणसमः prakaraṇa-samaḥ, synonymous with the subject under consideration.

48. **Equal to the question** is the reason which provokes the very question, for the solution of which it was employed.—7.

Proposition—Sound is non-eternal,

Reason which is *equal to the question*.—Because it is not possessed of the attribute of eternality.

'Non-eternal' is the same as 'not possessed of the attribute of eternality.' In determining the question, whether sound is non-eternal, the reason given is that sound is non-eternal, or, in other words, the reason begs the question.

साध्याविशिष्टस्साध्यत्वात् "साध्यसमः" ॥ १ । २ । ८ ॥

साध्याविशिष्टः sâdhya-avis'ṣṭaḥ, not distinguished from what is to be established ; साध्यत्वात् sâdhya-tvât, requiring to be established ; साध्यसमः sâdhya-samaḥ, synonymous with what is to be established.

49. The **unproved** is the reason which stands in need of proof, in the same way as the proposition does—8.

Proposition.—Shadow is a substance.

Unproved reason.—Because it possesses motion.

Here, unless it is actually proved that shadow possesses motion, we cannot accept it as the reason for the proposition that shadow is a substance. Just as the proposition stands in need of proof, so does the reason itself. It is possible that the motion belongs to the person who causes that obstruction of light which is called shadow.

कालात्ययापदिष्टः "कालातीतः" ॥ १ । २ । ९ ॥

कालात्ययापदिष्टः kâla atyaya-apadiṣṭaḥ, assigned after lapse of time; कालातीतः kâla-atîtaḥ, time-expired, mistimed.

50. The **mistimed** is the reason which is adduced when the time is passed in which it might hold good.—9.

Proposition.—Sound is durable.

Mistimed reason.—Because it is manifested by union, as a colour.

The colour of a jar is manifested when the jar comes into union with a lamp, but the colour existed before the union took place, and will continue to exist after the union has ceased. Similarly, the sound of a drum is manifested when the drum comes into union with a rod, and the sound must, after the analogy of the colour, be presumed to have existed before the union took place, and to continue to exist after the union has ceased. Hence, sound is durable. The reason adduced here is mistimed, because the manifestation of sound does not take place at the time when the drum comes into union with the rod, but at a subsequent moment when the union has ceased. In the case of colour, however, the manifestation takes place just at the time when the jar comes into union with the lamp. Because the time of their manifestation is different, the analogy between colour and sound is not complete; therefore, the reason is mistimed.

Some interpret the aphorism as follows :—The *mistimed* is the reason which is adduced in a wrong order among the five members, for instance, as, if the reason is stated before the proposition. But this interpretation, according to Vâtsyâyana, is wrong; for a word bears its legitimate connection with another word (in a Sanskrit sentence) even if they are placed at a distance from each other, and, on the other hand, even the closest proximity is of no use if the words are disconnected in their sense.* Moreover, the placing of members in a wrong order is noticed in the Nyâya-sûtra as a *nigrahasthâna* (occasion for rebuke), called *aprâpta-kâla* (inopportune). (V. ii. 11.)

वचनविघातोऽर्थविकल्पोपपत्त्या "छलम्" ॥१।२।१०॥

वचनविघातः vachana-vighâtaḥ, opposition to statement; अर्थविकल्पोपपत्त्या artha-vikalpa-upapattyâ, by the assumption of an alternative import; छलम् chhalam, quibble, finding fault with.

* (Quoted by Vatsyâyana in the Nyâya-bhâṣya, p. 250).

51. **Quibble** is the opposition offered to a proposition by the assumption of an alternative meaning.—10.

"तत्त्रिविधं" वाक्छलं सामान्यच्छलमुपचारच्छलं चेति- ॥ १ । २ । ११ ॥

तत् tat, it ; त्रिविधं tri-vidham, three-fold ; वाक्छलं vâk-chhalam, quibble in respect of a word ; सामान्यछलं sâmânya-chhalam, quibble in respect of a genus ; उपचारछलं upachâra-chhalam, quibble in respect of a metaphor; चेति cha iti, and.

52. It is of *three* kinds, *viz.*, quibble in respect of a term, quibble in respect of a genus, and quibble in respect of a metaphor.—11.

अविशेषाभिहितेऽर्थे वक्तुरभिप्रायादर्थान्तरकल्पना "वाक्-छलम्" ॥ १ । २ । १२ ॥

अविशेषाभिहिते a-viśeṣa-abhihite, stated in a general way ; अर्थे arthe, in respect of an object वक्तुः vaktuḥ, speaker's ; अभिप्रायात् abhiprâyât, from the intention ; अर्थान्तरकल्पना artha-antara-kalpanâ, supposition of a different object ; वाक्छलं vâk-chhalam, quibble in respect of words.

53. **Quibble in respect of a term** consists in wilfully taking the term in a sense other than that intended by a speaker who has happened to use it ambiguously.—12.

A speaker says: "This boy is *nava-kambala* (possessed of a new blanket)."

A quibbler replies: "This boy is not certainly *nava-kambala* (possessed of nine blankets), for he has only one blanket."

Here the word *nava*, which is ambiguous, was used by the speaker in the sense of "new," but has been wilfully taken by the quibbler in the sense of "nine."

सम्भवतोऽर्थस्यातिसामान्ययोगादसम्भूतार्थकल्पना "सामान्यच्छलम्" ॥ १ । २ । १३ ॥

सम्भवतः sambhavataḥ, possible ; अर्थस्य arthasya, of import ; अतिसामान्ययोगात् atisâmânya-yogât, from the application of a higher genus ; असम्भूतार्थकल्पना a-sambhûta-artha-kalpanâ, supposition of an impossible import; सामान्यछलं sâmânya-chhalam, quibble in respect of a genus.

54. **Quibble in respect of a genus** consists in asserting the impossibility of a thing which is really possible, on the ground that it belongs to a certain genus which is very wide.—13.

A speaker says: "This Brâhmaṇa is possessed of learning and conduct."

An objector replies: "It is impossible, for how can it be inferred that this person is possessed of learning and conduct because he is a Brâhmaṇa? There are little boys who are Brâhmaṇas, yet not possessed of learning and conduct."

Here the objector is a quibbler, for he knows well that possession of learning and conduct was not meant to be an attribute of the whole class of Brâhmaṇas, but it was ascribed to "this" particular Bráhmaṇa who lived long enough in the world to render it possible for him to pursue studies and acquire good morals.

धर्म्मविकल्पनिर्द्देशेऽर्थसद्भावप्रतिषेध "उपचारच्छलम्" ॥ १ । २ । १४ ॥

धर्मविकल्पनिर्देशे dharma-vikalpa-nirdeśe, in the case of transference of epithet; अर्थसद्भावप्रतिषेधः artha-sadbhâva-pratiṣedhaḥ, denial of the possibility of sense; उपचारछलं upachâra-chhalam, quibble in respect of a metaphor.

55. **Quibble in respect of a metaphor** consists in denying the proper meaning of a word by taking it literally, while it was used metaphorically, and *vice versa*.—14.

A speaker says: "The scaffolds cry out."

An objector replies: "It is impossible for scaffolds to cry out, for they are inanimate objects."

Here the objector is a quibbler, for he knew well that the word *scaffolds* was used to signify those standing on the scaffolds.

वाक्छलमेवोपचारच्छलं तदविशेषात ॥ १ । २ । १५ ॥

वाक्छलं vâk-chhalam, verbal quibble, playing on words; एव eva, itself; उपचारछलं upachâra-chhalam, metaphorical quibble, playing on metaphors; तदविशेषात् tat-aviśeṣât, there being no difference from it.

56. It may be said that quibble in respect of a metaphor is in

reality quibble in respect of a term, for the first is not different from the second.—15.

न तदर्थान्तरभावात् ॥ १ । २ । १६ ॥

न na, not ; तदर्थान्तरभावात् tat-artha-antara-bhâvât, being different objects. Denial of the possibility of sense is not the same as the supposition of a different sense.

57. But it is not so, for there is a distinction between them.—16.

Words are taken in their direct (literal) meanings in the case of 'quibble in respect of a term,' while they are taken in their direct (literal) as well as indirect (secondary) meanings in the case of 'quibble in respect of a metaphor.'

अविशेषे वा किञ्चित्साधर्म्यादेकच्छलप्रसङ्गः ॥ १ । २ । १७ ॥

अविशेषे aviśeṣe, in the absence of distinction ; वा vâ, or ; किञ्चित् साधर्म्यात् kiñchit sâdharmyât, through partial similarity ; एकछलप्रसंगः eka-chhala-prasaṅgaḥ, one quibble only will result.

58. If you do not admit that one is differant from another simply because there is some similarity between them, then we should have only one kind of quibble.—17.

If 'quibble in respect of a metaphor' were not different from 'quibble in respect of a term,' then these two also would not be different from 'quibble in respect of a genus,' because there is some similarity among all of them. This is absurd, hence the three kinds of quibble are different from one another.

साधर्म्यवैधर्म्याभ्यां प्रत्यवस्थानं "जातिः" ॥ १ । २ । १८ ॥

साधर्म्य वैधर्म्याभ्यां sâdharmya-vaidharmyâbhyâm, by means of similarity and dissimilarity ; प्रत्यवस्थानं pratyavasthânam, opposition ; जातिः jâtiḥ, futility.

59. **Futility** consists in offering objections founded on mere similarity or dissimilarity.—18.

A disputant says : "The soul is inactive, because it is all-pervading as ether."

His opponent replies : "If the soul is inactive because it bears similarity to ether as being all-pervading, why is it not active because it bears similarity to a pot as being a seat of union ?"

The reply is futile, because it overlooks the universal connection between the middle term and the major term which is existent in the arguments of the disputant, but wanting in the arguments of the opponent. Whatever is all-pervading is inactive, but whatever is a seat of union is not necessarily active.

Or again :

Disputant.—Sound is non-eternal, because unlike ether it is a product.

Opponent.—If sound is non-eternal because as a product it is dissimilar to ether, why is it not eternal because as an object of auditory perception it is dissimilar to a pot ?

The reply is futile, because it overlooks the universal disconnection between the middle term and the absence of the major term. There is a universal disconnection between "a product" and "not non-eternal," but there is no such disconnection between "an object of auditory perception" and "not eternal."

विप्रतिपत्तिरप्रतिपत्तिश्च "निग्रहस्थानम्" ॥ १ । २ । १९ ॥

विप्रतिपत्तिः vipratipattiḥ, wrong deduction ; अप्रतिपत्तिः apratipattiḥ, indecision ; च cha, and ; निग्रहस्थानं nigraha-sthânam, occasion for rebuke, ground of defeat.

60. **An occasion for rebuke** arises when one misunderstands, or does not understand at all.—19.

If a person begins to argue in a way which betrays his utter ignorance, or wilfully misunderstands and yet persists in showing that he understands well, it is of no avail to employ counter arguments. He is quite unfit to be argued with, and there is nothing left for his opponent but to turn him out or quit his company, rebuking him as a blockhead or a knave.

An instance of *occasion for rebuke* :—

Whatever is not quality, is substance.

Because there is nothing except colour, etc (quality)

A person who argues in the above way is to be rebuked as a fool, for his reason (which admits only quality) opposes his proposition (which admits both quality and substance)

Another instance :

Disputant.—Fire is not hot,

Opponent.—But the evidence of touch disproves such a statement.

Disputant, in order to gain the confidence of the assembled people, says—"O learned audience, listen, I do not say that fire is not hot," etc.

It is only meet that the opponent should quit the company of a man who argues in this way.

तद्विकल्पाज्जातिनिग्रहस्थानबहुत्वम् ॥ १ । २ । २० ॥

तद्विकल्पात् tat-vikalpât, from their varieties; जातिनिग्रहस्थान बहुत्वं játi-nigrahasthâna-bahutvam, multiplicity of futility and ground of defeat.

61. Owing to the variety of kinds, there is multiplicity of futilities and occasions for rebuke.—20.

There are 24 kinds of futility and 22 kinds of occasion for rebuke which will be treated respectively in Chapter I and Chapter II of Book V.

इति श्रीगौतममहर्षिप्रणीते न्यायदर्शने प्रथमस्याध्यायस्य द्वितीयमाह्निकम् ॥ १ । २ ॥

Book II, Chapter I.

समानानेकधर्म्माध्यवसायादन्यतरधर्म्माध्यवसायाद्वा न संशयः ॥ २ । १ । १ ॥

समानानेक धर्माध्यवसायात् samâna-aneka-dharma-adhyavasâyât, from the asecrtainment of common or more than one attributes of two objects; अन्यतरधर्माध्यवसायात् anyatara-dharma adhyavasâyât, from the ascertainment of the attributes of one of them; वा vâ, or; न na, not, संशयः samśayaḥ, doubt.

62. Some say that doubt cannot arise from the recognition of common and uncommon properties, whether conjointly or separately.–1.

Conjointly.—It is said that doubt about an object is never produced if *both* the common and uncommon properties of the object are recognised. For instance, if we see in the twilight a tall object which moves, we do not doubt whether it is a man or a post. We at once decide that it is a man, for though tallness is a property possessed in common by man and post, locomotion is a property which distinguishes a man from a post.

Separately.—Likewise, doubt about an object is said never to be produced if *only* the common or the uncommon properties are recognised. For instance, if we see a tall object in the twilight, we have no reason to doubt whether it is a man or a post. Tallness is certainly a property possessed in common by man and post, but the tallness of a man is not identical with that of a post: it merely resembles it. Now, the knowledge of similarity between the tallness of a man and that of a post presupposes a knowledge of the man and the post, of which two kinds of tallness are attributes. If there is already a knowledge of the man and the post, there cannot be any doubt about them, for knowledge is the vanquisher of doubt.

विप्रतिपत्त्यव्यवस्थाध्यवसायाच्च ॥ २ । १ । २ ॥

विप्रतिपत्त्यव्यवस्थाध्यवसायात् vipratipatti-avyavasthâ-adhyavasâyât, from the ascertainment of contradiction or of irregularity of perception and non-perception. च cha, and.

63. It is further said that doubt cannot arise, either from conflicting testimony, or from the irregularity of perception and non-perception.—2.

विप्रतिपत्तौ च सम्प्रतिपत्तेः ॥ २ । १ । ३ ॥

विप्रतिपत्तौ vipratipattau, if contradiction be a cause of doubt; च cha, also; सम्प्रतिपत्तेः sampratipatteḥ, from agreement.

64. In the case of conflicting testimony there is, according to them, a strong conviction (on each side).—3.

Suppose a disputant (Naiyâyika) says: there is soul. His opponent (Buddhist) replies: there is no soul.

The disputant and his opponent are quite sure that their respective statements are correct. Hence there is no doubt, but on the contrary there is conviction, in the minds of both.

अव्यवस्थात्मनि व्यवस्थितत्वाच्चाव्यवस्थायाः ॥२।१।४॥

अव्यवस्था avyavasthâ, irregularity; आत्मनि âtmani, in itself; व्यवस्थितत्वात् vyavasthita-tvât, being regular; च cha, and; अव्यवस्थायाः a-vyavasthâyâḥ, from irregularity.

65. Doubt, they say, does not arise from the irregularity of perception and non-perception, because in the irregularity itself there is regularity.—4.

An irregularity may be designated as such with reference to something else, but with reference to itself it is a settled fact. If the irregularity is settled in itself, it is regular and cannot cause doubt. On the other hand, if the irregularity is not settled in itself, it is devoid of its own character and cannot cause doubt.

तथाऽत्यन्तसंशयस्तद्धर्म्मसातत्योपपत्तेः ॥ २ । १ । ५ ॥

तथा tathâ, similarly; अत्यन्त संशयः atyanta-saṃśayaḥ, endless doubt; तद्धर्मसातत्योपपत्तेः tat-dharma-sâtatya-upapatteḥ, from continuous existence of the attributes thereof.

66. Likewise, there is, they say, the chance of an endless doubt, owing to the continuity of its cause.—5.

Recognition of properties common to many objects is, for instance, a cause of doubt. The common properties continue to exist, and hence there will, they say, be no cessation of doubt.

यथोक्ताध्यवसायादेव तद्विशेषापेक्षात्संशयेनासंशयो नात्यन्तसंशयो वा ॥ २ । १ । ६ ॥

यथोक्ताध्यवसायात् yathâ-ukta-adhyavasâyât, from the ascertainment as stated by the opponent ; एव eva, certainly ; तद्विशेषापेक्षात् tat-viśeṣa-apekṣât, in which there is need of the differentia ; संशये saṃśaye, doubt arising ; न na, not ; असंशयः a-saṃśayaḥ, absence of doubt ; न na, not ; अत्यन्त संशयः atyanta-saṃśayaḥ, endless doubt ; वा vâ, or.

67. In reply, it is stated that the recognition of properties common to many objects, etc., are certainly causes of doubt, if there is no reference to the precise characters of the objects : there is no chance of *no* -doubt or of *endless*-doubt.—6.

It is admitted that doubt does not arise from the recognition of common and uncommon properties conjointly. Aphorism 2-1-1 brings forth the objection that doubt is not produced even by the recognition of common or uncommon properties alone. It is said that, while we see a tall object in the twilight, we at once think of a man and a post, both of which are tall. Thus there is knowledge rather than doubt about the man and post suggested by the tall object. The present aphorism dismisses the objection, by stating that there is certainly a common (non-distinctive) knowledge about a man and a post suggested by the tall object, but there is no precise (distinctive) knowledge about them. Precise knowledge (that is, knowledge of the precise character which distinguishes a man from a post) being absent, doubt must arise. Similar arguments will apply to doubt arising from the recognition of non-common properties alone.

Aphorisms 2-1-2 and 2-1-3 raise the objection that doubt does not arise from conflicting testimony, as the disputant and his opponent are both confident of their respective contentions. The present aphorism disposes of the objection, by pointing out that, in the case of conflicting statements, one is led to believe that both statements are worth consideration, but is unable to penetrate into the precise characters of the statements. Hence, though the disputant and his opponent remain fixed, the umpire and the audience are thrown into doubt by their conflicting statements.

Aphorism 2-1-4 raises the objection that doubt cannot arise from the irregularity of perception and non-perception, as the irregularity is settled in itself. The present aphorism meets the objection by stating that the irregularity cannot be concealed by mere verbal tricks. The irregularity, though settled in itself, does not lose its own character until the objects which cause it are removed.

Aphorism 2-1-5 gives rise to the fear that there is the possibility of an endless doubt, inasmuch as the cause is continuous. The present aphorism removes the fear by stating that, though materials of doubt, such as common properties, etc., continue to exist, we do not always recognise them. Unless there is recognition of the common properties, etc., there cannot be doubt.

यत्र संशयस्तत्रैवमुत्तरोत्तरप्रसङ्गः ॥ २ । १ । ७ ॥

यत्र yatra, wherever ; संशयः saṃśayaḥ, doubt ; तत्र tatra, there ; एवं evam, in this way ; उत्तरोत्तरप्रसंगः uttara-uttara-prasañgaḥ, sequence of arguments one after another.

68. **Examination** should be made in this way of each case where there is room for doubt.—7.

It has been stated that knowledge about the true nature of the categories consists in the true knowledge of their enunciation, definition, and examination. In case of well-known facts admitted by all, there should be no examination. We are to examine only those cases where there is room for doubt. The author explains, therefore, first the nature of doubt, and then proceeds to examine the other categories, lest there should be any room for doubt in them.

प्रत्यक्षादीनामप्रामाण्यं त्रैकाल्यासिद्धेः ॥ २ । १ । ८ ॥

प्रत्यक्षादीनां pratyakṣa-âdînâm, of perception and the rest ; अप्रामाण्यं a-prâmâṇyam, absence of the characteristic of being the means of right knowledge ; त्रैकाल्यासिद्धेः traikâlya-asiddheḥ, because of their non-operation in any of the three divisions of time, past, present, and future.

69. Perception and other means of knowledge, says an objector, are invalid, as they are impossible at all the three times,—8.

According to the objector, perception is impossible at the present, past and future times, or, in other words, perception can neither be prior to, nor posterior to, nor simultaneous with, the objects of sense.

पूर्व्वं हि प्रमाणसिद्धौ नेन्द्रियार्थसन्निकर्षात्प्रत्यक्षोत्पत्तिः ॥ २ । १ । ९ ॥

पूर्वं pûrvam, before ; हि hi, because ; प्रमाणसिद्धौ pramâṇa-siddhau, if the means of right knowledge, perception, etc., come into existence ; न na, not ; इन्द्रियार्थसन्निकर्षात् indriya-artha-sannikarṣât, from the contact of the sense and object; प्रत्यक्षोत्पत्तिः pratyakṣa-utpattiḥ, production of perception.

70. If perception occurred anteriorly it could not, he says, have arisen from the contact of a sense with its object.—9.

With reference to the perception of colour, for instance, it is asked whether the colour precedes perception or the perception precedes colour. If you say that perception occurred anteriorly or preceded the colour, you must give up your definition of perception, *viz.*, that perception arises from the contact of a sense with its object.

पश्चात्सिद्धौ न प्रमाणेभ्यः प्रमेयसिद्धिः ॥२।१।१०॥

पश्चात् paśchât, after; सिद्धौ siddhau, if it comes into existence; न na, not; प्रमाणेभ्यः pramâṇebhyaḥ, from the means of right knowledge; प्रमेयसिद्धिः prameya-siddhiḥ, establishment of what is to be proved.

71. If perception is supposed to occur posteriorly you cannot, he continues, maintain the conclusion that objects of sense are established by perception.—10.

The objection stands thus:—The means of right knowledge are stated by you to be perception, inference, comparison and verbal testimony. All objects of right knowledge are said to be established by them. The objects of sense, for instance, are supposed to be established by perception: colour is said to be established by visual perception. This conclusion will have to be abandoned if you say that perception occurs posteriorly to the objects.

युगपत्सिद्धौ प्रत्यर्थनियतत्वात्क्रमवृत्तित्वाभावो बुद्धीनाम् ॥ २ । १ । ११ ॥

युगपत् yugapat, simultaneously; सिद्धौ siddhau, if it comes into existence; प्रत्यर्थनियतत्वात् prati-artha-niyata-tvât, being restricted to each object; क्रमवृत्तित्वाभावः krama-vṛitti-tva-abhâvaḥ, absence of the characteristic of being in successive order; बुद्धीनाम् buddhînâm, of cognitions.

72. If perception were simultaneous with its object there would not, says the objector, be any order of succession in our cognitions, as there is no such order in their corresponding objects.—11.

Various objects of sense can exist at one time, *e.g*, colour and smell exist in a flower at the same time. If we hold that perception is simultaneous with its object, we must admit that the colour and the smell can be perceived at the same time, that is, our perception of colour must be admitted to be simultaneous with our perception of smell. This is absurd, because two acts of perception, nay, two cognitions cannot take place at the same time. As there is an order of succession in our cognitions, perception cannot be simultaneous with its object. The aphorism may also be explained as follows:—

In knowing a colour we perform, we may say, two kinds of knowledge simultaneously, *viz.*, perception and inference. As soon as our eye comes in contact with the colour, perception results which does not, however, enable us to be aware of the colour. The colour is brought home to us by inference which, we may say, is performed simultaneously with the perception. Now, says the objector, perception and inference being two different kinds of knowledge cannot be simultaneous, as the mind which is an atomic substance cannot be instrumental in producing more than one kind of knowledge at a time.

त्रैकाल्यासिद्धेः प्रतिषेधानुपपत्तिः ॥ २ । १ । १२ ॥

त्रैकाल्यासिद्धेः traikâlya-asiddheḥ, from the non-existence (of the means of right knowledge) in all the three times ; प्रतिषेधानुपपत्तिः pratiṣedha-an-upapattiḥ, non-establishment of denial or negation.

73. In reply, it is stated that if perception and other means of right knowledge are impossible, the denial of them is also impossible.–12.

Owing to absence of the matter to be denied, the denial is inoperative.

सर्वप्रमाणप्रतिषेधाच्च प्रतिषेधानुपपत्तिः ॥ २।१।१३॥

सर्वप्रमाणप्रतिषेधात् sarva-pramâṇa pratiṣedhât, owing to the denial of all the means of right knowledge ; च cha, and ; प्रतिषेधानुपपत्तिः pratiṣedha-an-upapattiḥ, non-existence of denial

74. Moreover, the denial itself cannot be established, if you deny all means of right knowledge.—13.

If you are to establish anything (*e g.*, denial), you can do so only by one or more of the means of right knowledge, *viz.*, perception, inference, comparison, etc. If you deny them, there will be left nothing which will lead you to the establishment of the thing. Hence you will not be able to establish the denial itself.

तत्प्रामाण्ये वा न सर्वप्रमाणविप्रतिषेधः ॥२।१।१४॥

तत्प्रामाण्ये tat-prâmâṇye, if denial is valid; वा vâ, or; न na, not; सर्वप्रमाणविप्रतिषेधः sarva-pramâṇa-vipratiṣedhaḥ, denial of all the means of right knowledge.

75. If you say that your denial is based on a certain means of right knowledge, you do thereby acknowledge the validity of the means.—14.

Suppose you deny a thing, because it is not perceived. You do thereby acknowledge that perception is a means of right knowledge. Similarly, inference, etc., are also to be acknowledged as means of right knowledge.

त्रैकाल्याप्रतिषेधश्च शब्दादातोद्यसिद्धिवत्तत्सिद्धेः ॥२।१।१५॥

त्रैकाल्याप्रतिषेधः trai-kâlya-apratiṣedhaḥ, non-denial by reference to three times; च cha, and; शब्दात् śabdât, from sound; आतोद्यसिद्धिवत् âtodya-siddhivat, like the proof of the existence of the drum; तत्सिद्धेः tat-siddheḥ, from the proof of their existence.

76. The means of right knowledge cannot, therefore, be denied. They are established in the manner that a drum is proved by its sound. —15.

There is, says Vâtsyâyana, no fixed rule that the means of right knowledge should precede objects of right knowledge or should succeed them or be simultaneous with them. The order of precedence is never uniform. Look at the analogous cases: a drum precedes its sound, and illumination succeeds the sun, while smoke is synchronous with fire.

प्रमेया च तुलाप्रामाण्यवत् ॥ २ । १ । १६ ॥

प्रमेया prameyâ, what is to be established; च cha, and; तुला tulâ, something possessing weight, a pair of scales, a measure of weight; प्रामाण्यवत् prâmâṇya-vat, like its being a means of right knowledge by being used as a weight.

77. The character of an object of right knowledge resembles that of a balance by which a thing is weighed.—16.

Just as a balance is an instrument for measuring weight, but is a measured object when it is itself weighed in another balance, so the senses, etc, are said to be instruments of right knowledge from one point of view, and objects of right knowledge from another point of view. The eye, for instance, is ani nstrument of perception as well as an object of perception. So also the means of right knowledge may, if occasion arises, be also regarded as objects of right knowledge.

प्रमाणतस्सिद्धेः प्रमाणानां प्रमाणान्तरसिद्धिप्रसङ्गः ॥२।१।१७॥

प्रमाणतः pramâṇa-taḥ, from the means of right knowledge ; सिद्धेः siddheḥ, knowledge or proof being; प्रमाणानां pramâṇânâm, of the means of right knowledge ; प्रमाणान्तरसिद्धिप्रसङ्गः pramâna-antara.siddhi-prasaṅgaḥ, implication of the existence of other means of right knowledge.

78. If an object of right knowledge, continues the objector, is to be established by a means of right knowledge, this latter needs also to be established by another means of right knowledge.—17.

The objection stands thus :—

You say that an object of right knowledge is to be established by a means of right knowledge. I admit this, and ask how you establish the means of right knowledge itself. Since a means of right knowledge may also be regarded as an object of right knowledge, you are required to establish the so-called means of right knowledge. by another means of right knowledge, and so on.

तद्विनिवृत्तेर्वा प्रमाणसिद्धिवत्प्रमेयसिद्धिः ॥२।१।१८॥

तद्विनिवृत्तेः tat-vinivṛittehḥ, in case of the cessation of the other means after the cognition of the means of right knowledge ; वा vâ, on the other hand ; प्रमाणसिद्धिवत् pramâṇa-siddhi-vat, as in the case of the proof or knowledge of the means of right knowledge ; प्रमेयसिद्धिः prameya-siddhiḥ, proof of the object of right knowledge.

79. Or, he continues, if a means of right knowledge does not require another means of right knowledge for its establishment, let an object of right knowledge be also established without any means of right knowledge.—18.

A means of right knowledge stands in the same category as an object of right knowledge, if you are to establish either of them. If the means of right knowledge is accepted as self-established, the object of right knowledge must also, according to the objector, be accepted as self-established. In such a contingency perception, inference, etc., will be superfluous.

न प्रदीपप्रकाशसिद्धिवत्तत्सिद्धेः ॥ २ । १ । १९ ॥

न na, no ; प्रदीपप्रकाशसिद्धिवत् pradîpa-prakâśa-siddhi-vat, like proof of illumination of the lamp ; तत्सिद्धेः tat-siddheḥ, because of the proof thereof *i. e.* the means of right knowledge.

80. It is not so : the means of right knowledge are established like the illumination of a lamp.—19.

A lamp illumines a jar and our eye illumines the lamp. Though it is sometimes the lamp, and sometimes the eye, that illumines, you are bound to admit a general notion of illuminator. Similarly, you must admit a general notion of the means of right knowledge as distinguished from that of the objects of right knowledge. The means will not, of course, be regarded as such when included under the category of an object.

[The aphorism is also interpreted as follows :—Just as a lamp illumines itself and the other objects, the means of right knowledge establish themselves and the objects of right knowledge. Hence perception establishes itself and the objects of sense].

Note.—Objections raised in aphorisms 8, 9, 10, 11, 16, 17 and 18 emanated from the Buddhist philosophy. The reply given in aphorisms 12, 13, 14, 15 and 19, represents the views of Brâhmanic philosophers who regard perception as a real act and objects as self-existent entities. According to the Buddhist philosophers, however, neither perception nor objects have any self-existence. They acquire an apparent or conditional existence, in virtue of a certain relation which exists between them. Cause and effect, long and short, prior and posterior, etc., are all relative terms. The whole world is a net-work of relations. The relations themselves are illusory, as the objects which are related have no self-existence. Hence the world is an illusion, or has a mere conditional existence. But where there is conditionality, there is no truth. Truth and conditionality are incompatible terms. That which neutralises all relations is the void or absolute which lies beyond the conditional world. To speak the truth, the world is an absolute nothing, though it has a conditional existence. *Vide* my Translation of the Mâdhyamika aphorisms in the Journal of the Buddhist Text Society, Calcutta, for 1895, 1896, 1897, 1898 and 1899.

क्वचिन्निवृत्तिदर्शनादनिवृत्तिदर्शनाच्च क्वचिदनेकान्तः ॥ २।१।२० ॥

क्वचित् kvachit, in some cases, e. g. lamp ; निवृत्तिदर्शनात् nivṛitti-darśanât, from the observation of cessation ; अनिवृत्तिदर्शनात् anivṛitti-darśanât, from the observation of non-cessation or non-absence ; च cha, and ; क्वचित् kvachit, in some cases, e. g. jar ; अनेकान्तः an-eka-antaḥ, not-one-ended, uncertain.

81. Seeing that in some cases other proofs are not required and

that in some cases there is need of other proofs, your argument is indecisive—20.

This is in reply to those who argue that just as a light does not require another light to illuminate it, even so the proofs, i. e. the means of right knowledge also may not require anything else to prove them ; in other words, that every means of right knowledge is also the means of its own right knowledge. The reply is that the example cannot be stretched so far, because there is nothing to distinguish the hetu (reason), viz. to be the illuminator, from the udâharaṇa (example), viz. the lamp, in this respect The means of right knowledge and a lamp both illuminate objects ; a lamp also illuminates itself ; but it does not therefore follow that the means of right knowledge also illuminates itself. For a lamp which illuminates objects, can also be illuminated by another lamp ; and it would then follow on the same analogy that the means of right knowledge which illuminates objects, may be also illuminated by other means. Thus your argument leads to opposite conclusions.

प्रत्यक्षलक्षणानुपपत्तिरसमग्रवचनात् ॥ २ । १ । २१ ॥

प्रत्यक्षलक्षणानुपपत्तिः pratyakṣa-lakṣaṇa-an-upapattiḥ, non-establishment of the definition of perception ; असमग्रवचनात् A-samagra-vachanât, from incomplete statement.

82. An objector may say that the definition of perception as given before is untenable, because incomplete.—21.

Perception has been defined as knowledge which arises from the contact of a sense with its object. This difinition is said to be defective, because it does not notice the conjunction of soul with mind, and of mind with sense, which are also causes of perception.

नात्ममनसोस्सन्निकर्षाभावे प्रत्यक्षोत्पत्तिः ॥ २ । १ । २२॥

न na, not; आत्ममनसः âtma-mansoḥ, of soul and mind ; सन्निकर्षाभावे sannikarṣa-abhâve, in the absence of contact ; प्रत्यक्षोत्पत्तिः : pratyakṣa-utpattih, production of perception.

83. Perception, it is said, cannot arise unless there is conjunction of soul with mind.—22.

From the contact of a sense with its object no knowledge arises unless, it is said, there is also conjunction of soul with mind. A sense coming in contact with its object produces knowledge in our soul, only if the sense is conjoined with the mind. Hence the conjunction of soul with mind should be mentioned as a necessary element in the definition of perception.

दिग्देशकालाकाशेष्वप्येवं प्रसङ्गः ॥ २ । १ ।२३ ॥

दिग्देशकालाकाशेषु dik-deśa-kâla-âkâśeṣu, in respect of direction, space, time and ether; अपि api, also; एवं evam, similar; प्रसंगः prasaṅgaḥ, implication.

84. Were it so, observes one of the assembly then direction, space, time and ether should also be enumerated among the causes of perception.—23.

Direction, space, time and ether are also indispensable conditions in the production of knowledge. But even the objector does not feel the necessity of enumerating these among the causes of perception.

ज्ञानलिङ्गत्वादात्मनो नानवरोधः ॥ २ । १ । २४ ॥

ज्ञानलिङ्गत्वात् jñâna-liṅga-tvât, because cognition or knowledge is its mark; आत्मनः âtmanaḥ, of soul; न na, not; अनवरोधः anavarodhaḥ, non-exclusion.

85. The soul, we point out, has not been excluded from our definition, inasmuch as knowledge is a mark of the soul.—24.

Perception has been described as knowledge, and knowledge implies the soul which is its abode. Consequently, in speaking of knowledge, the soul has, by implication, been mentioned as a condition in the production of perception.

तदयौगपद्यलिङ्गत्वाच्च मनसः ॥ २ । १ । २५ ॥

तदयौगपद्यलिङ्गत्वात् tat-ayaugapadya-liṅga-tvât, because non-simultaneity of cognitions is its mark; च cha, and; न na, not; मनसः manasaḥ, of mind.

86. The mind, too, has not been omitted from our definition, inasmuch as we have spoken of the non-simultaneity of acts of knowledge.—25.

Perception has been defined as knowledge. An essential characteristic of knowledge is that more than one act of knowing cannot take place at a time. This characteristic is due to the mind, an atomic substance, which is conjoined with the sense, when knowledge is produced. Hence, in speaking of knowledge, we have, by implication, mentioned the mind as a condition of perception.

प्रत्यक्षनिमित्तत्वाच्चेन्द्रियार्थयोस्सन्निकर्षस्य स्वशब्देन

वचनम् ॥ २ । १ । २६ ॥

प्रत्यक्षनिमित्तत्वात pratyakṣa nimitta-tvât, because it is the condition of perception ; इन्द्रियार्थयोः indriya-arthayoḥ, of sense and object ; सन्निकर्षस्य sannikarṣasya, of contact ; स्वशब्देन sva-śabdena, by identical term, specific ; वचनं vachanam, statement.

87. The contact of a sense with its object is mentioned as the special cause of perception —26.

There are many kinds of knowledge, such as perception, recollection, etc. Conjunction of soul with mind is a cause which operates in the production of all kinds of knowledge, while the contact of a sense with its object is the cause which operates only in perception. In our definition of perception we have mentioned only the special cause, and have omitted the common causes which precede not only perception, but also other kinds of knowledge.

सुप्तव्यासक्तमनसाञ्चेन्द्रियार्थयोस्सन्निकर्षनिमित्तत्वात ॥ २ । १ । २७ ॥

सुप्तव्यासक्तमनसां supta-vyâsakta-manasâm, of minds asleep and inattentive; च cha, and ; इन्द्रियार्थयोः indriya-arthayoḥ, of sense and object ; सन्निकर्षनिमित्तत्वात् sannikarṣa-nimitta- tvât, because contact is the condition.

88. The contact of a sense with its object is certainly the main cause, as perception is produced even when one is asleep or inattentive.—27.

Even a sleeping person hears the thundering of a cloud if his ear is open to it, and a careless person experiences heat if his skin is exposed to it.

तैश्चापदेशो ज्ञानविशेषाणाम् ॥ २ । १ । २८ ॥

तैः taiḥ, by these ; च cha, also ; अपदेशः apadeśaḥ, differenciation ; ज्ञानविशेषाणां jñâna-viśeṣâṇâm, of particular cognitions.

89. By the senses and their objects are also distinguished the special kinds of knowledge.—28.

The special kinds of knowlege are the five varieties of perception, *viz.*, by sight, hearing, smell, taste and touch. These are distinguished by the senses in whose spheres they lie, or by the objects which they illumine. Thus the visual perception is called eye-knowledge or colour-knowledge, the auditory perception is called ear-knowledge or sound-knowledge, the olfactery perception is called nose-knowledge or smell-knowledge, the gustatory perception is called tongue-knowledge or taste-knowledge and the tactual perception is called skin-knowledge or touch-knowledge.

व्याहतत्वादहेतुः ॥ २ । १ । २९ ॥

व्याहतत्वात् vyâhata-tvât, because it is precluded or obstructed ; अहेतुः a-hetuḥ, no argument.

90. (The above, says the objector, is) no argument, because it is precluded.—29.

The conclusion reached in the preceding three aphorisms is that the contact of the sense and the object, and not the contact of the sense and mind nor the contact of the soul and mind, should be stated to be the cause of perception. To this the objector puts in a rejoinder. The meaning is that if in certain circumstances, e. g. where the person is asleep or inattentive, perception takes place without the contact of the soul and mind, then there would be nothing to prevent several cognitions from being produced at one and the same time, and thus the tenet that the non-production of several cognitions simultaneously is the mark of the mind (Nyâya-sûtra, I. i. 16) would be violated. Therefore the sûtra I. i. 16 precludes, or is precluded by, the argument advanced in the preceding three aphorisms.

नार्थविशेषप्राबल्यात् ॥ २ । १ । ३० ॥

न na, not ; अर्थविशेषप्राबल्यात् artha viśeṣa-prâbalyât, on account of the prevalence or intensity of a particular percept or sensible object.

91. (We reply that there is) no (such preclusion or violation). (In the case of a person who is asleep or inattentive perception takes place) through the intensity of the sensible object.—30.

The three aphorisms in question, Nos 87-89, do not imply that the contact of the soul and mind sometimes is, and sometimes is not, the the cause of perception. They merely emphasise the fact that the contact of the sense and object is the principal cause of perceptual cognition. For the intensity of the object and the keenness of the sense directly establish contact of the object with the sense, and not of the sense with mind and the soul.

प्रत्यक्षमनुमानमेकदेशग्रहणादुपलब्धेः ॥ २ । १ । ३१ ॥

प्रत्यक्षं pratyakṣam, perception ; अनुमानं anumânam, inference ; एकदेशग्रहणात् eka-deśa-grahaṇât, because of apprehension of a part ; उपलब्धेः upalabdheḥ, of cognition.

92. Perception, it may be urged, is inference, because it illumines only a part as a mark of the whole.—31.

We are said to perceive a tree, while we really perceive only a part of it. This knowledge of the tree, as a whole, derived from the knowledge of a part of it is, according to the objectors, a case of inference.

न प्रत्यक्षेण यावत्तावदप्युपलम्भात् ॥ २ । १ । ३२ ॥

न na, no ; प्रत्यक्षेण pratyakṣeṇa, by perception ; यावत् तावत् yâvat tâvat, so much as that ; अपि api, even ; उपलम्भात् upalambhât, because there is cognition.

93. But this is not so, for perception is admitted of at least that portion which it actually illumines.—32.

The objectors themselves admit that a part is actually perceived. Hence, perception as a means of knowledge is not altogether denied, and it is accepted as different from inference.

साध्यत्वादवयविनि सन्देहः ॥ २ । १ । ३३ ॥

साध्यत्वात् sâadhya-tvât, because it is what is to be established ; अवयविनि avayavini, in respect of the whole ; सन्देहः sandehaḥ, doubt.

94. There is, some say, doubt about the whole, because the whole has yet to be established.—33.

The objectors say that parts alone are realities and that there is no whole behind them. A tree, for instance, is yellow in some parts and green in other parts. If the tree was one whole, then the contradictory qualities of yellowness and greenness could not have belonged to it simultaneously. Hence the parts alone must, according to them, be regarded as real.

सर्व्वाग्रहणमवयव्यसिद्धेः ॥ २ । १ । ३४ ॥

सर्वाग्रहणं sarva-agrahaṇam, non-apprehension of all ; अवयव्यसिद्धेः avayavi-asiddheḥ, in case of non-existence of the whole.

95. If there were no whole, there would, it is replied, be non-perception of all.—34.

All signifies substance, quality, action, generality, particularity and intimate relation. None of these would be perceptible, if the whole were denied. Suppose that the parts alone are real. Then, since a part is not of fixed dimension, it may itself be divided into parts, these latter again into further parts, and so on, until we reach the atoms which are the ultimate parts. Now the atoms which possess no bulk are not perceptible. Similarly, the quality, action, etc., which inhere in the atoms, are also not perceptible. Consequently, if we deny that there is a 'whole,' neither the substance nor quality, etc., would be perceptible.

धारणाकर्षणोपपत्तेश्च ॥ २ । १ । ३५ ॥

धारणाकर्षणोपपत्तेः dhâraṇa-âkarṣaṇa upapatteḥ, because of the fact of holding and pulling ; च cha, and.

96. There is a *whole*, because we can hold, pull, etc.—35.

If there were no whole, we could not have held or pulled an entire thing by holding or pulling a part of it. We say, 'one jar,' 'one man,' etc. This use of 'one' would vanish, if there were no whole.

सेनावनवद्ग्रहणमिति चेन्नातीन्द्रियत्वादणूनाम् ॥२।१।३६॥

सेनावनवत् senâ-vana-vat, like an army and a forest ; ग्रहणं grahaṇam, apprehension ; इति iti, so ; चेत् chet, if ; न na, no ; अतीन्द्रियत्वात् ati-indriya-tvât, because of their being beyond the senses ; अणूनां aṇûnâm, of the atoms.

97. The illustration from an army or a forest does not hold good, for atoms cannot be detected by the senses.—36.

If any one were to say that just as a single soldier or a single tree may not be seen from a distance, but an army consisting of numerous soldiers or a forest consisting of numerous trees is seen, so a single atom may not be perceptible, but a jar consisting of numerous atoms will be perceptible, and these atoms being called 'one jar,' the use of 'one' will not vanish, the analogy, we reply, does not hold good, because the soldiers and trees possess bulk and so are preceptible, whereas the atoms do not possess bulk and so are individually not perceptible. It is absurd to argue that, because soldiers and trees are perceptible in the mass, atoms are perceptible in the mass also : to avoid this conclusion, we must admit the existence of a whole beyond the parts.

रोधोपघातसादृश्येभ्यो व्यभिचारादनुमानमप्रमाणम् ॥२।१।३७॥

रोधोपघातसादृश्येभ्यः rodha-upaghâta-sâdṛiśyebhyaḥ, from obstruction (as in the case of a stream), disturbance (as in the case of an ants' nest) and (artificial) similarity ; व्यभिचारात् vyabhichârât, as it errs ; अनुमानं anumânam, inference ; अप्रमाणं apramâṇam, not a means of right knowledge.

98. **Inference**, some say, is not a means of right knowledge, as it errs in certain cases *e, g*, when a river is banked, when something is damaged, and when similarity misleads, &c.—37.

If we see a river swollen, we infer that there has been rain ; if we see the ants carrying off their eggs, we infer that there will be rain ; and if we hear a peacock scream, we infer that clouds are gathering. These inferences, says an objector, are not necessarily correct, for a river may be swollen because embanked, the ants may carry off their eggs because their nests have been damaged, and the so-called screaming of a peacock may be nothing but the voice of a man.

नैकदेशत्राससादृश्येभ्योऽर्थान्तरभावात् ॥ २।१।३८ ॥

न na, no ; एकदेशत्राससादृश्येभ्यः ekadeśa-trâsa-sâdṛiśyebhyaḥ, from the part, fear, and similarity ; अर्थान्तरभावात् artha-antara-bhâvât, because it is something different.

99. It is not so, because our inference is based on something else than the part, fear and likeness.—38.

The swelling of a river caused by rain is different from that which results from the embankment of a part of it ; the former is attended by a great rapidity of currents, an abundance of foam, a mass of floating fruits, leaves, wood, etc. The manner in which ants carry off their eggs just before rain is quite different from the manner in which they do so when their nests are damaged. The ants run away quickly in a steady line when rain is imminent, but fear makes them fly in disorder when their nests are damaged. The screaming of a peacock which suggests gathering clouds is quite different from a man's imitation of it, for the latter is not natural. If in such cases any wrong inference is drawn, the fault is in the person, not in the process.

वर्त्तमानाभावः पततः पतितपतितव्यकालोपपत्तेः ॥२।१।३९॥

वर्त्तमानाभावः vartamâna-abhâvaḥ, non-existence of present time ; पततः patataḥ, of the falling ; पतितपतितव्यकालोपपत्तेः patita-patitavya-kâla-upapatteḥ, because of proof of the time through which it has fallen and the time through which it will fall.

100. There is, some say, no present time because when a thing falls, we can know only the time through which it has fallen and the time through which it will yet fall.—39.

Inference has reference to three times. In the *a priori* inference we pass from the past to the present, in the *a posteriori* from the present to the past, and in the '*commonly seen*' from the present to the present. It is, therefore, proper that we should examine the three times. The reason which leads some people to deny the present time is that when a fruit, for instance, falls from a tree, we recognise only the past time taken up by the fruit in traversing a certain distance and the future time which will yet be taken up by the fruit in traversing the remaining distance. There is no intervening distance which the fruit can traverse at the so-called present. time. Hence, they say, there is no present time.

तयोरप्यभावो वर्तमानाभावे तदपेक्षत्वात् ॥२।१।४०॥

तयेाः tayoḥ, of these two ; अपि api, also ; अभावः abhâvaḥ non-existence ; वर्त्तमानाभावे vartamâna-abhâve, in the case of the non-existence of the present ; तदपेक्षत्वात् tat-apekṣa-tvât, because of being related to it.

101. If there is no present time, there will, it is replied, be no past and future times, because they are related to it.—40.

The past is that which precedes the present, and the future is that which succeeds it. Hence, if there is no present time, there cannot be any past or future time.

नातीतानागतयोरितरेतरापेक्षासिद्धिः ॥ २ । १ । ४१ ॥

न na, not ; अतीतानागतयेाः atîta-anâgatayoḥ, of the past and the future ; इतरेतरापेक्षासिद्धिः itara-itara-apekṣâ-siddhiḥ, establishment by mutal dependence.

102. The past and future cannot be established by a mere mutual reference.—41.

If the past is defined as that which is not the future and the future is defined as that which is not the past, the definition would involve a fallacy of mutual dependency. Hence we must admit the present time, to which the past and future are related.

वर्तमानाभावे सर्व्वाग्रहणम्प्रत्यक्षानुपपत्तेः ॥२।१।४२॥

वर्त्तमानाभावे vartamâna-abhâve, in the case of the non-existence of the present; सर्व्वाग्रहणं sarva-agrahaṇam, non-apprehension of all; प्रत्यक्षानुपपत्तेः pratyakṣa-an-upapatteḥ, owing to impossibility of perception.

103. If there were no present time, sense perception would be impossible, knowledge would be impossible.—42.

If you deny the present time, there cannot be any perception which illumines only what is present in time; and, in the absence of perception, all kinds of knowledge would be impossible. Hence the present time is established by confutation or the principle of *reductio ad absurdum*.

कृतताकर्त्तव्यतोपपत्तेरुभयथा ग्रहणम् ॥ २ । १ । ४३ ॥

कृतताकर्त्तव्यतोपपत्तेः kṛitatâ-kartavyatâ-upapatteḥ, from the possibility of a thing having been accomplished and remaining to be accomplished; उभयथा ubhayathâ, bothways; ग्रहणं grahaṇam, apprehension.

104. We can know both the past and the future, for we can conceive of a thing as made and as about to be made—43.

The present time is indicated by what continues, the past by what has been finished, and the future by what has not yet begun.

अत्यन्तप्रायैकदेशसाधर्म्यादुपमानासिद्धिः ॥२।१।४४॥

अत्यन्तप्रायैकदेशसाधर्म्यात् atyanta-prâya-ekadeśa-sâdharmyât, from absolute, almost complete or partial similarity; उपमानासिद्धिः upamâna-asiddiḥ, non-establishment of comparison.

105. **Comparison,** some say, is not a means of right knowledge, as it cannot be established either through complete or considerable or partial similarity.—44.

On the ground of complete similarity we never say "a cow is like a cow," on the ground of considerable similarity we do not say that "a buffalo is like a cow," and on the gronnd of partial similarity we do not say that "a mustard seed is like Mount Meru." Hence comparison is regarded by some as not a means of right knowledge, for it has no precise standard.

प्रसिद्धसाधर्म्यादुपमानसिद्धेर्यथोक्तदोषानुपपत्तिः ॥२।१।४५॥

प्रसिद्धसाधर्म्यात् prasiddha-sâdharmyât, from wellknown similarity; उपमानसिद्धेः upamâna-siddheḥ, because of establishment of comparison; उक्तदोषानुपपत्तिः ukta-doṣa-anupapattiḥ, non-application of the defect urged.

106. This objection does not hold good, for comparison is established through similarity in a high degree.—45.

The similarity in a high degree exists between such well-known objects as a cow and a bos gavæus, etc.

प्रत्यक्षेणाप्रत्यक्षसिद्धेः ॥ २ । १ । ४६ ॥

प्रत्यक्षेण pratyakṣeṇa, by perception ; अप्रत्यक्षसिद्धेः apratyakṣa-siddheḥ, because of establishment of what is not an object of perception.

107. Comparison, some say, is not different from inference, for both seek to establish the unperceived by means of the perceived —46.

We recognise a bos gavæus at first sight through its special similarity to a cow which we have often perceived. This knowledge of a previously unperceived object derived through its similarity to a perceived object is, it has been said, nothing but a case of inference.

नाप्रत्यक्षे गवये प्रमाणार्थमुपमानस्य पश्यामः ॥२।१।४७॥

न na, not ; अप्रत्यक्षे apratyakṣe, unperceived ; गवये gavaye, in a bos gavæus ; प्रमाणार्थम् pramâna-artham, the purpose of proof, utility as proof ; उपमानस्य upamânasya, of comparison ; पश्यामः paśyâmaḥ, we see.

108. It is not in a bos gavæus *unperceived* that we find the real matter of comparison.—47.

The matter of comparison is similarity, *e.g.*, between a cow and a bos gavæus. The bos gavæus in which we notice the similarity is first perceived, that is, on perceiving a bos gavæus we notice its similarity to a cow Hence comparison supplies us with knowledge of a *perceived* thing, through its similarity to another thing also *preceived.* This characteristic distinguishes it from inference, which furnishes us with knowledge of an *unperceived* thing through that of a thing *perceived.*

तथेत्युपसंहारादुपमानसिद्धेर्नाविशेषः ॥ २ । १ । ४८ ॥

तथा tathâ iti, and thus ; उपसंहारात् upasaṃhârât, from conclusion, summation ; उपमानसिद्धेः upamâna-siddheḥ, from the establishment of comparison ; न na, not ; अविशेषः a-viśeṣaḥ, non-difference.

109. There is non-difference, inasmuch as comparison is established through the compendious expression "so."—48.

It is not true that comparison is identical with inference, because the former is established through the compendious expression "so." 'As is a cow, *so* is a bos gavæus'—this is an instance of comparison. This use of 'so' makes it clear that comparison is a distinct means of right knowledge.

शब्दोऽनुमानमर्थस्यानुपलब्धेरनुमेयत्वात् ॥२।१।४९॥

शब्दः śabdaḥ, word ; अनुमानं anumânam, inference ; अर्थस्य arthasya, of the object ; अनुपलब्धेः an-upalabdheḥ, because of non-cognition ; अनुमेयत्वात् anumeyatvât, because of its having to be inferred.

110. **Verbal testimony**, say some, is inference, because the object revealed by it is not perceived but inferred.—49.

Inference gives us the knowledge of an unperceived object, through the knowledge of an obiect which is perceived. Similarly, verbal testimony enables us to acquire the knowledge of an unperceived object, through the knowledge of a word which is perceived. The verbal testimony is,therefore, supposed by some to be inference, as the object reveald by both is unperceived.

उपलब्धेरद्विप्रवृत्तित्वात् ॥ २ । १ । ५० ॥

उपलब्धेः upalabdheḥ, of consciousness, cognition, apprehension ; अद्विप्रवृत्तित्वात् a-dvi-pravṛitti-tvât, not having a dual application.

111. In respect of perceptibility the two cases are not, continues the objector, different.—50.

In infereuce as well as in verbal testimony we pass to an unperceived object through an object which is perceived. In respect of perceptibility of the object through which we pass, the inference does not, continues the objector, differ from the verbal testimony.

सम्बन्धाच्च ॥ २ । १ । ५१ ॥

सम्बन्धात् sambandhât, from relation or connection ; च cha, and.

112. There is, moreover, adds the objector, the same connection.—51.

Just as in inference there is a certain connection between a sign (*e.g.*, smoke) and the thing signified by it (*e. g.*, fire), so in verbal testimony there is connection between a word and the object signified by it. So inference, says the objector, is not different from verbal testimony.

आप्तोपदेशसामर्थ्याच्छब्दादर्थसम्प्रत्ययः ॥२।१।५२॥

आप्तोपदेशसामर्थ्यात् âpta-upadeśa-sâmarthyât, through force derived from the declaration by a reliable person ; शब्दार्थसंप्रत्ययः śabda-artha-sampratyayaḥ, complete intuition of the object from the word,

113. In reply, we say that there is reliance on the matter signified by a word, because the word has been used by a reliable person.—52.

In reference to the objections raised in aphorisms 49 and 50, we say that we rely on unseen matter, not simply because it is signified by words, but because they are spoken by a reliable person. There are, some say, paradise, nymphs, Uttarakurus, seven islands, ocean human settlements, etc. We accept them as realities, not because they are known through words, but because they are spoken of by persons who are reliable. Hence verbal testimony is not inference. The two agree in conveying knowledge of an object through its sign, but the sign in one is different from the sign in the other. In the case of verbal testimony, the special point is to decide whether the sign (word) comes from a reliable person.

Aphorism 51 speaks of a certain connection between a word and the object signified by it. The present aphorism points out that the connection is not a natural one. We acknowledge that a word indicates a certain object, but we deny that the object is naturally or necessarily connected with the word. Hearing, for instance, the word "cow," we think of the animal signified by it, nevertheless the word and the animal are not connected with each other by nature or necessity. In the case of inference, however, the connection between a sign (*e.g.*, smoke) and the thing signified (*e.g.*, fire) is natural and necessary. Therefore, the connection involved in inference is not of the same kind as that involved in verbal testimony.

पूरणप्रदाहपाटनानुपलब्धेश्च सम्बन्धाभावः ॥२।१।५३॥

पूरणप्रदाहपाटनानुपलब्धेः pûraṇa-pradâha-pâṭana-anupalabdheḥ, from non-apprehension of filling, burning, and splitting; च cha, and; सम्बन्धाभावः sambandha-abhâvaḥ, non existence of connection.

114. There is no natural connection between a word and the object signified by it, as we do not find that the words food, fire and hatchet, are accompanied by the actions filling, burning and splitting.—53.

If a word were naturally connected with the object signified by it, then by uttering the words food, fire and hatchet we should have found our mouth filled up (with food), burnt (with fire) and split (by a hatchet). But such is never the case. Hence there is no natural connection between a word and the object signified by it, and consequently verbal testimony is not inference.

शब्दार्थव्यवस्थानादप्रतिषेधः ॥ २ । १ । ५४ ॥

शब्दार्थव्यवस्थानात् śabda artha-vyavasthânât, from the fixity of (the intuition) of object from word ; अप्रतिषेधः a-pratiṣedhaḥ, non-contradiction.

115. It cannot, says an objector, be denied that there is a fixed connection between words and their meanings.—54.

A particular word denotes a particular meaning, *e.g.* the word 'cow' denotes the animal of that name, but it does not denote a horse, a jar, or any other thing. There is, therefore, in the case of verbal testimony, a fixed connection between a word and its meaning as there is in the case of inference a fixed connection between a sign and the thing signified. Hence verbal testimony is considered by the objector to be a case of inference.

न सामयिकत्वाच्छब्दार्थसम्प्रत्ययस्य ॥ २ । १ । ५५ ॥

न na, not ; सामयिकत्वात् sâmayika-tvât, from being conventional ; शब्दार्थसंप्रत्ययस्य śabda-artha-sampratyayasya, of the intuition of object from word.

116. We reply, it is through convention that the meaning of a word is understood.—55.

The connection between a word and its meaning is conventional and not natural. The connection, though fixed by man, is not inseparable and cannot therefore be the basis of an inference.

जातिविशेषे चानियमात् ॥ २ । १ । ५६ ॥

जातिविशेषे jâti-viśeṣe, with particular classes ; च cha, and ; अनियमात् aniyamât, from absence of natural uniformity.

117. There is no universal uniformity of connection between a word and its meaning.—56.

The ṛiṣis, âryas and mlechchhas use the same word in different senses, *e.g* the word "yava" is used by the âryas to denote a long-awned grain, but by the mlechchhas to denote a panic-seed. So the connection between a word and its meaning is not everywhere uniform, and consequently verbal testimony cannot be considered as inference.

तदप्रामाण्यमनृतव्याघातपुनरुक्तदोषेभ्यः ॥२।१।५७॥

तत् tat, that, word ; अप्रामाण्यं a-prâmâṇyam, not a means of right knowledge, invalid; अनृतव्याघात पुनरुक्त दोषेभ्यः anṛita-vyâghâta-punarukta-doṣebhyaḥ, owing to the defects of falsity, futility and repetition.

118. The **Veda**, some say, is unreliable, as it involves the faults of untruth, contradiction and tautology.—57.

The Veda, which is a kind of verbal testimony, is not, some say, a means of right knowledge. It is supposed by them to be tainted with the faults of untruth, contradiction and tautology. For instance, the Veda affirms that a son is produced when the sactifice for the sake of a son is performed. It often happens that the son is not produced, though the sacrifice has been performed.

There are many contradictory injunctions in the Veda, *e.g.*, it declares "let one sacrifice when the sun has risen," also "let one sacrifice when the sun has not risen," etc. There is such tautology as "let the first hymn be recited thrice," "let the last hymn be recited thrice," etc.

न कर्मकर्त्तृसाधनवैगुण्यात् ॥ २ । १ । ५८ ॥

न na, not ; कर्मकर्तृसाधनवैगुण्यात् karma-kartṛi-sâdhana-vaiguṇyât, from defect in the act, agent, or materials.

119. The so-called untruth in the Veda comes from some defect in the act, operator or materials of sacrifice.—58.

Defect in the act consists in sacrificing not according to rules, defect in the operator (officiating priest) consists in his not being a learned man, and defect in the materials consists in the fuel being wet, butter being not fresh, remuneration (to the officiating priest) being small, etc. A son is sure to be produced as a result of performing the sacrifice, if these defects are avoided. Therefore, there is no untruth in the Veda.

अभ्युपेत्य कालभेदे दोषवचनात् ॥ २ । १ । ५९ ॥

अभ्युपेत्य abhyupetya, arriving at a decision ; कालभेदे kâla-bhede, in the case of alteration of the time ; दोषवचनात् doṣa-vachanât, there being the declaration of the defect.

120. Contradiction would occur if there were alteration of the time agreed upon.—59.

Let a person perform sacrifice before sunrise or after sunrise if he has agreed upon doing it at either of the times. Two alternative courses being open to him, he can perform the sacrifice before sunrise or after sunrise, according to his agreement or desire. The Veda cannot be charged with the fault of contradiction, if it enjoins such alternative courses.

अनुवादोपपत्तेश्च ॥ २ । १ । ६० ॥

अनुवादोपपत्तेः anuvâda-upapatteḥ, from the possibility of its being a re-inculcation ; च cha, and.

121. There is no tautology, because re inculcation is of advantage.—60.

Tautology means a useless repetition, which never occurs in the Veda. If there is any repetition there, it is either for completing a certain number of syllables, or for explaining a matter briefly expressed, etc. "Let the first hymn be recited thrice," "let the last hymn be recited thrice"—such instances embody a useful repetition.

वाक्यविभागस्य चार्थग्रहणात् ॥ २ । १ । ६१ ॥

वाक्यविभागस्य vâkya-vibhâgasya, of the division of speech ; च cha, and; अर्थग्रहणात् artha-grahaṇât, from apprehension of different objects.

122. And because there is necessity for the classification of Vedic speech.—61.

It is necessary to divide the Vedic speech into classes based on special characters.

विध्यर्थवादानुवादवचनविनियोगात् ॥ २ । १ । ६२ ॥

विध्यर्थवादानुवादवचनविनियोगात् vidhi-arthavâda-anuvâda-vachana-viniyogât, from the distribution of speech as injunction, persuasion and re-inculcation.

123. The Vedic speech being divided on the principle of injunction, persuasion and re-inculcation —62.

The two main divisions of the Veda are (1) hymn and (2) ritual. The ritual portion admits of three sub-divisions, *viz*, injunctive, persuasive and re-inculcative.

विधिः विधायकः ॥ २ । १ । ६३ ॥

विधिः vidhiḥ, injunction ; विधायकः vidhâyakaḥ, that which prescribes something positive.

124. An injunction is that which exhorts us to adopt a certain course of action [as the means of attaining good].—63.

The following is an injunction :—" Let him who desires paradise perform the fire-sacrifice." This is a direct command.

स्तुतिर्निन्दा परकृतिः पुराकल्प इति अर्थवादः ॥२।१।६४॥

स्तुतिः stutiḥ, praise ; निन्दा nindâ, blame ; परकृतिः para kṛitiḥ, doing of others, failures of others ; पुराकल्पः purâ-kalpaḥ, tradition, customs of old ; इति iti, such ; अर्थवादः artha-vâdaḥ, persuasion.

125. Persuasion is effected through praise, blame, warning, and prescription.—64.

Praise is speech which persuades us to a certain course of action by extolling its consequences, *e.g.*, "By the Sarvajit sacrifice gods conquered all, there is nothing like Sarvajit sacrifice, it enables us to obtain everything and to vanquish every one, etc." Here there is no direct command, but the Sarvajit sacrifice is extolled in such a way that we are persuaded to perform it.

Blame is speech which persuades us to adopt a certain course of action by acquainting us with the undesirable consequences of neglecting it, *e g.*, "One who performs any other sacrifice, neglecting the Jyotiṣṭoma, falls into a pit and decays there." Here one is persuaded to perform the Jyotiṣṭoma sacrifice, the neglect of which brings about evil consequences.

Warning is the mentioning of a course of action, the obstruction of which by some particular person led to bad consequenees, *e.g.*, on presenting oblation one is to take the fat first and the sprinkled butter afterwards, but alas ! the Charaka priests first took the sprinkled butter which was, as it were, the life of fire, etc. Here the foolish course of action adopted by the Charaka priests should serve as a warning to other priests who ought to avoid the course.

Prescription implies the mention of something as commendable on account of its antiquity, *e g.*, "By this the Brâhmaṇas recited the Sâma hymn, etc."

विधिविहितस्यानुवचनम् अनुवादः ॥ २ । १ । ६५ ॥

विधिविहितस्य vidhi-vihitasya, of what is prescribed by injunction ; अनुवचनम् anu-vachanam, repetition ; अनुवादः anuvâdaḥ reinculcation.

126. Re-inculcation is the repetition of that which has been enjoined by an injunction.—65.

Re-inculcation may consist of (1) the repetition of an *injunction*, or (2) the repetition of that which has been *enjoined*. The first is called verbal re-inculcation and the second objective re-inculcation. In the Veda there is re-inculcation, as in ordinary use there is repetition. "Non eternal not eternal"—this is a verbal repetition. "Non-eternal, possessing the character of extinction"—this is objective repetition.

नानुवादपुनरुक्तयोर्विशेषः शब्दाभ्यासोपपत्तेः ॥२।१।६६॥

न na, not; अनुवादपुनरुक्तयोः anuvâda-punaruktayoḥ, of reinculcation and repetition; विशेषः viśeṣaḥ, difference; शब्दाभ्यासोपपत्तेः śabda-abhyâsa-upapatteḥ, because of the existence of the repetition of words.

127. There is, some say, no difference between re-inculcation and tautology, as there is in either case a repetition of some expression already used.—66.

Re-inculcation is supposed by some to be a fault, inasmuch as it does not, according to them, differ from tautology.

शीघ्रतरगमनोपदेशवदभ्यासान्नाविशेषः ॥२।१।६७॥

शीघ्रतरगमनोपदेशवत् śîghratara-gamana-upadeśa-vat, like the direction of going faster and faster which indicates intensity of action; अभ्यासात् abhyâsât, from repetition; न na, not; अविशेषः a-viśeṣaḥ, non-difference.

128. There is a difference, because re-inculcation serves some useful purpose, as, *e.g.*, a command to go faster.—67.

Tautology consists of a useless repetition, but the repetition in the case of re-inculcation is useful, *e.g.*, "go on, go on"—signifies " go faster."

मन्त्रायुर्वेदप्रामाण्यवच्च तत्प्रामाण्यमाप्तप्रामाण्यात् ॥२।१।६८॥

मन्त्रायुर्वेदप्रामाण्यवत् mantra âyurveda-prâmâṇya-vat, like the validity of mantra or chant and of medical science; च cha, and; तत्प्रामाण्यम् tat prâmâṇyam, its validity; आप्तप्रामाण्यात् âpta-prâmâṇyât, from the authority of the reliable speaker.

129. The Veda is reliable like the spell and the medical science, because of the reliability of their authors.—68.

The spell counteracts poison, etc., and the medical science prescribes correct remedies. The authority which belongs to them is derived from their authors, the sages, who were reliable persons. The sages themselves were reliable, because (1) they had an intuitive perception of truths, (2) they had great kindness for living beings and (3) they had the desire of communicating their knowledge of the truths. The authors, (*lit.*, the seers and speakers) of the Veda were also the authors of the spell and medical science. Hence, like the spell and medical science, the Veda must be accepted as authoritative. The view that the Veda is authoritative because eternal, is untenable.

इति श्रीगौतममहर्षिप्रणीते न्यायदर्शने द्वितीयस्याऽध्यायस्य प्रथममाह्निकम् ॥ २ । १ ॥

Book II, Chapter II.

न चतुष्ट्वमैतिह्यार्थापत्तिसम्भवाभावप्रामाण्यात् ॥२।२।१॥

न na, not ; चतुष्ट्वम् chatuṣṭvam, to be four ; ऐतिह्यार्थापत्तिसम्भवाभावप्रामाण्यात् aitihya-arthâpatti-sambhava-abhâva-prâmâṇyât, because tradition, presumption, probability and non-existence are also means of right knowledge.

130. Some say that the means of right knowledge are more than four, because rumour, presumption, probability and non-existence are also valid.—1.

In Book I, chapter I, aphorism 3, the means of right knowledge have been stated to be four, *viz.*, perception, inference, comparison and verbal testimony. Some say that there are other means of right knowledge, such as rumour, presumption, probability and non-existence.

Rumour is an assertion which has come from one to another without any indication of the source from which it first originated, *e.g.*, in this fig tree there live goblins.

Presumption is the deduction of one thing from the declaration of another thing : *e.g.*, from the declaration that 'unless there is cloud, there is no rain,' we deduce that 'there is rain, if there is cloud.' A more familiar instance of presumption is this : the fat Devadatta does not eat during the day time. Here the presumption is that he eats in the night for it is impossible for a person to be fat if he does not eat at all.

Probability consists in cognising the existence of a thing from that of another thing in which it is included, *e. g.*, cognising the measure of an *âḍhaka* from that of a *droṇa* of which it is a fourth part, and cognising the measure of a *prastha* from that of an *âḍhaka* of which it is a quarter.

Of two opposite things, the *non-existence* of one establishes the existence of the other, *e.g.* the non existence of rain establishes the combination of wind and cloud. When there is a combination of wind and cloud, drops of water cannot fall, in spite of their weight.

शब्द ऐतिह्यानर्थान्तरभावादनुमानेऽर्थापत्तिसम्भवाभावानर्थान्तरभावाच्चाप्रतिषेधः ॥ २ । २ । २ ॥

शब्दे śabde. in word ; ऐतिह्यानर्थान्तरभावात् aitihya-an-artha-antara-bhâvât, from existence of tradition as a non-different object ; अनुमाने anumâne, in inference ; अर्थापत्तिसम्भवाभावानर्थान्तरभावात् arthâpatti-sambhava-abhâva-anartha-antara-bhâvât, from existence of presumption, probability and non-existence as non-different objects ; च cha, and ; अप्रतिषेधः a-pratiṣedhaḥ, non-contradiction.

131. This, we reply, is no contradiction, since rumour is included in verbal testimony, and presumption, probability and non-existence are included in inference —2.

Those who maintain that rumour, presumption, probability and non existence are valid, do not really oppose our division of the means of right knowledge into four, *viz.*, perception, inference, comparison and verbal testimony.

Rumour partakes of the general characteristics of verbal testimony, and is a special kind of it.

Presumption is explained as the knowledge of a thing derived through the consideration of it from the opposite standpoint. For instance, the fat Devadatta does not eat during the day time : here the presumption is that he eats in the night. The fact of his eating in the night has not been expressly stated, but is ascertained from this consideration that a person who does not eat during the day cannot be strong unless he eats in the night. It is evident that presumption, like inference, passes from a perceived thing to an unperceived one, because they are in some way connected.

Probability is inference, because it is the cognizance of a part from knowledge of a whole with which it is inseparably connected.

Non-existence is inference, inasmuch as it really infers the obstruction of a cause from the non-existence of its effect through a certain connection, *viz.*, if the obstruction occurs, the effect cannot occur.

Hence rumour, etc., are not independent means of right knowledge, but are included in the four, enumerated in Book I, Chapter I, aphorism 3.

अर्थापत्तिरप्रमाणमनैकान्तिकत्वात् ॥ २ । २ । ३ ॥

अर्थापत्तिः arthâpattiḥ, presumption ; अप्रमाणं apramâṇam, not a means of right knowledge ; अनैकान्तिकत्वात् anaikântikatvât, because it is not one-pointed.

132.—Presumption, some say, is not valid, because it leads to uncertainty.—3.

" If there is no cloud, there will be no rain"—from this we are said to presume that if there is a cloud there will be rain. But it often happens that a cloud is not followed by rain So presumption does not always lead to certainty.

अनर्थापत्तावर्थापत्त्यभिमानात् ॥ २ । २ । ४ ॥

अनर्थापत्तौ anarthâpattau in respect of what is not a presumption; अर्थापत्त्यभिमानात् arthâpatti-abhimânât, from attribution of being presumption.

133. We reply : if there is any uncertainty, it is due to your supposing that to be a presumption which is not really so.—4.

" If there is no cloud, there will be no rain"—from this we are entitled to presume that if there is rain there must have been a cloud. But if you pretend to presume that " if there is a cloud, there will be rain," your so-called presumption will be an invalid one.

प्रतिषेधाप्रामाण्यञ्चानैकान्तिकत्वात् ॥ २ । २ । ५ ॥

प्रतिषेधाप्रामाण्यं pratiṣedha-aprâmâṇyam, invalidity of the contradiction; च cha, and ; अनैकान्तिकत्वात् anaikântikatvât, from being not-one-pointed.

134. The objection itself, we say, is invalid, because it leads to uncertainty.—5.

"Presumption is not valid, because it leads to uncertainty"—this is your objection. In it there are two points for consideration, *viz*, (1) the validity of presumption and (2) the existence of presumption. Your objection refers to one of the points, *viz.* the validity of presumption. So you do not deny the existence of presumption. In some instances, however, your objection may refer to more points than one. In fact, the nature of your objection is not definite in itself, or, in other words, it leads to uncertainty. Hence your objection is invalid.

तत्प्रामाण्ये वा नार्थापत्त्यप्रामाण्यम् ॥ २ । २ । ६ ॥

तत्प्रामाण्ये tat-prâmâṇye, if the contradiction be valid ; वा vâ, or ; न na, not ; अर्थापत्त्यप्रामाण्यं arthâpatti-aprâmâṇyam, invalidity of presumption.

135. Or, if that be valid, then our presumption is not invalid.—6.

Perhaps you will say that your objection is valid, because you can ascertain in each case whether one or more points are referred to by the objection. Similarly, we shall say that our presumption is not invalid, because we can ascertain in each case whether the presumption is capable of leading to more conclusions than one. Hence, if you say that your objection is valid, we shall say that our presumption is also valid.

नाभावप्रामाण्यं प्रमेयासिद्धेः ॥ २।२।७ ॥

न na, not; अभावप्रामाण्य abhâva-prâmâṇyam, non-existence to be a means of right knowledge ; प्रमेयासिद्धेः prameya-asiddheḥ, because of the non-existence of what is to be the object of right knowledge.

136. Some say that **non-existence** is not a means of right knowledge, because there is no ohject which is known by it.—7.

लक्षितेष्वलक्षणलक्षितत्वादलक्षितानां तत्प्रमेयसिद्धेः ॥२।२।८॥

लक्षितेषु lakṣiteṣu, in marked objects ; अलक्षण लक्षिततत्वात alakṣaṇa-lakṣitatvât, from being marked by what is not a mark ; अलक्षितानां alakṣitânâm, of unmarked objects ; तत्प्रमेयसिद्धेः tat-prameya-siddheḥ, from their affirmation as objects of knowledge.

137. Non-existence, we reply, serves to mark out an object unmarked by the mark which characterises other objects.—8.

Suppose a person wants to bring a pot which is not blue. The absence of blueness is a mark which will enable him to mark out the particular pot he wants to bring, and to exclude the other pots which are blue. Thus an object may be known through the non-existence (absence) of its mark.

असत्यर्थे नाभाव इति चेन्नान्यलक्षणोपपत्तेः ॥२।२।९॥

असति asati, non-existent ; अर्थे arthe, in the case of an object ; न na, not ; अभावः abhâvaḥ, non-existence or absence of mark ; इतिचेत iti chet, if so ; न na, no ; अन्यलक्षणोपपत्तेः anya-lakṣaṇa-upapatteḥ, from affirmation of other marks.

138. If you say that the non-existence (absence) of a mark is impossible where there was no mark at all, it is, we reply, not so, because the non-existence (absence) is possible in reference to a mark elsewhere.—9.

We can, says an objector, talk of a mark being non-existent (absent), if it was previously existent (present). A pot is said to be not blue only in reference to its being blue previously. In reply, we say that it is not so. "Not-blue" is no doubt possible only in reference to "blue," but that blueness may exist elsewhere. For instance, we can talk of this pot being not blue, in contrast to that pot which is blue.

तत्सिद्धेरलक्षितेष्वहेतुः ॥ २ । २ । १० ॥

तत्सिद्धेः tat-siddheḥ, from presence therein i. e. in marked objects ; अलक्षितेषु alakṣiteṣu, in respect of unmarked objects ; अहेतुः ahetuḥ no mark.

139. Though a mark may distinguish the object which is marked, the non-existence (absence) of the mark cannot, some say, distinguish the object which is not marked.—10.

A blue pot is distinguished by the blueness which is its mark. But how can we, says the objector, distinguish an unmarked object by the non-existence (absence) of the mark which it does not possess ?

न लक्षणावस्थितापेक्षासिद्धेः ॥ २ । २ । ११ ॥

न na, no ; लक्षणावस्थितापेक्षासिद्धेः lakṣaṇa-avasthita-apekṣâ-siddheḥ, from establishment by reference to objects in which marks are present.

140. This is not so, because the non-existence (absence) of a mark serves as a mark, in relation to the presence of the mark.—11.

We can speak of a pot being not blue, in relation to one which is blue. Hence, though not-blueness is not a positive mark, it serves as a (negative) mark, in relation to blueness.

प्रागुत्पत्तेरभावोपपत्तेश्च ॥ २ । २ । १२ ॥

प्राक् prâk, prior ; उत्पत्तेः utpatteḥ, to production ; अभावोपपत्तेः abhâva-upapatteḥ, from affirmation of non-existence ; च cha, and

141. Moreover, we perceive non-existence as a mark antecedent to the production of a thing.—12.

There are two kinds of non-existence, *viz.*, antecedent non-existence and subsequent non-existence. When we say that there will be a jar, we perceive the mark of non-existence of the jar in the halves which are destined to compose it. This is antecedent non existence. Similarly, when we say that a jar has broken, we perceive the mark of non existence of the jar in the parts which composed it. This is subsequent non-existence.

आदिमत्त्वादैन्द्रियकत्वात् कृतकवदुपचाराच्च ॥२।२।१३॥

आदिमत्त्वात् âdi-mat-tvât, because it has a beginning ; ऐन्द्रियकत्वात् aindriy-aka-tvât, because it is sensuous ; कृतकवदुपचारात् kṛitaka vat-upachârât, because it is treated as any other product च cha, and.

142. **Sound is not eternal, because it has a beginning and is cognised by our sense and is spoken of as artificial.—13.**

Sound is non-eternal, because it begins or arises from the concussion of two hard substances, *e.g.*, an axe and a tree, etc. Another ground for the non-eternality of sound is that it is cognised by our sense. Moreover, we attribute to sound the properties of an artificial object, *e.g.*, we speak of a sound being grave, acute, etc. This would be impossible, if it had been eternal.

Some say that the so called beginning of a sound is merely a manifestation of it, that is, sound does not really begin, but is merely manifested by the concussion of two hard substances. In reply, we say that the concussion does not manifest, but produces a sound. You cannot suppose the concussion to be the manifester and sound the manifested, unless you can prove that the concussion and sound are simultaneous. But the proof is impossible, as a sound is heard at a great distance even after the concussion of the substances has ceased. So sound is not manifested by the concussion. It is, however, legitimate to suppose that sound is produced by the concussion, and that one sound produces another sound, and so on, until the last sound is heard at a great distance.

न घटाभावसामान्यनित्यत्वान्नित्येष्वप्यनित्यवदुपचाराच्च ॥ २ । २ । १४ ॥

न na, no ; घटाभावसामान्यनित्यत्वात् ghaṭa-abhâva-sâmânya-nitya-tvât, because the non-existence of a pot after destruction and the genus which is cognisable through contact with the sense are eternal ; नित्येषु nityeṣu, in the case of eternal objects ; अनित्यवत् anitya-vat, as non-eternal ; उपचारात् upachârât, from treatment ; च cha, and.

143. **Some will not accept this argument, because the non-existence of a jar and the genus of it are eternal, and eternal things are also spoken of as if they were artificial.—14.**

Some say that it is not true that whatever has a beginning is non-eternal. Look ! the non-existence (destruction) of a jar which began when the jar was broken is eternal (indestructible). Whatever is cognised by our sense is non-eternal : this is also said to be an unsound argument. When, for instance, we perceive a jar, we perceive also its genus (*i.e.*, jarness), which is eternal. It is further said that we often attribute to eternal things the properties of an artificial object, *e.g.*, we speak of the extension of ether as we speak of the extension of a blanket.

तत्त्वभाक्तयोर्नानात्वविभागादव्यभिचारः ॥२।२।१५॥

तत्त्वभाक्तयोः tattva-bhâktayoḥ, of true and false eternals ; नानात्वविभागात् nânâ-tva-vibhâgât, from division as many ; अव्यभिचारः a-vyabhichârah, absence of uncertainty.

144. There is, we reply, no opposition because there is distinction between what is really eternal and what is partially eternal —15.

That which is really eternal belongs to the three times But the non-existence (destruction) of a jar does not belong to three times, as it was impossible before the jar was broken Hence the non-existence (destruction) of a jar which has a beginning is not really eternal.

सन्तानानुमानविशेषणात् ॥ २ । २ १६ ॥

सन्तानानुमानविशेषणात् santâna-anumâna-viśeṣaṇât, from the inference of continuity which is the distinguishing characteristic (of sound).

145. It is only the things cognised by our sense as belonging to a certain genus that must, we say, be inferred to be non-eternal.—16.

The objectors have said that things cognised by our sense are not necessarily non-eternal, *e.g.*, as we perceive a jar, we also perceive its genus jar-ness, which is eternal. In reply, we say that not all things cognised by our sense are non-eternal, but only those that belong to a certain genus. A jar, for instance. is non-eternal, because we perceive it as belonging to the genus jar-ness. But jar-ness which is cognised by our sense is not non-eternal, because it does not belong to a further genus, named jar-ness-ness. Similarly, sound is non-eteranl, because it is cognised by our sense as belonging to the genus called sound-ness.

The aphorism may also be interpreted as follows :—Sound is non-eternal, because it is inferred to advance in a series.

We do not say that whatever is cognised by our sense is non-eternal: our intention is to say that things cognised by our sense as advancing in a series are non-eternal. Sound is cognised in that manner (*i.e.*, sound advances like a wave), and hence sound is non-eternal.

कारणद्रव्यस्य प्रदेशशब्देनाभिधानात् नित्येष्वप्यव्यभिचार इति ॥ २ । २ । १७ ॥

कारणद्रव्यस्य kâraṇa-dravyasya, of the causal substance ; प्रदेशशब्देन pradeśa-śabdena, in terms of extension ; अभिधानात् abhidhânât, from declaration or designation ; नित्येषु nityeṣu, in the case of eternal objects ; अपि api, also अव्यभिचार: a vyabhichârah, absence of uncertainty.

146. We further say that only artificial things are designated by the term extension.—17.

When we speak of the extension of ether, we really mean that the extension belongs to an artificial thing, which has for its substratum the ether. Hence we do not in reality attribute to eternal things the properties of artificial objects.

प्रागुच्चारणादनुपलब्धेरावरणाद्यनुपलब्धेश्च ॥२।२।१८॥

प्राक् prâk, prior ; उच्चारणात् uchhâraṇât, to pronunciation ; अनुपलब्धे: an-upalabdheḥ, from non-apprehension ; आवरणाद्यनुपलब्धे: âvaraṇa-âdi-an-upalabdheḥ, from non-apprehension of the causes of non-apprehension ; च cha, and.

147. Sound is non-eternal, because neither do we perceive it before pronunciation, nor do we notice any veil which covers it.—18.

If sound were eternal, it would be perceived before pronunciation. You cannot say that sound really existed before pronunciation but was covered by some veil, for we do not notice any such veil.

तदनुपलब्धेरनुपलम्भादावरणोपपत्तिः ॥ २ । २ । १९ ॥

तदनुपलब्धे: tat-an-upalabdheḥ, of its non-apprehension ; अनुपलम्भात् an-upalambhât, from non-apprehension , आवरणोपपत्ति: âvaraṇa-upapattiḥ, establishment of the causes of non-apprehension.

148. The veil, some say, really exists, because we do not perceive the non-perception thereof.—19.

The objectors say :—If you deny the veil because it is not perceived, we deny the non-perception of the veil because it is also not perceived. The denial of non-perception is the same as the acknowledgment of perception, or, in other words, the veil is acknowledged to be existent.

अनुपलम्भादप्यनुपलब्धिसद्भाववन्नावरणानुपपत्तिरनुपलम्भात् ॥ २ । २ । २० ॥

अनुपलम्भात् an upalambhât, from non-apprehension ; अपि api, even ; अनुपलब्धिसद्भाववत् an-upalabdhi-sadbhâvavat, like existence of non-apprehension ; न na, not ; आवरणानुपपत्ति: âvaraṇa an-upapattiḥ, non-establishment of the causes of non-apprehension. अनुपलम्भात् an-upalambhât, from non-apprehension.

149. If you assert non-perception of the veil, though the non-perception is not perceived, we, continue the objectors, assert the e is-tence of the veil, though it is not perceived,—.0.

You admit non-perception of the veil, though you do not perceive it (non-perception). Similarly, we, the objectors, admit the existence of the veil, though we do not perceive it.

अनुपलम्भात्मकत्वादनुपलब्धेरहेतुः ॥ २ । २ । २१ ॥

अनुपलम्भात्मकत्वात् an-upalambha-âtmaka-tvât, from the nature of its being non-apprehension ; अनुपलब्धेः an-upalabdheḥ, of non apprehension ; अहेतुः a-hetuḥ, not a mark.

150. This, we reply, is no reason, because non-perception consists of absence of perception.—21.

A veil is a thing fit to be perceived. Our non-perception of it indicates its absence. On the other hand, the non perception of a veil is not a thing fit to be perceived. Hence, non-perception of the non-perception leads us to nothing real,

अस्पर्शत्वात् ॥ २ । २ । २२ ॥

अस्पर्शत्वात् a-sparśa-tvât, being intangible.

151. Some say that sound is eternal, because it is intangible.—22.

Ether which is intangible is eternal. Sound must, similarly, acording to some, be eternal, because it is intangible.

न कर्मानित्यत्वात् ॥ २ । २ । २३ ॥

न na, no ; कर्मानित्यत्वात् karma-anitya-tvât, because action is non-eternal.

152. This we deny, because action is non-eternal.—23.

Action is non-eternal, though it is intangible. Hence, intangibiliy does not establish eternality.

नाणुनित्यत्वात् ॥ २ । २ । २४ ॥

न, na, no ; अणुनित्यत्वात् aṇu-nitya-tvât, because atom is eternal.

153. An atom, on the other hand, is eternal though not intangible.—24.

Tangibility is not incompatible with eternality, *e.g.* atoms are tangible, yet eternal

सम्प्रदानात् ॥ २ । २ । २५ ॥

सम्प्रदानात् sampradânât, from delivery.

154. Sound, some say, is eternal, because of the traditionary teaching —25.

A preceptor could not have imparted knowledge to his pupils by means of sounds, if these were perishable (non-eternal). In fact, the traditionary teaching would, according to the objectors, be impossible, if the sounds were non eternal.

तदन्तरालानुपलब्धेरहेतुः ॥ २ । २ । २६ ॥

तद् न्तरालानुपलब्धेः tat-antarâla-an-upalabdheḥ, from non-apprehension in the interval between them ; अहेतुः a-hetuḥ, not a mark.

155. This is, we reply, no reason, because sound is not perceived in the interval —26.

Suppose a preceptor delivers certain sounds (in the form of a lecture) which are received by his pupil. The sounds are not audible in the interval between the preceptor giving them and the pupil receiving them. They would never be inaudible, if they were eternal.

अध्यापनादप्रतिषेधः ॥ २ । २ । २७ ॥

अध्यापनात् adhyâpanâ , from teaching ; अप्रतिषेधः a-pratiṣedhaḥ, absence of contradiction.

156. This, say the objectors, is no argument, because there is the teaching.—27.

The objectors say :—If the sounds, as soon as they came out of the preceptor, were destroyed and did not reach the pupil, there could not be any teaching carried on. But there is the teaching, hence sound does not perish; or, in other, words, it is eternal.

उभयोः पक्षयोरन्यतरस्याध्यापनादप्रतिषेधः ॥२।२।२८॥

उभयोः ubhayoḥ, in both ; पक्षयोः pakṣayoḥ, views ; अन्यतरस्य anyatarasya, of the one or the other ; अध्यापनात् adhyâpanât, from teaching ; अप्रतिषेधः a-pratiṣedhaḥ, non-opposition.

157. In whichever of the two senses it is accepted, the teaching does not offer any opposition.—28.

The word "teaching" may be interpreted either as (1) the pupil's receiving the sounds given by his preceptor, or as (2) the pupil's imitating the sounds of his preceptor, as one imitates dancing. Neither of these interpretations would support the eternality of sound. In consonance with the first interpretation we shall say that the sound coming out of the preceptor produces another sound, and so on, until the last sound reaches the pupil. This would make sound non-eternal. It is obvious that the second interpretation similarly proves the non-eternality of sound.

अभ्यासात् ॥ २ । २ । २९ ॥

अभ्यासात् abhyâsât, from repetition.

158. Sound, continue the objectors, is eternal, because it is capable of repetition.—29.

That which is capable of repetition is persistent or not perishable, *e.g.*, one and the same colour can be repeatedly looked at, because it is persistent. One and the same sound can similarly be repeatedly uttered, hence it is persistent or not perishable.

नान्यत्वेऽप्यभ्यासस्योपचारात् ॥ २ । २ । ३० ॥

न na, no ; अन्यत्वे anya-tve, were it otherwise ; अपि api, even ; अभ्यासस्य abhyâsasya, of repetition ; उपचारात् upachârât, from treatment or use.

159. It is, we reply, not so, because even if sounds were "other" (different), repetition could take place.—30.

Repetition does not prevent perishableness, because repetition is possible even if the things repeated are "other" or different, *e.g.*, he sacrifices twice, he dances thrice, etc. Here the two sacrifices are different, and yet we use the repetitive word 'twice'; similarly the three dancings are different, and yet we use the repetitive word 'thrice.'

अन्यदन्यस्मादनन्यत्वादनन्यदित्यन्यताऽभावः ॥२।२।३१॥

अन्यत् anyat, other ; अन्यस्मात् anyasmât, from other ; अनन्यत्वात् an-anyatvât, from not being other ; अनन्यत् an-anyat, not other ; इति iti, thus ; अन्यताऽभावः anya-tâ-abhâvaḥ, non-existence of otherness.

160. Some say that there is no such thing as otherness, because what is called "other," in reference to some other, is not other in reference to itself.—31.

We maintain that repetition is possible even if the things repeated are "other" or different. Our position is said to be untenable : the term "other" is described as unmeaning, as nothing is other than itself.

तदभावे नास्त्यनन्यता तयोरितरेतरापेक्षसिद्धेः ॥ २ । २ । ३२॥

तदभावे tat-abhâve, in the absence of otherness ; न na, not ; अस्ति asti, is ; अनन्यता an-anya-tâ, the being not-other ; तयोः tayoḥ, of these ; इतरेतरापेक्षसिद्धेः: itara-itara-apekṣa-siddheḥ, because existence depends of one upon that of the other.

161. In the absence of otherne s there would, we reply, be no sameness, because the two exist in reference to each other.—32.

If there was no otherness, there would be no sameness. This would lead us to absurdity, as it would disprove both persistency and perishableness. Hence we must admit otherness, and if there is "other," there will be no flaw in our expression, *viz.*, repetition is possible even if things were "other" or different.

विनाशकारणानुपलब्धेश्च ॥ २ । २ । ३३ ॥

विनाशकारणानुपलब्धेः: vinâśa-kâraṇa-an-upalabdheḥ, because of non-apprehension of cause of destruction ; च cha, and.

162. Sound, some say, is eternal, because we perceive no cause why it should perish.—33.

Whatever is non-eternal is destroyed by some cause. Sound is said to have no cause of destruction, hence sound is held by some to be not non-eternal, (*i.e.*, is regarded as eternal)

अश्रवणकारणानुपलब्धेस्सततश्रवणप्रसङ्गः ॥२।२।३४॥

अश्रवणकारणानुपलब्धेः: a-śravaṇa-kâraṇa-an-upalabdheḥ, from non-apprehension of cause of non-hearing ; सततश्रवणप्रसङ्गः: satata-śravaṇa-prasaṅgaḥ, implication of perpetual hearing.

163. But by the same argument, we are afraid, non-perception of the cause of inaudition would mean constant audition.—34.

If non-perception is to establish non-existence, we should not cease to hear, because we do not perceive any cause of our not hearing. But such a conclusion is absurd.

उपलभ्यमाने चानुपलब्धेरसत्त्वादनपदेशः ॥ २ । २ । ३५ ॥

उपलभ्यमाने upalabhyamâne, in the case of being apprehended ; च cha, and; अनुपलब्धेः an-upalabdheḥ, of non-apprehension ; असत्त्वात् a-sat-tvât, from being non-existent ; अनपदेशः an-apadeśaḥ, not a mark.

164. Your position, we further say, is untenable, because there is no non-perception ; on the contrary, there is perception of the cause of inaudition.—35.

Suppose that a sound is produced by an axe striking against a tree. This sound will perish after producing another sound, which will again perish, giving rise to another, and so on, until the last sound is destroyed by some obstacle. In fact every sound that is produced is destined to perish. Hence there is no non perception of the cause of inaudition ; on the contrary, there is perception of such a cause. Consequently, sound is not eternal.

पाणिनिमित्तप्रश्लेषाच्छब्दाभावे नानुपलब्धिः ॥२।२।३६॥

पाणिनिमित्त प्रश्लेषात् pâṇi-nimitta-praśleṣât, from contact with the gong due to action of the hand ; शब्दाभावे śabda-abhâve, in the absence of sound; न na, not; अनुपलब्धिः an-upalabdhiḥ, non apprehension.

165. There is, we again say, no non-perception, because the sound [of a gong] ceases on the contact of our hand [with the gong].—36

You cannot say that there is non-perception of the cause of cessation of sound, because we actually perceive that by the contact of our hand we can stop the sound of a gong.

विनाशकारणानुपलब्धेश्चावस्थाने तन्नित्यत्वप्रसङ्गः ॥२।२।३७॥

विनाशकारणानुपलब्धेः vinâśa-kâraṇa-an-upalabdheḥ, from non-apprehension of the cause of destruction ; च cha, and ; अवस्थाने avasthâne, in persistence ; तन्नित्यत्वप्रसङ्गः tat-nitya-tva-prasaṅgaḥ, implication of its eternality.

166. We call a thing eternal (persistent) if it continues to exist, and if we cannot perceive any cause why it should cease.—37.

Sound does not continue to exist, and the cause of its cessation is also perceived. Hence sound is not eternal.

अस्पर्शत्वादप्रतिषेधः ॥ २ । २ । ३८ ॥

अस्पर्शत्वात् a-sparśa-tvât, from being intangible ; अप्रतिषेधः a-pratiṣedhaḥ non-contradiction.

167. That the substratum of sound is intangible is no counter-argument.—38.

Sound has not for its substratum any of the tangible substances, *viz*, earth, water, fire and air, for, it is found to be produced even where these do not exist. For instance, sound is produced in a vacuum which is devoid of smell, taste, colour and touch, which are the qualities of tangible substances. The reason why the sound produced in a vacuum does not reach our ears is that there is no air to carry it. Hence the substratum of sound is an intangible substance, *viz*., ether.

It is a peculiarity of sound that it cannot co-abide with colour, etc. A tangible substance (*e.g.*, earth) which is the abode of smell may also be the abode of colour, taste or touch. But the substance, in which sound abides, cannot be the abode of any other qualities. This distinguishes the substratum of sound from the substrata of other qualities. This peculiar substratum is called ether.

The fact of having an intangible substratum is no bar to the non-eternality of sound. Sound, though its substratum is the intangible ether, is produced by the contact of two hard substances. One sound produces another sound (or a certain vibration), which again causes another sound (or vibration), and so on, until the last sound (or vibration) ceases owing to some obstacle. Sound is therefore non-eternal.

विभक्त्यन्तरोपपत्तेश्च समासे ॥ २ । २ । ३९ ॥

विभक्त्यन्तरोपपत्तेः vibhakti-antara-upapatteḥ, from affirmation of different divisions or inflections ; **च** cha, and ; **समासे** samâse, in the case of co-inherence, or of a compound.

168. Sound cannot be supposed to co-abide with other qualities, for there are also varieties of it.—39

In each tangible substance there is only one kind of smell, taste, touch or colour. If we suppose that sound abides with one or more of these qualities in a tangible substance, we must admit that sound is of one kind only. But sound is of various kinds, such as grave, acute, etc. ; and even the same sound may vary in degrees, according to the nature of the obstruction it meets. This proves that sound does not abide with other qualities in a tangible substance. It further proves that sound is not unalterable or eternal.

Also signifies that this aphorism is to be considered along with aphorism 2—2—33, in which a reason for the non-eternality of sound is given.

विकारादेशोपदेशात् संशयः ॥ २ । २ । ४० ॥

विकारादेशोपदेशात् vikâra-âdeśa-upadeśât, from the rule of modification and substitution ; संशयः saṃśayaḥ, doubt.

169. From the injunction about modification and substitute there arises doubt.—40.

The word 'dadhi,' conjoined with the word 'atra,' becomes 'dadhyatra,' by the rule of Sanskrit grammar. Looking at 'dadhi-atra' and 'dadhyatra,' we notice that there is *i* in the former and *y* in the latter. Here some say that *i* undergoes modification as *y*, while others say that *y* comes as a substitute for *i*. Consequently we are thrown into doubt whether letters really undergo modifications or take up substitutes.

प्रकृतिविवृद्धौ विकारविवृद्धेः ॥ २ । २ । ४१ ॥

प्रकृतिविवृद्धौ prakṛiti-vivṛiddhau, on the augmentation of the root; विकारविवृद्धेः vikâra-vivṛiddheḥ, because there is augmentation of the modification.

170. If letters underwent modification, an increase of bulk in the original material would be attended by an increase of bulk in the modification.—41.

If we accept the theory of modification, the letter *y* which originated from the short *i* must be supposed to be less in bulk than the *y* which originated from the long *î*. But in reality the *y* in both the cases is of the same bulk. Hence it is concluded that letters do not undergo modification, but take up other letters as substitutes.

न्यूनसमाधिकोपलब्धेर्विकाराणामहेतुः ॥ २ । २ । ४२ ॥

न्यूनसमाधिकोपलब्धेः nyûna-sama adhika-upalabdheḥ, from apprehension of less, same, and more ; विकाराणाम् vikârâṇâm, of modifications ; अहेतुः a-hetuḥ, not a mark.

171. The foregoing argument, some say, is futile, because we find modification less than, equal to, and greater than, the original material.—42.

The bulk of the modification does not, in all cases, correspond to the bulk of the original material, *e.g.*, thread is of less bulk than cotton which is its original material, a bracelet is equal in bulk to the gold of which it is made, and a banyan tree is greater in bulk than the seed from which it springs. Hence the argument against the theory of modification is, according to the objectors, baseless.

द्विविधस्यापि हेतोरभावादसाधनं दृष्टान्तः ॥२।२।४३॥

द्विविधस्य dvi-vidha-sya, of twofold ; अपि api, even ; हेतोः hetoḥ, reasons; अभावात् abhâvât, owing to absence ; असाधनं a-sâdhanam̱, not a means of proof ; दृष्टान्तः dri̱ṣṭântaḥ, example .

172. On account of the absence of both the positive and negative marks of inference, we say, the example does not establish the point.—43.

The examples cited by the opponent are irrelevant. They are neither similar nor dissimilar to the case under consideration: they belong altogether to a different category. An example which can establish a point must contain the reason which is found present in the thing to be established. Not only are the examples not a means of proof here, but they are also not the examples required.

नातुल्यप्रकृतीनां विकारविकल्पात् ॥ २ । २ । ४४ ॥

न na, no ; अतुल्यप्रकृतीनां a-tulya-prakṛitînâm, of different roots ; विकार-विकल्पात् vikâra-vikalpât, from difference of modifications .

173. It is not so, because we spoke of those modifications which originated from different materials.—44.

A modification may not correspond in bulk to its orignal material. But if the original materials are different, their modifications are expected to be different. Here *i* being different from *î*, their modifications are expected to be different. But *y* issues from *i* as well as *î*. Hence *y* is not a modification of *i* or *î*.

द्रव्यविकारे वैषम्यवद्वर्णविकारविकल्पः ॥ २ । २ । ४५ ॥

द्रव्यविकारे dravya-vikâre; in the case of the modification of substance in general ; वैषम्यवत् vaiṣamya-vat, as there is dissimilarity ; वर्णविकार-विकल्पः varṇa-vikâra-vikalpaḥ, difference of the modification of letter in general.

174. There is, says an objector, difference between a letter and its modification, as there is between a substance and its modification.—45.

According to the objector, there is difference between the letter *i* (or *î*) and its modification *y*, as there is difference between the substance cotton and its modification thread.

न विकारधर्मानुपपत्तेः ॥ २ । २ । ४६ ॥

न na, no ; विकारधर्मानुपपत्तेः vikâra-dharma-an- upapatteḥ, because of non-establishment of the character of a modification.

175. In reply, we say that it is not so, because the character of a modification does not exist here —16.

A modification must be of the same nature as its original material, though the former may not correspond in bulk to the latter. A bracelet is no doubt a modification of gold or silver, but a horse is not a modification of a bull. Similarly, *y*, which is a semi-vowel, is not a modification of *i* (or *î*) which is a full vowel.

विकारप्राप्तानामपुनरापत्तेः ॥ २ । २ । ४७ ॥

विकारप्राप्तानाम् vikâra-prâptânâm, of those which have undergone modification ; अपुनरापत्तेः a-punaḥ-âpatteḥ, from non-return to original form.

176. A thing which has undergone modification does not again return to its original form.—17.

Milk modified into curd does not again attain the state of milk. But *i* having reached the condition of *y* may again revert to its original form. Hence *y* is not a modification of *i*.

सुवर्णादीनां पुनरापत्तेरहेतुः ॥ २ । २ । ४८ ॥

सुवर्णादीनाम् suvarṇa-âdînâm. of gold and the like ; पुनरापत्तेः punaḥ-âpatteḥ, from return to original ; अहेतुः a-hetuḥ, not a mark.

177. Some say that this is untenable, because golden ornaments may again be converted into their original forms —48.

A golden bracelet is converted into a mass of gross gold which again may be modified into a bracelet. The objector, relying on the analogy of golden ornaments, says that in the case of letters the theory of modification does not suffer by *i* reaching the condition of *y* and again returning to its original form.

न तद्विकाराणां सुवर्णभावाव्यतिरेकात् ॥ २ । २ । ४९ ॥

न na, not ; तद्विकारानां tat-vikârâṇàm, of its modifications ; सुवर्णभावाव्यतिरेकात् suvarṇa-bhâva-a-vyatirekât, from not giving up the nature of gold.

178. The analogy, we say, is inapt, because the modifications of gold (called ornaments) do not relinquish the nature of gold.—49.

A mass of gold when made into ornaments does not relinquish its own nature. But *i* when converted into *y* loses its own nature. Hence the analogy is unsuitable.

नित्यत्वे अविकारादनित्यत्वे चानवस्थानात् ॥ २ । २ । ५० ॥

नित्यत्वे nitya tve, were letters eternal ; अविकारात् a-vikârât, from non-modification ; अनित्यत्वे a-nitya-tve, were they non-eternal ; च cha, and ; अनवस्थानात् an-avasthânât, from non-persistence.

179. If the letter were eternal it could not be modified, and if it were impermanent it could not abide long enough to furnish the material for modification.—50.

On the supposition of the letters being eternal, *i* cannot be modified into *y* ; and on the supposition of their being impermanent, *i* must perish before it can be modified into *y*.

नित्यानामतीन्द्रियत्वात्तद्धर्म्मविकल्पाच्च वर्णविकाराणामप्रतिषेधः ॥ २ । २ । ५१ ॥

नित्यानां nityânâm, of eternals ; अतीन्द्रियत्वात् ati-indriya-tvât, from being super-sensuous ; तद्धर्म्मविकल्पात् tat-dharma-vikalpât, from difference of attributes ; वर्णविकाराणां varṇa-vikârâṇâm, of the modifications of letters ; अप्रतिषेधः a-pratiṣedhaḥ, non-contradiction.

180. Though the letters be eternal, their modification, says an objector, cannot be denied, as some of the eternal things are beyond the grasp of the senses, while others possess a different character.—51.

Just as some eternal things (as ether) are supersensuous while others (such as cowhood) are cognisable by the sense, so some eternal things as ether may be unmodifiable while others such as letters may be susceptible to modification.

अनवस्थायित्वे च वर्णोपलब्धिवत्तद्विकारोपपत्तिः ॥२।२।५२॥

अनवस्थायित्वे an-avasthâyi-tve, in case of not persisting ; च cha, and ; वर्णोपलब्धिवत् varṇa-upalabdhi-vat, like apprehension of letters ; तद्विकारोपपत्तिः tat-vikâra-upapattiḥ, establishment of their modifications.

181. Even if the letters are impermanent, their modification, like their perception, is, according to the objector, possible.—52.

Even if you say that letters are impermanent, you admit that they abide long enough to be capable of being perceived. Why then cannot they abide long enough to be capaple of being modified ?

विकारधर्म्मित्वे नित्यत्वाभावात्कालान्तरे विकारोपपत्तेश्चाप्रतिषेधः ॥ २ । २ । ५३ ॥

विकारधर्मित्वे vikâra-dharmi-tve, where there is the character of undergoing modification ; नित्यत्वाभावात् nitya-tva-abhâvât, from absence of eternality ; कालान्तरे kâla-antare, at another time ; विकारोपपत्तेः vikâra-upapatteḥ, from establishment of modification ; च cha, and ; अप्रतिषेधः a-pratiṣedhaḥ, non-contradiction.

182. In reply, we say that our position is unassailable, because there is no eternalness where there is the character of modification and because your so-called modification presents itself at a time subsequent to the destruction of the original material.—53.

The letters cannot be modified if you say that they are eternal, because modification is the reverse of eternalness. When a thing is modified it assumes another nature, abandoning its own. Again, the letters cannot be modified if you say that they are impermanent, because there is no time for *i* (of dadhi) to be modified into *y* when *a* (of atra) follows. The sound 'dadhi' is produced (pronounced) at the first moment, exists (continuously) during the second moment, and perishes at the third moment. The sound "atra" is produced (pronounced) at the second moment, exists (continues) during the third moment, and perishes at the fourth moment. Now, *i* (of dadhi) cannot be modified into *y* until *a* (of atra) has come into existence. But *a* comes into existence at the third moment, when *i* has already perished. So, on the supposition of impermanency of letters, modification is impossidle.

प्रकृत्यनियमाद्वर्णविकाराणाम् ॥ २ । २ । ५४ ॥

प्रकृत्यनियमात् prakṛiti-a-niyamât, from non-restriction to the root ; वर्णविकाराणां varṇa-vikârâṇâm, of the modifications of letters.

183. Letters are not modified, because there is no fixity as to the original material of their modification.—54.

In the case of real modifications there is a fixity as regards their original materials, *e.g.*, milk is the original material of curd, but not *vice versa*. In the case of letters, however, there is no fixed rule, *e.g.*, *i* is the original material of *y* in dadhyatra (dadhi+atra), but *y* is the original material of *i* in vidhyati (vyadh+ya+ti). Hence the operation of modification is not really applicable to letters.

अनियमे नियमान्नानियमः ॥ २ । २ । ५५ ॥

अनियमे a-niyame, in the case of non-restriction ; नियमात् niyamât, because of restriction, i, e. rule or uniformity ; न na, not ; अनियमः a-niyamaḥ, non-restriction.

184. Some say that there is no lack of fixity, because the absence of fixity itself is fixed.—55.

I is sometimes modified into *y*, and *y*, sometimes into *i*. So in respect of letters there is no fixity as to the original materials of their modification. This much, however, is fixed that there is no fixity, or in other words, the absence of fixity is fixed. Hence the objector, who is a quibbler, contends that there is fixity at least as to the negative aspect of modification.

नियमानियमविरोधादनियमे नियमाच्चाप्रतिषेधः ॥ २।२।५६॥

नियमानियम विरोधात् niyama-aniyama-virodhât, owing to contradiction of restriction and non-restriction ; अनियमे aniyame, in respect of non-restriction ; नियमात् niyamât, there being restriction ; च cha, and ; अप्रतिषेधः a-pratiṣedhaḥ, non-contradiction.

185. By saying that the absence of fixity is fixed, you cannot set aside our reason, because the fixity and its absence are contradictory terms.—56.

Our reason is that in respect of letters there is no fixity as to their modification. You contend that, though there is no fixity, the absence of fixity is fixed. Our reply is that, though the absence of fixity is fixed, it does not establish fixity as a positive fact, because fixity is incompatible with the absence of fixity.

गुणान्तरापत्त्युपमर्द्दह्रासवृद्धिलेशश्लेषेभ्यस्तु विकारोपपत्तेर्वर्णविकारः ॥ २ । २ । ५७ ॥

गुणान्तरापत्त्युपमर्द्दह्रासवृद्धिलेशश्लेषेभ्यः guṇa-antara-âpatti-upamarda-hrâsa-vṛiddhi-leśa-śleṣebhyaḥ, from the ensuing of a different quality, overcoming, shortening, lengthening, dropping and incoming ; तु tu, but ; विकारोपपत्तेः vikâra-upapatteḥ, from establishment of modification ; वर्णविकारः varṇa-vikâraḥ, modification of letters,

186. There is an apparent modification of letters in the case of their attaining a different quality, taking up substitutes, becoming short or long and undergoing diminution or augmentation.—57.

A letter is said to attain a different quality when, for instance, the grave accentuation is given to what was acutely accented. As an instance of a letter accepting a substitute, we may mention *gam* as becoming *gachchh*. A long vowel is sometimes shortened, *e.g.*, nadî (in the vocative case), becomes nadi. A short vowel is lengthened, *e.g.*, 'muni' (in the vocative case) becomes 'mune". Diminution occurs in such cases as 'as+tas' becoming 'stas.' In 'devânâm' (deva+âm) *na* is an augment.

ते विभक्त्यन्ताः पदम् ॥ २ । २ । ५८ ॥

ते te, they, letters ; विभक्त्यन्ताः vibhakti-antâḥ, with inflections ; पदम् padam, word.

187. The letters ended with an affix form a **word**.—58.

Words are of two kinds: *nouns* and *verbs*. A noun ends in a *sup* affix, *e.g.* Râmas (Râma+su), while a verb ends in a *tiṅ* affix, *e.g.*, bhavati (bhû+ti).

तदर्थे व्यक्त्याकृतिजातिसन्निधावुपचारात् संशयः ॥२।२।५९॥

तदर्थे tat-arthe, as to the object or meaning of the word ; व्यक्त्याकृतिजातिसन्निधौ vyakti-âkṛiti-jâti-sannidhau, invariable association with an individual, form and class ; उपचारात् upachârât, from use ; संशयः saṃśayaḥ, doubt.

188. There is doubt what a word (noun) really means, as it invariably presents to us an **individual, form and genus.**—59.

The word 'cow' reminds us of an individual (a four-footed animal), its form (limbs) and its genus (cowhood). Now, it is asked, what is the real signification of a word (noun)—an individual, form or genus ?

याशब्दसमूहत्यागपरिग्रहसंख्यावृद्ध्युपचयवर्णसमासानुबन्धानां व्यक्तावुपचाराद्व्यक्तिः ॥ २ । २ । ६० ॥

या शब्दसमूहत्यागपरिग्रहसंख्यावृद्ध्युपचयवर्णसमासानुबन्धानाम् yâ-śabda-samûha-tyâga-parigraha-saṃkhyâ-vṛiddhi-upachaya-varṇa-samâsa-anubandhânâm, of the word, that, i e. any noun, collection, avoiding, accepting, number, growth, colour, connection, and propagation ; व्यक्तौ vyaktau, in the case of the individual ; उपचारात upachârât, from use, व्यक्तिः vyaktiḥ, individual.

189. Some say that the word (noun) denotes individual, because it is only in respect of individuals that we can use "that," "collection," "giving," "taking," "number," "waxing," "waning," "colour," "compound" and "propagation."—60.

"That cow is going"—here the term "that" can be used only in reference to an individual cow. Similarly, it is only in respect of individuals that we can use the expressions "collection of cows," "he gives the cow," "he takes the cow," "ten cows, "cow waxes," "cow wanes," "red cow," "cow-legs" and "cow gives birth to cow."

न तदनवस्थानात् ॥ २ । २ । ६१ ॥

न na, no ; तदनवस्थानात् tat-an-avasthânât, from its non-persistence.

190. A word (noun) does not denote an individual, because there is no fixation of the latter.—61.

Unless we take genus into consideration, the word cow will denote any individual of any kind. Individuals are infinite. They cannot be distinguished from one another, unless we refer some of them to a certain genus and others to another genus, and so on. In order to distinguish a cow-individual from a horse-individual, we must admit a genus called cow distinguished from a genus called horse.

सहचरणस्थानतादर्थ्यवृत्तमानधारणसामीप्ययोगसाधनाधिपत्येभ्यो ब्राह्मणमञ्चकटराजशक्तुचन्दनगङ्गाशटकान्न पुरुषेष्वतद्भावेऽपि तदुपचारः ॥ २ । २ । ६२ ॥

सहचरण स्थानतादर्थ्यवृत्तमानधारण सामीप्य योग साधनाधिपत्येभ्यः sahacharaṇa-sthâna-tâdarthya-vṛitta-mâna-dhâraṇa- sâmîpya-yoga-sâdhana âdhipatye-bhyaḥ, from association, place, purpose, function, measure, containing, vicinity, conjunction, sustenance and supremacy, ब्राह्मणमञ्चकटराज शक्तुचन्दन गङ्गा शटकान्न पुरुषेषु brâhmaṇa-mañcha-kaṭa râja-saktu chandana gaṅgâ-śakata-anna-puruṣeṣu, in respect of a brâhmaṇa, scaffold, mat, king flour, sandal wood, Gangâ, cart bullock, food and person ; अतद्भावे a-tat bhâve, in the absence of object or inherent meaning ; अपि api, even ; तदुपचारः tat-upachâ âḥ, its use.

191. Though a word does not literally bear a certain meaning, it is used figuratively to convey the same, as in the case of Brahmana, scaffold, mat, king, flour, sandalwood, Ganges, cart, food and man, in

consideration of association, place, design, function, measure, containing, vicinity, conjunction, sustenance and supremacy.—62.

If the word does not denote an individual, how is it that we refer to an individual cow by the expression "that cow is feeding"? The answer is that, though the word cow may not literally mean an individual, we may refer to the same figuratively. There are such instances as:—'Feed the staff' means 'feed the Brâhmaṇa holding a staff,' 'the scaffolds shout' means 'men on the scaffolds shout,' 'he makes a mat' means 'he aims at making a mat,' 'Yama' (chastiser) means 'a king,' 'a bushel of flour' means flour measured by a bushel, 'a vessel of sandal-wood' means 'sandal-wood placed in a vessel,' 'cows are grazing on the Ganges' means 'cows are grazing in the vicinity of the Ganges,' 'a black cart' means a cart marked with blackness, 'food' means 'life' and 'this person (Bharadvâja) is a clan' means 'this person is the head of a clan.'

आकृतिस्तदपेक्षत्वात् सत्त्वव्यवस्थानसिद्धेः ॥ २ । २ । ६३॥

आकृतिः âkṛitiḥ, form ; तदपेक्षत्वात् tat-apekṣa-tvât, as being dependent upon it ; सत्त्वव्यवस्थानसिद्धेः sattva-vyavasthâna-siddheḥ, from the establishment of the identity or position of an entity.

192. Some say that the word (noun) denotes form by which an entity is recognised.—63.

We use such expressions as 'this is a cow' and 'this is a horse' only with reference to the forms of the cow and the horse. Hence it is alleged by some that the word denotes form.

व्यक्त्याकृतियुक्तेऽप्यप्रसङ्गात्प्रोक्षणादीनां मृद्गवके जातिः ॥ २ । २ । ६४ ॥

व्यक्त्याकृतियुक्ते vyakti-âkṛiti-yukte, possessing individuality and form ; अपि api, also ; अप्रसंगात् a-prasaṅgât, from non-application. प्रोक्षणादीनाम् prokṣaṇa-âdînâm, of immolation, etc. ; मृद्गवके mṛit-gavake, in respect of an earthenware cow ; जातिः jâtiḥ. class or genus.

193. Others say that the word (noun) must denote genus, otherwise why in an earthenware cow, possessed of individuality and form, do we not find immolation, etc.?—64.

We can immolate a real cow, but not an earthenware cow, though the latter possesses individuality and form. The distinction between a real cow and an earthenware one is that the former comes under the genus cow, but the latter does not. Hence it is urged by some that a word (noun) denotes genus.

नाकृतिव्यक्त्यपेक्षत्वाज्जात्यभिव्यक्तेः ॥ २ । २ । ६५ ॥

न na, no ; आकृति व्यक्त्यपेक्षत्वात् âkriti-vyakti-apekṣa-tvat, from being dependent upon form and individuality ; जात्यभिव्यक्तेः jâti-abhivyakteh, of the manifestation of the genus.

194. In reply, we say that it is not genus alone that is meant by a word (noun), because the manifestation of genus depends on the form and individuality.—65.

The genus abides in the individual, and the individual cannot be recognised except by its form. Hence genus has reference both to the form and individual, for, in other words, the genus alone is not the signification of a word.

व्यक्त्याकृतिजातयस्तु पदार्थः ॥ २ । २ । ६६ ॥

व्यक्त्याकृतिजातयः vyakti âkriti-jâtayaḥ, individual, form and genus ; तु tu, but ; पदार्थः padârthaḥ the object denoted by the word.

195. The meaning of a word (noun) is, according to us, the genus, form and individual.—66.

The word (noun) signifies all the three, though prominence is given to one of them. For the purpose of distinction, the individual is prominent. In order to convey a general notion, per-eminence is given to the genus. In practical concerns, much importance is attached to the form. As a fact, the word 'noun' ordinarily presents to us the form, denotes the individual and connotes the genus.

व्यक्तिर्गुणविशेषाश्रयो मूर्त्तिः ॥ २ । २ । ६७ ॥

व्यक्तिः vyaktiḥ, individual ; गुणविशेषाश्रयः guṇa-viśeṣa-âśrayaḥ, the abode of particular attributes : मूर्त्तिः mûrtiḥ, body, substance.

196. An **individual** is that which has a definite form and is the abode of particular qualities.—67.

An individual is any substance which is cognised by the senses, as a limited abode of colour, taste, smell, touch, weight, solidity, tremulousness, velocity or elasticity.

आकृतिर्जातिलिङ्गाख्या ॥ २ । २ । ६८ ॥

आकृतिः âkṛitiḥ, form; जातिलिङ्गाख्या jâti-liṅga-âkhyâ, that by which the genus and the marks of the genus are manifested.

197. The **form** is that which is called the token of the genus.—68.

The genus cowhood, for instance, is recognised by a certain collocation of the dewlap which is a form. We cannot recognise the genus of a formless substance.

समानप्रसवात्मिका जातिः ॥ २ । २ । ६९ ॥

समानप्रसवात्मिका samâna-prasava-âtmikâ, that the nature of which is to produce the same idea or cognition ; जातिः jâtiḥ, genus, class.

198. **Genus** is that whose nature is to produce the same conception.—69.

Cowhood is a genus which underlies all cows. Seeing a cow somewhere, we acquire a general notion of cows (*i.e.*, derive knowledge of cowhood). This general notion enables us on all subsequent occasions to recognise individual cows.

Book III.—Chapter I.

दर्शनस्पर्शनाभ्यामेकार्थग्रहणात् ॥ ३ । १ । १ ॥

दर्शनस्पर्शनाभ्याम् darśana-sparśanâbhyâm, by means of sight and touch; एकार्थग्रहणात् eka-artha-grahaṇât, because of the apprehension of the same object.

199. A sense is not soul because we can apprehend an object through both sight and touch.

"Previously I saw the jar and now I touch it:" such expressions will be meaningless if "I" is not different from eye which cannot touch and from skin which cannot see. In other words, the "I" or soul is distinct from the senses.

न विषयव्यवस्थानात् ३ । १ । २ ॥

न na, no; विषयव्यवस्थानात् viṣaya-vyavasthânât, owing to the particular relation or allocation of the senses to the objects.

200. This is, some say, not so because there is a fixed relation between the senses and their objects.

Colour, for instance, is an exclusive object of the eye, sound of the ear, smell of the nose, and so on. It is the eye that, according to the objectors, apprehends colour, and there is no necessity for assuming a soul distinct from the eye for the purpose of explaining the apprehension of colour.

तद्व्यवस्थानादेवात्मसद्भावादप्रतिषेधः ॥ ३ । १ । ३ ॥

तद्व्यवस्थानात् tat-vyavasthânât, from that allocation; एव eva, itself; आत्मसद्भावात् âtma-sadbhâvât, because of the existence of the soul; अप्रतिषेधः a-pratiṣedhaḥ, non-opposition.

201. This is, we reply, no opposition because the existence of soul is inferred from that very fixed relation.

There is a fixed relation between the senses and their objects, e.g., between the eye and colour, the ear and sound, and so on. It is the eye and not the ear that can apprehend colour, and it is the ear and not the eye that can apprehend sound. If a sense were the soul it could apprehend only one object, but "I" can apprehend many objects, that is, "I" can see colour, hear sound, and so on. Hence the "I" or soul which confers unity on the various kinds of apprehension is different from the senses each of which can apprehend only one object.

शरीरदाहे पातकाभावात् ॥ ३ । १ । ४ ॥

शरीरदाहे śarîra-dâhe, in burning the body, पातकाभावात् pâtaka-abhâvât, as there would be absence of sin.

202. If the **body** were soul there should be release from sins as soon as the body was burnt.

If a person has no soul beyond his body he should be freed from sins when the body is destroyed. But in reality sins pursue him in his subsequent lives. Hence the body is not soul.

The aphorism admits of another interpretation :—

If the **body** were soul there could arise no sin from killing living beings.

Our body varies in dimension and character with every moment. The body which exists at the present moment is not responsible for the sin which was committed at a previous moment inasmuch as the body which committed the sin is now non existent In other words, no sin would attach to the person who killed living beings if the soul were identical with our transient body.

तदभावः सात्मकप्रदाहेऽपि तन्नित्यत्वात् ॥ ३ । १ । ५ ॥

तदभावः tat-abhâvaḥ, absence of sin ; सात्मकप्रदाहे sa-âtmaka pradâhe, in burning the body endowed with a soul ; अपि api, even ; तन्नित्यत्वात् tat-nityatvât, as the soul is eternal.

203. There would, says an objector, be no sin even if the body endowed with a soul were burnt, for the soul is eternal.

In the previous aphorism it was shown that the commission of sins would be impossible if we supposed the body to be the soul. In the present aphorism it is argued by an objector that we should be incapable of committing sins even on the supposition of the soul being distinct from our body, for such a soul is eternal and cannot be killed.

न कार्याश्रयकर्तृवधात् ॥ ३ । १ । ६ ॥

न na, no ; कार्याश्रयकर्तृवधात् kârya-âśraya kartṛi badhât, because there is killing of the body which is at once the cause and the field of experience, or killing of the field of experience i.e. the body and of its cause i e. the senses, or killing of the embodied life of the soul.

204. In reply we say that it is not so because we are capable of killing the body which is the site of operations of the soul.

Though the soul is indestructible we can kill the body which is the seat of its sensations. Hence we are not incapable of committing sins by killing or murder. Moreover, if we do not admit a permanent soul beyond our frail body we shall be confronted by many absurdities such as " loss of merited action " (kṛita-hâni) and " gain of unmerited action " (akṛitâbhyâgama). A man who has committed a certain sin may not suffer its consequences in this life and unless there is a soul continuing to his next life he will not suffer them at all. This is a " loss of merited action". Again, we often find a man suffering the consequences of action which he never did in this life. This would be a " gain of unmerited action," unless we believed that his soul did the action in his previous life.

सव्यदृष्टस्येतरेण प्रत्यभिज्ञानात् ॥ ३ । १ । ७ ॥

सव्यदृष्टस्य savya-dṛ ṣṭasya, of that which is seen by the left eye ; इतरेण itareṇa, by the other ; प्रत्यभिज्ञानात् pratyabhijñânât, because there is recognition.

205. [There is a soul beyond the **sense**] because what is seen by the left eye is recognised by the right.

A thing perceived previously by the left eye is recognised now by the right eye. This would have been impossible if the soul were identical with the left eye or the right eye on the principle that the seat of recognition must be the same as the seat of perception. Consequently we must admit that there is a soul which is distinct from the left and right eyes and which is the common seat of perception and recognition.

नैकस्मिन्नासास्थिव्यवहिते द्वित्वाभिमानात ॥ ३ । १ । ८ ॥

न na, no ; एकस्मिन् ekasmin, in one and the same ; नासास्थिव्यवहिते na â-asthi-vyavahite, separated by the nasal bone ; द्वित्वाभिमानात dvitva-abhimâ-nât, because there arises the conceit of duality of the eye.

206. Some say that the eyes are not **two**: the conceit of duality arises from the single organ of vision being divided by the bone of the nose.

The objectors argue as follows :—

If the eyes were really two, *viz*, right and left, we would have been bound to admit a soul distinct from the senses as the common seat of perception and recognition. But there is only one eye which is divided by the bridge of the nose and which performs the two functions of perception and recognition Hence there is, according to the objectors, no soul beyond the eye

एकविनाशे द्वितीयाविनाशान्नैकत्वम् ॥ ३ । १ । ९ ॥

एकविनाशे eka-vinâśe, on the destruction of the one ; द्वितीयाविनाशात् dvitîya-a-vinâśât, as there is non-destruction of the other ; न na, not ; एकत्वम् eka-tvam, unity

207. The eyes we reply, are really two because the destruction of one does not cause the destruction of the other.

If the organ of vision was only one, then on the destruction of that one (*i e.*, one eye) there would be total blindness.

अवयवनाशेऽप्यवयव्युपलब्धेरहेतुः ॥ ३ । १ । १० ॥

अवयवनाशे avayava nâśe, on the destruction of a part ; अपि api, even ; अवयव्युपलब्धेः avayavi upalabdheḥ, as the whole is cognised ; अहेतुः a hetuḥ no reason.

208. This is, some say, no argument, for the destruction of a part does not cause the destruction of the whole.

The objectors say :—Just as a tree does not perish though a branch of it has been destroyed, so there may not be total blindness though one eye (a part of the organ of vision) has been destroyed.

दृष्टान्तविरोधादप्रतिषेधः ॥ ३ । १ । ११ ॥

दृष्टान्तविरोधात् dṛṣṭânta-virodhât, owing to conflict with the familiar instance ; अप्रतिषेधः a pratiṣedhaḥ, non- opposition.

209. This is, we reply, no opposition to our argument inasmuch as your illustration is inapt.

The illustration of a tree and its branch is not quite apt, for a tree does not exist in its entirety but assumes a mutilated condition when a branch of it is cut off. The right eye, on the other hand, remains in a perfect condition and performs the full function of an eye even when the left eye is destroyed.

इन्द्रियान्तरविकारात् ॥ ३ । १ । १२ ॥

इन्द्रियान्तरविकारात् indriya-antara-vikârât, as there takes place modification of another sense.

210. The soul is distinct from the senses, because there is an excitement of one sense through the operation of another sense.

When we see an acid substance, water overflows our tongue. In other words, in virtue of the operation of our visual sense there is an excitement in the sense of taste. This would be impossible unless there was a soul distinct from the senses. The soul seeing the acid substance remembers its properties ; and the remembrance of the acid properties excites the sense of taste.

न स्मृतेः स्मर्त्तव्यविषयत्वात् ॥ ३ । १ । १३ ॥

न na, no ; स्मृतेः smriteḥ, of memory, recollection ; स्मर्त्तव्यविषयत्वात् smartavya-viṣaya-tvât, because it has the thing recollected as its object.

211. It is, some say, not so because **remembrance** is lodged in the object remembered.

Remembrance, according to the objectors, is lodged in the thing remembered and does not necessarily presuppose a soul.

तदात्मगुणसद्भावादप्रतिषेधः ॥ ३ । १ । १४ ॥

तदात्मगुणसद्भावात् tat âtma-guṇa-sadbhâvât, because of its existence as a quality of the soul ; अप्रतिषेधः a-pratiṣedhaḥ, non-oppositon.

212. This is, we reply, no opposition, because remembrance is really a quality of the soul.

Remembrance is based on perception, that is, one can remember only that thing which one has perceived. It often happens that seeing the colour of a thing we remember its smell. This would be impossible if remembrance was a quality of a sense, *e.g.*, the eye which has never smelt the thing. Hence remembrance must be admitted to be a quality of a distinct substance called soul which is the common seat of perceptions of colour and of smell.

नात्मप्रतिपत्तिहेतूनां मनसि सम्भवात् ॥ ३ । १ । १५ ॥

न na, no ; आत्मप्रतिपत्तिहेतूनां âtma-pratipatti-hetûnâm, of the reasons or proofs of the existence of a separate soul ; मनसि manasi, to the mind ; सम्भवात् sambhavât, because of applicability.

213. There is, some say, no soul other than the mind because the arguments which are adduced to establish the "soul" are applicable to the mind.

The substance of the objection is this:—

We can apprehend an object by both the eye and the skin. It is true that the acts of seeing and touching the object by one agent cannot be explained unless we suppose the agent to be distinct from both the eye and the skin (*i.e*, from the senses), let however the agent be identified with the mind.

ज्ञातुर्ज्ञानसाधनोपपत्तेः संज्ञाभेदमात्रम् ॥ ३ । १ । १६ ॥

ज्ञातुः jñâtuḥ, of the knower; ज्ञानसाधनोपपत्तेः jñâna-sâdhana-upapatteḥ, as there must be instruments of knowing; संज्ञाभेदमात्रम् saṃjñâ-bheda-mâtram, mere difference of name.

214. Since there is a knower endowed with an instrument of knowledge it is, we reply, a mere verbal trick to apply the name "mind" to that which is really the "soul."

To explain the acts of seeing, touching, etc. you admit an agent distinct from the senses which are called its instruments. The sense or instrument by which the act of thinking is performed is called the "mind." The agent sees by the eye, hears by the ear, smells by the nose, tastes by the tongue, touches by the skin and thinks by the "mind." Hence we must admit the agent (soul) over and above the mind. If you call the agent as "mind," you will have to invent another name to designate the instrument. This verbal trick will not, after all, affect our position. Moreover, the mind cannot be the agent as it is atomic in nature. An atomic agent cannot perform the acts of seeing, hearing, knowing, feeling, etc.

नियमश्च निरनुमानः ॥ ३ । १ । १७ ॥

नियमः niyamaḥ, rule; च cha, and; निरनुमानः nir-anumânaḥ, devoid of inference

215. Your conclusion is moreover opposed to inference.

We admit a mind apart from the soul. If you deny any one of them or identify one with the other, an absurd conclusion will folow. Unless you admit the mind you will not be able to explain the internal perception. By the eye you can see, by the ear you can hear, by the nose you can smell, by the tongue you can taste and by the skin you can touch. By what sense do you carry on internal perception, *viz.*, thinking, imagining, etc.? Unless you admit the mind for that purpose your conclusion will be opposed to inference.

पूर्वाभ्यस्तस्मृत्यनुबन्धाज्जातस्य हर्षभयशोकसंप्रतिपत्तेः ॥ ३ । १ । १८ ॥

पूर्वाभ्यस्तस्मृत्यनुबन्धात् pûrva-abhyasta-smṛiti-anubandhât, from association with, or sequence from, memory previously experienced ; जातस्य jâtasya, of the new-born, the child ; हर्षभयशोकसंप्रतिपत्तेः harṣa-bhaya-śoka-sampratipatteḥ, on account of the occurrence of pleasure, fear and grief.

216. (The soul is to be admitted) on account of joy, fear and grief arising in a child from the memory of things previously experienced.

A new-born child manifests marks of joy, fear and grief. This is inexplicable unless we suppose that the child perceiving certain things in this life remembers the corresponding things of the past life. The things which used to excite joy, fear and grief in the past life continue to do so in this life. The memory of the past proves the previous birth as well as the existence of the soul.

पद्मादिषु प्रबोधसंमीलनविकारवत्तद्विकारः ॥ ३ । १ । १९ ॥

पद्मादिषु padma-âdiṣu, in the case of the lotus, etc. ; प्रबोधसंमीलनविकारवत् prabodha-sammîlana vikâra-vat, like the modifications of opening and closing ; तद्विकारः tat-vikâraḥ. its modifications.

217. It is objected that the changes of countenance in a child are like those of expanding and closing up in a lotus.

The objection stands thus :—

Just as a lotus which is devoid of memory expands and closes up by itself, so a child expresses joy, fear and grief even without the recollection of the things with which these were associated in the previous life.

नोष्णशीतवर्षकालनिमित्तत्वात् पञ्चात्मकविकाराणाम् ॥ ३ । १ । २० ॥

न na, no ; उष्णशीतवर्षकालनिमित्तत्वात् uṣṇa śîta-varṣa-kâla-nimitta tvât, because of their being caused by heat, cold, rain and season ; पञ्चात्मकविकाराणाम् pañcha âtmaka-vikârâṇâm, of the modifications or changes in things constituted by the five (elements).

218. This is, we reply, not so because the changes in inanimate things are caused by heat, cold, rain and season.

The changes of expansion and contraction in a lotus are caused by heat and cold. Similarly the changes of countenance in a child must be caused by something. What is that thing? It is the recollection of pleasure and pain associated with the things which are perceived.

प्रेत्याहाराभ्यासकृतात् स्तन्याभिलाषात् ॥ ३ । १ । २१ ॥

प्रेत्य pretya, transmigrating; आहाराभ्यासकृतात् âhâra-abhyâsa-kritât, produced by the habit of eating (in the previous life); स्तन्याभिलाषात् stanya abhilâṣât, from the desire for the mother's milk.

219. A child's desire for milk in this life is caused by the practice of his having drunk it in the previous life.

A child just born drinks the breast of his mother through the remembrance that he did so in the previous life as a means of satisfying hunger. The child's desire for milk in this life is caused by the remembrance of his experience in the previous life. This proves that the child's soul, though it has abandoned a previous body and has accepted a new one, remembers the experiences of the previous body.

अयसोऽयस्कान्ताभिगमनवत्तदुपसर्पणम् ॥ ३ । १ । २२ ॥

अयसः ayasaḥ, of the iron; अयस्कान्ताभिगमनवत् ayaskânta-abhigamana-vat, like the approach to the loadstone; तदुपसर्पणम् tat-upa-sarpaṇam, the approach of the infant.

220. Some deny the above by saying that a new-born child approaches the breast of his mother just as an iron approaches a loadstone (without any cause).

The objection runs thus:—

Just as an iron approaches a loadstone by itself, so does a child approach the breast of his mother without any cause.

नान्यत्र प्रवृत्त्यभावात् ॥ ३ । १ । २३ ॥

न na, no; अन्यत्र anyatra, elsewhere; प्रवृत्त्यभावात् pravṛitti-abhâvât, on account of absence of activity.

221. This is, we reply, not so because there is no approach towards any other thing.

You say that there is no cause which makes an iron approach a loadstone, or a child the breast of his mother. How do you then explain that an iron approaches only a loadstone but not a clod of earth and a child approaches only the breast of his mother and not any other thing? Evidently there is some cause to regulate these fixed relations.

वीतरागजन्मादर्शनात् ॥ ३ । १ । २४ ॥

वीतरागजन्मादर्शनात् vîta râga-janma-a-darśanât, because the rebirth of one who is free from desire is not observed.

222. We find that none is born without desire.

Every creature is born with some desires which are associated with the things enjoyed by him in the past life. In other words, the desire proves the existence of the creature or rather of his soul in the previous lives. Hence the soul is eternal.

सगुणद्रव्योत्पत्तिवत्तदुत्पत्तिः ॥ ३ । १ । २५ ॥

सगुणद्रव्योत्पत्तिवत् sa-guṇa-dravya-utpatti- vat, like the production of substances endowed with qualities ; तदुत्पत्तिः tat-utpattiḥ, its production.

223. Some say that the soul is not eternal because it may be produced along with desire as other things are produced along with their qualities.

The objection stands thus :—

Just as a jar, when it is produced, is distinguished by its colour, etc, so the soul when it is produced is marked by its desire, etc. Hence the desires do not pre-suppose the soul in the previous lives or, in other words, the soul is not eternal,

न संकल्पनिमित्तत्वाद्रागादीनाम् ॥ ३ । १ । २६ ॥

न na, no ; संकल्पनिमित्तत्वात् saṃkalpa-nimitta-tvât, because of their being caused by saṃkalpa, i.e. volition (springing from the recollection of past experience) ; रागादीनाम् râga âdînâm, of desire, etc.

224. This is, we reply, not so because the desire in a new-born child is caused by the ideas left in his soul by the things he enjoyed in his previous lives.

The desire implies that the soul existed in the previous lives or, in other words, the soul is eternal.

पार्थिवं गुणान्तरोपलब्धेः ॥ ३ । १ । २७ ॥

पार्थिवं pârthivam, earthy ; गुणान्तरोपलब्धेः guṇa-antara-upalabdheḥ, because of the perception of the quality of the earth.

225. Our body is earthy because it possesses the special qualities of earth.

In other worlds there are beings whose bodies are watery, fiery, airy or ethereal. Though our body is composed of all the five elements we call it earthy owing to the preponderance of earth in it.

पार्थिवाप्यतैजसं तद्गुणोपलब्धेः ॥ ३ । १ । २८ ॥

पार्थिवाप्यतैजसं ârthiva-âpya-taijasam, composed of elements of earth, water, and fire; तद्गुणोपलब्धेः tat-guṇa-upalabdheḥ, because of the perception of their attributes.

226. The body is composed of the elements of earth, water and fire, as the attributes of these elements are perceived in it.

निःश्वासोच्छ्वासोपलब्धेश्चातुर्भौतिकम् ॥३।१।२९॥

निःश्वासोच्छ्वासोपलब्धेः niḥśvâsa-uchchhvâsa-upalabdheḥ, because of the perception of in-breathing and out-breathing; चातुर्भौतिकं châturbhautikam, composed of four elements.

227. The body is composed of four elements, because it performs the operations of in-breathing and out breathing.

गन्धक्लेदपाकव्यूहावकाशदानेभ्यः पाञ्चभौतिकम् ॥३।१।३०॥

गन्धक्लेदपाकव्यूहावकाशदानेभ्यः gandha-kleda- pâka-vyûha-avakâśa-dânebhyaḥ, by reason of smell, wetness, digestion, circulation of blood, and room for movement; पाञ्चभौतिकं pâñcha bhautikam, composed of five elements.

228. The body is composed of five elements, as it possesses smell, wetness, digestion, circulation of blood and room for movement.

In the body there are smell and moisture which are attributes of earth and water respectively. Digestion and circulation of blood are done respectively by fire and air. There is also in the body room for the movement of the other elements in it, and therefore ether is also present in it.

Gotama has not taken the trouble to refute these doubtful reasonings in the above three aphorisms. They are generally refuted by the authority of the Veda in the next aphorism.

श्रुतिप्रामाण्याच्च ॥ ३ । १ । ३१ ॥

श्रुतिप्रामाण्यात् śruti-prâmâṇyât, from the authority of the Veda ; च cha, and.

229. In virtue of the authority of scripture too.

That our body is earthy is proved by our scripture. In the section on "Dissolution into the primordial matter," there are such texts as: May the eye be absorbed into the sun, may the body be absorbed into the earth, etc. The sun is evidently the source of the eye and the earth of the body.

कृष्णसारे सत्युपलम्भाद्व्यतिरिच्य चोपलम्भात्संशयः ॥ ३ । १ । ३२ ॥

कृष्णसारे kṛiṣṇasâre, the eyeball ; सति sati, there being ; उपलम्भात् upalambhât, because there is perception (of colour) ; व्यतिरिच्य vyatirichya, screening, removing ; च cha, and ; उपलम्भात् upalambhât, because there is perception ; संशयः saṃśayaḥ, doubt.

230 It is doubtful as to whether a sense is material or all-pervading because there is perception when there is (contact with) the eye-ball and there is perception even when the eye-ball is far off.

The eye-ball is said by some to be a material (elemental) substance inasmuch as its function is limited by its contact. A thing is seen when it has contact with the eye-ball, but it is not seen when the eye-ball is not connected. In other words, the eye-ball, like any other material substance, exercises its function only in virtue of its contact with things. Others hold that the eye-ball is a non-material all-pervading substance inasmuch as it can perceive things with which it has not come in contact. The eye-ball does not touch the things which it sees from a distance. Hence the question arises as to whether the eye-ball is a material or an all-pervading substance.

महदणुग्रहणात् ॥ ३ । १ । ३३ ॥

महदणुग्रहणात् mahat-aṇu-grahaṇât, because it apprehends both the large and the small.

231. It is contended that the eye-ball is not a material substance because it can apprehend the great and the small.

If the eye-ball had been a material substance it could have apprehended only those things which coincided with itself in bulk. But we find it can apprehend things of greater and smaller bulk. So it is contended that the eye ball is not a material substance.

रश्म्यर्थसन्निकर्षविशेषात्तद्ग्रहणम् ॥ ३ । १ । ३४ ॥

रश्म्यर्थसन्निकर्षविशेषात् raśmi-artha-sannikarṣa viśeṣât, from a special contact of the ocular ray with the object ; तद्ग्रहणम् tat-grahaṇam, the apprehension of the large and the small.

232. (The Naiyayika's reply to the above is that!) it is by the contact of the ray that the thi gs great and small are apprehended.

The Naiyâyikas say that even on the supposition of the eye-ball being a material sabstance the apprehension by it of the great and the small will not be impossible. Their explanation is that though the eye-ball itself does not coincide with things which are greater or smaller in bulk, yet the rays issuing from the eye-ball reach the things in their entire extent. Hence in spite of the eye-ball being a material substance there is no impossibility for it to apprehend the great and the small.

तदनुपलब्धेरहेतुः ॥ ३ । १ । ३५ ॥

तदनुपलब्धेरहेतुः tat-an-upalabdheḥ, because of its non-perception ; अहेतुः a-hetuḥ, not a cause.

233. Contact is not the cause because we do not perceive the ray.

The contact of a ray with a thing is not the cause of apprehension of the thing because we perceive no ray issuing from the eye ball.

नानुमीयमानस्य प्रत्यक्षतोऽनुपलब्धिरभावहेतुः ॥३।१।३६॥

न na, not ; अनुमीयमानस्य anumîyamânasya, of that which can be inferred ; प्रत्यक्षतः pratyakṣataḥ, by perception ; अनुपलब्धिः an-upalabdhiḥ, non-apprehension ; अभावहेतुः abhâva-hetuḥ, a mark of non-existence.

234. That we do not apprehend a thing through perception is no proof of non-existence of the thing because we may yet apprehend it through inference.

The ray issuing from the eye is not perceived as it is supersensuous. But it is established by inference like the lower half of the earth or the other side of the moon.

द्रव्यगुणधर्मभेदाच्चोपलब्धिनियमः ॥ ३ । १ । ३७ ॥

द्रव्यगुणधर्मभेदात् dravya-guṇa dharma-bhedât, according to differences of the nature of the substance and the attribute, च cha, and ; उपलब्धिनियमः upalabdhi-niyamaḥ, rule of perception.

235 And perception dependes upon the special character of the substance and its qualites.

A substance unless it possesses magnitude, or a quality unless it possesses obviousness, is not perceived. From the absence of magnitude and obvious colour the ray of the eye-ball is not perceived.

अनेकद्रव्यसमवायात् रूपविशेषाच्च रूपोपलब्धिः ॥३।१।३८॥

अनेकद्रव्यसमवायात् an eka dravya-samavâyât, from combination in more than one substance ; रूपविशेषात् rûpa viśeṣat, from peculiarity, i.e. perceptible intensity, of colour ; च cha, and ; रूपोपलब्धिः rûpa-upalabdhiḥ, perception of colour.

236. A colour is perceived only when it abides in many things intimately and possesses obviousness.

The sun's ray is perceived as it possesses an obviousness in respect of colour and touch. But the ray of the eye-ball is not perceived as it is obvious neither in respect of colour nor in respect of touch.

कर्मकारितश्चेन्द्रियाणां व्यूहः पुरुषार्थतन्त्रः ॥ ३ । १ । ३९ ॥

कर्मकारितः karma-kâritaḥ, determined or organised by karma or deserts ; च cha, and ; इन्द्रियाणाम् indriyâṇâm, of the senses ; व्यूहः vyûhaḥ, order or assemblage ; पुरुषार्थतन्त्रः puruṣa artha-tantraḥ, subservient to the purposes of the puruṣa or man.

237. And the senses subservient to the purposes of man have been set in order by his deserts.

The order referred to is as follows :—

The eye emits ray which does not possess the quality of obviousness and cannot consequently burn the thing it touches. Moreover, had there been obviousness in the ray it would have obstructed our vision by standing as a screen between the eye and the thing. This sort of arrangement of the senses was made to enable man to attain his purposes according to his merits and demerits.

मध्यन्दिनोल्काप्रकाशानुपलब्धिवत्तदनुपलब्धिः ॥३।१।४०॥

मध्यन्दिनोल्काप्रकाशानुपलब्धिवत् madhyandina-ulkâ prakâśa-an-upalabdhi-vat, like the non-perception of the light of a meteor at midday ; तदनुपलब्धिः tat-an-upalabdhiḥ, its non-perception.

238. Some say that the ray of the eye (possesses obviousness of colour but it) is not perceived just as the light of a meteor at midday is not perceived.

The light of a meteor though possessing obviousness of colour is not perceived at midday because it is then overpowered by the light of the sun. Similarly, some say, the ray of the eye possesses obviousnesss of colour but it is not perceived during the day time on account of its being overpowered by the light of the sun.

न रात्रावप्यनुपलब्धेः ॥ ३ । १ । ४१ ॥

न na, no रात्रौ râtrau, at night; अपि api, even; अनुपलब्धेः anupalabdheḥ, from its non-perception.

239. It is, we reply, not so because even in the night the ray of the eye is not perceived.

Had the ray of the eye possessed obviousness of colour it would have been perceived during the night when it cannot be overpowered by the light of the sun. As the ray of the eye is not perceived even during the night we must conclude that it does not possess obviousness of colour.

वाह्यप्रकाशानुग्रहाद्विषयोपलब्धेरनभिव्यक्तितोऽनुपलब्धिः ॥ ३ । १ । ४२ ॥

बाह्यप्रकाशानुग्रहात् bâhya-prakâśa-anugrahât, through conjunction with, or co-operation of, external light; विषयोपलब्धेः viṣaya-upalabdheḥ, because perception of objects (takes place) ; अनभिव्यक्तितः an-abhivyakti-taḥ, from non-manifestation ; अनुपलब्धिः an-upalabdhiḥ, non-perception.

240. The ray of the eye is not perceived in consequence of its unobviousness but not on account of its total absence because it reaches objects through the aid of external light.

In the eye there is ray which does not however possess an obvious colour. Had the eye possessed no ray it could not have perceived any object. Since the eye perceives objects, it possesses ray in it, and since it requires the aid of external light (such as the light of the sun) to perceive them it follows that the ray does not possess the quality of obviousness. This aphorism answers the objection raised in 3-1-35.

अभिव्यक्तौ चाभिभवात् ॥ ३ । १ । ४३ ॥

अभिव्यक्तौ abhivyaktau, in case of man festation ; च cha, and (where co-operation of external light is not required) ; अभिभवात् abhibhavât, because it is overpowered.

241. And the in isibility of the ray of the eye cannot be due to its being overpowered (by an external light such as the light of the sun) because the overpowering is possible only of a thing which possessed obviousness.

It is only a thing which possesses obviousness or manifestation that can be overpowered or obscured. But how can we throw a thing into obscurity which never possessed manifestation ? We cannot therefore say that tho ray of the eye is not perceived on account of its having been overpowered by an external light.

नक्तञ्चरनयनरश्मिदर्शनाच्च ॥ ३ । १ । ४४ ॥

नक्तञ्चरनयनरश्मिदर्शनात् naktañchara nayana-raśmi-darśanât, because the ray of the eye is seen in the case of prowlers by night , च cha, and.

242. There must be ray in the eye of man as we see it in the eye of animals that move about in the night.

We see that animals wandering by night, such as cats, possess ray in their eyes. By this we can conjecture that there is ray in the eye of man.

अप्राप्य ग्रहणं काचाभ्रपटलस्फटिकान्तरितोपलब्धेः ॥३।१।४५॥

अप्राप्य aprâpya, without reaching ; ग्रहणं grahaṇam, apprehension ; काचाभ्रपटलस्फटिकान्तरितोपलब्धेः kâcha-abhra-paṭala-sphaṭika-antarita-upalabdheḥ, because of perception of things screened by glass, mica, and crystal.

243. Some say that the eye can perceive a thing even without coming in go tast with it by means of its rays just as things sereened from us by glass, mica, membra e or crystal are seen.

The objection raised in this aphorism controverts the Nyâya theory of contact (in pratyakṣa) and seeks to prove that the senses are not material substances.

कुड्यान्तरितानुपलब्धेरप्रतिषेधः ॥ ३ । १ । ४६ ॥

कुड्यान्तरितानुपलब्धेः kuḍya antarita an-upalabdheḥ, because of non-perception of what is screened from view by a wall ; अप्रतिषेधः a-pratiṣedhaḥ, non-contradiction.

244. (The foregoing objection is not valid) because we cannot perceive what is screened from us by walls.

The eye cannot really perceive a thing without coming in contact with it by means of its rays. For instance, a thing which is screened from us by a wall is not perceived by our eyes.

अप्रतिघातात् सन्निकर्षोपपत्तिः ॥ ३ । १ । ४७ ॥

अप्रतिघातात् a-pratighâtât, from non-obstruction ; सन्निकर्षोपपत्तिः sannikarṣa-upapattiḥ, establishment of contact.

245. There is a real contact because there is no actual obstruction (caused by glass, mica, membrane or crystal)

The ray issuing from the eye can reach an external object through glass, mica, etc., which are transparent substances. There being no obstruction caused by these substances, the eye comes really in contact with the external object.

आदित्यरश्मेः स्फटिकान्तरेऽपि दाह्येऽविघातात् ॥ ३।१।४८॥

आदित्यरश्मेः âditya-raśmeḥ, of the sun's ray ; स्फटिकान्तरे sphaṭika-antare, being screened by a crystal ; अपि api, even ; दाह्ये dâhye, towards a combustible substance ; अविघातात् ; a-vighâtât, from non-obstruction.

246. A ray of the sun is not prevented from reaching a combustible substance though the latter is screened by a crystal.

This is an example which supports the theory of contact, *viz.*, a ray issuing from the eye passes actually through a crystal to an object lying beyond it.

नेतरेतरधर्म्मप्रसङ्गात् ॥ ३ । १ ४९ ॥

न na, no ; इतरेतरधर्मप्रसंगात् itara-itara-dharma-prasaṅgât, on account of implication of mutual properties.

247. It is, some say, not so because the character of one presents itself in the other.

The objection stands thus :—

If a ray issuing from the eye can reach an object screened by a stal, why can it not reach another object which is screened by a wall ?

According to the objector the property of the crystal presents itself in the wall.

आदर्शोदकयो: प्रसादस्वाभाव्याद्रूपोपलब्धिवत्तदुपलब्धि: ॥ ३ । १ । ५० ॥

आदर्शोदकयो: âdarśa-udakayoḥ, in a mirror and in water; प्रसादस्वाभाव्यात् prasâda svâbhâvyât, from natural clearness or transparency; रूपोपलब्धिवत् rûpa-upalabdhi-vat, like the perception of colour or form; तदुपलब्धि: tat-upalabdhiḥ, its perception.

248. In reply we say that the perception of a thing screened by a crystal takes place in the same manner as that of a form in a mirror or water owing to the possession of the character of transparency.

The form of a face is reflected on a mirror because the latter possesses transparency. Similarly, a thing is reflected on a crystal inasmuch as the latter is transparent. A wall which does not possess transparency can reflect nothing. It is therefore entirely due to the nature of the screens that we can or cannot perceive things through them.

दृष्टानुमितानां नियोगप्रतिषेधानुपपत्ति: ॥ ३ । १ । ५१ ॥

दृष्टानुमितानां driṣṭa-anumitânâm, of things seen and inferred; नियोगप्रतिषेधानुपपत्ति: niyoga-pratiṣedha-an-upapattiḥ, inapplicability of injunctions and prohibitions, assertions and denials.

249. It is not possible to impose injunctions and prohibitions on facts which are perceived or inferred to be of some fixed character.

A crystal and a wall are found respectively to be transparent and non transparent. It is not possible to alter their character by saying "let the crystal be non-transparent" and "let the wall be transparent." Likewise, a ray of the eye in passing to a thing is obstructed by a wall but not by a crystal. This is a perceived fact which cannot be altered by our words. Hence the theory of contact remains intact.

स्थानान्यत्वे नानात्वादवयविनानात्वादवयविनानास्थानत्वाच्च संशय: ॥ ३ । १ । ५२ ॥

स्थानान्यत्वे sthâna-anya-tve, from occupying different places; नानात्वात् nânâ-tvát, because of diversity; अवयविनानास्थानत्वात् avayavi-nânâ-sthâna-tvât, from a whole occupying different places; च cha, and; संशय: saṃśayaḥ, doubt.

250. Since many things occupy many places and since also one thing possessing different parts occupies many places, there arises doubt as to whether the senses are more than one.

There is doubt as to whether there are as many senses as there are sensuous functions or whether all the functions belong to one sense possessing different parts.

त्वगव्यतिरेकात् ॥ ३ । १ । ५३ ॥

त्वक् tvak, skin, touch ; अव्यतिरेकात् a vyatirekât, from its non-exclusion.

251. Some say that the senses are not many as none of them is independent of touch (skin).

The eye, ear, nose and tongue are said to be mere modifications of touch (skin) which pervades them, that is, there is only one sense, *viz.*, touch (skin), all others being merely its parts.

न युगपदर्थानुपलब्धेः ॥ ३ । १ । ५४ ॥

न na, no ; युगपत् yugapat, simultaneously ; अर्थानुपलब्धेः artha-an-upa-labdheḥ, from non-perception of objects.

252. Touch is not the only sense because objects are not perceived simultaneously.

Had there been only one sense, *viz.*, touch, it would have in conjunction with the mind produced the functions of seeing, hearing, smelling, tasting, etc., simultaneously. But we cannot perform different functions at once. This proves that the senses are many : the mind which is an atomic substance being unable to come in contact with the different senses at a time cannot produce different functions simultaneously.

विप्रतिषेधाच्च नत्वगेका ॥ ३ । १ । ५५ ॥

विप्रतिषेधात् vipratiṣedhât, because there is obstruction ; च cha, and ; न na, not ; त्वक् tvak, touch ; एका ekâ, only one.

253. Touch cannot be the only sense prohibiting the function of other senses.

Touch can perceive only those objects which are near (contiguous) but it cannot perceive objects which are far off. As a fact we can perceive colour and sound from a great distance. This is certainly not the function of touch but of some other sense which can reach distant objects.

इन्द्रियार्थपञ्चत्वात् ॥ ३ । १ । ५६ ॥

इन्द्रियार्थपञ्चत्वात् indriya- artha pañcha-tvât, because the objects of the senses are five.

254. Senses are five because there are five objects.

There are five objects, *viz.*, colour, sound, smell (odour), taste (savour) and touch which are cognised respectively by the eye, ear, nose, tongue and skin. There are therefore five senses corresponding to the five objects.

न तदर्थबहुत्वात् ॥ ३ । १ । ५७ ॥

न na, no ; तदर्थबहुत्वात् tat-artha-bahu-tvât, because their objects are many.

255. Some say that the senses are not five because there are more than five objects.

The objects of sense are said to be many such as good smell, bad smell, white colour, yellow colour, bitter taste, sweet taste, pungent taste, warm touch, cold touch, etc. According to the objector there must be senses corresponding to all these objects.

गन्धत्वाद्यव्यतिरेकाद्गन्धादीनामप्रतिषेधः ॥ ३ । १ । ५८ ॥

गन्धत्वाद्यव्यतिरेकात् gandha-tva-âdi-a-vyatirekât, because of the non-exclusion of the character of smell, etc. ; गन्धादीनां gandha-âdînâṃ, of smell, etc. ; अप्रतिषेधः a-pratiṣedhaḥ, non-exclusion.

256. There is, we reply, no objection because odour (smell), etc. are never devoid of the nature of odour (smell), etc.

Good odour, bad odour, etc. are not different objects of sense but they all come under the genus odour. It is the nose alone that cognises all sorts of odour—good or bad. Similarly all colours—white, yellow, blue or green—are cognised by the eye. In fact there are only five objects which are cognised by the five senses.

विषयत्वाव्यतिरेकादेकत्वम् ॥ ३ । १ । ५९ ॥

विषयत्वाव्यतिरेकात् viṣaya-tva-a-vyatirekât, because of the non-exclusion of the character of their being objects of sense ; एकत्वम् eka-tvam, unity,

257. Some say that there is only one sense as the so-called different objects of sense are n t devoid of the character of an object.

The objection raised in this aphorism is as follows:—

The so-called different objects, *viz.*, colour, sound, smell (odour) taste (savour) and touch agree with one another in each of them being an object of sense. As they all possess the common characteristic of being an object of sense it is much simpler to say that the object of sense is only one. If there is only one object of sense, the sense must also be one only.

न बुद्धिलक्षणाधिष्ठानगत्याकृतिजातिपञ्चत्वेभ्यः ॥३।१।६०॥

न na, no, बुद्धिलक्षणाधिष्ठानगत्याकृतिजातिपञ्चत्वेभ्यः buddhi-lakṣaṇa-adhiṣṭhâna-gati-âkṛiti-jâti-pañcha-tvebhyaḥ, because of fivefoldness of the states of consciousness which the senses produce, their sites, their movements, their shapes and their origins.

258. It is, we reply, not so because the senses possess five-fold character corresponding to the characters of knowledge, sites, processes, forms and materials.

The senses must be admitted to be five on the following grounds:—

(*a*) The characters of knowledge—There are five senses correspon-ding to the five characters of knowledge, *viz.*, visual, auditory, olfactory, gustatory and tactual.

(*b*) The sites—The senses are five on account of the various sites they occupy. The visual sense rests on the eyeball, the auditory sense on the ear-hole, the olfactory sense on the nose, the gustatory sense on the tongue, while the tactual sense occupies the whole body.

(*c*) The processes—There are five senses involving five different processes, *e. g.*, the visual sense apprehends a colour by approaching it through the (ocular) ray while the tactual sense apprehends an object which is in association with the body, and so on.

(*d*) The forms—The senses are of different forms, *e g.*, the eye partakes of the nature of a blue ball, and the ear is not different from ether, etc.

(*e*) The materials—The senses are made up of different materials : the eye is fiery, the ear is ethereal, the nose is earthy, the tongue is watery, and the skin (touch) is airy.

भूतगुणविशेषोपलब्धेस्तादात्म्यम् ॥ ३ । १ । ६१ ॥

भूतगुणविशेषोपलब्धेः bhûta-guṇa-viśeṣa-upalabdheḥ, on account of the perception of the specific attributes of the elements ; तादात्म्यम् tadâtmyam, identity.

259. The senses are essentially identical with the elements in consequence of the possession of their special qualities.

The five senses, *viz.*, the eye, ear, nose, tongue and skin (touch), are essentially identical with the five elements, *viz.*, fire, ether, earth, water and air, whose special qualities, *viz.*, colour, sound, smell (odour), savour (taste) and tangibility, are exhibited by them.

गन्धरसरूपस्पर्शशब्दानां स्पर्शपर्य्यन्ताः पृथिव्याः॥ ३।१।६२॥

गन्धरसरूपस्पर्शशब्दानां gandha-rasa-rûpa-sparśa śabdânâm, of smell, taste, form, touch, and sound ; स्पर्शपर्यन्ताः sparśa-paryantâḥ, those ending with touch ; पृथिव्याः prithivyâḥ, of the earth.

260. Of odour (smell), savour (taste), colour, tangibility (touch) and sound those ending with tangibility belong to earth.

अप्तेजोवायूनां पूर्व्वं पूर्व्वमपोह्याकाशस्योत्तरः ॥३।१।६३॥

अप्तेजोवायूनाम् ap-tejo-vâyûnâm, of water, fire and air ; पूर्वम्पूर्वम् pûrvam pûrvam, each preceding one ; अपोह्य apohya, discarding ; आकाशस्य âkâśasya, of ether ; उत्तरः uttaraḥ, the last.

261. Rejecting each preceding one in succession they belong respectively to water, fire and air ; the last (sound) belongs to ether.

The earth possesses four qualities, *viz.*, odour (smell), savour (taste), colour and tangibility. In water there are three qualities, *viz.*, savour, colour and tangibility; colour and tangibility are known to be the qualities of fire while tangibility and sound belong respectively to air and ether.

न सर्व्वगुणानुपलब्धेः ॥ ३ । १ । ६४ ॥

न na, no ; सर्वगुणानुपलब्धेः sarva-guṇa-an-upalabdheḥ, an account of the non-perception of all the attributes.

262. An objector says that it is not so because an element is not apparently found to possess more than one quality.

The substance of the objection is that the earth does not possess four qualities but only one quality, *viz.*, odour (smell) which is apprehended by the nose. Water does not possess three qualities but possesses only one quality, *viz.*, savour (taste) which is apprehended by the tongue. Similarly the other elements do, each of them, possess only one quality.

एकैकश्येनोत्तरोत्तरगुणसद्भावादुत्तराणां तदनुपलब्धिः ॥ ३ । १ । ६५ ॥

एकैकश्येन eka-eka-śyena, one to one ; उत्तरोत्तरगुणसद्भावात uttara-uttara-guṇa-sadbhâvât, because of the existence of the attributes in each succeeding one ; उत्तराणम् uttarâṇâm, in the succeeding ones ; तदनुपलब्धिः tat-an-upa-labdhiḥ, non-perception thereof.

263. The objector further says that the qualities belong to the elements, one to one, in their respective order so that there is non-perception of other qualities in them.

The substance of the objection is this :—

Odour (smell) is the only quality of the earth. Consequently the other three qualities, *viz.*, savour (taste), colour and tangibility, alleged to belong to the earth, are not found in it. Savour (taste) is the only quality of water, hence the other two qualities, *viz.*, colour and tangibility alleged to belong to water, are not found in it. Colour is the only quality of fire, and hence the other quality, *viz.*, tangibility alleged to belong to fire, is not found in it. Tangibility is of course the quality of air and sound of ether.

विष्टं ह्यपरम्परेण ॥ ३ । १ । ६६ ॥

विष्टं viṣṭam, covered, interpenetrated ; हि hi, for ; अपरं aparam, one ; अपरेण apareṇa, by another.

264. Of the elements one is, according to the objector, often interpenetrated by others.

The objection is explained as follows:

The earth is often interpenetrated by water, fire and air and is consequently found to possess savour (taste), colour and tangibility besides odour (smell). Similar is the case with water, etc.

न पार्थिवाप्ययोः प्रत्यक्षत्वात ॥ ३ । १ । ६७ ॥

न na, no ; पार्थिवाप्ययोः pârthiva-âpyayoḥ, of the earthy and the watery, of the terrene and aqueous ; प्रत्यक्षत्वात pratyakṣa-tvât, because of being perceptible.

265. It is, we reply, not so because there is visual perception of the earthy and t e watery.

The Naiyayikas meet the foregoing objections by saying that the earth really possesses four qualities, water three, fire two, air one, and ether one. Had the earth possessed only odour (smell) and the water only savour (taste) then it would have been impossible for us to see the earthy and watery things. We are competent to see only those things which possess colour, and if the earth and water had not possessed colour how could we have seen them? Since we can see the earthy and the watery it follows that they possess colour. If you say that earth and water are visible because they are mixed with the fiery things which possess colour, why then the air and ether are also not visible? There is no rule that it is only the earth and water that can be mixed with fiery things but that the air and ether cannot be so mixed. Proceeding in this way we find that the earth, etc. do not each possess only one quality.

पूर्व्वपूर्व्वगुणोत्कर्षात्तत्तत्प्रधानम् ॥ ३ । १ । ६८ ॥

पूर्वपूर्वगुणोत्कर्षात् pûrva-pûrva guṇa-utkarṣât, owing to the predominance of each preceding attribute ; तत्तत्प्रधानं tat-tat-pradhânam, each is predominant attribute of each corresponding element.

266. Owing to the predominance of one quality in an element, a sense is characterised by the quality which pre-dominates in its corresponding element.

The nose is characterised by odour (smell) which predominates in its corresponding element the earth ; the tongue is characterised by savour (taste) which predominates in its corresponding element the water; the eye is characterised by colour which predominates in its corrresponding element the fire ; the skin (touch) is characterised by tangibility which abides in its corresponding element the air while the ear is characterised by sound which is the special quality of its corresponding element the ether.

तद्व्यवस्थानन्तु भूयस्त्वात् ॥ ३ । १ । ६९ ॥

तद्व्यवस्थानं tat- vyavasthânam, distribution thereof ; तु tu, however ; भूयस्त्वात् bhûyastvât, according to their fitness.

267. A sense as distinguished from its corresponding element is determined by its fineness.

A sense (*e g* , the nose) which is the fine part of an element (*e.g* , the earth) is able to perceive a special object (*e.g*, odour) owing to the act-force (*saṃskâra, karma*) of the person possessing the sense. A sense cannot perceive more than one object because it possesses the predominant quality of an element, *e g.*, the nose possesses only odour which is the predominant quality of the earth, the tongue the savour of water, the eye the colour of fire, and so on.

सगुणानामिन्द्रियभावात् ॥ ३ । १ । ७० ॥

सगुणानां saguṇânâm, of those attended with attributes ; इन्द्रियभावात् indriya-bhâvât, being themselves the senses.

268. A sense is really called as such when it is attended by its quality.

Some may say why a sense (the nose for instance) cannot perceive its own quality (odour) The reply is that a sense consists of an element endowed with its quality It is only when a sense is attended by the quality that it can see an object. Now in perceiving an object the sense is attended by the quality but in perceiving its own quality it is not so attended. Consequently a sense cannot perceive its own quality.

तेनैव तस्याग्रहणाच्च ॥ ३ । १ । ७१ ॥

तेन tena, by that ; एव eva, alone ; तस्य tasya, its ; अग्रहणात् a-grahaṇât, on account of non-apprehension ; च cha, and.

269. Moreover an object is never perceived by itself.

An eye can see an external object but it cannot see itself. On the same principle a sense cannot perceive its own quality.

न शब्दगुणोपलब्धेः ॥ ३ । १ । ७२ ॥

न na, no ; शब्दगुणोपलब्धेः śabda-guṇa-upalabdheḥ, because of perception of the attribute of sound.

270. It is, some say, not so because the quality of sound is perceived by the ear.

The objection stands thus:—

It is not true that a sense cannot perceive its own quality. The ear, for instance, can perceive sound which is its own quality.

तदुपलब्धिरितरेतरद्रव्यगुणवैधर्म्यात् ॥ ३ । १ । ७३ ॥

तदुपलब्धिः tat-upalabdhiḥ, its perception ; इतरेतरद्रव्यगुणवैधर्म्यात् itara-itara-dravya-guṇa- vaidharmyât, from difference from the attribute of every other substance.

271. The perception of sound furnishes a contrast to that of other qualities and their corresponding substrata.

The nose, tongue, eye and skin can respectively smell earth, taste water, see colour and touch air only when they are attended by their own qualities, *viz*, odour (smell), savour (taste), colour and tangibility. But an ear when it hears sound is not attended by any quality. In fact the ear is identical with the ether and hears sound by itself. By indirect inference we can prove that sound is the special quality of the ether: odour is the predominant quality of the earth, savour of water, colour of the eye, and tangibility of the skin (touch): sound must therefore be the quality of the remaining element, *viz.*, the ether.

Book III, Chapter II.

कर्म्माकाशसाधर्म्यात् संशयः ॥ ३ । २ । १ ॥

कर्माकाशसाधर्म्यात् karma-âkâśa-sâdharmyât, owing to its resemblance to action and ether ; संशयः samśayaḥ, doubt.

272. Since the intellect resembles both action and ether there is doubt as to whether it is transitory or permanent.

Inasmuch as the intellect bears likeness to both action and ether in respect of intangibility, there arises the question whether it is transitory like an action or permanent like the ether. We find in the intellect the function of origination and decay which marks transitory things as well as the function of recognition which marks permanent things. "I knew the tree," "I know it" and "I shall know it"—these are expressions which involving the ideas of origination and decay indicate our knowledge to be transitory, "I who knew the tree yesterday am knowing it again today"—this is an expression which involving the idea of continuity indicates our knowledge to be permanent. Hence there is doubt as to whether the intellect which exhibits both kinds of knowledge is really transitory or permanent.

विषयप्रत्यभिज्ञानात् ॥ ३ । २ । २ ॥

विषयप्रत्यभिज्ञानात् viṣaya-pratyabhijñânât, because of recognition of objects.

273. Some say that the intellect is permanent because there is recognition of objects.

The Sâṃkhyas maintain the permanency of the intellect on the ground of its capacity for the recognition of objects. A thing which was known before is known again now—this sort of knowledge is called recognition. It is possible only if knowledge which existed in the past continues also at the present, that is, if knowledge is persistent or permanent. Recognition would have been impossible if knowledge had been transitory. Hence the Sâṃkhyas conclude that the intellect which recognises objects is permanent.

साध्यसमत्वादहेतुः ॥ ३ । २ । ३ ॥

साध्यसमत्वात् sâdhya-sama-tvât, because the proof is the same as the thing to be proved ; अहेतुः a-hetuḥ, no mark.

274. The foregoing reason is not, we say, valid inasmuch as it requires proof like the very subject in dispute..

Whether the intellect is permanent or not—this is the subject in dispute. The Sâṃkhyas affirm that it is permanent and the reason adduced by them is that it can recognise objects. The Naiyâyikas dispute not only the conclusion of the Sâṃkhyas but also their reason. They say that the intellect does not recognise objects but it is the soul that does so. Knowledge cannot be attributed to an unconscious instrument, the intellect, but it must be admitted to be a quality of a conscious agent, the soul. If knowledge is not a quality of the soul, what else can be its quality? How is the soul to be defined? There is therefore no proof as to the validity of the reason, *viz.*, that the intellect recognises objects.

न युगपदग्रहणात् ॥ ३ । २ । ४ ॥

न na, no ; युगपत् yugapat, simultaneously; अग्रहणात् a-grahaṇât, because of non-perception.

275. Knowledge is neither a mode of the permanent intellect nor identical with it because various sorts of knowledge do not occur simultaneously.

The Sâṃkhyas affirm that knowledge is a mode of the permanent intellect from which it is not different. Knowledge, according to them, is nothing but the permanent intellect modified in the shape of an object which is reflected on it through the senses The Naiyâyikas oppose this view by saying that if knowledge as a mode of the permanent intellect is not different from it, then we must admit various sorts of knowledge to be permanent. But as a fact various sorts of knowledge are not permanent, that is, we cannot receive various sorts of knowledge simultaneously. Hence knowledge is not identical with the permanent intellect.

अप्रत्यभिज्ञाने च विनाशप्रसङ्गः ॥ ३ । २ । ५ ॥

अप्रत्यभिज्ञाने a-pratyabhijñâne, during non-recognition ; च cha, and ; विनाशप्रसंगः vinâśa-prasaṅgaḥ, implication of destruction.

276. And in the cessation of recognition there arises the contingency of cessation of the intellect.

If knowledge as a mode of the intellect is not different from it, then the cessation of recognition which is a kind of knowledge should be followed by the cessation of the intellect. This will upset the conclusion of the Sâṃkhyas that the intellect is permanent. Hence knowledge is not identical with the intellect.

क्रमवृत्तित्वादयुगपद्ग्रहणम् ॥ ३ । २ । ६ ॥

क्रमवृत्तित्वात् krama vṛitti-tvât, owing to its operation being successive ; अयुगपत् a-yugapat, non-simultaneous ; ग्रहणम् grahaṇam, reception, apprehension.

277. The reception of different sorts of knowledge is non-simultaneous owing, according to us, to our mind coming in contact with different sen es in succession.

The Naiyâyikas say that if knowledge as a mode of the permanent intellect had been identical with it, then there would have been neither a variety of knowledge nor origination and cessation of it. The different sorts of knowledge do not occur simultaneously because they are produced, according to the Naiyâyikas, by the mind which is atomic in dimension coming in contact with the senses in due succession.

अप्रत्यभिज्ञानञ्च विषयान्तरव्यासङ्गात् ॥३।२।७॥

अप्रत्यभिज्ञानं a-pratyabhijñânam, non-recognition; च cha, and, विषयान्तर-व्यासङ्गात् viṣaya-antara-vyâsaṅgât, due to occupation with another object.

278. The recognition (or knowledge) of an object cannot take place when the mind is drawn away by another object.

We cannot hear a sound by our ear when the mind conjoined with the eye is drawn away by a colour. This shows that knowledge is different from the intellect, and that the mind which is atomic in dimension serves as an instrument for the production of knowledge.

न गत्यभावात् ॥ ३ । २ । ८ ॥

न na, no ; गत्यभावात् gati-abhâvât, because of absence of motion.

279. The intellect cannot be conjoined with the senses in succession because there is no motion in it.

The mind which, according to the Naiyâyikas, is atomic in dimension can move from one sense-organ to another in succession to produce different kinds of knowledge. This is impossible in the case of the intellect which, according to the Sâṃkhyas, is not only permanent but also all-pervading and as such cannot change its place, that is, does not possess the tendency to be conjoined with the different sense-organs in succession. In fact there is only one internal sense called the mind, the other two so-called internal senses—intellect (Buddhi) and self-conceit

(Ahaṃkâra)—being superfluous. It is not all-pervading, and knowledge is not its mode. Knowledge classified as visual, olfactory, etc. is of different kinds which belong to the soul.

स्फटिकान्यत्वाभिमानवत्तदन्यत्वाभिमानः ३।२।९॥

स्फटिकान्यत्वाभिमानवत् sphaṭika-anyatva-abhimâna-vat, like conceit that a crystal is other than what it is ; तदन्यत्वाभिमानः tat-anya-tva-abhimânaḥ, the conceit of its being other than what it is.

280. A conceit of difference is said to arise in the intellect in the same way as the appearance of difference in a crystal.

As a single crystal appears to assume the different colours of different objects which are reflected on it, so the intellect though one appears, according to the Sâṃkhya, to be modified into different sorts of knowledge under the influence of different objects reflected on it through the senses.

स्फटिकेऽप्यपरापरोत्पत्तेः क्षणिकत्वाद्व्यक्तीनामहेतुः॥३।२।१०॥

स्फटिके sphaṭike, in the case of a crystal ; अपि api, even ; अपरापरोत्पत्तेः apara-apara-utpatteḥ, of diverse manifestations one after another ; क्षणिकत्वात् kṣaṇika-tvât, being momentary ; व्यक्तीनां vyaktînâm, of the individual maifestations ; अहेतुः a-hetuḥ, no mark.

281. It is said to be absurd even in the case of a crystal being replaced by newer and newer ones which grow up owing to all individuals being momentary.

The Sâṃkhya says that as a crystal seems to be modified by the colours which are reflected on it, so the intellect seems to be modified by the objects which are reflected on it through the senses. In reality there is, according to the Sâṃkhya, neither any modification of the crystal nor that of the intellect. This theory has in the preceding aphorism been controverted by the Naiyâyikas and is in the present aphorism opposed by the Buddhists. According to the latter all things, including even our body, are momentary. A thing which exists at the present moment grows up into another thing at the next moment so that there is no wonder that in the course of moments there should grow up crystals of different colours or intellects of different modes. Hence the conclusion of the Sâṃkhyas that a crystal remains unaltered is, according to the Buddhists, untenable.

नियमहेत्वभावाद्यथादर्शनमभ्यनुज्ञा ॥ ३ । २ । ११ ॥

नियमहेत्वभावात् niyama-hetu-abhâvât, owing to the absence of any reason for the rule (of growth and decay); यथादर्शनं yathâ darśanam, exactly as seen; अभ्यनुज्ञा abhyanujñâ, assent.

282. Owing to the absence of any absolute rule we shall give our assent according to the nature of each occurrence.

It is not true that in every case there are at each moment newer growths. Our body no doubt undergoes increase and decrease but a piece of stone or a crystal does not, so that the doctrine of growth applies to the first case but not to the second. Hence there is no general rule that a thing at the lapse of a moment should be replaced by another thing which grows up in its place.

नोत्पत्तिविनाशकारणोपलब्धेः ॥ ३ । २ । १२ ॥

न na, no ; उत्पत्तिविनाशकारणोपलब्धेः utpatti-vinâśa-kâraṇa-upalabdheḥ, because of the perception of the cause of production and destruction.

283. There is no absence of link as we perceive the cause of growth and decay.

The growth of a thing is the increase of its parts while the decay is the decrease of them An ant-hill gradually increases in dimension before it attains its full growth while a pot decreases in dimension before it reaches its final decay. We never find an instance in which a thing decays without leaving any connecting link for another thing which grows in its place. There is in fact no linkless growth or linkless decay.

क्षीरविनाशे कारणानुपलब्धिवद्दध्युत्पत्तिवच्च तदुपपत्तिः ॥ ३ । २ । १३ ॥

क्षीरविनाशे kṣîra-vinâśe, in the case of the destruction of milk ; कारणानुपलब्धिवत् kâraṇa-anupalabdhi-vat, like the non-perception of the cause ; दध्युत्पत्तिवत् dadhi-utpatti vat, like the production of curd ; च cha, and ; तदुपपत्तिः tat-utpattiḥ, its production.

284. The growth of newer crystals in the place of an old one is comparable, according to some, to the growth of curd in the place of milk the cause of whose decay is not perceived.

The Buddhist says that there are things which grow and decay without the gradual increase and decrease of their parts. Of such things we do not find the cause of the first growth (origination) and the last decay (cessation), that is, there is no link between the thing which ceases and another thing which grows in its palce. The milk, for instance, ceases without leaving any connecting link for the curd which grows in its place. Similarly new crystals grow to take the place of an old one which decays without leaving any mark. The crystal which exists at the present moment is not the same one that existed at the previous moment. There is no connection whatsoever between them.

लिङ्गतो ग्रहणान्नानुपलब्धिः ॥ ३ । २ । १४ ॥

लिङ्गत: liṅgataḥ, from the mark ; ग्रहणात् grahaṇât, from perception ; न na, not ; अनुपलब्धि: an-upalabdhiḥ, non-perception.

285. There is no non-perception of the cause of final decay as it is cognisable by its mark.

The Naiyâyikas say that it is not true that we do not perceive the final decay of the milk which is the cause of the first growth of the curd. The mark attending the final decay of milk (that is, the disappearance of sweet flavour) is the cause of the destruction of the milk, and that attending the first growth of curd (that is, the appearance of acid flavour) is the cause of its production. So through the mark we really perceive the cause of decay of milk and growth of curd. But there is no such mark perceptible in the case of a crystal which at the lapse of a moment is said to be replaced by another crystal of a different character.

न पयसः परिणामगुणान्तरप्रादुर्भावात् ॥ ३ । २ । १५ ॥

न na, not ; पयस: payasaḥ, of milk ; परिणामगुणान्तरप्रादुर्भावात् pariṇâma-guṇa antara-prâdurbhâvât, owing to the appearance or evolution of a different attribute or quality in virtue of transformation.

286. There is, it is alleged, no destruction of the milk but only a change of its quality.

The Sâmkhya says that the milk as a substance is not destroyed to produce another substance called curd. In reality a quality of the milk, *viz* sweet flavour, is changed into another quality, *viz.*, acid flavour.

व्यूहान्तराद्द्रव्यान्तरोत्पत्तिदर्शनं पूर्व्वद्रव्यनिवृत्तेरनुमानम् ॥ ३ । २ । १६ ॥

व्यूहान्तरात् vyûha-antarât, from one set (of causes) ; द्रव्यान्तरोत्पत्तिदर्शनं dravya-antara-utpatti-darśanam, observation of the production of another substance ; पूर्वद्रव्यनिवृत्तेः pûrva-dravya-nivṛitteḥ, of the cessation of the previous substance ; अनुमानम् anumânam, inference.

287. Seeing that a thing grows from another thing whose parts are disjoined, we infer that the latter thing is destroyed.

Seeing that a thing grows after the component parts of another thing have been disjoined, we infer that the latter thing has really been destroyed The curd, for instance, is not produced until the component parts of the milk have been destroyed. This shows that the growth of curd follows the decay of milk.

क्वचिद्विनाशकारणानुपलब्धेः क्वचिच्चोप-
लब्धेरनेकान्तः ॥ ३ । २ । १७ ॥

क्वचित् kvachit, in some cases ; विनाशकारणानुपलब्धेः vinâśa-kâraṇa-an-upalabdheḥ, from the non-perception of the cause of destruction ; क्वचित् kva chit, in some cases ; च cha, and ; उपलब्धेः upalabdheḥ, from perception; अनेकान्तः an-eka-antaḥ, not-one-ended, uncertain.

288. There will be an uncertainty of conclusion on the assumption that the cause of destruction is perceived in some cases and not perceived in others.

In the case of a jar being produced out of a piece of clay you say you perceive the cause of destruction of the clay and production of the jar, but in the case of the curd growing out of milk you say that you do not perceive the cause of destruction of the milk and production of the curd. This sort of perception in certain cases and non-perception in others will lead to an uncertainty of conclusion. As a fact in every case there is perception of the cause of destruction. Milk, for instance, is destroyed when there is the contact of an acid substance.

नेन्द्रियार्थयोस्तद्विनाशेऽपि ज्ञानावस्थानात् ॥ ३।२।१८ ॥

न na, not ; इन्द्रियार्थयोः indriya-arthayoḥ, of the sense and of the object; तद्विनाशे tat-vinâśe, on their destruction ; अपि api, also ; ज्ञानावस्थानात् jñâna-avasthânât, from the continuance of cognition.

289. Knowledge belongs neither to the sense nor to the object because it continues even on the destruction thereof.

If knowledge had been a quality of the sense, it could not continue after the sense had been destroyed. But knowledge in the form of memory is found actually to abide even after the sense has perished. Hence the sense is not the abode of knowledge. Similarly it may be proved that knowledge does not abide in the object.

युगपज्ज्ञेयानुपलब्धेश्च न मनसः ॥ ३ । २ । १९ ॥

युगपत् yugapat, simultaneously ; ज्ञेयानुपलब्धेः jñeya-an-upalabdheḥ, from the non-perception of the knowaoles ; च cha, and ; न na, not ; मनसः manasaḥ, of the mind.

290. It does not also belong to the mind the existence of which is inferred from the knowables not being perceived simultaneously.

As two or more things cannot be known (perceived) simultaneously, it is to be concluded that the mind which is an instrument of our knowledge is atomic in dimension. If we supposed this mind to be the abode of knowledge we could not call it an instrument in the acquisition of the same ; and knowledge as a quality of an atom would in that case become imperceptible. An atomic mind as the abode of our knowledge would stand moreover in the way of a *yogi* perceiving many things simultaneously through many sensuous bodies formed by his magical power.

तदात्मगुणत्वेऽपि तुल्यम् ॥ ३ । २ । २० ॥

तत् tat, it, the objection ; आत्मगुणत्वे âtma-guṇa-tve, were (cognition) an attribute of the soul ; अपि api, also ; तुल्यम् tulyam, the same.

291. Even if knowledge were a quality of the soul it would, says some one, give rise to similar absurdities..

The objection stands thus:—If the soul which is all-pervading were the abode of knowledge, there would be the simultaneous perceptions of many things in virtue of different sense-organs coming in contact with the soul simultaneously. But two or more things are never perceived simultaneously : the soul cannot therefore be the abode of knowledge, that is, knowledge cannot be a quality of the soul.

इन्द्रियैर्मनसः सन्निकर्षाभावात् तदनुत्पत्तिः ॥३।२।२१॥

इन्द्रियैः indriyaiḥ, with the senses ; मनसः manasaḥ, of the mind ; सन्निकर्षाभावात् sannikarṣa-abhâvât, owing to absence of contact or connection ; तदनुत्पत्तिः tat-an-utpattiḥ, non-production of simultaneous cognitions.

292. There is, we reply, non-production of simultaneons cognitions on account of the absence of contact of the mind with many sense-organs at a time..

The Naiyâyikas say that the soul cannot perceive an object unless the latter comes in contact with a sense which is conjoined with the mind. Though many objects can come in proximity with their corresponding senses simultaneously, the mind which is atomic in dimension can come in conjunction with only one sense at a time. Hence two or more things are not perceived simultaneously although the soul which perceives them is all-pervading.

नोत्पत्तिकारणानपदेशात् ॥३।२।२२॥

न na, no ; उत्पत्तिकारणानपदेशात् utpatti-kâraṇa-an-apadeśât, owing to non-predication of cause of production.

293 This is held by some to be untenable as there is no ground for the production of knowledge.

The objection stands thus:—It has been argued by the Naiyâyikas that there is absence of production of simultaneous cognitions on account of the lack of contact of the senses with the mind. An opponent takes exception to the word " production " and says that knowledge cannot be said to be produced if it is regarded as a quality of the soul which is eternal.

विनाशकारणानुपलब्धेश्चावस्थाने तन्नित्यत्वप्रसङ्गः॥३।२।२३॥

विनाशकारणानुपलब्धेः vinâśak-âraṇa-an-upalabdheḥ, owing to non-perception of the cause of destruction ; च cha, and ; अवस्थाने avasthâne, in the case of the existence (of cognition in the soul) ; तन्नित्यत्वप्रसङ्गः tat-nitya-tva-prasaṅgaḥ, implication of its eternality.

294. If knowledge is supposed to abide in the soul there is the contingency of its being eternal as there is perceived no cause of its destruction.

Knowledge can never be destroyed if it is supposed to be a quality of the soul. A quality may be destroyed in two ways—(1) either by the destruction of its abode, or (2) by the production of an opposite quality in its place. In the case of knowledge neither of these is possible as the soul which is its abode is eternal and as we find no opposite quality taking its place. Hence it follows that if knowledge is a quality of the soul it is eternal. But as knowledge is not eternal it is not a quality of the soul.

अनित्यत्वग्रहाद्बुद्धेर्बुद्ध्यन्तराद्विनाशः शब्दवत् ॥३।२।२४॥

अनित्यत्वग्रहात् a-nitya-tva-grahât, from the observation of non-eternality ; बुद्धेः buddheḥ, of cognition ; बुद्ध्यन्तरात् buddhi-antarât, from another cognition ; विनाशः vinâśaḥ, destruction ; शब्दवत् śabda-vat, as in the case of sound.

295. Cognitions being found to be non-eternal there is, we reply, destruction of one cognition by another like that of a sound.

We realize that cognition (knowledge) is not eternal when we observe that at one time there arises in us a certain kind of cognition (knowledge) and at the next time that cognition (knowledge) vanishes giving rise to another kind of cognition (knowledge). It has been asked how cognitions undergo destruction. Our reply is that one cognition vanishes as soon as it is replaced by another cognition which is opposed to it just as a sound-wave is destroyed by another sound-wave which takes its place.

ज्ञानसमवेतात्मप्रदेशसन्निकर्षान्मनसः स्मृत्युत्पत्तेर्न युगपदुत्पत्तिः ॥ ३ । २ । २५ ॥

ज्ञानसमवेतात्मप्रदेशसन्निकर्षात् jñâna-samaveta-âtma-pradeśa-sannikarṣât, from contact with a certain part of the soul in which cognition (in the form of impression) inheres ; मनसः manasaḥ of the mind ; स्मृत्युत्पत्तेः smṛiti-utpatteḥ, because of the production of recollection ; न na, not ; युगपद् yugapat, simultaneous उत्पत्तिः utpattiḥ, production.

29 . Since recollection (memory) is produced, according to some, by the conjunction of the mind with a certain part of the soul in which knowledge (impression) inheres, there is no simultaneous production of many recollections.

If knowledge be a quality of the soul there is the possibility of many recollections being produced simultaneously inasmuch as the many impressions deposited in our soul by our past perceptions are liable at once to be revived and developed into recollections by the mind whose contact with the soul always remains constant. Some say that there is no such possibility of simultaneousness because recollections are produced, according to them, by the mind coming in contact with particular parts of the soul in which particular impressions inhere. As the mind cannot come in contact with all parts of the soul simultaneously, the many impressions deposited in different parts of the soul are not revived and developed into recollections at once.

नान्तःशरीरवृत्तित्वान्मनसः ॥ ३ । २ । २६ ॥

न na, not; अन्तःशरीरवृत्तित्वात् antaḥ-śarîra-vṛitti-tvât, because it has its operation within the body; मनसः manasaḥ, of the mind.

297. This is, we reply, not so because it is within the body that the mind has its function.

It has been said in the preceding aphorism that recollections are produced by the mind coming in due order in conjunction with particular parts of the soul in which impressions inhere. This is, according to the Naiyâyikas, untenable because the mind cannot come in conjunction with the soul except in the body, and if the conjunction takes place in the body then there remains the possibility of simultaneous recollections.

साध्यत्वादहेतुः ॥ ३ । २ । २७ ॥

साध्यत्वात् sâdhya-tvât, because it is the thing to be established; अहेतुः a-hetuḥ, not a mark.

298. This is, some say, no reason because it requires to be proved.

The Naiyâyikas say that the mind comes in conjunction with the soul only within the limit of the body. Some oppose this by saying that until they receive sufficient proof they cannot admit that the conjunction takes place only in the body.

स्मरतः शरीरधारणोपपत्तेरप्रतिषेधः ॥३।२।२८॥

स्मरतः smarataḥ, of the person recollecting; शरीरधारणोपपत्तेः śarîra-dhâraṇa-upapatteḥ, because of the fact of his sustaining the body; अप्रतिषेधः a-pratiṣedhaḥ, non-contradiction.

299. It is, we reply, not unreasonable because a person is found to sustain his body even while he performs an act of recollection.

If we suppose that a recollection is produced by the mind coming in conjunction with a particular part of the soul outside the body, we cannot account for the body being sustained during the time when the recollection is performed. The body in order that it may be sustained requires an effort which is supplied by the mind coming in conjunction with the soul. Now the effort which arises from the conjunction is of two kinds, *viz.*, (1) the effort for sustaining, and (2) that for impelling (setting in motion). The body will be devoid of the first kind of effort if we suppose the mind to wander away from it for conjunction with the soul.

न तदाशुगतित्वान्मनसः ॥३।२।२९ ॥

न na, no; तत् tat, this; आशुगतित्वात् âśu-gati-tvât, owing to swiftness; मनसः manasaḥ, of the mind.

300. This is, some say, not so because the mind moves swiftly.

Some meet the objection raised in the preceding aphorism by saying that the mind while producing a recollection by its conjunction with the soul outside the body can, on account of its swift motion, come back at once to the body to produce the effort required for the sustenance of the same.

न स्मरणकालानियमात् ॥ ३।२।३० ॥

न na, no; स्मरणकालानियमात् smaraṇa-kâla-aniyamât, as there is no rule as to the time of recollection.

301. It is, we reply, not so because there is no fixed rule as to the duration of recollection.

The Naiyâyikas oppose the view expressed in the foregoing aphorism on the ground that the mind, if it is to be conjoined with the soul outside the body, may take a pretty long time to produce a recollection there, so that it may not come back to the body with sufficient quickness to produce the effort required for the sustenance of it.

आत्मप्रेरणयदृच्छाज्ञताभिश्च न संयोगविशेषः ॥ ३।२।३१ ॥

आत्मप्रेरणयदृच्छाज्ञताभिः âtma-preraṇa-yat-ṛichchhâ jña-tâ-bhiḥ, in virtue of a direction of the soul, spontaneity or chance, and the characteristic of its being the knower; च cha, and; न na, no; संयोगविशेषः saṃyoga-viśeṣaḥ, particular conjunction.

302. There is no peculiar conjunction of the soul with the mind either in virtue of the former sending the latter in search of what it wishes to recollect or through the latter being congnizant of what is to be recollected or through arbitrariness.

If we suppose the soul to send the mind to recollect a particular thing we encounter the absurdity of admitting that the soul already possesses the memory of what it is going to recollect. If on the other hand we suppose the mind to move out of its own accord for a particular recollection, we shall have to assume that the mind is the knower but in reality it is not so. We cannot even hold that the mind comes in conjunction with the soul arbitrarily for in that case there will remain no order then as to the occurrence of the objects of recollection.

व्यासक्तमनसः पादव्यथनेन संयोगविशेषेण समानम्॥३।२।३२॥

व्यासक्तमनसः vyâsakta-manasaḥ, of a man whose mind is absorbed in something else; पादव्यथनेन pâda-vyathanena, by the hurting of his foot; संयोगविशेषेण somyoga-viśeṣeṇa, with the particular conjunction; समानम् samânam, similar.

303. This is, some say, parallel to the particular conjunction which occurs in a man who while rapt in mind hurts his foot.

If a man while looking eagerly at dancing hurts his foot with a thorn, he feels pain because his mind comes instantly in conjunction with his soul at the foot which has been hurt. Similarly the peculiar conjunction referred to in the foregoing aphorism takes place, according to some, through the mind being cognizant of what is to be recollected.

प्रणिधानलिङ्गादिज्ञानानामयुगपद्भावादयुगपत्स्मरणम्॥३।२।३३॥

प्रणिधानलिङ्गादिज्ञानानां praṇidhâna-liṅga-âdi-jñânânâm, of concentration and cognition of the marks, etc; अयुगपद्भावात् âyugapat bhâvât owing to non-simultaneousness; अयुगपत् a-yugapat, non-simultaneous; स्मरणं smaraṇam, recollection.

304. Recollections are not simultaneous owing to the non-simultaneousness of the efforts of attention, operations of stimuli, etc.

A recollection is produced by the mind coming in conjunction with the soul in which impressions inhere. The production of recollection also presupposes efforts of attention, operations of stimuli, etc. As these do not occur simultaneously there is no simultaneousness of recollections.

ज्ञस्येच्छाद्वेषनिमित्तत्वादारम्भनिवृत्त्योः ॥ ३ । २ । ३४ ॥

ज्ञस्य jñasya, of the knower; इच्छाद्वेषनिमित्तत्वात् ichchhâ-dveṣa-nimitta-tvât, because of their being caused by desire and aversion; आरम्भनिवृत्त्योः ârambha-nivṛittyoh, of action and inaction.

305. Desire and aversion belong to the soul inasmuch as they are the causes of its doing an act or forbearing from doing the same.

The Sâṃkhyas say that knowledge is a quality of the soul (Purusa) while desire, aversion, volition, pleasure and pain are the qualities of the internal sense (the mind). This is, according to the Naiyâyikas, unreasonable because a person does an act or forbear from doing it on account of a certain desire for or aversion against the same. The desire and aversion again are caused by the knowledge of pleasure and pain respectively. Hence it is established that knowledge, desire, aversion, volition, pleasure and pain have all of them a single abode, that is, they are the qualities of a single substance called the soul.

तल्लिङ्गत्वादिच्छाद्वेषयोः पार्थिवाद्येष्वप्रतिषेधः ॥३।२।३५॥

तल्लिङ्गत्वात् tat-linga-tvât, because they are their marks इच्छाद्वेषयोः ichchhâ dveṣayoḥ, of desire and aversion; पार्थिवाद्येषु pârthiva-âdyeṣu, in respect of the terrene, etc; अप्रतिषेधः a-pratiṣedhaḥ non-obstruction.

306. It cannot, some say, be denied that desire and aversion belong to the body inasmuch as they are indicated by activity and forbearance from activity.

The Chârvâkas say that activity and forbearance from activity are the marks respectively of desire and aversion which again are the effects of knowledge. Now the body which is made of earth, etc. is the abode (field) of activity and forbearance from activity. Hence it is also the abode of knowledge, desire, aversion, etc.

परश्वादिष्वारम्भनिवृत्तिदर्शनात् ॥ ३ । २ । ३६ ॥

परश्वादिषु paraśu-âdiṣu, in the axe, etc; आरम्भनिवृत्तिदर्शनात् ârambha-nivṛitti-darśanât, from the observation of action and inaction.

307. This is, we reply, unreasonable because activity and forbearance from activity are found in the axes and the like.

Just as an axe, which is found sometimes to split a tree and at other times not to split it, is not a receptacle of knowledge, desire and aversion, so the body which is made of earth, etc. is not an abode of knowledge, etc., though we may find activity and forbearance from activity in it.

नियमानियमौ तु तद्विशेषकौ ॥ ३ । २ । ३७ ॥

नियमानियमौ niyama-aniyamau, regularity and irregularity; तु tu, but; तद्विशेषकौ tat-viśeṣakau, their distinguishing marks.

308. The regularity and irregularity of possession demarcate the soul and matter.

A material thing is by nature inactive but becomes endowed with activity when it is moved by a conscious agent. There is no such irregularity or uncertainty as to the possession of activity, etc by the soul. Knowledge, desire, aversion, etc. abide in the soul through an intimate connection, while these belong to matter through a mediate connection. We cannot account for the function of recognition, etc. if we assume knowledge to abide in the material atoms a conglomeration of which forms the body. Those who suppose the body to be the seat of knowledge cannot admit the efficacy of deserts and can offer no consolation to sufferers.

यथोक्तहेतुत्वात् पारतन्त्र्यादकृताभ्यागमाच्च न मनसः ॥३।२।३८॥

यथोक्तहेतुत्वात् yathokta-hetu-tvât, for the reasons already given; पारतन्त्र्यात् pâratantryât, from subserviency; अकृताभ्यागमात् a-kṛita-abhyâgamât, from usurpation of the unearned; च cha, and; न na, not; मनसः manasaḥ, of the mind.

309. The mind is not the seat of knowledge on account of reasons already given, on account of its being subject to an agent and owing to its incapacity to reap the fruits of another's deeds.

The mind cannot be the seat of knowledge because it has already been shown in aphorism 1. 1. 10 that desire, aversion, volition, pleasure and pain are the marks of the soul. Had the mind been the abode of knowledge it could have come in contact with the objects of sense independent of any agent. Since it cannot do so it is to be admitted to be a material thing serving the purpose of an instrument in the acquisition of knowledge. If you say that the mind itself is the agent you will have to admit that it is not an atom but possessed of magnitude like the soul so that it can apprehend knowledge, etc. which are its qualities. In order to avoid the simultaneousness of many perceptions it will further be necessary to assume an internal sense of an atomic dimension like the mind as we understand it. These assumptions will lead you to accept in some shape the tenets of the Naiyâyikas. On the supposition of the mind (or body) being the seat of knowledge and consequently of merits and demerits, it will be possible for work done by a person not to produce its effects on him after death and it may even necessitate a person to suffer for work not done by him. Hence the mind is not the seat of knowledge, desire, aversion, volition, pleasure and pain.

परिशेषाद्यथोक्तहेतूपपत्तेश्च ॥ ३ । २ । ३९ ॥

परिशेषात् pariśeṣât, by exhaustion; यथोक्तहेतूपपत्तेः yathâ-ukta-hetu-upapatteḥ, from the operation of the reasons already given; च cha, and.

310. Knowledge, etc. must be admitted to be qualities of the soul by the principle of exclusion and on account of arguments already adduced.

Knowledge is a quality which inheres in a substance. That substance is neither the body nor the sense nor the mind. It must therefore be the soul. The body cannot be the abode of knowledge because it is a material substance like a pot, cloth, etc. Knowledge cannot belong to the sense as the latter is an instrument like an axe. Had the sense been the abode of knowledge there could not be any recollection of things which were experienced by the sense before it was destroyed. If knowledge were a quality of the mind many perceptions could be simultaneous. But this is impossible. Hence the abode of knowledge is not the mind, but it is the soul which is permanent so that it can perceive a thing now as well as remember one perceived in the past.

स्मरणन्त्वात्मनो ज्ञस्वाभाव्यात् ॥ ३ । २ । ४० ॥

स्मरणं smarṇam, recollection; तु tu, but; आत्मनः âtmanaḥ, of the soul; ज्ञस्वाभाव्यात् jña-svâbhâvyât, because its nature is to be the knower.

311. Memory belongs to the soul which possesses the character of a knower.—43.

The soul is competent to recollect a thing because it possesses the knowledge of the past, present and future.

प्रणिधाननिबन्धाभ्यासलिङ्गलक्षणसादृश्यपरिग्रहाश्रयाश्रितसम्बन्धानन्तर्य्यवियोगैककार्य्यविरोधातिशयप्राप्तिव्यवधानसुखदुःखेच्छाद्वेषभयाऽर्थित्वक्रियारागधर्म्माधर्म्मनिमित्तेभ्यः ॥ ३ । २ । ४१ ॥

प्रणिधाननिबन्धाभ्यासलिङ्गलक्षणसादृश्यपरिग्रहाश्रयाश्रितसम्बन्धानन्तर्य्यवियोगैककार्य्यविरोधातिशयप्राप्तिव्यवधानसुखदुःखेच्छाद्वेषभयाऽर्थित्वक्रियारागधर्म्माधर्म्मनिमित्तेभ्यः; praṇidhâna-nibandha abhyâsa liṅga-lakṣaṇa-sâdṛiśya parigraha-âśraya-âṣrita-sambandha-ânantarya-viyoga-eka-kârya-virodha-atiśaya-prâpti-vyavadhâna-sukha-duḥkha-ichchhâ-dveṣa-bhaya-arthitva-kṛiyâ-râga-dharma-adharma-nimittebhyaḥ, from the causes of concentration, context, repetition, mark, characteristic, similarity, relationship, container, contained, connection, immediacy, separation, co-efficient, opposition, excess, acquisition, distance, pleasure, pain, desire, aversion, fear, entreaty, action, passion, merit and demerit.

312. Memory is awakened by such causes as attention, context, exercise, signs, marks, likeness, possession, relation of refuge and refugee, immediate subsequency, separation, similar employment, opposition, excess, receipt, intervention, pleasure and pain, desire and aversion, fear, entreaty, action, affection and merit and demerit.

Attention—enables us to fix the mind on one object by checking it from wandering away to any other object.

Context—is the connection of subjects such as proof, that which is to be proved, etc.

Exercise—is the constant repetition which confirms an impression.

Signs—may be (1) connected, (2) inseparable (intimate), (3) correlated or (4) opposite, *e.g.*, smoke is a sign of fire with which it is connected; horn is a sign of a cow from which it is inseparable an arm is a sign of a leg with which it is correlated; and the non-existent is a sign of the existent by the relation of opposition.

Mark—a mark on the body of a horse awakens the memory of the stable in which it was kept.

Likeness—as the image of Devadatta drawn on a board reminds us of the real person.

Possession—such as a property awakens the memory of the owner and *vice versa*.

Refuge and refugee—such as a king and his attendants.

Immediate subsequency—as sprinkling the rice and pounding it in a wooden mortar.

Separation—as of husband and wife.

Similar employment—as of fellow-disciples.

Opposition—as between a snake and ichneumon.

Excess—awakening the memory of that which exceeded.

Receipt—reminding us of one from whom something has been or will be received.

Intervention—such as a sheath reminding us of the sword.

Pleasure and pain—reminding us of that which caused them.

Desire and aversion—reminding us of one whom we liked or hated.

Fear—reminding us of that which caused it, *e. g.*, death.

Entreaty—reminding us of that which was wanted or prayed for.

Action—such as a chariot reminding us of the charioteer.

Affection—as recollecting a son or wife.

Merit and demerit—through which there is recollection of the causes of joy and sorrow experienced in a previous life.

कर्म्मानवस्थायिग्रहणात् ॥ ३ । २ । ४२ ॥

कर्मानवस्थायिग्रहणात् karma-anavasthâyi-grahaṇât, because of the cognisance of momentary events by action.

313. Knowledge perishes instantly because all actions are found to be transitory.

Does knowledge perish instantly like a sound or does it continue like a pot? Knowledge perishes as soon as it is produced in virtue of its being an action. In analysing an action, such as the falling of an arrow, we find that the arrow undergoes a series of movements in the course of its falling to the ground. Similarly in examining an act of knowledge we find that a series of steps are undergone by the act in the course of its production. These steps perish one after another in due succession. Hence it is clear that knowledge is transitory. If knowledge were permanent we could say, "I am preceiving a pot," even after the pot has been removed from our sight. Since we cannot use such an expression we must admit that knowledge is not permanent but transitory.

अव्यक्तग्रहणमनवस्थायित्वात् विद्युत्सम्पाते रूपाव्यक्तग्रहणवत् ॥ ३ । २ । ४३ ॥

अव्यक्तग्रहणं a-vyakta-grahaṇam, cognition of the indistinct; **अनवस्थायित्वात्** an-avasthâyi-tvât, being unenduring; **विद्युत्संपाते** vidyut-sampâte, on the flash of lightning; **रूपाव्यक्तग्रहणवत्** rûpa-avyakta-grahaṇa-vat, like the indistinct cognition of form.

314. An opponent fears that if knowledge were transitory no object could be known distinctly just as there is no distinct apprehension of colour during a flash of lightning.

The fear of the opponent arises thus :—If knowledge were transitory it could not at a moment apprehend an object in its entirety, that is, could not apprehend the infinite number of its properties at once. Hence the object could only be known indistinctly. As a fact, however, we can know things distinctly. Hence knowledge is not transitory.

हेतूपादानात् प्रतिषेद्धव्याभ्यनुज्ञा ॥ ३ । २ । ४४ ॥

हेतूपादानात् hetu upâdânât, from the reason advanced; प्रतिषेद्धव्याभ्यनुज्ञा pratiṣeddhavya-abhyanujñâ, admission of what is sought to be disproved.

315. From the argument advanced you have, we reply, to admit that which you went to disprove.

In the previous aphorism the opponent feared that if knowledge were transitory no object could be apprehended distinctly. The Naiyâyika removes the fear by saying that objects are apprehended indistinctly not owing to the transitoriness of knowledge but on account of our apprehending only their general qualities. The knowledge which takes cognizance of objects as possessed of both the general and special qualities is distinct but that which concerns itself only with the general qualities is indistinct.

The aphorism may be explained in another way:—The very illustration cited by you, *viz.*, that there is distinct apprehension during a flash of lightning leads you to admit the transitoriness of knowledge which you went to disprove.

* प्रदीपार्चिःसन्तत्यभिव्यक्तग्रहणवत्तद्ग्रहणम् ॥३।२।४५॥

प्रदीपार्चिःसन्तत्य भिव्यक्तग्रहणवत् pradîpa-archiḥ-santati-abhivyakta-grahaṇa-vat, like the apprehension of that which is illuminated by the stream of the rays of the lamp; तद्ग्रहणं tat-grahaṇam, distinct apprehension.

316. Although knowledge is transitory there is distinct apprehension through it as there is one through the series of momentary rays of a lamp.

Though the series of rays emitted by a lamp are transitory the apprehension through them is distinct. Similarly though our knowledge is transitory there is no obstacle to our apprehension being distinct.

द्रव्ये स्वगुणपरगुणोपलब्धेः संशयः ॥ ३ । २ । ४६ ॥

द्रव्ये dravye, in a substance; स्वगुणपरगुणोपलब्धेः sva-guṇa-paraguṇa-

* Vâchaspati reads a न. to show that the opponent's apprehension is unfounded.

upalabdheḥ, from the perception of its own as well as of other attributes; संशयः saṃśayaḥ, doubt.

317. From our perceiving in a substance the qualities of itself as well as of others there arises, says an opponent, a doubt as to whether the knowledge perceived in our body is a quality of its own.

In water we perceive liquidity which is one of its natural qualities as well as warmth which is an adventitious one. One may therefore ask as to whether the knowledge perceived in our body is a natural quality of the latter or is a mere adventitious one.

यावच्छरीरभावित्वाद्रूपादीनाम् ॥ ३ । २ । ४७ ॥

यावच्छरीरभावित्वात् yâvat-śarîra-bhâvi-tvât, because (form, etc.) endure as long as the body does; रूपादीनां rûpa-âdînâm, of form, etc.

318. [Knowledge is not a natural quality of the body because it furnishes a contrast to] colour, etc. which as natural qualities of the body do exist as long as the latter continues.

Knowledge, according to the Naiyâyika, is not a natural quality of the body because it may not continue quite as long as the body does. But such is not the case with colour, etc. which as natural qualities of the body do always exist with it. Hence knowledge is merely an adventitious quality of the body.

न पाकजगुणान्तरोत्पत्तेः ॥ ३ । २ । ४८ ॥

न na, no; पाकजगुणान्तरोत्पत्तेः pâka-ja-guṇa-antara-utpatteḥ, because of the production of other attributes caused by the action of heat.

319. It is, says an opponent, not so because other qualities produced by maturation do arise.

It has been stated that a substance and its natural qualities co-exist with each other and that knowledge not being always co-existent with the body is not a natural quality of the latter. An opponent in order to maintain that a substance and its natural qualities are not necessarily coexistent cites the instance of a jar whose natural colour is blue but which assumes a red colour through maturation in fire.

प्रतिद्वन्द्विसिद्धेः पाकजानामप्रतिषेधः ॥३।२।४९॥

प्रतिद्वन्द्विसिद्धेः pratidvandvi-siddheḥ, from the production of opposites; पाकजानाम् pâkajânâm, in the case of attributes caused by the action of heat; अप्रतिषेधः a-pratiṣedhaḥ, non-contradiction.

320. This is, we reply, no opposition becauses maturation occurs if there is production of opposite qualities.

A jar which was blue may through maturation become red but it is never totally deprived of colour which is its natural quality. But a body (dead) may be totally devoid of knowledge which is therefore not a natural quality of it. In the case of maturation moreover a quality is replaced by an opposite one with which it cannot co-abide, *e. g.*, the blueness of a jar may through maturation assume redness but cannot co-abide with the same. In the case of the body however knowledge is not replaced by an opposite quality. Hence knowledge is not a natural quality of the body.

शरीरव्यापित्वात् ॥ ३ । २ । ५० ॥

शरीरव्यापित्वात् śarîra-vyâpi-tvât, because it pervades the body.

321. [Knowledge, says an opponent, is a natural quality] because it pervades the whole body.

The opponent tries to prove that knowledge is a natural quality of the body because it pervades, according to him, the whole body and the numerous parts of it. But this, according to the Naiyâyika, is unreasonable as it leads to the assumption of numerous seats of knowledge, that is, souls in the body destructive of all order and system as to the feeling of pleasure, pain, etc.

न केशनखादिष्वनुपलब्धेः ॥ ३ । २ । ५१ ॥

न na, no; केशनखादिषु keśa-nakha-âdiṣu, in the hair, nails, etc; अनुपलब्धेः an-upalabdheḥ, because of non-perception.

322. [Knowledge does not pervade the whole body] as it is not found in the hair, nails, etc.

Knowledge does not pervade the whole body, *e. g*, it is not found in the hair, nails, etc. It cannot therefore be a natural quality of the body.

This aphorism may also be explained as follows:—

It is not true that a substance should be entirely pervaded by its natural qualities. Colour, for instance, is a natural quality of the body but it does not pervade the hair, nails etc.

त्वक्पर्य्यन्तत्वाच्छरीरस्य केशनखादिष्वप्रसङ्गः ॥३।२।५२॥

त्वक्पर्यन्तत्वात् tvak-paryanta-tvât, because of ending with the skin; शरीरस्य śarîrasya, of the body केशनखादिषु keśa nakha-âdiṣu, in the hair, nails, etc ; अप्रसंग: a-prasangaḥ, non-following.

323. The body being bounded by touch (cuticle) there is, says an opponent, no possiblity of knowledge abiding in the hair, nails, etc.

The hair, nails, etc. are not, according to the opponent, part of the body as they are not bounded by touch (cuticle). Knowledge cannot consequently abide in them

The aphorism may also be interpreted as follows :—

The body being bounded by touch (cuticle) there is no possibility of colour abiding in the hair, nails, etc.

शरीरगुणवैधर्म्यात् ॥ ३ । २ । ५३ ॥

शरीरगुणवैधर्म्यात् śarîra-guṇa-vaidharmyât, from dissimilarity to attributes of the body

324. Knowledge, we reply, is not a quality of the body because of its difference from the well-known qualities of the same.

The Naiyâyika says :—

The qualities of the body are of two kinds, *viz*: (1) those which are cognised by the external senses *e. g.*, colour, and (2) those which are not cognised by them, *e. g*, gravity. Knowledge does not come under either of the categories as it is uncognizable by the external senses and is at the same time cognizable on account of our being aware of the same.

The aphorism may also be explained as follows :—

The qualities of the body are cognized by the external senses but knowledge is not so cognized. Consequently knowledge cannot be a quality of the body.

न रूपादीनामितरेतरवैधर्म्यात् ॥ ३ । २ । ५४ ॥

न na, no ; रूपादीनां rûpa-âdînâm, of form, etc ; इतरेतरवैधर्म्यात् itara-itara-vaidharmyât, from dissimilarity of one to another.

325. This is, says the opponent, not so because of the mutual difference in character of the colour, etc.

The opponent argues :—

If you say that knowledge is not a quality of the body because it differs in character from other well-known qualities of the same, I should say that the well-known qualities themselves differ from each other, *e. g.*, the colour is cognized by the eye but the touch is not. You cannot on this ground say that colour is a quality of the body but touch is not.

ऐन्द्रियकत्वाद्रूपादीनामप्रतिषेधः ॥ ३ । २ । ५५ ॥

ऐन्द्रियकत्वात् aindriyaka-tvât, from being sensible; रूपादीनाम् rûpa-âdînâm, of form, etc; अप्रतिषेधः a-pratiṣedhaḥ, non-contradiction.

326. There is, we reply, no objection to colour, etc. being qualities of the body because these are cognized by senses.

The colour, etc. may differ from touch, etc. in respect of certain aspect of their character but they all agree in one respect, *viz.*, that they are all cognisable by one or another of the external senses. But knowledge is not so cognized and cannot therefore be a quality of the body.

ज्ञानायौगपद्यादेकं मनः ॥ ३ । २ । ५६ ॥

ज्ञानायौगपद्यात् jñâna-ayaugapadyât, from non-simultaneity of cognitions; एकं ekam, one; मनः manaḥ, mind.

327. The mind is one on account of the non-simultneousness of cognitions.

If there were more minds than one, they could come in contact with many senses at a time so that many cognitions could be produced simultaneously. As many cognitions are never produced at once the mind must be admitted to be one.

न युगपदनेकक्रियोपलब्धेः ॥ ३ । २ । ५७ ॥

न na, no; युगपत् yugapat, simultaneously; अनेकक्रियोपलब्धेः an-eka-kriyâ-upalabdheḥ, from the pereeption of more than one action or change.

328. It is, says an opponent, not so because we do cognize many acts simultaneously.

The objection stands thus:–A certain teacher while walking on a road holds a waterpot in his hand. Hearing wild sounds he, out of fear, looks at the road, recites a sacred text and thinks of the nearest place of safety. The teacher is supposed in this instance to perform visual perception, auditory perception, recollection, etc., simultaneously. This would be impossible if there were only one mind.

अलातचक्रदर्शनवत्तदुपलब्धिराशुसञ्चारात् ॥ ३ । २ । ५८ ॥

अलातचक्रदर्शनवत् alâta-chakra-darśana-vat, like the observation of a circle of fire caused by a revolving firebrand; तदुपलब्धिः tat-upalabdhiḥ, their perception; आशुसंचारात् âśu-sañchârât, from rapid movement.

329. The appearance of simultaneousness is, we reply, due to the mind coming in contact with different senses in rapid succession like the appearance of a circle of firebrand.

Just as a firebrand while whirling quickly appears to form a continuous circle, so the mind moving from one sense to another in rapid succession appears to come in contact with them simultaneously. Hence the cognitions produced by the contact appear to the simultaneous though in reality they are successive.

यथोक्तहेतुत्वाच्चाणु: ॥ ३ । २ । ५९ ॥

यथोक्तहेतुत्वात् yathâ-ukta-hetu-tvât, from the reasons already stated; च cha, and; अणुः aṇuh, atomic.

330. And on account of the aforesaid reasons the mind is an atom.

If the mind were possessed of magnitude it could come in contact with many senses at a time so that many cognitions could take place simultaneously. Since this has been found to be impossible the mind is an atom.

पूर्वकृतफलानुबन्धात्तदुत्पत्तिः ॥ ३ । २ । ६० ॥

पूर्वकृतफलानुबन्धात् pûrva-kṛita-phala-anubandhât, following as the fruit of acts previously done; तदुत्पत्तिः tat-utpattiḥ, its production.

331. The body is produced as the fruit of our previous deeds (deserts).

Our present body has been made up of elements endowed with the fruits of merit and demerit of our previous lives.

भूतेभ्यो मूर्त्त्युपादानवत् तदुपादानम् ॥ ३ । २ । ६१ ॥

भूतेभ्यः bhûtebhyaḥ, from the elements; मूर्त्युपादानवत् mûrti-upâdâna-vat, like the formation of bodies; तदुपादानम् tat-upâdânam, its production.

332. The formation of our body of elements, says an opponent, resembles that of a statue of stone, etc.

The objection stands thus:—Just as a statue is formed of stone, clay, etc., which are devoid of deserts, our body has been made up of elements which are not endowed with the fruits of our previous merits and demerits.

न साध्यसमत्वात् ॥ ३ । २ । ६२ ॥

न na, no ; साध्यसमत्वात् sâdhya-sama-tvât, because this is the same as the thing to be established.

333. It is, we reply, not so because the statement requires proof.

To prove that our body is formed of elements which are devoid of deserts, the opponent cites the instance of a statue made up of clay or stone, which is supposed to bear no connection whatsoever with deserts. The Naiyâyika replies that the very example cited requires to be verified for clay, etc. are made of atoms which have actually a reference to deserts as they comport themselves in such a way as to work out the designs of Retributive Justice.

नोत्पत्तिनिमित्तत्वान्मातापित्रोः ॥ ३ । २ । ६३ ॥

न na, no ; उत्पत्तिनिमित्तत्वात् utpatti-nimitta-tvât, because of their being the conditions of production ; मातापित्रोः mâtâ-pitroḥ, of the blood and the seed.

334. Not so because father and mother are the cause of its production.

The formation of our body cannot be compared to that of a clay-statue because the body owes its origin to the sperm and blood of our father and mother while the statue is produced without any seed at all.

तथाहारस्य ॥ ३ । २ । ६४ ॥

तथा tathâ, so ; आहारस्य âhârasya, of the food.

335. So too eating is a cause.

The food and drink taken by the mother turns into blood which develops the embryo (made up of the sperm of the father) through the various stages of formation of the *arbuda* (a long round mass), *mâṃsa-peśî* (a piece of flesh), *kalala* (a round lump), *kaṇḍarā* (sinews), *śiraḥ* (head), *pāṇi* (hands), *pāda* (legs), etc. Eating is therefore a cause of production of our body but not of a clay-statue.

प्राप्तौ चानियमात् ॥ ३ । २ । ६५ ॥

प्राप्तौ prâptau, in the case of union ; च cha, and ; अनियमात् aniyamât, because there is no uniformity.

336. And there is desert because of uncertainty even in the case of union.

All unions between husband and wife are not followed by the production of a child (body). Hence we must acknowledge the desert of the child to be a co-operative cause of its birth.

शरीरोत्पत्तिनिमित्तवत् संयोगोत्पत्तिनिमित्तं कर्म्म ॥३।२।६६॥

शरीरोत्पत्तिनिमित्तवत् śarîra-utpatti-nimitta-vat, as it is the condition of the production of the body ; संयोगोत्पत्तिनिमित्तं saṃyoga-utpatti-nimittam, condition of the production of (generative) union ; कर्म karma, desert.

337. Desert is the cause not only of the production of the body but also of its conjunction with a soul.

Just as the earth, etc., independent of a person's desert, are unable to produce his body, so the body itself as a seat of particular pleasures and pains is unable to be connected with a soul without the intervention of the desert of the latter.

एतेनानियमः प्रत्युक्तः ॥ ३ । २ । ६७ ॥

एतेन etena, by this ; अनियमः a-niyamaḥ, absence of uniformity ; प्रत्युक्तः prati-uktaḥ, answered.

338. By this the charge against inequality is answered.

Some persons are found to possess a healthy body while others an unhealthy one ; a certain body is beautiful while another ugly. This inequality in the formation of the body is due to the desert acquired by the persons in their previous lives.

The aphorism may also be interpreted as follows :—

338. By this the charge against uncertainty is answered.

It is due entirely to the interference of the desert that the union between husband and wife is not always followed by the production of a child (body).

तददृष्टकारितमिति चेत् पुनस्तत्प्रसङ्गोऽपवर्गे ॥३।२।६८॥

तत् tat, that; **अदृष्टकारितम्** adṛiṣṭa kâritam, caused by adṛiṣṭa; **इतिचेत्** iti chet, should you say, **पुनः** punaḥ, again, **तत्प्रसंगः** tat-prasaṅgaḥ its implication; **अपवर्गे** apavarge, in the case of release.

339. If the the body was attached to a soul only to remove the inexperience of the latter, then the same inexperience would recur after the soul had been emancipated (released).

An opponent says that there is no necessity for admitting the desert and that the body which is made up of elements is connected with a soul only to enable the latter to experience objects and realize its distinction from matter (prakṛiti). As soon as the soul satisfies itself by the experience and attains emancipation (release) it is separated from the body for ever. The Naiyâyika asks: "Why is not the soul, even after emancipaion (release), again connected with a body to regain its experiential power?" Since the opponent does not admit desert there is nothing else to stop the connection.

मनःकर्म्मनिमित्तत्वाच्च संयोगानुच्छेदः ॥ ३।२।६९॥

मनःकर्मनिमित्तत्वात् manaḥ-karma-nimitta-tvât, from its being caused by the action of the mind; **च** cha, and; **संयोगानुच्छेदः** saṃyoga-an-uchchhedaḥ, non-termination of conjunction.

340 And there will be no cessation of the conjunction if it is caused by the desert of the mind.

Those who maintain that the desert is a quality of the mind cannot explain why there should at all be a separation of the body from the mind which is eternal If it is said that the very desert which connected the body with the mind does also separate it therefrom, we shall be constrained to admit an absurd conclusion that one and the same thing is the cause of life and death.

नित्यत्वप्रसङ्गश्च प्रायणानुपपत्तेः ॥ ३ । २ । ७० ॥

नित्यत्वप्रसंगः nitya-tva-prasaṅgaḥ, implication of eternality; **च** cha, and; **प्रायणानुपपत्तेः** prâyaṇa-an-upapatteḥ, from non-proof of departure.

341. Owing to there being no reason for destruction we should find the body to be eternal.

If the body is supposed to be produced from elements independent of deserts, we should not find anything the absence of which will caues its destruction. In the event of the destruction being arbitrary, there will be no fixed cause to effect emancipation or rebirth thereafter as the elements will always remain the same.

अणुश्यामतानित्यत्ववदेतत स्यात् ॥ ३ । २ । ७१ ॥

अणुश्यामतानित्यत्ववत् aṇu-śyâma-tâ-nitya-tva-vat, like the eternality of the darkness of the atom; एतत् etat, this; स्यात् syât, may be.

342. The disappearance of the body in emancipation (release) is, according to an opponent, eternal like the blackness of an atom.

The opponent says:—Just as the blackness of an atom suppressed by redness through contact with fire does not reappear, so the body which has once attained emancipation (release) will not reappear.

नाकृताभ्यागमप्रसङ्गात ॥ ३ । २ । ७२ ॥

न na, no; अकृताभ्यागमप्रसंगात् a-kṛita-abhyâgama-prasaṅgât, from implication of the acquisition of the unearned.

343. This is, we reply, not so because it would lead us to admit what was undemonstrable.

The argument employed in the previous aphorism is, according to the Naiyâyika, futile for it cannot be proved that the blackness of an atom is suppressed by redness through contact with fire, for it is possible that the blackness is altogether destroyed.

The aphorism may also be interpreted as follows;—

This is, we reply, not so, because it would lead us to acknowledge the consequence of actions not done by us.

Unless we acknowledge deserts there will be no principle governing he enjoyment of pleasure and suffering of pain. The absence of such a principle will be repugnant to all evidences—perception, inference and scripture.

BOOK IV.—CHAPTER I.

प्रवृत्तिर्यथोक्ता ॥ ४ । १ । १ ॥

प्रवृत्तिः pravṛittiḥ, activity ; यथोक्ता yathâ-uktâ, as explained.

344. Activity, as it is, has been explained.

The definition of activity is to be found in aphorism 1-1-17.

तथा दोषाः ॥ ४ । १ । २ ॥

तथा tathâ, similarly ; दोषाः doṣâḥ, faults.

345. So the faults.

The definition of faults has been given in aphorism 1-1-18. The faults which co-abide with intellect in the soul are caused by activity, produce rebirths and do not end until the attainment of final release (apavarga).

तत्त्रैराश्यं रागद्वेषमोहार्थान्तरभावात् ॥ ४ । १ । ३ ॥

तत्त्रैराश्यम् tat-trai-râśyam, their threefoldness ; रागद्वेषमोहार्थान्तरभावात् râga-dveṣa-moha-artha-antara-bhâvât, according to the differences of affection, aversion, and stupidity, or attraction, repulsion and confusion.

346. The faults are divisible in three groups, as all of them are included in affection, aversion and stupidity.

The faults are divided in three groups, *viz.*, affection, aversion and stupidity. Affection includes lust, avarice, avidity and covetousness. Aversion includes anger, envy, malignity, hatred and implacability. Stupidity includes misapprehension, suspicion, arrogance and carelessness.

नैकप्रत्यनीकभावात् ॥ ४ । १ । ४ ॥

न na, no ; एकप्रत्यनीकभावात् eka-prati-anîka-bhâvât, because they are only the opposites of the same thing, namely true knowledge.

347. It is, some say, not so, because they are the opposites of one single thing.

The objection stands thus :—There is no distinction between affection, aversion and stupidity, as all of them are destructible by one single thing, *viz.*, perfect knowledge. The three, in so far as they are destructible by one single thing, are of a uniform character.

व्यभिचारादहेतुः ॥ ४ । १ । ५ ॥

व्यभिचारात् vyabhichârât, on account of erring; **अहेतुः** a-hetuḥ, not a mark.

348. This reason, we reply, is not good, because it is erratic.

To prove that there is no distinction between affection, aversion and stupidity, the opponent has advanced the reason that all the three are destructible by one single thing. This reason is declared by the Naiyâyika to be erratic, because it does not apply to all cases, *e. g.*, the blue, black, green, yellow, brown and other colours, although they are different from one another, are destructible by one single thing, *viz.*, contact with fire.

तेषां मोहः पापीयान्नामूढस्येतरोत्पत्तेः ॥ ४ । १ । ६ ॥

तेषां teṣâm, among them; **मोहः** mohaḥ, stupidity, confusion; **पापीयान्** pâpîyân the worst; **न** na, not; **अमूढस्य** a-mûdhasya, of the non stupid; **इतरोत्पत्तेः** itara-utpatteḥ, because of the production of the other two.

349. Of the three, stupidity is the worst, because in the case of a person who is not stupid, the other two do not come into existence.

There are three faults, *viz.*, affection, aversion and stupidity, of which the last is the worst, because it is only a stupid person who may be influenced by affection and aversion.

निमित्तनैमित्तिकभावादर्थान्तरभावो दोषेभ्यः ॥४।१।७॥

निमित्तनैमित्तिकभावात् nimitta-naimittika-bhâvât, owing to the relation of cause and effect; **अर्थान्तरभावः** artha-antara bhâvaḥ, condition of being a different object; **दोषेभ्यः** doṣebhyaḥ, from faults.

350. There is then, says an opponent, a difference between stupidity and other faults owing to their interrelation of cause and effect.

The opponent argues as follows:—Since stupidity is the cause of the other two faults, it must be different from them. In fact there cannot be the relation of cause and effect between two things which are not different from each other.

न दोषलक्षणावरोधान्मोहस्य ॥ ४ । १ । ८ ॥

न na, no ; दोषलक्षणावरोधात् doṣa-lakṣaṇa-avarodhât, from inclusion by the definition of fault ; मोहस्य mohasya, of stupidity.

351. It is, we reply, not so, because faults as already defined include stupidity.

Stupidity is indeed a fault because it is homogeneous with or possesses the character of the same as defined in aphorism 1-1-18.

निमित्तनैमित्तिकोपपत्तेश्च तुल्यजातीयानामप्रतिषेधः ॥४।१।९॥

निमित्तनैमित्तिकोपपत्तेः nimitta-naimittika-uppapatteḥ, from the relation of cause and effect ; च cha, and ; तुल्यजातीयानां tulya-jâtîyânâm, of homogeneous things ; अप्रतिषेधः a-pratiṣedhaḥ, non-contradiction,

352. And there is, we reply, no prohibition for homogeneous things to stand in the relation of cause and effect.

It is not proper to exclude stupidity from the faults on the mere ground that they stand to each other in the relation of cause and effect. In fact the homogeneous things such as two substances or two qualities may stand to each other in the relation of cause and effect, *e. g.*, in the case of a jar being produced from its two halves we notice the relation of cause and effect between the jar and the halves which are homogeneous with each other.

आत्मनित्यत्वे प्रेत्यभावसिद्धिः ॥ ४ । १ । १० ॥

आत्मनित्यत्वे âtma-nitya-tve, the soul being eternal. प्रेत्यभावसिद्धिः pretya-bhâva-siddhiḥ, proof of re-birth, of existence after passing away.

353. Transmigration is possible if the soul is eternal.

Transmigration defined in 1-1-19 belongs to the soul and not to the body. The series of births and deaths included in it is possible only if the soul is eternal. If the soul were destructible, it would meet with two unexpected chances, *viz.*, destruction of actions done by it (kṛita-hâni) and suffering from actions not done by it (akṛitâbhyâgama).

व्यक्ताद्व्यक्तानां प्रत्यक्षप्रामाण्यात् ॥ ४ । १ । ११ ॥

व्यक्तात् vyaktât, from the manifested ; व्यक्तानाम् vyaktânâm, of the manifested; प्रत्यक्षप्रामाण्यात् pratyakṣa-prâmâṇyât, from the authority of perception.

354. There is evidence of perception as to the production of the distinct from the distinct.

It is found that jars, etc., which are distinct, are produced from earth, etc., which are also distinct. Similarly our body is produced from the elements.

न घटाद् घटानिष्पत्तेः ॥ ४ । १ । १२ ॥

न na, no; घटात् ghaṭât, from the pot; घटानिष्पत्तेः ghata-a-niṣpatteh from the non-production of the pot.

355. It is, some say, not so, because a jar is not produced from another jar.

The objection stands thus:—You cannot say that there is the production of a distinct thing from another distinct thing, *e. g.*, a jar is not produced from another jar.

व्यक्ताद्घटनिष्पत्तेरप्रतिषेधः ॥ ४ । १ । १३ ॥

व्यक्तात् vyaktât, from the manifested, i.e earth; घटनिष्पत्तेः ghaṭa-niṣpatteḥ, from the production of the pot; अप्रतिषेधः a-pratiṣedhaḥ, non-contradiction.

356. There is, we reply, no prohibition for a jar being produced from a distinct thing.

A jar may not be produced from another jar but it is certainly produced from another distinct thing, *viz.*, from its bowl-shaped halves. There is therefore no bar against the production of the distinct from the distinct.

अभावाद्भावोत्पत्तिर्नानुपमृद्य प्रादुर्भावात् ॥ ४ । १ । १४॥

अभावात् abhâvât, from non existence; भावोत्पत्तिः bhâva-utpattiḥ, production of existence; न na, no; अनुपमृद्य an-upamṛidya, without destroying; प्रादुर्भावात् prâdurbhâvât, as there is production.

357. Some say that entity arises from non-entity, as there is no manifestation unless there has been destruction.

A sprout cannot come into existence, unless the seed from which it comes has been destroyed. This shows that there is no manifestation of effect without the destruction of its cause.

व्याघातादप्रयोगः ॥ ४ । १ । १५ ॥

व्याघातात vyâghâtât, on account of obstruction, inconsistency; अप्रयोगः a-prayogaḥ, non-application of the argument.

358. It is, we reply, not so, because such an expression, inconsistent as it is, cannot be employed

To say that a thing comes into existence by destroying another thing which is its cause, is a contradiction in terms, for if that which, according to you, destroys the cause and takes the place thereof, was not existent prior to the destruction, then it cannot be said to be a destroyer, and if it existed prior to the cause, then it cannot be said to come into existence on the destruction thereof.

नातीतानागतयोः कारकशब्दप्रयोगात् ॥ ४ । १ । १६ ॥

न na, not : अतीतानागतयोः atîta anâgatayoḥ, to the past and the future; कारकशब्दप्रयोगात् kâraka-śabda-prayogât, from application of the word doer.

359. There is, says the objector, no inconsistency, because terms expressive of action are figuratively applied to the past and future.

The objecter says as follows :—There is no impropriety in the statement that a thing comes into existence by destroying another thing which is its cause, for terms expressive of action are figuratively employed to denote that which is not existent now but which existed in the past or will exist in the future, *e. g.*, he congratulates himself on the son that is to be born. In the sentence "a sprout comes into existence by destroying its cause" —the term expressive of destruction is figuratively applied to the sprout that will come into existence in the future.

न विनष्टेभ्योऽनिष्पत्तेः ॥ ४ । १ । १७ ॥

न na, no ; विनष्टेभ्यः vinaṣṭebhyaḥ, from what has been destroyed ; अनिष्पत्तेः a-niṣpatteḥ, as there is no production.

360. It is, we reply, not so because nothing is produced from things destroyed.

A sprout does not spring from a seed already destroyed. Hence we can lay down the general rule that entity does not arise from non-entity.

क्रमनिर्देशादप्रतिषेधः ॥ ४ । १ । १८ ॥

क्रमनिर्द्देशात् krama-nirdeśât, from the declaration of order or procession ; अप्रतिषेधः a-pratiṣedhaḥ, non-contradiction.

361. There is no objection if destruction is pointed out only as a step in the processes of manifestation.

In connection with earth, water, heat, etc., a seed undergoes destruction of its old structure and is endowed with a new structure. A sprout cannot grow from a seed, unless the old structure of seed is destroyed and a new structure is formed. It is in this sense allowable to say that manifestation is preceded by destruction. This does not preclude a seed from being the cause of a sprout But we do not admit an unqualified assertion that production springs from destruction or entity arises from non-entity.

ईश्वरः कारणं पुरुषकर्म्माफल्यदर्शनात् ॥ ४ । १ । १९ ॥

ईश्वरः îśvaraḥ, the lord ; कारणं kâraṇam, cause ; पुरुषकर्म्माफल्यदर्शनात् puruṣa-karma-â-phalya-darśanât, from seeing the failure of the acts of man.

362. God, says some one, is the sole cause of fruits, because man's acts are found occasionally to be unattended by them.

Seeing that man does not often attain success proportionate to his exertions, some one infers that tnese are entirely subservient to God who alone can provide them with fruits.

न पुरुषकर्म्माभावे फलानिष्पत्तेः ॥४।१।२०॥

न na, no ; पुरुषकर्म्माभावे puruṣa-karma-abhâve, in the absence of the act of man ; फलानिष्पत्तेः phala-a-niṣpatteḥ, because of non-production of fruit.

363. This is, some are afraid, not so, because in the absence of man's acts there is no production of fruits.

The fear referred to arises thus :—If God were the only source of fruits, man could attain them even without any exertions.

तत्कारितत्वादहेतुः ॥ ४ ।१ । २१ ॥

तत्कारितत्वात् tat-kârita-tvât, from their being caused to arise by him ; अहेतुः a-hetuḥ, not a cause.

364. Since fruits are awarded by God, man's acts, we conclude, are not the sole cause thereof.

Man performs acts which are endowed with fruits by God. The acts become fruitless without His grace. Hence it is not true that man's acts produce fruits by themselves

God is a soul specially endowed with qualities. He is freed from misapprehension, carelessness, etc., and is enriched with merit, knowledge and concentration. He possesses eight supernatural powers (such as the power of becoming as small as an atom) which are the consequence of His merit and concentration. His merit, which conforms to His will, produces merit and demerit in each person and sets the earth and other elements in action. God is, as it were, the father of all beings. Who can demonstrate the existence of Him who transcends the evidences of perception, inference and scripture ?

अनिमित्ततो भावोत्पत्तिः कण्टकतैक्ष्ण्यादिदर्शनात ॥४।१।२२॥

अनिमित्ततः a-nimitta-taḥ, from no cause ; भावोत्पत्तिः bhâva-utpattiḥ, production of existence or entity ; कण्टकतैक्ष्ण्यादिदर्शनात् kaṇṭakataikṣṇya-âdi-darśanât, from the observation of the sharpness of a thorn, and the like.

365. From an observation of the sharpness of thorn, etc., some say that entities are produced from no cause.

The objectors argue as follows:—Thorns are by nature sharp, hills beautiful, and stones smooth. None has made them so. Similarly our bodies, etc., are fortuitous effects which did not spring from a cause, that is, were not made by God.

अनिमित्तनिमित्तत्वान्नानिमित्ततः ॥ ४ । १ । २३ ॥

अनिमित्तनिमित्तत्वात् a-nimitta-nimitta-tvât, being caused by no-cause ; न na, not ; अनिमित्ततः a-nimitta-taḥ, from no cause.

366. Entities cannot be said to be produced from no-cause, because the no-cause is, according to some, the cause of the production.

An opponent has said that entities are produced from no-cause. Some critics point out that the use of the fifth case-affix in connection with no-cause indicates that it is the cause.

निमित्तानिमित्तयोरर्थान्तरभावादप्रतिषेधः ॥ ४ । १ । २४ ॥

निमित्तानिमित्तयोः nimitta a-nimittayoḥ, between cause and no cause; अर्थान्तरभावात् artha-antara-bhâvât, there being the relation of two different objects; अप्रतिषेधः a-pratiṣedhaḥ, non-contradiction.

367. The aforesaid reason presents no opposition, because cause and no-cause are two entirely different things.

Cause and no-cause cannot be identical, *e. g*, a jar which is waterless cannot at the same time be full of water. The doctrine involved in this aphorism does not differ from the one explained in 3-2-66 [according to which our body cannot be made up independent of our desert (Karma).

सर्व्वमनित्यमुत्पत्तिविनाशधर्म्मकत्वात् ॥ ४ । १ । २५ ॥

सर्वं sarvam, all; अनित्यं a nityam, non eternal; उत्पत्तिविनाशधर्म्मकत्वात् utpatti-vinâśa-dharmaka tvât, because of their possessing the character of production and destruction.

368. All, says some one, are non-eternal, because they possess the character of being produced and destroyed.

All things including our body which is material and our intellect which is immaterial are non-eternal inasmuch as they are subject to the law of production and destruction. All things which are produced and destroyed are non-eternal.

नानित्यतानित्यत्वात् ॥ ४ । १ । २६ ॥

न na, no; अनित्यतानित्यत्वात् a-nitya-tâ-nitya-tvât, non-eternalness being eternal.

369. These are, we reply, not so, because of the non-eternalness being eternal.

If non-eternalness pervades all things you must admit it to be eternal Hence, all are not non- eternal, for there is at least one thing, *viz.*, non-eternalness, which is eternal.

तदनित्यत्वमग्नेर्दाह्यं विनाश्यानुविनाशवत् ॥४।१।२७॥

तदनित्यत्वम् tat-a-nitya-tvam, non-eternalness of that (*i.e.* non-eternalness); अग्नेः agneḥ, in the case of fire; दाह्यं dâhyam, combustible, fuel; विनाश्यानुविनाशवत् vinâśya-anu-vinâśa-vat, like the destruction following after the destructible.

370. Some hold non-eternalness to be not eternal on the analogy of a fire which dies out after the combustibles have perished.

The objection is explained as follows:—Just as a fire dies out as soon as the things which caught it have perished, so the non-eternalness disappears as soon all non-eternal things have passed away. Hence, non-eternalness is not eternal.

नित्यस्याप्रत्याख्यानं यथोपलब्धि व्यवस्थानात् ॥४।१।२८॥

नित्यस्य nityasya, of the eternal ; अप्रत्याख्यानं a-pratyâkhyânam, non-denial ; यथोपलब्धि yathâ-upalabdhi, according to perception or knowledge; व्यवस्थानात् vyavasthânât, from regulation.

371. There is no denial of the eternal, as there is a regulation as to the character of our perception.

Whatever is perceived to be produced or destroyed is non-eternal and that which is not so is eternal, *e. g*, there is no perceptual evidence as to the production or destruction of ether, time, space, soul, mind, generality, particularity and intimate relation. Consequently these are eternal.

सर्व्वं नित्यम्पञ्चभूतनित्यत्वात् ॥ ४ । १ । २९ ॥

सर्वं sarvam, all ; नित्यं nityam, eternal ; पञ्चभूतनित्यत्वात् pañcha-bhûta-nitya-tvât, owing to the eternalness of the five elements.

372. Some say that all are eternal, because the five elements are so.

The elements which are the material causes of all things are eternal, consequently the things themselves are eternal.

नोत्पत्तिविनाशकारणोपलब्धेः ॥ ४ । १ । ३० ॥

न na, no; उत्पत्तिविनाशकारणोपलब्धेः utpatti-vinâśa-kârana-uplabdheḥ, owing to perception of the causes of production.

373. These are, we reply, not so, because we perceive the causes of production and destruction.

All things are non-eternal because we find them to be produced and destroyed. Whatever is produced or destroyed is non-eternal.

तल्लक्षणावरोधादप्रतिषेधः ॥ ४ । १ । ३१ ॥

तल्लक्षणावरोधात् tat-lakṣaṇa-avarodhât, from inclusion by its definition ; अप्रतिषेधः a-pratiṣedhaḥ, non-contradiction.

374. This is, some say, no refutation, because the character of the elements is possessed by the things which are produced or destroyed.

The objector says as follows:—A thing which is made up of an element, possesses the character of the element. Since the element is eternal, the thing also must be so.

नोत्पत्तितत्कारणोपलब्धेः ॥ ४ । १ । ३२ ॥

न na, no ; उत्पत्तितत्कारणोपलब्धेः utpatti-tat-kâraṇa-upalabdheḥ, owing to perception of production and its cause.

375. This is, we reply, no opposition because we perceive production and the cause thereof.

An effect inherits the character of its cause but the two are not identical, *e g.*, ether is the cause of sound, although the former is eternal and the latter non-eternal.

Moreover we actually perceive that things are produced which convince us of their non-eternalness If production is regarded as a mere vision of a dream, then the whole world is no better than an illusion which can serve no practical purpose.

If all things were eternal there could be no effort or activity on our part to attain any object. Hence all are not eternal.

न व्यवस्थानुपपत्तेः ॥ ४ । १ । ३३ ॥

न na, no; व्यवस्थानुपपत्तेः vyavasthâ-an-upapatteḥ, from the impossibility of uniformity.

376. If all things were eternal there would be no regulation of time.

Some say that things are eternal, because they existed even before they were produced and will continue even after they are destroyed. But this view, contends the Naiyâyika, is absurd. It destroys all regulation with regard to time, for if all things were perpetually existent, there could not be any use of such expressions as "was produced" and "will be destroyed" which presuppose a thing which was non-existent to come into existence or one which is existent to lose its existence.

सर्व्वं पृथग्भावलक्षणपृथक्त्वात् ॥ ४ । १ । ३४ ॥

सर्वं sarvam, all ; पृथक् prithak, diverse ; भावलक्षणपृथक्त्वात् bhâva-lakṣaṇa-prithak-tvât, owing to diversity of the marks of existence.

377. Some say that all are aggregates because each consists of several marks.

A jar, for instance, is an aggregate consisting of several parts, such as bottom, sides, back, etc., and several qualities, such as, sound, smell, taste, colour, touch, etc. There is not a single entity devoid of its several parts or qualities.

[This refers to the Buddhist doctrine which denies a substance apart from its qualities and a whole apart from its parts as is evident from the writings of Nâgârjuna*, Ârya Deva† and others.]

नानेकलक्षणैरेकभावनिष्पत्तेः ॥ ४ । १ । ३५ ॥

न na, no ; अनेकलक्षणैः an-eka-lakṣaṇaiḥ, by several marks ; एकभावनिष्पत्तेः eka-bhâva-niṣpatteḥ, because of constitution of one entity.

378. These are, we reply, not so because by several marks one single entity is constituted.

The Naiyâyika says that there is certainly a substance apart from its qualities and a whole apart from its parts, *e. g.*, we must admit an entity called a jar as the substratum of its several qualities, such as colour, smell, etc , and its several parts such as bottom, sides, back, etc.

[The Buddhists‡ oppose this view by saying that the substance

---

* लक्ष्याल्लक्षणमन्यच्चेत् स्यात्तल्लक्ष्यमलक्षणम् ।
तयोरभावोऽनन्यत्वे विस्पष्टं कथितं त्वया ॥

(Mâdhyamika Sûtra. Chap. I. page 64 ; Prof. Poussin's edition.)

रूपादिव्यतिरेकेण यथा कुम्भो न विद्यते ।
वाय्वादिव्यतिरेकेण तथा रूपो न विद्यते ॥ इति ॥

(Mâdhyamika Sûtra, Chap. I, page 71 ; Poussin's edition.)

† सर्व एव घटोऽदृष्टो रूपे दृष्टे हि जायते ।
ब्रूयात् कस्तत्त्वविन्नाम घटः प्रत्यक्ष इत्यपि ॥
एतेनैव विचारेण सुगन्धि मधुरं मृदु ।
प्रतिषेधयितव्यानि सर्वाण्युत्तमबुद्धिना ॥

(Śataka quoted in the Mâdhyamika Vritti, p. 71.)

‡ इह तु काठिन्यादिव्यतिरिक्तपृथिव्याद्यसम्भवे सति न युक्तो विशेषणविशेष्यभावः । तीर्थिकैर्व्यतिरिक्तलक्ष्याभ्युपगमात्तदनुरोधेन विशेषणाभिधानमदुष्टमितिचेत् । नैतदेवं नहि तीर्थिकपरिकल्पिता युक्तिविधुराः पदार्थाः स्वसमयेऽभ्युपगन्तुं न्याय्याः । प्रमाणान्तरादेरप्यभ्युपगमप्रसङ्गात् ।

(Mâdhyamikâ Vritti. Chap. I. p. 66 ; Poussin's edition.)

independent of its qualities and the whole independent of its parts admitted by the Naiyâyikas are opposed to reason and cannot be accepted as realities though there is no harm in acknowledging them as "appearances"* for the fulfilment of our practical purposes.]

लक्षणव्यवस्थानादेवाप्रतिषेधः ॥ ४ । १ । ३६ ॥

लक्षणव्यवस्थानात् lakṣaṇa-vyavasthânât, from the distribution of marks; एव eva, surely ; अप्रतिषेधः a-pratiṣedhaḥ, non-contradiction.

379. There is, moreover, no opposition on account of the very distribution of the marks.

The Naiyâyika says as follows:—Our conclusion is unassailable owing to the marks abiding in one single entity. A jar, for instance, possesses two marks, *viz.*, tangibility and colour, by each of which it can be identified.

If there were no jar beyond its tangibility and colour we could not use such expression as "I see the jar which I touched yesterday." To enable us to ascertain the identity there must be a substance called jar beyond its tangibility and colour which are two distinct qualities belonging to the same substance.

The opponent has said that "all are aggregates." Whence, we ask, does the aggregate arise if there are no units? The very reason given that "each consists of several marks" presupposes an "each" or unity or entity beyond the marks or aggregate.

सर्वमभावो भावेष्वितरेतराभावसिद्धेः ॥ ४ । १ । ३७ ॥

सर्वं sarvam, all ; अभावः a-bhâvaḥ, non-existence ; भावेषु bhâveṣu, in entities ; इतरेतराभावसिद्धेः itara-itara-abhâva-siddheḥ, from proof of mutual non-existence.

380. All are non-entities because the entities are non-existent in relation to one another,

In the expression "a horse is not a cow" there is the non-existence of "cow" in the "horse" and in the expression "a cow is not a horse" there is the non-existence of "horse" in the "cow." As a fact every thing is non-existent in so far as it is not identical with another thing.

* घटः प्रत्यक्ष इत्यत्र तु नहि घटो नाम कश्चिद्योऽप्रत्यक्षः पृथगुपलब्धो यस्योपचारात्प्रत्यक्षत्वं स्यात् । नीलादिव्यतिरिक्तस्य घटस्याभावादौपचारिकं प्रत्यक्षत्वमिति चेत् । एवमपि सुतरामुपचारो न युक्त उपचर्यमाणस्याश्रयस्याभावात् । नहि खरविषाणे तैक्ष्ण्यमुपचर्यते ।

(Mâdhyamikâ Vṛitti. p. 70, Chap. I ; Poussin's edition.)

न स्वभावसिद्धेर्भावानाम् ॥ ४ । १ । ३८ ॥

न na, no ; स्वभावसिद्धेः sva-bhâva-siddheḥ, from existence by own nature ; भावानाम् bhâvânâm, of entities.

381. It is, we reply, not so because the entities are existent in reference to themselves.

A cow is a cow though it is not a horse : a thing is existent in reference to itself though it is non-existent in so far as it is not another thing.

न स्वभावसिद्धिरापेक्षिकत्वात् ॥ ४ । १ । ३९ ॥

न, no ; स्वभावसिद्धिः sva bhâva siddhiḥ, proof of own nature ; आपेक्षिकत्वात् âpekṣika-tvât, being relative.

382. Some say that entities are not self-existent inasmuch as they exist in relation to one another.

The objection is explained as follows :—

A thing is called short only in relation to another thing which is long, and *vice versa* ; the long and short are inter-related.

[This refers to the Mâdhyamika Buddhist doctrine* of "relation" according to which all things are inter-dependent and nothing is self-existent,]

व्याहतत्वादयुक्तम् ॥ ४ । १ । ४० ॥

व्याहतत्वात् vyâhata-tvât, being inconsistent ; अयुक्तम् a-yuktam, not rational.

383. The doctrine, we reply, is unreasonable because it hurts itself.

If the long and short are inter-dependent then neither of them can be established in the absence of the other ; if neither of them is self-existent, then it will be impossible to establish the inter-relation ; and in the absence of all relations the doctrine of the opponent will fall to the ground.

---

* न सम्भवः स्वभावस्य युक्तः प्रत्ययहेतुभिः ।
स्वभावः कृतको नाम भविष्यति पुनः कथम् ॥
(Mâdhyamika Sûtra, Chap. XV, p. 93 ; B. T. Society's edition.)

[The Mâdhyamikas say that there is no reality* underlying any entity, and that the entities exist only by virtue of their mutual relations which are mere illusions. Viewed from the standpoint of absolute truth the world is void, Śûnya,† but measured by the standard of "relation" or "condition" it possesses an apparent existence which serves all our practical purposes.]

सङ्ख्यैकान्तासिद्धिः कारणानुपपत्त्युपपत्तिभ्याम् ॥४।१।४१॥

सङ्ख्यैकान्तासिद्धिः saṅkhyâ-eka-anta-a-siddhiḥ, non-proof of the fixity of number; कारणानुपपत्त्युपपत्तिभ्याम् kâraṇa-an-upapatti-upapattibhyâm, by proof and disproof of cause.

384. Neither through the reason being given nor through the reason being omitted there is the establishment of the fixity of number.

Some say that there is only *one* thing (Brahma) pervading all the so-called varieties. Others say that things are of *two* kinds, *viz.*, the eternal and the non-eternal. Certain philosophers find *three* things, *viz.*, the knower, knowledge and the knowable, while others treat of *four* things, *viz.*, the agent of knowledge, means of knowledge, object of knowledge and act of knowledge. In this way the philosophers indulge themselves in a fixed number of things. The Naiyâyikas oppose them by saying that there is no reason to establish the fixity of number. The fixed number is the *Sâdhya* or that which is to be proved and the reason is that which is to prove it. Now, is the reason included in the *Sâdhya* or excluded from it? In either case the fixity of number will be unfixed. If, on the other hand, the reason is not different from the *Sâdhya*, there is no means to establish the *Sâdhya*.

न कारणावयवभावात् ॥ ४ । १ । ४२ ॥

न na, no; कारणावयवभावात् kâraṇa-avayava-bhâvât, the cause being a member or part.

---

* शून्यविद्यं नहि विद्यते क्वचित् अन्तरिक्षि शकुनस्य वा पदम् ।
यश्च विद्यति स्वभावतः क्वचित् सा न जातु परहेतु भविष्यति ॥

(Ârya Ratnâkara Sûtra quoted in Mâdhyamika Vṛitti, Chap. I. 24; B. T. Society's edition.)

† स्वभावं परभावञ्च भावञ्चाभावमेव च ।
ये पश्यन्ति न पश्यन्ते तत्त्वं हि बुद्धशासने ॥

(Mâdhyamika Sûtra, Chap. XV, p. 96; B. T. Society's edition.)

385. This is, some say, not so, because the reason is a part of the number.

The objection is this:—

The number of things is fixed, and there is no disturbance of the fixity on the score of the reason being included in, excluded from, or identical with, the number, for the reason is a part of the number and as such is not different from it.

निरवयवत्वादहेतुः ॥ ४ । १ । ४३ ॥

निरवयवत्वात् nir-avayava-tvât, being without a member or part ; **अहेतुः** a-hetuḥ, no reason.

386. The reason, we reply, is not valid because there is no part available for the purpose.

The opponent has argued that the number is fixed and that the reason is only a part of it. The Naiyâyika counterargues that the number cannot be fixed until the reason is fixed and it will be absurd to fix the number with an unfixed reason. The reason which is asserted by the opponent to be a part of the number will remain unfixed until the number itself is fixed.

The doctrine of the fixity of number, opposed as it is to the evidences of perception, inference and scripture, is a false doctrine which cannot refute the variety of things established through the speciality of their characters. If there is an agreement as to the number of things on the ground of their general characters, and difference on the ground of their special characters, then the doctrine of fixity is admittedly to be abandoned.

सद्यः कालान्तरे च फलनिष्पत्तेः संशयः ॥ ४ । १ । ४४ ॥

सद्यः sadyaḥ, immediately ; **कालान्तरे** kâla-antare, at another time ; **च** cha, and ; **फलनिष्पत्तेः** phala-nispatteḥ, on account of production of fruit ; **संशयः** saṃśayaḥ, doubt.

387. There arises doubt as to the fruit which is produced either instantly or after a long interval.

Seeing that some action such as *cooking* produces its effect immediately while another action such as *ploughing* does not bring about any effect until sometime has passed away, a certain person asks whether the fruit of maintaining the sacred fire will be produced immediately or after a considerable lapse of time.

कालान्तरेणानिष्पत्तिर्हेतुविनाशात् ॥ ४ । १ । ४५ ॥

कालान्तरेण kâla-antareṇa, after a lapse of time ; अनिष्पत्तिः a niṣpattiḥ, non-production ; हेतुविनाशात् hetu-vinâśât, because of the destruction of the cause.

388. It cannot, says some one, be produced after a lapse of time because the cause has disappeared.

The objection is this:—

The fruit (*viz.*, the attainment of heaven) cannot be produced after our death because the action (*viz.*, maintaining the sacred fire) calculated to produce the fruit was destroyed before our death.

प्राङ्निष्पत्तेर्वृक्षफलवत्तत् स्यात् ॥ ४ । १ । ४६ ॥

प्राक् prâk, prior ; निष्पत्तेः niṣpatteḥ, to production ; वृक्षफलवत् vṛikṣa-phala-vat, like the fruit of a tree ; तत् tat, that स्यात् syât, will be.

389. This fruit, we reply, before it is produced, bears analogy to the fruit of a tree.

Just as a tree, whose roots are now nourished with water, will be able to produce fruits in the future, so the sacred fire which is maintained now will enable the maintainer to attain heaven after death. The doctrine involved here has been explained in aphorism 3-2- 60.

नासन्न सन्न सदसदसत्सतोर्वैधर्म्यात् ॥ ४ । १ । ४७ ॥

न na, no ; असत् a-sat, non-existent ; न na, not ; सत् sat, existent ; न na, not ; सदसत् sat-a-sat, existent-and-non-existent ; असत्सतोः asat-satoḥ, of the non-existent and existent ; वैधर्म्यात् vaidharmyât, owing to dissimilarity, difference.

390. Some say that the fruit, anterior to its production, is neither existent nor non-existent nor both, because existence and non-existence are incongruous.

The fruit (or any effect) anterior to its production was not non-existent because the material causes are so regulated that each one thing is not produced from each other thing promiscuously. We cannot suppose the fruit to have been existent prior to its production because a thing cannot be said to come into existence if it had already an existence. The fruit was not both existent and non-existent prior to its production because existence and non-existence are incompatible with each other.

[The aphorism refers to the Mâdhyamika Buddhist philosophy which maintains that the effect, before it is produced, is neither existent nor non-existent nor both, as is evident from the writings of Nâgârjuna* and Ârya Deva†.]

उत्पादव्ययदर्शनात् ॥ ४ । १ । ४८ ॥

उत्पादव्ययदर्शनात् utpâda-vyaya-darśanât, from the observation of production and destruction.

391. It is, we reply, a fact that the fruit before it was produced was non-existent because we witness the production and destruction.

When a jar is produced we find that it was non-existent prior to the production.

बुद्धिसिद्धन्तु तदसत् ॥ ४ । १ । ४९ ॥

बुद्धिसिद्धं buddhi-siddham, established by the understanding ; तु tu, but ; तत् tat, that ; असत् a-sat, non-existent.

392. That it was non-existent, is established by our understanding.

It is only when a thing is non-existent that we can apply ourselves to the production of it by means of suitable materials. A weaver, for instance, sets himself to work for a web which is non-existent but which he knows he can make by means of threads.

आश्रयव्यतिरेकाद्वृक्षफलोत्पत्तिवदित्यहेतुः ॥४।१।५०॥

---

* सतश्च तावदुत्पत्तिरसतश्च न युज्यते ।
न सतश्चासतश्चेति पूर्वमेवोपपादितम् ॥
नैवासतो नैव सतः प्रत्ययार्थस्य युज्यते ।
न सन्नासन्न सदसत् धर्म्मो निर्वर्त्तते सदा ॥

(Nâgârjuna's Mâdhyamika Sûtra, Chap. VII, p. 51 ; B. T. Society's edition.)

† सदसत्सदसच्चेति यस्य पक्षो न विद्यते ।
उपालम्भश्चिरेणापि तस्य वक्तुं न शक्यते ॥

(Ârya Deva's Śataka quoted in the Mâdhyamika Vṛitti, Chap. I p. 4 ; B. T. Society's edition.)

आश्रयव्यतिरेकात âśraya-vyatirekât, in the absence of a receptacle; वृक्षफलोत्पत्तिवत् vriksa phala-utpatti-vat, like the production of the fruit of a tree; इति iti, this; अहेतुः a-hetuḥ, no reason.

393. Some say that the analogy to the fruit of a tree is ill-founded because a receptacle is awanting.

It has been stated that the fruit obtainable from maintaining the sacred fire bears analogy to the fruit of a tree. An opponent finds fault with the analogy by showing that the tree which produces fruits now is the same tree which was previously nourished with water, but the body which is alleged to attain heaven after death is not the same body which maintained the sacred fire. The two bodies being different their analogy to the tree is ill-founded.

प्रीतेरात्माश्रयत्वादप्रतिषेधः ॥ ४ । १ । ५१ ॥

प्रीतेः prîteḥ, of pleasure, satisfaction; आत्माश्रयत्वाद् âtmâ âśraya-tvât, having the soul as its receptacle or support; अप्रतिषेधः a-pratiṣedhaḥ, non-contradiction.

394. The foregoing objection, we reply, is unreasonable because the soul is the receptacle of happiness.

It is not our body that maintains the sacred fire or attains heaven. In reality the soul is the receptacle for both these acts. The soul which maintained the secred fire is identical with the soul which enjoys happiness in heaven. Consequently a receptacle is not awanting and the analogy to the tree is not ill-founded.

न पुत्रपशुस्त्रीपरिच्छदहिरण्यान्नादिफलनिर्देशात ॥४।१।५२॥

न na, no; पुत्रपशुस्त्रीपरिच्छदहिरण्यान्नादिफलनिर्देशात putra-paśu-strî-parichchhada-hiraṇya-anna âdi-phala-nirdeśât, because the fruits declared are son, cattle, wife, clothes, gold, food etc.

395. The soul, some say, cannot be the receptacle for the fruits which are mentioned, *viz.*, a son, a wife, cattle, attendants, gold, food, etc.

The objection is this:—

If the fruit consists merely of happiness it can be lodged in the soul. But the soul cannot be the receptacle for such fruits as a son, a wife, cattle, etc. which are mentioned in the scripture.

तत्सम्बन्धात् फलनिष्पत्तेस्तेषु फलवदुपचारः ॥४।१।५३॥

तत्सम्बन्धात् tat-sambandhât, through connection with them ; फलनिष्पत्तेः phala-niṣpatteḥ, because of production of fruit ; तेषु teṣu, in them ; फलवदुपचारः phala-vat-upachârah, predication as fruit.

396. The fruit, we reply, is attributed to them because it is produced through their conjunction.

In reality the fruit is happiness. We attribute the name fruit to a son, wife, etc., because happiness is produced through them.

विविधबाधनायोगाद्दुःखमेव जन्मोत्पत्तिः ॥४।१।५४॥

विविधबाधनायोगात् vividha-bâdhanâ-yogât, through connection with various distresses दुःखं duḥkham, pain ; एव eva, surely ; जन्मोत्पत्तिः janma-utpattiḥ, production of birth.

397. Birth is a pain because it is connected with various distresses.

Birth is stated to be a pain because it signifies our connection with the body, the senses and the intellect which bring us various distresses. The body is the abode in which pain resides, the senses are the instruments by which pain is experienced, and the intellect is the agent which produces in us the feeling of pain. Our birth as connected with the body, the senses and the intellect is necessarily a source of pain.

न सुखस्यान्तरालनिष्पत्तेः ॥ ४ । १ । ५५ ॥

न na, not ; सुखस्य sukhasya, of pleasure ; अन्तरालनिष्पत्तेः antarâlaniṣpatteḥ, because of production during intervals.

398. Pleasure is not denied because it is produced at intervals.

We cannot altogether deny the existence of pleasure which often arises amidst pains.

बाधनाऽनिवृत्तेर्वेदयतः पर्य्येषणदोषादप्रतिषेधः ॥४।१।५६॥

बाधनाऽनिवृत्तेः bâdhanâ-a-nivṛtteḥ, there being non-cessation of distress ; वेदयतः vedayataḥ, of the feeling person; पर्य्येषणदोषात् paryeṣaṇa-doṣât, from the fault of pursuit ; अप्रतिषेधः a-pratiṣedhaḥ, non-contradiction.

399. This is, we reply, no opposition because distresses do not disappear from a person who enjoys one pleasure and seeks another.

The substance of the Naiyâyika's reply is this:— Pleasure itself is to be regarded as pain because even a person who enjoys pleasure is tormented by various distresses. His objects may be completely frustrated or fulfilled only partially, and while he attains one object he cannot resist the temptation of pursuing another which causes him uneasiness.

दुःखविकल्पे सुखाभिमानाच्च ॥ ४ । १ । ५७ ॥

दुःखविकल्पे duḥkha-vikalpe, in a form of pain; सुखाभिमानात् sukha-abhimânât, from a conceit of pleasure; च cha, and.

400. And because there is conceit of pleasure in what is only another name for pain.

Some persons thinking that pleasure is the *summum bonum* are addicted to the world which causes them various distresses through birth, infirmity, disease, death, connection with the undesirable, separation from the desirable, etc. It is therefore clear that one who pursues pleasure does in reality pursue pain, or, in other words, pleasure is a synonym for pain.

ऋणक्लेशप्रवृत्त्यनुबन्धादपवर्गाभावः ॥ ४ । १ । ५८ ॥

ऋणक्लेशप्रवृत्त्यनुबन्धात् ṛina-kleśa-pravṛitti-anubandhât, because debts, troubles and activity pursue us to the end; अपवर्गाभावः apavarga-abhâvaḥ, absence of release.

401. There is, some say, no opportunity for us to attain release because of the continual association of our debts, troubles and activities.

The objection stands thus:— The scripture declares that as soon as we are born we incur three debts which we must go on clearing off until the time of our decay and death; and troubles are our constant companions, while activities pursue us throughout our life. There is then no opportunity for us to attain release.

The three debts are:—

Debt to sages (Ṛishi-ṛiṇa)—which can be cleared off only by undergoing a course of student life.

Debt to gods (Deva-ṛiṇa)—from which we can be freed only by performing sacrifices.

Debt to our progenitors (Pitṛi-ṛiṇa)—which cannot be cleared off except by begetting children.

Activity has been defined in 1-1-17 and 1-1-18.

प्रधानशब्दानुपपत्तेर्गुणशब्देनानुवादो निन्दाप्रशंसोपपत्तेः ॥

॥ ४ । १ । ५९॥

प्रधानशब्दानुपपत्तेः pradhâna-śabda-an-upapatteḥ, from failure of the word in the principal sense ; गुणशब्देन guṇa śabdena, by the word in the secondary sense ; अनुवादः anuvâdaḥ, interpretation ; निन्दाप्रशंसोपपत्तेः nindâ-praśaṃsâ-upapatteḥ, because of the establishment of blame and praise.

402. If an expression is inadmissible in its literal sense we are to accept it in its secondary meaning to suit blame or praise.

"As soon as a person is born he incurs three debts"—this expression, inadmissible as it is in its literal sense, is to be taken in its secondary meaning, *viz.*, "as soon as a person enters the life of a householder, he incurs three debts the clearing off of which brings him credit." The expression "until the time of our decay and death" signifies that "as long as we do not arrive at the fourth stage when we are to adopt the life of a mendicant." If the scriptural texts are interpreted in this way, it becomes clear that our whole life does not pass away in the mere clearing off of our debts.

समारोपणादात्मन्यप्रतिषेधः ॥ ४ । १ । ॥ ६० ॥

समारोपणात् samâropaṇat, through transferring ; आत्मनि âtmani, to the soul ; अप्रतिषेधः a-pratiṣedhaḥ, non-contradiction.

403. There is no lack of opportunity for our release because the sacrifices (to be performed for clearing off our debts) are trusted to the soul.

A Brahman, while old, should refrain from all searches after sons, wealth and retinue. Śruti (Veda) instructs him to retire from the world when he has trusted to his soul the sacrifices which he used to perform to clear off his debts. By so doing he will imagine that his soul is the sacrificial fire in which his physical actions are offered as oblations. Freed from all debts, he will live on alms and find an ample opportunity for effecting his own release.

As regards the division of life into stages, there is the authority of Itihâsa, Purâṇa and Dharma Śâstra.

पात्रचयान्तानुपपत्तेश्च फलाभावः ॥ ४ । १ । ६१ ॥

पात्रचयान्तानुपपत्तेः pâtra-chaya-anta-an-upapatteḥ, because of the non-proof of performances ending with the collection of the sacrificial vessels at death; च cha, and; फलाभावः phala-abhâvaḥ, absence of fruit.

404. Because the performances ending with the collection of the sacrificial vessels at death cannot reasonably be supposed (to have been prescribed for all without distinction), there would be an absence of fruits (which could impede release)

For a householder keeping alive the sacrificial fire it is prescribed that at his death the sacrificial vessels should be collected and burnt with his body. Such a man continues to perform acts till the end and these acts must produce results which must be exhausted by experiencing them before release can be attained But these acts are not meant for those who retire from the world and have no desire for sons, wealth or other worlds. Therefore, so far as such men are concerned, the Vedic injunctions in respect of the sacrificial vessels and the like do not cause any obstacle to the attainment of release.

सुषुप्तस्य स्वप्नादर्शने क्लेशाभाववदपवर्गः ॥ ४ । १ । ६२ ॥

सुषुप्तस्य suṣuptasya, of one in deep sleep; स्वप्नादर्शने svapna-a-darśane, in not seeing dreams; क्लेशाभाववत् kleśa-a-bhâva-vât, like absence of troubles; अपवर्गः apavargaḥ, release.

405. As there is no distress in a person who is sound asleep and sees no dream, so there is no association of troubles in one who attains release.

A person who has, through the knowledge of Brahma, attained release, is freed from all bonds of lust, pleasure, pain, etc.

[The word *kleśa* (here rendered as trouble) is a technical term very extensively used in the Buddhist Sanskrit and Pâli literature to signify depravity, defilement, corruption or passion. *Kleśa*, called in Pali *kileso*, is the cause of all sinful actions and consequently of rebirths. Arhatship consists in the annihilation of *kleśa*. The Pâli Piṭakas enumerate ten *kilesas*, of which five are prominent. The ten *kilesas* are:—

लोभो (greed), दोसो (hatred), मोहो (stupidity), मानो (pride), दिट्ठि (heretical view), विचिकिच्छा (doubt), थीनम् (sloth), उद्धच्चम् (arrogance), अहिरिका (shamelessness) and अनोत्तप्पम् (recklessness).

The Buddhist Sanskrit books enumerate six *kleśas* and twenty-four *upakleśas*.

षट्क्लेशाः ॥

रागः प्रतिघो मानोऽविद्या कुदृष्टिर्विचिकित्सा चेति ॥

(Dharmasaṁgraha LXVII.,

चतुर्विंशतिरूपक्लेशाः । तद्यथा ॥

क्रोध उपनाहो म्रक्षः प्रदाश ईर्ष्या मात्सर्यं शाठ्यं माया मदो विहिंसाह्रीरनपत्रपा स्त्यानमश्राद्ध्य कौसीद्य प्रमादो मुषितस्मृतिर्विक्षेपोऽसंप्रजन्यं कौकृत्यं मिद्धं वितर्को विचारश्चेति ॥

(Dharmasaṁgraha LXIX.)

The word *kleśa* used in the Nyâya Sûtra 4-1-58, 4-1-62, 4-1-63 and 4-1-64 evidently conveys the meaning of moral depravity. *Hîna-kleśa* (हीनक्लेश) used in 4-1-63 rings in my ears as a phrase borrowed from the Buddhist philosophy.]

न प्रवृत्तिः प्रतिसन्धानाय हीनक्लेशस्य ॥ ४ । १ । ६३ ॥

न na, no ; प्रवृत्तिः pravṛittiḥ, activity ; प्रतिसन्धानाय prati sandhânâya, for binding again to birth ; हीनक्लेशस्य hîna-kleśa-sya, of one whose troubles have disappeared.

406. The activity of one who has got rid of the troubles does not tend to obstruction.

Activity does not present any obstacle to release (apavarga) in respect of a person who is freed from the troubles of lust, hatred and stupidity. In his case activity produces neither merit nor demerit, and consequently no re-birth.

न क्लेशसन्ततेः स्वाभाविकत्वात् ॥ ४ । १ । ६४ ॥

न na, no ; क्लेशसन्ततेः kleśa-santateḥ, of the stream of troubles; स्वाभाविकत्वात् svâbhâvika-tvât, being natural.

407. There is, some say, no end of troubles because these are natural.

The objection raised here is this:—None can attain release because it is impossible to get rid of troubles which are natural (beginningless).

प्रागुत्पत्तेरभावानित्यत्ववत्स्वाभाविकेऽप्यनित्यत्वम् ॥४।१।६५॥

प्राक् prâk, prior ; उत्पत्तेः utpatteḥ, to production; अभावानित्यत्ववत् abhâva-a-nitya-tva vat, like the non-eternality of non-existence ; स्वाभाविके svâbhâvike, in the natural ; अपि api, also ; अनित्यत्वम् a-nitya-tvam, non-eternality.

408. Even the natural, says some one, are non-eternal like the non-existence that was antecedent to production.

The objection raised in the previous aphorism is answered by some one as follows:—

A non-existence antecedent to production is natural (beginningless) but it disappears as soon as the production takes place. Similarly the troubles are natural (beginningless) but they terminate as soon as release is attained.

A jar before it is produced is non-existent. This non-existence is called antecedent non-existance. It has no beginning but it has an end for it disappears as soon as the jar is produced. The troubles like the antecedent non-existence are beginningless but not endless.

[It is only an existence, that is, an existent thing, that can be called eternal or non-eternal. We cannot apply the epithets " eternal " and " non-eternal " to non-existence except in a figurative sense.]

अणुश्यामताऽनित्यत्ववद्वा ॥ ४ । १ । ६६ ॥

अणुश्यामताऽनित्यत्ववत् aṇu-śyâma-tâ-a-nitya-tva-vat, like the non-eternality of the darkness of the atom ; वा vâ, or.

409. Or non-eternal like the blackness of an atom.

An earthy atom, which is naturally black, changes its colour when it is baked red in the kiln. Likewise the troubles which are natural disappear as soon as release is attained.

न सङ्कल्पनिमित्तत्वाच्च रागादीनाम् ॥ ४ । १ । ६७ ॥

न na, no ; संकल्पनिमित्तत्वात sankalpa-nimitta-tvât, being caused by will or deliberation ; च cha, and ; रागादीनां râga-âdînâm, of desire, etc.

410. It is, we reply, not so because affection, etc. are caused by misapprehension.

The Naiyâyika says:—There is no necessity for us here to admit that a thing which is natural (beginningless) may not be endless. The troubles are not in fact natural (beginningless) because they are caused by activity which springs from our affection, aversion and stupidity. These last are generated by our misapprehension. The troubles not being natural, there is no lack of opportunity for us to attain release.

Book IV.—Chapter II.

दोषनिमित्तानां तत्त्वज्ञानादहङ्कारनिवृत्तिः ॥ ४ । २ । १ ॥

दोषनिमित्तानां doṣa-nimittânâm, of the causes of faults ; तत्त्वज्ञानात् tattva-jñânât, through knowledge of the truth ; अहंकारनिवृत्तिः ahaṅkâra-nivṛittiḥ, cessation of ahamkâra.

411. Through knowledge about the true nature of the causes of faults, there is cessation of egotism.

Egotism is stupidity of the form "I am." It consists of the notion, "I am," entertained by a person in respect of what is not self. It disappears as soon as we attain knowledge about the true nature of the faults which are caused by all objects such as body, etc. enumerated in aphorism 1—1—9

दोषनिमित्तं रूपादयो विषयाः सङ्कल्पकृताः ॥ ४ । २ । २ ॥

दोषनिमित्तं doṣa-nimittam, the cause of faults ; रूपादयः rûpa-âdayaḥ, form, etc ; विषयाः viṣayâḥ, objects ; संकल्पकृताः saṅkalpa-kṛitâḥ, adopted by the will.

412. The colour and other objects, when regarded as good, become the causes of faults.

It is only when we look upon colour or any other object as a source of enjoyment that it becomes a cause of our affection, aversion or stupidity.

तन्निमित्तन्त्ववयव्यभिमानः ॥ ४ । २ । ३ ॥

तन्निमित्तं tat-nimittam, their cause ; तु tu, but ; अवयव्यभिमानः avayavi-abhimânaḥ, regard as a whole.

413. The faults are caused through a conception of the *whole* apart from its *parts*.

The faults are produced if a man or woman looks upon each other as a *whole, viz.*, as a male or female with all his or her paraphernalia of teeth, lips, eyes, nose, etc., together with their secondary marks ; and they are shunned if he or she looks upon each other by *parts* only, *viz.*, upon his or her hair, flesh, blood, bone, nerve, head, phlegm, bile, excrement, etc., all of which are frail. The notion of the *whole* engenders lust while that of the *parts* produces equanimity, We must regard every thing from the standpoint of evil, *e. g.*, the rice boiled with poison is looked upon by a wordly man as rice and by an ascetic as poison.

विद्याऽविद्याद्वैविध्यात् संशयः ॥ ४ । २ । ४ ॥

विद्याऽविद्याद्वैविध्यात् vidyâ-a-vidyâ dvaividhyât, from twofoldness of knowledge and of ignorance ; संशयः samśayaḥ, doubt.

414. Owing to the apprehension and non-apprehension being each of two kinds, there arises a doubt as to the existence of a whole apart from its parts.

There are two kinds of apprehension, *viz*, real and unreal. The apprehension of water in a tank is real while that of mirage as a mass of water is unreal. The non-apprehension is also of two kinds, *viz.*, real and unreal. The non-apprehension of a hare's horn (which is non-existent) is a real non-apprehension while that of the ether (which is existent) is an unreal non-apprehension. The apprehension and non-apprehension being both real and unreal there arises a doubt as to whether there is really a whole apart from its parts. If we apprehend a whole apart from its parts, our apprehension may be unreal. If we do not apprehend a whole, our non-apprehension too may be unreal.

तदसंशयः पूर्वहेतुप्रसिद्धत्वात् ॥ ४ । २ । ५ ॥

तदसंशयः tat-a-samśayaḥ, no doubt about it; पूर्वहेतुप्रसिद्धत्वात् pûrva-hetu-prasiddha-tvât, having been established by reasons already stated.

415. There is no room for doubt with regard to the existence of a whole already established through arguments.

No one has yet set aside the arguments employed in aphorism 2—1—34 to establish a whole apart from its parts.

वृत्त्यनुपपत्तेरपि तर्हि न संशयः ॥ ४ । २ । ६ ॥

वृत्त्यनुपपत्तेः vritti-an-upapatteḥ, from absence of proof of inclusion ; अपि api, also ; तर्हि tarhi, then ; न na, not ; संशयः samśayaḥ doubt.

416. There is, says some one, no room for doubt even with regard to the non-existence of a whole on account of the impossibility of the whole residing anywhere.

In the preceding aphorism the Naiyâyika has said that there is no doubt as to the existence of a whole apart from its parts as demonstrated in aphorism 2—1—34. In the present aphorism his opponent says that there is no doubt as to the non-existence of a whole apart from its parts because neither the whole can reside in its parts nor the latter in the former. One affirms that there is a whole while the other affirms that there is a no-whole. In either case there is no room for doubt.

कृत्स्नैकदेशावृत्तित्वादवयवानामवयव्यभावः ॥ ४ । २ । ७ ॥

कृत्स्नैकदेशावृत्तित्वात् kritsna-eka-deśa-a-vritti-tvât, because of not being co-extensive with the whole; अवयवानाम् avayavânâm, of the parts; अवयव्यभावः avayavi-abhâvaḥ, non-existence of the whole.

417. There is, says the objector, no whole because its parts reside in it neither totally nor partially.

A part does not occupy the whole in its totality owing to the difference of their dimension; neither does it occupy the whole partially because the part can reside neither in itself nor in another part.

तेषु चावृत्तेरवयव्यभावः ॥ ४ । २ । ८ ॥

तेषु teṣu, in them; च cha, and; अवृत्तेः a-vritteḥ, because of non-residence; अवयव्यभावः avayavi-abhâvaḥ, non-existence of the whole.

418. Also because the whole does not, continues the objector, reside in its parts.

The whole does not reside in each of its parts separately on account of the difference of their dimension. Neither does it reside in some of its parts collectively because in that case it loses its connection with the other parts.

पृथक् चावयवेभ्योऽवृत्तेः ॥ ४ । २ । ९ ॥

पृथक् prithak, other; च cha, and; अवयवेभ्यः avayavebhyaḥ, than the parts; अवृत्तेः a-vritteḥ, because of non-residence.

419. Owing to the lack of residence, affirms the objector, there is no whole apart from its parts.

The *whole* does not exist as the relation between it and its parts is not that of the container and the contained.

न चावयव्यवयवाः ॥ ४ । २ । १० ॥

न na, not; च cha, and; अवयवी avayavî, the whole; अवयवाः avayavâḥ, parts

420. And the parts are not the whole.

The objector says that the relation between the whole and its parts is not that of identity. No one says that the thread is the web or the pillar is the house.

एकस्मिन् भेदाभावाद्भेदशब्दप्रयोगानुपपत्तेरप्रश्नः ४।२।११॥

एकस्मिन् ekasmin, in one ; भेदाभावात् bheda-abhâvât, owing to absence of difference ; भेदशब्दप्रयोगानुपपत्तेः bheda-śabda-prayoga-an-upapatteḥ, because of impropriety of use of the word difference ; अप्रश्नः a-praśnaḥ, no question.

421. There is, we reply, no room for the question owing to the impropriety in the use of the term "variety" in reference to what is *one*.

In aphorism 4—2—7 an opponent raised the question as to whether the whole occupied its parts totally or partially. The Naiyâyika disposes of the question by saying that there is no room for it because the terms "totally" and "partially" cannot be applied to "*one.*" The term "totally" is employed only in the case of several things of which no one has been left out while the word "partially" refers to an aggregate of which some parts have been left out. Now, neither the term "totally" nor the term "partially" is applicable to what is "one", that is, to a "whole." In the case of a whole the employment of language implying variety is unjustifiable.

अवयवान्तराभावेप्यवृत्तेरहेतुः ॥ ४ । २ । १२ ॥

अवयवान्तराभावे avayava-antara-abhâve, in the absence of another part; अपि api, also ; अवृत्तेः a-vṛitteḥ, owing to non-residence or non-function ; अहेतुः a-hetuḥ, no mark or reason or argument.

422. The question, we further reply, is unreasonable because even if one part could be the residence of another part, it would not be the residence of the *whole*.

When we speak of a whole residing in its parts we must not understand that the term residence refers to any space, in fact it refers to the relation of refuge and refugee. A refuge is that with which the refugee is inseparably connected and without which it can never exist. Hence there is no impossibility of the whole residing in its parts.

केशसमूहे तैमिरिकोपलब्धिवत्तदुपलब्धिः ॥ ४ । २ । १३ ॥

केशसमूहे keśa-samûhe, in respect of a collection of hairs; तैमिरिकोपलब्धिवत् taimirika-upalabdhi-vat, like the perception of one affected with a dimness of sight; तदुपलब्धिः tat -upalabdhiḥ, its perception.

423. The perception of a "whole" bears analogy to that of a collection of hairs by a person affected with a dimness of sight.

Just as a person of dim sight cannot perceive hairs separately but can perceive them in a mass, so we cannot perceive the atoms separately but can perceive them in a mass in the form of a jar or the like.

स्वविषयानतिक्रमेणेन्द्रियस्य पटुमन्दभावाद्विषयग्रहणस्य तथा भावो नाविषये प्रवृत्तिः ॥ ४ । २ । १४ ॥

स्वविषयानतिक्रमेण sva-viṣaya-an-atikrameṇa, by reason of its not going beyond its own object ; इन्द्रियस्य indriyasya, of the sense ; पटुमन्दभावात् paṭu-manda-bhâvât, according to keenness and dullness ; विषयग्रहणस्य viṣaya-grahaṇa-sya, of the apprehension of object ; तथा tathâ, like ; भावः bhávaḥ, condition ; न na, no ; अविषये a-viṣaye, to what is not its object ; प्रवृत्तिः pravṛittiḥ, operation.

424. A sense is inoperative in reference to what is not its object because its acuteness or dullness of apprehension is restricted to its own object which it connot transcend..

The eye, whether it is acute or dim, cannot apprehend a sound. Similarly the ear, sharp or dull, cannot see a colour. All senses have their special objects to which their operation is restricted. An atom which is supersensuous, cannot be apprehended by any of our senses—no matter whether these aro acute or dim. Each hair being perceptible, its collection also is capable of being perceived whereas the atoms being imperceptible their collection cannot be perceived. As we can perceive the collection of atoms in the shape of a jar or the like, we must admit that the collection or the whole is a reality independent of its parts (the atoms).

अवयवावयविप्रसङ्गश्चैवमाप्रलयात् ॥ ४ । २ । १५ ॥

अवयवावयविप्रसंगः avayava avayavi-prasaṅgaḥ, relation of whole and parts ; च cha, and ; एवं evam, then ; आ â, up ; प्रलयात् pralayât, to pralaya, dissolution.

425. The whole and its parts should in that case be supposed to continue up to the time of annihilation.

Even if we admit the existence of a whole and its parts, we cannot suppose them to continue for ever because they are subject to destruction at the time of annihilation. A whole has got its parts and the parts again have their parts which do not cease until they become non-existent at the time of annihilation.

न प्रलयोऽणुसद्भावात् ॥ ४ । २ । १६ ॥

न na, no ; प्रलयः pralayaḥ, dissolution ; अणुसद्भावात् Aṇu-sad-bhâvât, owing to the existence of the atom.

426. There is, we reply, no annihilation because there are atoms.

There will never come a time when there will be an utter annihilation, for things will even then continue to exist in the state of atoms. An atom is a thing of the smallest dimension, that is, a thing which is not capable of being of smaller dimension.

परं वा त्रुटेः ॥ ४ । २ । १७ ॥

परं param, beyond ; वा vâ, or ; त्रुटेः truṭeḥ, of truṭi, a minute part.

427. An atom is that which is not capable of being divided.

An atom is not divisible into further parts.

[Two atoms make a *dvyaṇuka* (dyad) and three *dvyaṇukas* make a *tryasareṇu* (triad). All things which we perceive are composed of *tryasareṇus*. An atom (aṇu) is finer than a *dvyaṇuka* and the latter finer then a *tryasareṇu*]

आकाशव्यतिभेदात तदनुपपत्तिः ॥ ४ । २ । १८ ॥

आकाशव्यतिभेदात ákáśa-vyatibhedât, owing to interpenetration of ether ; तदनुपपत्तिः tat-an-upapattiḥ, its non-proof.

428. There is, says some one, an impossibility of such a thing, as it is divided throughout by ether.

The Naiyayika defines the atom as a whole which has no parts, that is, a thing which is not divisible into further parts. Some one controverts the definition by saying that an atom is not devoid of parts because it is intersected by ether *within* and *without*.

आकाशासर्वगतत्वं वा ॥ ४ । २ । १९ ॥

आकाशासर्वगतत्वं akáśa-a-sarva-gata-tvam, non-omnipenetration of ether ; वा vâ, or.

429. Else there would not be the omnipresence of the ether.

The ether would not be called omnipresent if it could not reside within the atoms

अन्तर्बहिश्च कार्य्यद्रव्यस्य कारणान्तरवचनादकार्य्ये तदभावः ॥ ४ । २ । २० ॥

अन्तः antaḥ, in ; बहिः bahiḥ, out ; च cha, and ; कार्य्यद्रव्यस्य kârya-dravya-sya, of the effect substance; कारणान्तरवचनात kâraṇa-antara-vachanât, owing to declaration of another cause ; अकार्य्ये a-karye, in a non-effect ; तदभावः tat-a-bhâvaḥ, its absense.

430. There is no " within" "without " of an eternal thing. The terms are applicable only to factitious things inasmuch as they imply constituents other than those which are seen.

The word " within " refers to that constituent of a thing which is enclosed by another constituet thereof while the word " without " refers to the constituent which encloses another constituennt, but is not enclosed by it. These terms cannot be applied to eternal things such as atoms which do not possess constituents some of which may enclose the rest.

शब्दसंयोगविभवाच्च सर्व्वगतम् ॥ ४ । २ । २१ ॥

शब्दसंयोगविभवात śabda-saṃyoga-bibhavât, owing to universality of conjunction of sound ; च cha, and ; सर्वगतं sarva-gatam, all-penetrating.

431. The ether is omnipresent because of the universality of its conjunction which is a cause of sound.

Owing to sound being produced everywhere it is inferred that the ether is omnipresent. If a certain place were devoid of contact with ether there would be no sound there. There is in fact a conjunction of ether everywhere.

अव्यूहाविष्टम्भविभुत्वानि चाकाशधर्माः ॥ ४ । २ । २२ ॥

अव्यूहाविष्टम्भविभुत्वानि a-vyûha-viṣṭambha-vibhu-tvâni, characteristics of not being massed, not offering obstruction, and being universal ; च cha, and ; आकाशधर्माः âkâśa-dharmâḥ, the attributes or properties of ether.

432. The ether possesses three properties, *viz.*, that it is not repelled, that it does not obstruct and that it is all-pervading.

The ether is not repelled because it does not possess any form, it does not obstruct because it is intangible, and it is all-pervading because it is omnipresent.

मूर्त्तिमताञ्च संस्थानोपपत्तेरवयवसद्भावः ॥ ४ । २ । २३ ॥

मूर्त्तिमतां mûrti-matâm, of things possessing a form ; च cha, and ; संस्थानोपपत्तेः samsthâna-upapatteḥ from proof of position, shape ; अवयवसद्भावः avayava-sad-bhâvaḥ, existence of parts.

433. There are, says some one, parts in an atom because a thing that is endowed with a form must also possess a collocation of parts.

The objection stands thus:—

An atom is divisible into parts because it possesses a form, that is, it is of a limited dimension.

[The ether, soul, space and time being of unlimited dimensions are not divisible into parts.]

संयोगोपपत्तेश्च ॥ ४ । २ । २४ ॥

संयोगोपपत्तेः saṃyoga-upapatteḥ, from proof of conjunction ; च cha, and.

434. An atom, continues the objector, must possess parts because it is capable of being conjoined with another atom.

The objection is this:—

The fact that atoms possess the quality of conjunction proves that they have parts, because an atom can come in conjunction with another only in some of its parts.

अनवस्थाकारित्वादनवस्थानुपपत्तेश्चाप्रतिषेधः ॥ ४ । २ । २५ ॥

अनवस्थाकारित्वात् an-avasthâ-kâri-tvât, as causing instability, regression; अनवस्थानुपपत्तेः an-avasthâ-an- upapatteḥ, because of unreasonableness of regression ; च cha, and ; अप्रतिषेधः a-pratiṣedhaḥ, non-contradiction.

435. The doctrine of the indivisibility of atom cannot, we reply, be refuted because such a refutation would give rise to a *regressus ad infinitum* which is not proper.

If you say that an atom is divisible into parts, you will have to admit that those parts again are divisible into futher parts. This would give rise to a *regressus ad infinitum* which should, if possible, be avoided. If all things were indefinitely divisible we should find a large thing and a small one to be of equal dimension as both would possess an infinite number of parts. A thing although indefinitely divided should not lose itself. There must remain a particle, *viz.*, an atom which should not perish even at the time of annihilation.

बुद्ध्या विवेचनात्तु भावानां याथात्म्यानुपलब्धिस्तन्त्वपकर्षणे पटसद्भावानुपलब्धिवत तदनुपलब्धिः ॥ ४ । २ । २६ ॥

बुद्ध्या buddhyâ, by the understanding ; विवेचनात vivechanât, from separation ; तु tu, but ; याथात्म्यानुपलब्धिः yâthâtmya-an upalabdhiḥ, non-perception of reality ; तन्त्वपकर्षणे tantu-apakarṣaṇe, on the separation of the threads ; पटसद्भावानुपलब्धिवत paṭa-sadbhâva-an-upalabdhi-vat, like the non-perception of the existence of fabric ; तदनुपलब्धिः tat-an-upalabdiḥ, its non-perception ;

436. Things, some say, do not possess a reality if they are separated from our thoughts, just as there is no reality in a web separated from its threads.

The objection is this:—

Things do not possess a reality independent of our thoughts just as a web does not possess a reality independent of its threads. Hence it is our thoughts alone that are real, external things are all unreal. [This aphorism refers to the doctrine of the Yogâchâra Buddhist philosophy explained in the Laṅkâvatâra Sûtra.] *

व्यहतत्वादहेतुः ॥ ४ । २ । २७ ॥

व्याहतत्वात् vyâhata-tvât, being obstructed ; अहेतुः a-hetuḥ, not a mark.

437. The reason, we reply, is not good as it hurts itself.

---

* बुद्ध्या विविच्यमानानां स्वभावो नावधार्य्यते ।
यस्मात् तस्माद् अनभिलाप्यास्ते निःस्वभावाश्च देशिताः ।

(लंकावतार सूत्र, २ परिवर्त्त, पृष्ठ ५०)

बुद्ध्या विविच्यमानानां स्वभावो नावधार्य्यते ।
यस्मादनभिलाप्यास्ते निःस्वभावाश्च देशिताः ॥
लंकावतार सूत्र १० परिवर्त्त, पृ० ११५ ॥

The Naiyâyika says that his opponent's reason, *viz.*, that things do not possess a reality if they are separated from our thoughts, is self-destructive because if things are capable of being separated from our thoughts they cannot be said to be unreal, and on the other hand if things are unreal they are incapable of being separated from our thoughts. The opponent commits a contradiction by saying that things are unreal and at the same time by going to separate them from our thoughts.

तदाश्रयत्वादपृथग्ग्रहणम् ॥ ४ । २ । २८ ॥

तदाश्रयत्वात् tat-áśraya-tvât, because an effect is dependent on the cause. अपृथक्ग्रहणम् a-pṛithak-grahaṇam, non-apprehension as separate.

438. There is, we reply, no separate perception of a refuge and its refugee.

A web being the refuge of its threads, the perception of the former includes that of the latter so that there are no separate perceptions of them. If our thoughts were the refuge of external things, then there would be no separate perceptions of them. But the opponent's argument, *viz.*, that "if things are separated from our thoughts," makes it manifest that our thoughts are not the refuge of external things.

प्रमाणतश्चाऽर्थप्रतिपत्तेः॥ ४ । २ । २९ ॥

प्रमाणतः pramáṇa-taḥ, by means of proof ; च cha, and ; अर्थप्रतिपत्तेः artha-pratipatteḥ, because of establishment of object.

439 And things are established by evidences.

The reality of things is proved by evidences such as perception. Every thing requires an evidence for its establishment. The very assertion that "things are not real if they cannot be separated from our thoughts" must be based on an evidence if it is to commend itself to our acceptance. Hence we cannot deny things if they are establised by evidences.

प्रमाणानुपपत्त्युपपत्तिभ्याम् ॥ ४ । २ । ३० ॥

प्रमाणानुपपत्त्युपपत्तिभ्याम् pramáṇa-an-upapatti-upapatti-bhyâm, by reason of application and non-application of proofs.

440. The non-reality of things is demonstrated neither by evidence nor without them.

The proposition that "there is nothing" cannot be proved in any way. If you say that there is an evidence to prove it, you hurt your own proposition, *viz.*, that, there is nothing. If again you say that there is no evidence, how do you then establish your porposition ?

स्वप्नविषयाभिमानवदयं प्रमाणप्रमेयाभिमानः ॥ ४।२।३१ ॥

स्वप्नविषयाभिमानवत् svapna-viṣaya-abhimâna-vat, like the idea of objects seen in a dream ; अयं ayaṃ, this ; प्रमाणप्रमेयाभिमानः pramâṇa-prameya-abhimânaḥ, idea of proof and the object of proof.

441. The concept of the means and the objects of knowledge, says some one, bears analogy to that of things appearing in a dream.

The means and the objects of knowledge are as delusive as things appearing in a dream.

[The aphorism 4-2-31 and 4-2-32 evidently refer to the Buddhist doctrine of "non-reality" expounded in the Ârya Upâli-pṛicchâ-Samâdhi râja-sûtra, Ârya-gagana-gañja-sûtra, Mâdhyamika-sûtra, Ârya-ratnâvalî, Lalitavistara-sûtra and other Mahâyâna works.*]

मायागन्धर्व्वनगरमृगतृष्णिकावद्वा ॥ ४ । २ । ३२ ॥

मायागन्धर्वनगरमृगतृष्णिकावत् mâyâ-gandharva-nagara-mṛiga-trisṇikâ-vat, like illusion, the city of the celestial musicians, and mirage ; वा vâ, or.

442. It may, continues the objector, be likened to jugglery, the city of the celestial quiristers or a mirage.

The means and the objects of knowledge are as unreal as things exhibited in jugglery, etc.

हेत्वभावादसिद्धिः ॥ ४ । २ । ३३ ॥

हेत्वभावात् hetu-a-bhâvât, owing to non-existence of cause ; असिद्धिः a-siddhiḥ non-proof.

---

* यथा माया यथा स्वप्नो गन्धर्वनगरं यथा ।
तथोत्पादस्तथा स्थानं तथा भङ्ग उदाहृतम् ॥ Mâdhyamika-Sûtra, Chap. VII.
यथैव गन्धवपुरं मरीचिका यथैव माया सुपिनं यथैव ।
स्वभावशून्या तु निमित्तभावना तथोपमान् जानत सर्वधर्म्मान् ॥
(Quoted in Mâdhyamikâ Vṛitti, p. 57).
माया मरीचि समो हि विकल्पः । (Ârya-Upâlipṛiccha, quoted in M. V. 63)
मायोपमा गगनविद्युत्समोदकचन्द्रसन्निभमरीचिसमाः । (Ârya-Samâdhirâja-Bhaṭṭâraka quoted in Mâdhamikâ Vṛitti, Chap. XXI.)

443. This cannot, we reply, be proved, as there is no reason for it.

There is no reason that the concept of the means and the objects of knowledge should bear an analogy to the concept of things appearing in a dream but not to that of things appearing in our wakeful state. If you, to prove the unrealty of things in a dream, adduce the reason that these are not perceived in our wakeful state, we would, to prove the reality of the means and the objects of knowledge, adduce the reason that these are perceived in our wakeful state.

स्मृतिसङ्कल्पवच्च स्वप्नविषयाभिमानः ॥ ४ । २ । ३४ ॥

स्मृतिसङ्कल्पवत् smṛiti-saṅkalpa-vat, like memory and imagination; च cha, and ; स्वप्नविषयाभिमानः svapna-viṣaya-abhimânaḥ, idea of object seen in a dream.

444. The concept of things in a dream arises in the same way as remembrance and imagination.

The things that appear in a dream are not unreal. We can conceive of them in a dream just as we can do in our wakeful state. Our concept of things in the dream is due to our memory and imagination.

It is by a reference to the knowledge in our wakeful condition, that we ascertain our knowlenge in the dream to be unreal. But in the event of there being only one condition, *viz.*, that of wakefulness, the analogy to the dream would not be appropriate.

मिथ्योपलब्धिविनाशस्तत्त्वज्ञानात् स्वप्नविषयाभिमानप्रणाशवत् प्रतिबोधे ॥ ४ । २ । ३५ ॥

मिथ्योपलब्धिविनाशः mithyâ-upalabdhi-vinâśaḥ, destruction of false perception or cognition ; तत्त्वज्ञानात् tattva-jñânât, from knowlege of reality ; स्वप्नविषयाभिमानप्रणाशवत् svapna-viṣaya-abhimâna-praṇâśa-vat, like the destruction of the idea of things seen in a dream ; प्रतिबोधे prati-bodhe, on awakening.

445. Our false apprehension is destroyed by a knowledge of the truth, just as our concept of objects in a dream comes to an end on our awaking.

In the case of jugglery, the city of the celestial quiristers and the mirage, our apprehension, if it is false, consists of our imputing "that" to what is "not that" just as when we mistake a post for a man. The objects of the apprehension are, however, not unreal, inasmuch as they arise from our memory and imagination.

Jugglery (mâyâ) consists of a false apprehension produced in others by an artifice through the use of materials similar to those originally announced by him.

Just as our concept of objects in a dream passes away as soon as we are awake, so also our false apprehension of objects disappears as soon as we attain a true knowledge of those objects.

बुद्धेश्चैवं निमित्तसद्भावोपलम्भात् ॥ ४ । २ । ३६ ॥

बुद्धेः buddheḥ, of the understanding, of (false) knowledge; च cha, also; एवं evam, likewise ; निमित्तसद्भावोपलम्भात् nimitta-sadbhâva-upalambhât, from perception or cognition of the cause and its existence.

446. There is therefore no denial of false knowledge, inasmuch as we perceive that there is a cause for that knowledge.

It has already been shown that our *concept* of objects in a dream is unreal, inasmuch as we do not actually perceive them at that time, but that the *objects* of the dream are not unreal, inasmuch as they arise from our memory and imagination. In fact, the objects that give rise to false knowledge are never unreal, although the knowledge itself may be false.

तत्त्वप्रधानभेदाच्च मिथ्याबुद्धेर्द्वैविध्योपपत्तिः ॥४।२।३७॥

तत्त्वप्रधानभेदात् tattva-pradhâna -bhedât, owing to the distinction of the reality and the primary idea or appearance; मिथ्याबुद्धेः mithyâ-buddheḥ, of false knowledge ; द्वैविध्योपपत्तिः dvai-vidhya-upapattiḥ, proof of twofoldness.

447. And false knowledge involves a two-fold character on account of the distinction between the essence and appearance of its object.

When we mistake a post for a man, our knowledge assumes the form "that is man." Our knowledge of the post, in so far as it is called "that", is a true knowledge, but in so far as it is described as "man", is a false knowledge. This falsity of knowledge is due to our recognition of certain properties common to the post and the man.

समाधिविशेषाभ्यासात् ॥ ४ । २ । ३८ ॥

समाधिविशेषाभ्यासात् samâdhi -viśeṣa-abhyâsât, from the practice of a particular contemplation.

448. The knowledge of truth is rendered habitual by a special practice of meditation.

Meditation is the soul's union with the mind abstracted from the senses whose contact with objects does not produce any perception. The knowledge of the truth is rendered habitual by the repeated practice of this maditation.

नार्थविशेषप्राबल्यात् ॥ ४ । २ । ३९ ॥

न na, no ; अर्थविशेषप्राबल्यात् artha-viśeṣa-prâbalyât, owing to predominance of certain objects.

449. Meditation, some say, is not practicable by reason of the predominance of certain external objects.

There are innumerable obstacles to meditation, *e. g.*, hearing the thundering noise of a cloud, one is prevented from practising meditation.

क्षुदादिभिः प्रवर्त्तनाच्च ॥ ४ । २ । ४० ॥

क्षुधादिभिः kṣut-âdi-bhiḥ, by hunger, etc. ; प्रवर्त्तनात् pravarttanât, from incitement ; च cha, and.

450. And by reason of our being impelled to action by hunger, etc.

Hunger and thirst, heat and cold, disease, etc. sometimes prevent us from practising meditation.

पूर्वकृतफलानुबन्धात तदुत्पत्तिः ॥ ४ । २ । ४१ ॥

पूर्वकृतफलानुबन्धात pûrva-kṛita-phala-anubandhât, from sequence of fruits of previous acts ; तदुत्पत्तिः tat-utpattiḥ, its production.

451. It arises, we reply, through possession of the fruits of our former works.

We acquire a habit of practising meditation in consequence of our good deeds of a previous life.

अरण्यगुहापुलिनादिषु योगाभ्यासोपदेशः ॥ ४ । २ । ४२ ॥

अरण्यगुहापुलिनादिषु araṇya-guhâ-pulina-âdi-ṣu, in forests, caves and river bank ; योगाभ्यासोपदेशः yoga-abhyâsa-upadeśaḥ, instruction of the practice of yoga or contemplation.

452. We are instructed to practise meditation in such places as a forest, a cave or a sand-bank.

The meditation practised in these places is not seriously disturbed by any obstacle.

अपवर्गेऽप्येवं प्रसङ्गः ॥ ४ । २ । ४३ ॥

अपवर्गे apavarge, in release ; अपि api, also ; एवं evam̤, similar ; प्रसंगः prasaṅgaḥ, implication.

453. Such possibilities may occur even in release.

Even a person who has attained release may be disturbe l by the violence of an external object.

न निष्पन्नावश्यम्भावित्वात् ॥ ४ । २ । ४४ ॥

न na, no ; निष्पन्नावश्यम्भावित्वात nispanna-avaśyambhâvi-tvât, being inevitable only where (a body has already been) formed.

454. It is, we reply, not so, because knowledge must spring up only in a body already in the state of formation.

A violent external object produces knowledge only in a body which has been formed, in consequence of our previous deeds, and which is endowed with senses, etc.

तदभावश्चापवर्गे ॥ ४ । २ । ४५ ॥

तदभावः tat-abhâvaḥ, its non-existence ; च cha, and ; अपवर्गे apa-varge, in release.

455. And there is absence of a body in cur release.

Our merits and demerits having already been exhausted, we cannot get a body after we have attained release. Release is the perfect freedom from all sufferings : it consists in a complete destruction of all the seeds and seats of sufferings.

तदर्थं यमनियमाभ्यामात्मसंस्कारो योगाच्चाध्यात्मविध्युपायैः ॥ ४ । २ । ४६ ॥

तदर्थं tat-artham, to that end ; यमनियमाभ्यां yama-niyamâbhyâm, by means of external and internal self-control ; आत्मसंस्कारः âtma-sam̤skâraḥ, purification of the soul ; योगात् yogât, from treatise on yoga or contemplation ; च cha, and ; अध्यात्मविध्युपायैः adhyâtma-vidhi-upâyaiḥ, by means of injunctions and practices regarding the soul.

456. For that purpose there should be a purifying of our soul by abstinence from evil and observance of certain duties as well as by following the spiritual injunctions gleaned from the Yoga institute.

In order to attain release we must practise meditation after the soul has been purified by our abstinence, etc. The injunctions gleaned from the Yoga institute refer to penances, the controlling of our breaths, the fixing of our mind, etc.

ज्ञानग्रहणाभ्यासस्तद्विद्यैश्च सह संवादः ॥ ४ । २ । ४७ ॥

ज्ञानग्रहणाभ्यासः jñâna-grahaṇa-abhyâsaḥ, study of the science of the soul and constant application to it ; तद्विद्यैः tat-vidyaiḥ, with those who are versed in it ; च cha, and ; सह saha, with ; संवादः saṃvâdaḥ, conversation.

457. To secure release, it is necessary to study and follow this treatise on knowledge as well as to hold discussions with those learned in that treatise.

The spiritual injunctions furnished by the Yoga institute cannot be properly assimilated unless we have already acquired a true knowledge of the categories explained in the Nyâya Śâstra. It is therefore very useful to study the Nyâya Śâstra and to hold discussions with persons learned in the Śâstra.

तं शिष्यगुरुसब्रह्मचारिविशिष्टश्रेयोर्थिभिरनसूयिभिरभ्युपेयात् ॥ ४ । २ । ४८ ॥

तं taṃ conversation ; शिष्यगुरुसब्रह्मचारिविशिष्टश्रेयोर्थिभिः śiṣya-guru-sabrahmachâri-viśiṣṭa-śreyorthibhiḥ, with disciples, preceptors, fellow students, and seekers after the supreme good ; अनसूयिभिः an-asûyibhiḥ, with unenvious ; अभ्युपेयात् abhyupeyât, resort to.

458. One should enter upon discussions with unenvious persons, such as disciples, preceptors, fellow-students and seekers of the *summum bonum*.

The epithet "unenvious" excludes those who do not seek truth but desire victory. Discussion has been defined in aphorism 1—2—1.

प्रतिपक्षहीनमपि वा प्रयोजनार्थमर्थित्वे ॥ ४ । २ । ४९ ॥

प्रतिपक्षहीनं pratipakṣa-hînam, without advancing opposition ; अपि api, even ; वा vâ, or ; प्रयोजनार्थं prayojana-artham, for the sake of the purpose ; अर्थित्वे arthi-tve, where one needs it.

459. In case of a necessity for the search of truth, discussion may be held even without an opposing side.

A person desirous of knowledge may submit his views for examination by simply expressing his curiosity for truth without an attempt to establish the views.

तत्त्वाध्यवसायसंरक्षणार्थं जल्पवितण्डे वीजप्ररोहसंरक्षणार्थं कण्टकशाखावरणवत् ॥ ४ । २ । ५० ॥

तत्त्वाध्यवसायसंरक्षणार्थं tattva-adhyavasâya-saṃrakṣaṇa-artham, for the sake of the conservation of the true and certain knowledge about reality ; जल्पवितण्डे jalpa-vitaṇḍe, sophistry and cavil ; वीजप्ररोहसंरक्षणार्थं vîja-praroha-saṃrakṣaṇa-arthaṃ, for the sake of the preservation of the shoots from seeds ; कण्टकशाखावरणवत् kaṇṭaka-śâkhâ-âvaraṇa-vat, like the fencing or covering of thorns and branches.

460. Wranglings and cavils may be employed to keep up our zeal for truth just as fences of thorny boughs are used to safeguard the growth of seeds.

Certain talkative people propound philosophies which are mutually opposed, while others violate all sense of rectitude out of a bias for their own side. Seeing that these people have not attained true knowledge and are not freed from faults, we may, in our disputation against them, employ wranglings and cavils which do not in themselves deserve any profit or encomium.

ताभ्यां विगृह्य कथनम् ॥ ४ । २ । ५१ ॥

ताभ्यां tâbhyâm, by means of them, sophistry and cavil ; विगृह्य vigṛihya, for overcoming ; कथनं kathanam, statement.

461. Sophistry and cavil should be employed also in declaring the truth to overcome the attack of the erratic.

Book V.—CHAPTFR I.

साधर्म्म्यवैधर्म्म्योत्कर्षापकर्षवर्ण्यावर्ण्यविकल्पसाध्यप्राप्त्य-प्राप्तिप्रसङ्ग प्रतिदृष्टान्तानुत्पत्ति संशयप्रकरणाहेत्वर्थापत्त्यवि-शेषोपपत्त्युपलब्ध्यनुपलब्धिनित्यानित्य कार्य्यसमाः॥५।१।१॥

साधर्म्यवैधर्म्योत् कर्षापकर्षवर्ण्यावर्ण्य विकल्पसाध्य प्राप्त्यप्राप्तिप्रसङ्ग प्रतिदृष्टान्तानुत्पत्ति संशयप्रकरणाहेत्वर्थापत्त्य विशेषोपपत्त्युपलब्ध्यनुपलब्धिनित्यानित्य कार्य्यसमाः sâdharmya-vaidharmya-utkarṣa-apakarṣa-varṇya-avarṇya-vikalpa-sâdhya-prâpti-aprâpti-prasaṅga-pratidṛiṣṭânta-anutpatti-saṃśaya-prakaraṇa-ahetu-arthâpatti-aviśeṣa-upaptti-upalabdhi-anupalabdhi-nitya-anitya-kârya-samâḥ, identicals in respect of resemblance, difference, addition, subtraction, questionable, unquestionable, alternative, thing to be established, presence, absence, regression, counter-example, non-production, doubt, topic, non-reason, presumption, non-difference, demonstration, perception, non-perception, eternal, non-eternal, and effect.

462. Futilities are as follows:—(1) Balancing the homogeneity, (2) balancing the heterogeneity, (3) balancing an addition, (4) balancing a subtraction, (5) balancing the questionable, (6) balancing the unquestionable, (7) balancing the alternative. (8) balancing the reciprocity, (9) balancing the co-presence, (10) balancing the mutual absence, (11) balancing the infinite regression, (12) balancing the counterexample, (13) balancing the non-produced, (14) balancing the doubt, (15) balancing the controversy, (16) balancing the non-reason, (17) balancing the presumption, (18) balancing the non-difference, (19) balancing the non-demonstration, (20) balancing the perception, (21) balancing the non-perception, (22) balancing the non-eternality, (23) balancing the eternality and (24) balancing the effect.

Futility, which is a fallacious argument, has been in general terms defined in aphorism 1-2-18. The twentyfour kinds of futility enunciated here will each be defined in due course. The fallacious characters of the twentyfour kinds will also be exposed in separate aphorisms.

साधर्म्म्यवैधर्म्म्याभ्यामुपसंहारे तद्धर्म्मविपर्य्ययोपपत्तेः साधर्म्म्यवैधर्म्म्यसमौ ॥ ५ । १ । २ ॥

साधर्म्यवैधर्म्याभ्याम् sâdharmya-vaidharmyâ-bhyâm, by means of resemblance and difference ; उपसंहारे upasaṃhâre, in case of a conclusion ; तद्धर्मविपर्य्ययोपपत्तेः tat-dharma-viparyaya-upapatteḥ, on account of the absence of that characteristic ; साधर्म्यवैधर्म्यसमौ sâdharmya-vaidharmya-samau, identicals in respect of resemblance and difference.

463. If against an argument based on a homogeneous or heterogeneous example one offers an opposition based on the same kind of example, the opposition will be called "balancing the homogeneity" or "balancing the heterogeneity".

Balancing the homogeneity.— A certain person, to prove the non-eternality of sound, argues as follows:—

Sound is non-eternal,
Because it is a product,
like a pot.

A certain other person offers the following futile opposition:—

Sound is eternal,
because it is incorporeal,
like the sky.

The argument, *viz.*, sound is non-eternal, is based on the homogeneity of sound with the non-eternal pot on the ground of both being products. The opposition, *viz.*, sound is eternal, is said to be based on the homogeneity of sound with the eternal sky on the alleged ground of both being incorporeal. This sort of opposition, futile as it is, is called "balancing the homogeneity", which aims at showing an equality of the arguments of two sides in respect of the homogeneity of examples employed by them.

Balancing the heterogeneity.—A certain person, to prove the non-eternality of sound, argues as follows:—

Sound is non-eternal,
because it is a product,
whatever is not non-eternal is not a product,
as the sky.

A certain other person offers a futile opposition thus:—

Sound is eternal,
because it is incorporeal,
whatever is not eternal is not incorporeal,
as a pot.

The argument, *viz.*, sound is non-eternal, is based on the heterogeneity of sound from the not-non-eternal sky, which are mutually incompatible. The opposition, *viz.*, sound is eternal, is said to be based on the heterogeneity of sound from the not-incorporeal pot which are alleged to be incompatible with each other. This sort of opposition, futile as it is, is called "balancing the heterogeneity", which aims at showing an equality of the arguments of two sides in respect of the heterogeneity of examples employed by them.

गोत्वाद्गोसिद्धिवत्तत्सिद्धिः ॥ ५ । १ । ३ ॥

गोत्वात् go-tvât, from bovineness, the generic idea of a cow ; गोसिद्धिवत् go-siddhi-vat, like the proof of a cow ; तत्सिद्धिः tat-siddhiḥ, its proof.

464. That is, we say, to be established like a cow through cowhood (or cow-type).

The Naiyâyika says:—If the opposition referred to in the previous aphorism is to be valid it must be based on the example, homogeneous or heterogeneous, exhibiting a universal connection between the reason and the predicate such as we discern between a cow and cowhood or a universal disconnection between the reason and the absence of the predicate such as we discern between a cow and absence of cowhood. In the argument—"sound is non-eternal, because it is a product, like a pot", the homogeneous example "pot" exhibits a universal connection between productivity and non-eternality, all products being non-eternal, but in the opposition —"sound is eternal, because it is incorporeal, like the sky"—the homogeneous example "sky" does not exhibit a universal connection between incorporeality and eternality because there are things, such as intellect or knowledge, which are incorporeal but not eternal. A similar observation is to be made with regard to the opposition called "balancing the heterogeneity." In the opposition "sound is eternal, because it is incorporeal, whatever is not eternal is not incorporeal, as a pot", the heterogeneous example "pot" does not exhibit a universal disconnection between incorporeality and absence of eternality because there are things, such as intellect or knowledge, which are incorporeal but not eternal.

साध्यदृष्टान्तयोर्धर्म्मविकल्पादुभयसाध्यत्वाच्चोत्कर्षापकर्षवर्ण्यावर्ण्यविकल्पसाध्यसमाः ॥ ५ । १ । ४ ॥

साध्यदृष्टान्तयोः sâdhya-dṛiṣṭântayoḥ, of the thing to be established and the example ; धर्म्मविकल्पात् dharma-vikalpât, from exchange or mutual transfer of properties; उभयसाध्यत्वात् ubhaya-sâdhya-tvât, both being in need of proof; च cha, and; उत्कर्षापकर्षवर्ण्यावर्ण्यविकल्पसाध्यसमाः utkarṣa-apakarṣa-varṇya-avarṇya-vikalpa-sâdhya-samâḥ, identicals in respect of addition, subtraction , doubtful, not-doubtful, alternative and the thing to be established.

465. The subject and example alternating their characters or both standing in need of proof, there occur (futilities called) "balancing an addition", "balancing a subtraction", "balancing the questionable", "balancing the unquestionable", "balancing the alternative" and "balancing the reciprocity.

Balancing an addition.—If against an argument based on a certain character of the example one offers an opposition based on an additional character thereof, the opposition will be called "balancing an addition."

A certain person, to prove the non-eternality of sound, argues as follows:—

Sound is non-eternal,
because it is a product,
like a pot.

A certain other person offers a futile opposition thus:—

Sound is non-eternal (and corporeal),
because it is a product,
like a pot (which is non-eternal as well as corporeal).

The opponent alleges that if sound is non-eternal like a pot, it must also be corporeal like it: if it is not corporeal let it be also not non-eternal. This sort of futile opposition is called "balancing an addition" which aims at showing an equality of the argument of two sides in respect of an additional character (possessed by the example and attributed to the subject).

Balancing a subtraction.—If against an argument based on a certain character of the example one offers an opposition based on another character wanting in it, the opposition will be called "balancing a subtraction."

A certion person, to prove the non-eternality of sound, argues as follows:—

Sound is non-eternal,
because it is a product,
like a pot.

A certain other person offers the following futile opposition:—

Sound is non-eternal (but not audible).
because it is a product,
like a pot (which is non-eternal but not audible.)

The opponent alleges that if sound is non-eternal like a pot, it cannot be audible, for a pot is not audible; and if sound is still held to be audible, let it be also not non-eternal. This sort of futile opposition is called "balancing a subtraction" which aims at showing an equality of the arguments of two sides in respect of a certain character wanting in the example (and consequently also in the subject).

Balancing the questionable.—If one opposes an argument by maintaining that the character of the example is as questionable as that of the subject, the opposition will be called "balancing the questionable."

A certain person, to prove the non-eternality of sound, argues as follows:—

Sound is non-eternal,
because it is a product,
like a pot.

A certain other person offers a futile opposition thus:—

A pot is non-eternal,
because it is a product,
like sound.

The opponent alleges that if the non-eternality of sound is called in question, why is not that of the pot too called in question, as the pot and sound are both products? His object is to set aside the argument on the ground of its example being of a questionable character. This sort of futile opposition is called "balancing the questionable" which aims at showing an equality of the arguments of two sides in respect of the questionable character of the subject as well as of the example.

Balancing the unquestionable.—If one opposes an argument by alleging that the character of the subject is as unquestionable as that of the example, the opposition will be called "balancing the unquestionable."

A certain person, to prove the non-eternality of sound, argues as follows:—

Sound is non-eternal,
because it is a product,
like a pot.

A certain other person offers a futile opposition thus:—

A pot is non-eternal,
because it is a product,
like sound.

The opponent alleges that if the non-eternality of a pot is held to be unquestionable, why is not that of sound too held to be so, as the pot and sound are both products? His object is to render the argument unnecessary on the ground of its subject being of an unquestionable character. This sort of futile opposition is called "balancing the unquestionable" which aims at showing the equality of the arguments of two sides in respect of the unquestionable character of the example as well as of the subject.

Balancing the alternative.—If one opposes an argument by attributing alternative character to the subject and the example, the opposition will be called "balancing the alternative."

A certain person, to prove the non-eternality of sound, argues as follows:—

Sound is non-eternal,
because it is a product,
like a pot.

A certain other person offers a futile opposition thus:—

Sound is eternal and formless,
because it is a product,
like a pot (which is non-eternal and has forms).

The opponent alleges that the pot and sound are both products, yet one has form and the other is formless: why on the same principle is not one (the pot) non-eternal and the other (sound) eternal? This sort of futile opposition is called "balancing the alternative" which aims at showing an equality of the arguments of two sides in respect of the alternative characters attributed to the subject and example.

Balancing the reciprocity.—If one opposes an argument by alleging a reciprocity of the subject and the example, the opposition will be called "balancing the reciprocity."

A certain person, to prove the non-eternality of sound, argues as follows:—

Sound is non-eternal,
because it is a product,
like a pot.

A certain other person offers a futile opposition thus:—

A pot is non-eternal,
because it is a product,
like sound.

The opponent alleges that the pot and sound being both products one requires proof for its non-eternality as much as the other does. Sound is to be proved non-eternal by the example of a pot and the pot is to be proved non-eternal by the example of sound. This leads to a reciprocity of the pot (example) and sound (subject) resulting in no definite conclusion as to the eternality or non-eternality of sound. This sort of futile opposition is called "balancing the reciprocity" which brings an argument to a stand-still by alleging the reciprocity of the subject and the example.

किंचित्साधर्म्म्यादुपसंहारसिद्धेर्वैधर्म्म्यादप्रतिषेधः ॥ ५ । १ । ५ ॥

किंचित kiñchit, partial ; साधर्म्म्यात sâdharmyât, from resemblance ; उपसंहारसिद्धेः upasaṃhâra-siddheḥ, from proof of the conclusion; वैधर्म्म्यात vaidharmyât, from difference ; अप्रतिषेधः a-pratiṣedhaḥ, non-contradiction.

466. This is, we say, no opposition because there is a difference between the subject and the example although the conclusion is drawn from a certain equality of their characters.

The Naiyâyika says:—The futilities called "balancing an addition," "balancing a subtraction," "balancing the questionable," "balancing the unquestonable" and "balancing the alternative" are all based on the false supposition of a complete equality of the subject and the example. Though there is no denial of an equality of the subject and the example in certain characters, there is indeed a great difference between them in other characters.

Sound is non-eternal.
because it is a product,
like a pot.

In this argument although there is an equality of "sound" and "pot" in respect of their being both products, there is a great difference between them in other respects. A cow possesses some characters in common with a *bos gavaeus* but there is no complete identity between them. No body can commit the futilities mentioned above if he bears in mind the equality of the subject and the example only in those characters which are warranted by the reason (middle term). In the case of the futility called "balancing an addition" it is clear that the equality supposed to exist between the pot and sound in respect of corporeality is not warranted by the reason (*viz.* being a product), because there are things, such as intellect or knowledge, which are products but not corporeal. Similarly with regard to the futility called "balancing a subtraction," the reason (*viz.* being a product) does not justify an equality of sound and pot in respect of their being not audible. As regards the futilities called "balancing the questionable" and "balancing the unquestionable," we cannot ignore the difference between the subject and the example without putting an end to all kinds of inference. The futility called "balancing the alternative" introduces an equality between the pot and sound in respect of a character (*viz.* being eternal) which is not warranted by the reason, *viz.* being a product.

साध्यातिदेशाच्च दृष्टान्तोपपत्तेः ॥ ५ । १ । ६ ॥

साध्यातिदेशात् sâdhya-atideśât, from extension of the thing to be established ; च cha, and ; दृष्टान्तोपपत्तेः dṛiṣṭânta-upapatteḥ, because of proof of the example.

467. And because the example happens to surpass the subject.

The futility called "balancing the reciprocity" is based on the false supposition that the example stands exactly on the same footing as the subject. But that one surpasses the other is evident from aphorism 1-1-25 which states that the example does not stand in need of proof as to its characters.

Sound is non-eternal,
because it is a product,
like a pot.

In this argument sound (the subject) may not be known by some to be non-eternal but a pot (the example) is known by all to be a product as well as non-eternal. "Balancing the reciprocity" is therefore a fallacious argument.

प्राप्य साध्यमप्राप्य वा हेतोः प्राप्त्या अविशिष्टत्वादप्राप्त्या असाधकत्वाच्च प्राप्त्यप्राप्तिसमौ ॥ ५ । १ । ७ ॥

प्राप्य prâpya, reaching, covering ; साध्यम् sâdhyam, the thing to be established ; अप्राप्य a-prâpya, not reaching ; वा vâ, or ; हेतोः hetoḥ, of the mark or reason ; प्राप्त्या prâptyâ, by the fact of covering or co-extension ; अविशिष्टत्वात् a viśiṣṭa-tvât, being undistinguished or identical ; अप्राप्त्या a-prâptyâ, by reason of non-co-extension ; असाधकत्वात् a sâdhaka-tvât, not being a means of establishment ; च cha, and ; प्राप्त्यप्राप्तिसमौ prâpti-aprâpti-samau, identicals in respect of presence and absence.

468. If against an argument based on the co-presence of the reason and the predicate or on the mutual absence of them one offers an opposition based on the same kind of co-presence or mutual absence, the opposition will, on account of the reason being non-distinguished from or being non-conducive to the predicate, be called "balancing the co-presence" or "balancing the mutual absence."

Balancing the co-presence.—If against an argument based on the co-presence of the reason and the predicate, one offers an opposition based on the same kind of co-presence, the opposition will, on account of the reason being non-distinguished from the predicate, be called "balancing the co-presence."

A certain person, to prove that there is fire in the hill, argues as follows:—

The hill has fire,
because it has smoke,
like a kitchen.

A certain other person offers a futile opposition thus:—

The hill has smoke,
because it has fire,
like a kitchen.

The arguer has taken the smoke to be the reason and the fire to be the predicate. The opponent raises a question as to whether the smoke is present at the same site which is occupied by the fire or is absent from that site. If the smoke is present with the fire at the same site, there remains, according to the opponent, no criterion to distinguish the reason from the predicate. The smoke is, in his opinion, as much a reason for the fire as the fire for the smoke. This sort of futile opposition is called "balancing the co-presence" which aims at stopping an argument on the alleged ground of the co-presence of the reason and the predicate.

Balancing the mutual absence.—If against an argument based on the mutual absence of the reason and the predicate, one offers an opposition based on the same kind of mutual absence, the opposition will, on account of the reason being non-conducive to the predicate, be called "balancing the mutual absence."

A certain person, to prove that there is fire in the hill, argues as follows:—

The hill has fire,
because it has smoke,
like a kitchen.

A certain other person offers a futile opposition thus:—

The hill has smoke.
because it has fire,
like a kitchen.

The opponent asks: "Is the smoke to be regarded as the reason because it is absent from the site of the fire ?" "Such a supposition is indeed absurd." The reason cannot establish the predicate without being connected with it, just as a lamp cannot exhibit a thing which is not within its reach. If a reason unconnected with the predicate could establish the latter, then the fire could be as much the reason for the smoke as the smoke for the fire. This sort of futile opposition is called "balancing the mutual absence" which aims at bringing an argument to a close on the alleged ground of the mutual absence of the reason and the predicate.

घटादिनिष्पत्तिदर्शनात् पीडने चाभिचारादप्रतिषेधः ॥ ५ । १ । ८ ॥

घटादिनिष्पत्तिदर्शनात् ghaṭa-ādi-niṣpatti-darśanāt, from the observation of the production of the pot and the like ; पीडने pîḍane, in the case of oppression ; च cha, and ; अभिचारात् abhichârât, from spells ; अप्रतिषेधः a-pratiṣedhaḥ, non-contradiction.

469. This is, we say, no opposition because we find the production of pots by means of clay as well as the oppression of persons by spells.

A potter cannot produce a pot without getting clay within his reach but an exorcist can destroy persons by administering spells from a distance. Hence it is clear that a thing is accomplished sometimes by the cause being present at its site and sometimes by being absent from it. "Balancing the co-presence" and "balancing the mutual absence" which attach an undue importance to the proximity or remoteness of sites, are therefore totally fallacious arguments.

दृष्टान्तस्य कारणानपदेशात् प्रत्यवस्थानाच्च प्रतिदृष्टान्तेन प्रसङ्गप्रतिदृष्टान्तसमौ ॥ ५ ॥ १ ॥ ९ ॥

दृष्टान्तस्य dṛiṣṭântasya, of the example ; कारणानपदेशात् kârana-an-apadeśât, from non-application of the cause ; प्रत्यवस्थानात् prati-avasthânât, from counter-opposition ; च cha, and ; प्रतिदृष्टान्तेन prati-dṛiṣṭântena, by a counter-example ; प्रसङ्गप्रतिदृष्टान्तसमौ prasaṅga-pratidṛiṣṭânta-samau, identicals in respect of regression and counter-example.

470. If one opposes an argument on the ground of the example having been established by a series of reasons or on the ground of the existence of a mere counter-example, the oppostion will be called "balancing the infinite regression" or "balancing the counter-example."

Balancing the infinite regression.—A certain person, to prove the non-eternality of sound, argues as follows:—

Sound is non-eternal,
because it is a product,
like a pot.

A certain other person offers a futile opposition thus:—

If sound is proved to be non-eternal by the example of a pot, how is the pot again to be proved as non-eternal? The reason which proves the non-eternality of the pot is to be proved by a further reason. This gives rise to an infinite regression which injures the proposition "sound is non-eternal" not less than the proposition "sound is eternal." This sort of futile opposition is called "balancing the infinite regression" which aims at stopping an argument by introducing an infinite regression which is said to beset the example.

Balancing the counter-example.—A certain person, to prove the non-eternality of sound, argues as follows :—

Sound is non-eternal,
because it is a product,
like a pot.

A certain other person offers a futile opposition thus:—

Sound is eternal,
like the sky.

The opponent alleges that if sound is held to be non-eternal by the example of a pot, why it should not be held to be eternal by the example of the sky? If the example of the sky is set aside, let the example of the pot too be set aside. This sort of futile opposition is called "balancing the counter-example" which aims at setting aside an argument by the introduction of a counter-example.

प्रदीपोपादानप्रसङ्गनिवृत्तिवत्तद्विनिवृत्तिः ॥ ५ । १ । १० ॥

प्रदीपोपादानप्रसंगनिवृत्तिवत्-pradîpa-upâdâna-prasṅga-nivṛitti-vat, like the cessation of the need for a collection of lamps ; तद्विनिवृत्तिः tat-vinivṛittiḥ. its cessation.

471. The example does not, we say, require a series of reasons for its establishment just as a lamp does not require a series of lamps to be brought in for its illumination.

The Naiyâyika says:—

An example is a thing the characters of which are wellknown to an ordinary man as well as to an expert. It does not require a series of reasons to reveal its own character or to reveal the character of the subject with which it stands in the relation of homogeneity or heterogeneity. In this respect it resembles a lamp which illumines itself as well as the things lying within its reach.

Sound is non-eternal,
because it is a product,
like a pot.

In this argument the pot is the example which is so well-known that it requires no proof as to its being a product or being non-eternal.

Hence the opposition called "balancing the infinite regression" is not founded on a sound basis.

प्रतिदृष्टान्तहेतुत्वे च नाहेतुर्दृष्टान्तः ॥ ५ । १ । ११ ॥

प्रतिदृष्टान्तहेतुत्वे pratidriṣṭânta-hetu-tve, the counter-example being a reason; च cha, and; न na, not; अहेतुः a-hetuḥ, not a reason; दृष्टान्तः driṣṭântaḥ, the example.

472. The example, we say, cannot be set aside as unreasonable only because a counter-example is advanced as the reason.

The Nâiyâyika says:—

The opponent must give a special reason why the counter-example should be taken as specially fitted to lead to a conclusion and the example should not be taken as such. Until such a special reason is given, the counter-example cannot be accepted as leading to a definite conclusion. In fact a mere counter-example without a reason (middle term) attending it cannot be conducive to any conclusion. Hence we must rely on an example attended by reason but not on a counter-example unattended by reason.

Sound is eternal,
like the sky.

This opposition which is founded on a mere counter-example is therefore to be rejected as unreasonable.

प्रागुत्पत्तेः कारणाभावादनुत्पत्तिसमः ॥ ५ । १ । १२ ॥

प्राक् prâk, prior; उत्पत्तेः utpatteḥ, to production; कारणाभावात् kâraṇa-abhâvât, from the non-existence of the cause; अनुत्पत्तिसमः an-utpatti-samaḥ, identical in respect of non-production.

473. If one opposes an argument on the ground of the property connoted by the reason being absent from the thing denoted by the subject while it is not yet produced, the opposition will be called "balancing the non-produced."

A certain person, to prove that sound is non-eternal, argues as follows:—

Sound is non-eternal,
because it is an effect of effort,
like a pot.

A certain other person offers a futile opposition thus:—

Sound is eternal,
because it is a non-effect of effort,
like the sky.

The opponent alleges that the property connoted by the reason, *viz.*, being an effect of effort, is not predicable of the subject, *viz.*, sound (while it is not yet produced). Consequently sound is not non-eternal, it must then be eternal. There is, according to the opponent, an apparent agreement between the two sides as to the sound being non-eternal on account of its being a non-effect-of-effort. This sort of futile opposition is called "balancing the non-produced" which pretends to show an equality of the argument of two sides assuming the thing denoted by the subject to be as yet non-produced.

तथाभावादुत्पन्नस्य कारणोपपत्तेर्न कारणप्रतिषेधः ॥ ५ । १ । १३ ॥

तथाभावात् tathâ-bhâvât, from the nature given to a thing when it is produced ; उत्पन्नस्य utpannasya, of the thing produced : कारणोपपत्तेः kâraṇa-upapatteḥ, owing to proof of the cause ; न na, not ; कारणप्रतिषेधः kâraṇa-pratiṣedhaḥ, contradiction of the cause.

474. This is, we say, no opposition against our reason so well predicable of the subject which becomes as such only when it is produced.

The Naiyâyika disposes of the futile opposition called "balancing the non-produced" by stating that the subject can become as such only when it is produced, and that there is then no obstacle to the property of the reason being predicated of it. The opposition, *viz.*, "sound (while non-produced) is eternal, because it is not then an effect of effort," carries no weight with it, since we do not take the sound to be the subject before it is produced. Sound, while it is produced, is certainly an effect of effort and as such is non-eternal.

सामान्यदृष्टान्तयोरैन्द्रियकत्वे समाने नित्यसाधर्म्यात् संशयसमः ॥ ५ । १ । १४ ॥

सामान्यदृष्टान्तयोः sâmânya-dṛiṣṭântayoḥ, of the genus and the (individual put forward as) example ; ऐन्द्रियकत्वे aindriyaka-tve, being sensible ; समाने samâne, equally ; नित्यानित्यसाधर्म्यात् nitya-anitya-sâdharmyât, from resemblance of things eternal (genus) and non-eternal (individual) ; संशयसमः saṃśaya-samaḥ, identical in respect of doubt.

475. If one opposes an argument on the ground of a doubt arising from the homogeneity of the eternal and the non-eternal consequent on the example and its genus (or type) being equally objects of perception the oppositon will be called "balancing the doubt."*

A certain person, to prove the non-eternality of sound, argues as follows:—

Sound is non-eternal
because it is a product,
like a pot.

A certain other person offers a futile opposition thus:—

Sound is non-eternal or eternal (?)
because it is an object of perception,
like a pot or pot-ness.

Tho opponent alleges that sound is homogeneous with a pot as well as pot-ness inasmuch as both are objects of perception; but the pot being non-eternal and pot-ness (the genus of pots or pot-type) being eternal there arises a doubt as to whether the sound is non-eternal or eternal. This sort of futile opposition is called "balancing the doubt" which aims at rejecting an argument in consequence of a doubt arising from the homogeneity of the eternal and the non-eternal.

साधर्म्यात्संशये न संशयो वैधर्म्यादुभयथा वा संशयेऽत्यन्तसंशयप्रसङ्गो नित्यत्वानभ्युपगमाच्च *सामान्यस्याप्रतिषेधः ॥ ५ । १ । १५ ॥

साधर्म्यात् sâdharmyât, from resemblance ; संशये saṃśaye, doubt arising; न na, and ; संशयः saṃśayaḥ, doubt ; वैधर्म्यात् vaidharmyât, from difference ; उभयथा ubhaya-thâ, in both ways ; वा vâ, or ; संशये saṃśaye, doubt arising ;

*The term *sâmânya* in the sense of "general notion, genus or type" was evidently taken form the Vaiśeṣika philosophy.

अत्यन्तसंशयप्रसंगः atyanta-saṃśaya-prasaṅgaḥ, implication of unending doubt ; नित्यत्वानभ्युपगमात् nitya-tva-an-abhyupagamât, from non admission of eternality ; च cha, and ; सामान्यस्य sâmânya-sya, of the genus ; अप्रतिषेधः a pratiṣedhaḥ, non-contradiction.

476. This is, we say, no opposition because we do not admit that eternality can be established by the homogeneity with the genus : a doubt that arises from a knowledge of the homogeneity vanishes from that of the heterogeneity, and that which arises in both ways never ends.

The Naiyâyika says:—

Sound cannot be said to be eternal on the mere ground of its homogeneity with pot-ness (the genus of pots or pot-type) but must be pronounced to be non-eternal on the ground of its heterogeneity from the same in respect of being a product. Though on the score of homogeneity we may entertain doubt as to whether sound is eternal or non-eternal, but on the score of heterogeneity we can pronounce it undoubtedly to be non-eternal. In this case we must bear in mind that we cannot ascertain the true nature of a thing unless we weigh it in respect of its homogeneity with as well as heterogeneity from other things. If even then there remains any doubt as to its true nature, that doubt will never end.

उभयसाधर्म्यात् प्रक्रियासिद्धेः प्रकरणसमः ॥ ५ । १ । १६ ॥

उभयसाधर्म्यात् ubhaya-sâdharmyât, from resemblance to both ; प्रक्रियासिद्धेः prakriyâ-siddheḥ, because of proof of the operation (of the subject and its opposite); प्रकरणसमः prakaraṇa-samaḥ, identical in respect of the topic.

477. "Balancing the controversy" is an opposition which is conducted on the ground of homogeneity with (or heterogeneity from) both sides.

A certain person, to prove the non-eternality of sound, argues as follows:—

Sound is non-eternal,
because it is a product,
like a pot.

A certain other person offers a futile opposition thus:—

Sound is eternal,
because it is audible.
like sound-ness.

The opponent alleges that the propositon, *viz.* sound is non-eternal, cannot be proved because the reason, *viz.*, audibility which is homogeneous with both sound (which is non-eternal) and soundness (which is eternal), provokes the very controversy for the settlement of which it was employed. This sort of futile opposition is called "balancing the controversy" which hurts an argument by giving rise to the very controversy which was to be settled.

प्रतिपक्षात् प्रकरणसिद्धेः प्रतिषेधानुपपत्तिः प्रतिपक्षोपपत्तेः ॥ ५ । १ । १७ ॥

प्रतिपक्षात् pratipakṣât, from the counter-subject ; प्रकरणसिद्धेः prakaraṇa-siddheḥ, because of proof of the topic ; प्रतिषेधानुपपत्तिः pratiṣedha-an-upapattiḥ, non-proof of the contradiction ; प्रतिपक्षोपपत्तेः pratipakṣa-upapatteḥ, becasue of proof of the counter-subject.

478. This is, we say, no opposition because it provokes a controversy which has an opposing side.

The Naiyâyika says:—The opposition called "balancing the controversy" cannot set aside the main argument because it leads to a controversy which supports one side quite as strongly as it is opposed by the other side.

त्रैकाल्यासिद्धेर्हेतोरहेतुसमः ॥ ५ । १ । १८ ॥

त्रैकाल्यासिद्धेः traikâlya-a-siddheḥ, because of non-operation in all the three times ; हेतोः hetoḥ, of the reason ; अहेतुसमः a-hetu-samaḥ, identical in respect of non-reason.

479. "Balancing the non- reason" is an opposition which is based on the reason being shown to be impossible at all the three times.

A certain person, to prove the non-eternality of sound, argues as follows:—

Sound is non-eternal,
because it is a product,
like a pot.

Here "being a product" is the reason or sign for "being non-eternal" which is the predicate or significate.

A certain other person offers a futile opposition thus:—

The reason or sign is impossible at all the three times because it cannot precede, succeed, or be simultaneous with the predicate or significate.

(*a*) The reason (or sign) does not precede the predicate (or significate) because the former gets its name only when it establishes the latter. It is impossible for the reason to be called as such before the establishment of the predicate.

(*b*) The reason (or sign) does not succeed the predicate (or significate) because what would be the use of the former if the latter existed already?

(*c*) The reason (or sign) and the predicate (or significate) cannot exist simultaneously for they will then be reciprocally connected like the right and left horns of a cow.

This sort of futile opposition is called "balancing the non-reason" which aims at setting aside an argument by showing that the reason is impossible at all the three times.

न हेतुतः साध्यसिद्धेस्त्रैकाल्यासिद्धिः ॥ ५ । १ । १९ ॥

न na, no ; हेतुतः hetu-taḥ, from the reason ; साध्यसिद्धेः sâdhya-siddheḥ, from the establishment of the thing to be established ; त्रैकाल्यासिद्धिः traikâlya-a-siddhiḥ, non-proof of operation in the three times.

480. There is, we say, no impossibility at the three times because the predicate or significate is established by the reason or sign.

The Naiyayika says:—The knowledge of the knowable and the establishment of that which is to be established take place from reason which must precede that which is to be known and that which is to be established.

प्रतिषेधानुपपत्तेः प्रतिषेद्धव्याप्रतिषेधः ॥ ५ । १ । २० ॥

प्रतिषेधानुपपत्तेः pratiṣedha-an-upapatteḥ, from non-proof of contradiction or opposition ; प्रतिषेद्धव्याप्रतिषेधः pratiṣeddhavya-a-prati-ṣedhaḥ, non-contradiction of the thing to be contradicted.

481. There is, we further say, no opposition of that which is to be opposed, because the opposition itself is impossible at all the three times.

It being impossible for the opposition to precede, succeed or be simultaneous with that which is to be opposed, the opposition itself is invalid and consequently the original argument holds good.

अर्थापत्तितः प्रतिपक्षसिद्धेरर्थापत्तिसमः ॥ ५ । १ । २१ ॥

अर्थापत्तितः arthâpatti-taḥ, from presumption ; प्रतिपक्षसिद्धेः prati-pakṣa-siddheḥ, from proof of counter-subject; अर्थापत्तिसमः arthâpatti-samaḥ, identical in respect of presumption.

482. If one advances an opposition on the basis of a presumption the opposition will be called "balancing the presumption."

A certain person, to prove the non-eternality of sound, argues as follows:—

Sound is non-eternal,
because it is a product,
like a pot.

A certain other person offers a futile opposition thus:—

Sound is presumed to be eternal,
because it is incorporeal,
like the sky.

The opponent alleges that if sound is non-eternal on account of its homogeneity with non-eternal things (*e.g.* in respect of its being a product), it may be concluded by presumption that sound is eternal on account of its homogenetiy with eternal things (*e.g.* in respect of its being incorporeal). This sort of futile opposition is called "balancing the presumption" which aims at stopping an argument by setting presumption as a balance against it.

अनुक्तस्यार्थापत्तेः पक्षहानेरुपपत्तिरनुक्तत्वादनैकान्तिकत्वाच्चार्थापत्तेः ॥ ५ । १ । २२ ॥

अनुक्तस्य an-ukta-sya, of thing not stated ; अर्थापत्तेः arthâpatteḥ, from presumption ; पक्षहानेः pakṣa-hâneḥ, of injury to, or loss of, position ; उपपत्तिः upapattiḥ, proof ; अनुक्तत्वात् an-ukta-tvât, because it is unsaid; अनैकान्तिकत्वात् an-aikantika-tvât, because of multifariousness; अर्थापत्तेः arthâpatteḥ, of presumption.

483. If things unsaid could come by presumption, there would, we say, arise a possibility of the opposition itself being hurt on account of the presumption being erratic and conducive to an unsaid conclusion.

Sound is eternal,
because it is incorporeal.
like the sky.

If by presumption we could draw a conclusion unwarranted by the reason, we could from the opposition cited above draw the following conclusion:—

Sound is presumed to be non-eternal,
because it is a product,
like a pot.

This would hurt the opposition itself. In fact the presumption as adduced by the opponent is erratic. If one says that "sound is non-eternal because of its homogeneity with non-eternal things", the preumption that naturally follows is that "sound is eternal because of its homogeneity with eternal things" and *vice versa*. There is no rule that presumption should be made in one case and not in the case opposed to it ; and in the event of two mutually opposed presumptions no definite conclusion would follow. Hence the opposition called "balancing the presumption" is untenable.

एकधर्म्मोपपत्तेरविशेषे सर्व्वाविशेषप्रसङ्गात् सद्भावोपपत्ते-रविशेषसमः ॥ ५ । १ । २३ ॥

एकधर्मोपपत्तेः eka-dharma-upapatteḥ, from proof of one property ; अविशेषे aviśeṣe, in case of non-difference ; सर्वाविशेषप्रसंगात् sarva-aviśeṣa-prasaṅgât, from implication of non-difference in all respects; सद्भावोपपत्तेः sabdhâva-upapatteḥ, because of proof of existence ; अविशेषसमः a-viśeṣa-samaḥ, identical in respect of non-difference.

484. If the subject and example are treated as non-different in respect of the possession of a certain property on account of their possessing in comn on the property connoted by the reason, it follows as a co clusion that all things are mutually non-different in respect of the posse sion of every property on account of their being existent : this sort of opposition is called "balancing the non-difference."

A certain person, to prove the non-eternality of sound, argues as follows:—

Sound is non eternal,
because it is a product,
like a pot.

A certain other person offers a futile opposition thus:—

If the pot and sound are treated as non-different in respect of non-eternality in consequence of their both being products, it follows as a conclusion that all things are mutually non-different in respect of the possession of every property in consequence of their being existent. Therefore, no difference existing between the eternal and the non-eternal, sound may be treated as eternal. This sort of opposition is called "balancing the non-difference" which aims at hurting an argument by assuming all things to be mutually non different.

क्वचिद्धर्म्मानुपपत्तेः क्वचिच्चोपपत्तेः प्रतिषेधाभावः ॥ ५ । १ । २४॥

क्वचित kva chit, in some cases ; धर्म्मानुपपत्त: dharma-anupapatteḥ, from non-proof of the property ; क्वचित kva chit, in some cases ; च cha, and ; उपपत्तेः upapatteḥ, from proof ; प्रतिषेधाभावः pratiṣedha-abhâvaḥ, absence of contradiction.

485. This is, we say, no opposition because the property possessed in common by the subject and the example happens in certain instances to abide in the reason while in other instances not to abide in it.

Sound is non-eternal,
because it is a product,
like a pot.

Here the pot and sound possessing in common the property of being a product are treated as non-different in respect of the possession of non-eternality. On the same principle if all things are treated as non-different in consequence of their being existent, we would like to know in what respect they are non-different. If they are treated as non-different in respect of non-eternality, then the argument would stand thus:—

All things are non-eternal,
because they are existent,
like (?)

In this argument "all things" being the subject, there is nothing left which may serve as an example. A part of the subject cannot be cited as the example because the example must be a well-established thing while the subject is a thing which is yet to be established. The argument, for want of an example, leads to no conclusion. In fact all things are not non-eternal since some at least are eternal. In other words, non-eternality abides in some existent things and does not abide in other existent things. Hence all things are not mutually non-different and the opposition called "balancing the non-difference" is unreasonable.

उभयकारणोपपत्तेरुपपत्तिसमः ॥ ५ । १ । २५ ॥

उभयकारणोपपत्तेः ubhaya kâraṇa-upapatteḥ, from proof of causes of both ; उपपत्तिसमः upapatti-samaḥ, identical in respect of proof.

486. If an opposition is offered by showing that both the demonstrations are justified by reasons the opposition will be called "balancing the demonstration."

A certain person demonstrates the non-eternality of sound as follows:—

Sound is non-eternal,
because it is a product,
like a pot.

A certain other person offers an opposition by the alleged demonstration of the eternality of sound as follows:—

Sound is eternal,
because it is incorporeal,
like the sky.

The reason in the first demonstration supports the non-eternality of sound while that in the second demonstration supports the eternality of sound, yet both the demonstrations are alleged to be right. The opponent advanced the second apparent demonstration as a balance against the first to create a dead-lock. This sort of opposition is called "balancing the demonstration".

उपपत्तिकारणाभ्यनुज्ञानादप्रतिषेधः ॥ ५ । १ । २६ ॥

उपपत्तिकारणाभ्यनुज्ञानात् upapatti-kâraṇa-abhyanujñânât, from admission of cause of proof (of the counter-subject) ; अप्रतिषेधः a-pratiṣedhaḥ non-contradiction.

487. This is, we say, no opposition because there is an admission of the first demonstration.

The Naiyâyika says:—

The opponent having asserted that both the demonstrations are justified by reasons, has admitted the reasonableness of the first demonstration which supports the non-eternality of sound. If to avoid the incompatibility that exists between the two demonstrations, he now denies the reason which supports non-eternality we would ask why does he not deny the other reason which supports eternality of sound, for he can avoid incompatibility by denying either of the reasons. Hence the opposition called "balancing the demonstration" is not well-founded.

निर्दिष्टकारणाभावेऽप्युपलम्भादुपलब्धिसमः ॥ ५ । १ । २७ ॥

निर्दिष्टकारणाभावे nirdiṣṭa-kâraṇa-abhâve, in the absence of the known cause ; अपि api, even ; उपलम्भाद् upalambhât, from perception ; उपलब्धिसमः upalabdhi-samaḥ, identical in respect of perception.

488. If an opposition is offered on the ground that we perceive the character of the subject even without the intervention of the reason, the opposition will be called "balancing the perception."

A certain person, to prove the non-eternality of sound, argues as follows:—

Sound is non-eternal
because it is a product,
like a pot.

A certain other person offers a futile opposition thus:—

Sound can be ascertained to be non-eternal even without the reason that it is a product, for we *perceive* that sound is produced by the branches of trees broken by wind. This sort of opposition is called "balancing the perception" which aims at demolishing an argument by setting up an act of perception as a balance against it.

कारणान्तरादपि तद्धर्मोपपत्तेरप्रतिषेधः ॥ ५ । १ । २८ ॥

कारणान्तरात् kâraṇa-antarât, from other causes ; अपि api, also तद्धर्मोपपत्तेः tat-dharma-upapatteḥ, from proof of that property ; अप्रतिषेधः a-pratiṣedhaḥ, non-contradiction.

489. This is, we say, no opposition because that character can be ascertained by other means as well.

The Naiyâyika says that the argument, *viz.*, "sound is non-eternal because it is a product, like a pot," implies that sound is proved to be non-eternal through the reason that it is a product. It does not deny other means, such as perception, etc., which also may prove sound to be non-eternal. Hence the opposition called "balancing the perception" does not set aside the main argument.

तदनुपलब्धेरनुपलम्भादभावसिद्धौ तद्विपरीतोपपत्तेरनुपलब्धिसमः ॥ ५ । १ । २९ ॥

तदनुपलब्धेः tat-an-upalabdheḥ, from non-cognition of that ; **अनुपलम्भात्** an-upalambhât, from non-perception ; **अभावसिद्धौ** abhâva-siddhau, non existence being established ; **तद्विपरीतोपपत्तेः** tat-viparîta-upapatteḥ from proof of its opposite ; **अनुपलब्धिसमः** an-upalabdhi-samaḥ, identical in respect of non-perception.

490. If against an argument proving the non existence of a thing by the non-perception thereof, one offers an opposition aiming at proving the contrary by the non-perception of the non-perception, the opposition will be called "balancing the non-perception."

In aphorsim 2-2-18 the Naiyâyika has stated that there is no veil which covers sound for we do not perceive such a veil. In aphorsim 2-2-19 his opponent has stated that there is a veil because we do not perceive the non-perception thereof. If the non-perception of a thing proves its non-existence, the non-perception of the non-perception must, in the opinion of the opponent, prove the existence of the thing. This sort of opposition is called "balancing the non-perception" which aims at counteracting an argument by setting up non-perception as a balance against it.

अनुपलम्भात्मकत्वादनुपलब्धेरहेतुः ॥ ५ । १ । ३० ॥

अनुपलम्भात्मकत्वात् an uplambhâtmaka-tvât, being of the nature of non-perception ; **अनुपलब्धेः** an-upalabdheḥ, of non-cognition ; **अहेतुः** a-hetuḥ, not a reason.

491. The reasoning through non-perception is not, we say, sound, because non-perception is merely the negation of perception.

The Naiyâyika says:—Perception refers to that which is existent while non-perception to that which is non-existent. The non-perception of non-perception which signifies a mere negation of non-perception cannot be interpreted as referring to an existent thing. Hence the opposition called "balancing the non-perception" is not well-founded.

ज्ञानविकल्पानाञ्च भावाभावसंवेदनादध्यात्मम् ॥५।१।३१॥

ज्ञानविकल्पानाम् jñâna-vikalpânâm, of diverse forms of cognition ; च cha, and भावाभावसंवेदनात् bhâva abhâva-saṃvedanât, from consciousness of existence and non existence ; अध्यात्मम् adhi-âtmam, in the soul.

492. There is, moreover, an internal perception of the existence as well as of the non-existence of the various kinds of knowledge.

There are internal perceptions of such forms as "I am sure," "I am not sure," "I have doubt," "I have no doubt", etc., which prove that we can perceive the non existence of knowledge as well as the existence thereof. Hence the non-perception itself is perceptible, and as there is no non-perception of non-perception, the opposition called "balancing the non-perception" falls to the ground.

साधर्म्यात्तुल्यधर्म्मोपपत्तेः सर्व्वानित्यत्वप्रसङ्गादनित्यसमः ॥ ५ । १ । ३२ ॥

साधर्म्यात् sâdharmyât, through resemblance ; तुल्यधर्म्मोपपत्तेः tulya-dharma-upapatteḥ, because of proof of equal properties ; सर्व्वानित्यत्वप्रसंगात् sarva-anityatva-prasaṅgât, from implication of non-eternality of all ; अनित्यसमः anitya-samaḥ, identical in respect of non-eternality.

493. If one finding that things which are homogeneous possess equal characters, opposes an argument by attributing non-eternality to all things, the opposition will be called "balancing the non-eternality".

A certain person, to prove the non-eternality of sound, argues as follows:—

Sound is non-eternal,
because it is a product,
like a pot.

A certain other person offers a futile opposition thus:—

If sound is non-eternal on account of its being homogeneous with a pot which is non-eternal, it will follow as a consequence that all things are non-eternal because they are in some one or other respect homogeneous with the pot— a consequence which will render all inferences impossible for want of heterogeneous examples. This sort of opposition is called "balancing the non-eternal" which seeks to counteract an argument on the alleged ground that all things are non-eternal.

साधर्म्म्यादसिद्धेः प्रतिषेधासिद्धिः प्रतिषेध्यसाधर्म्म्याच्च ॥
५ । १ । ३३ ॥

साधर्म्म्यात् sâdharmyât, through resemblance ; असिद्धेः a-siddheḥ, because of non-establishment ; प्रतिषेधासिद्धिः pratiṣedha-asiddhiḥ, non-establishment of contradiction ; प्रतिषेध्यसाधर्म्म्यात् pratiṣedhya-sâdharmyât, through resemblance to what is to be contradicted ; च cha, and.

494. The opposition, we say, is unfounded because nothing can be established from a mere homogeneity and because there is homogeneity even with that which is opposed.

The Naiyâyika says:—

We cannot ascertain the character of a thing from its mere homogeneity with another thing: in doing so we must consider the logical connection between the reason and the predicate. Sound, for instance, is non-eternal not merely because it is homogeneous with a non-eternal pot but because there is a universal connection between "being a product" and "being non-eternal." Hence it will be unreasonable to conclude that all things are non-eternal simply because they are homogeneous with a non-eternal pot in some one or other respect. Similarly a mere homogeneity of all things with the eternal sky in some one or other respect, does not prove all things to be eternal. The opposition called "balancing the non-eternal" is therefore not founded on a sound basis.

दृष्टान्ते च साध्यसाधनभावेन प्रज्ञातस्य धर्म्मस्य हेतुत्वा-
त्तस्य चोभयथाभावान्नाविशेषः ॥ ५ । १ । ३४ ॥

दृष्टान्ते dṛiṣṭânte, in the example ; च cha, and ; साध्यसाधनभावेन sâdhya-sâdhana-bhâvena, by the relation of the thing to be established and the means of establishing it ; प्रज्ञातस्य prajñâtasya, of the known ; धर्म्मस्य dharmasya, of property ; हेतुत्वात् hetu tvât, being the reason ; तस्य tasya, its ; च cha, and ; उभयथा ubhaya-thâ, both ways ; भावात् bhâvât, from existence ; न na, not ; अविशेषः a-viśeṣaḥ, non-difference.

495. There is, we say, no non-distinction, because the reason is known to be the character which abides in the example as conducive to the establishment of the predicate and because it is applied in both ways.

The Naiyâyika says that we are not justified in concluding that all things are non-eternal because there is no character in respect of which "all things" may be homogeneous with a pot. In order to arrive at a correct conclusion we must consider the reason as being that character of the example (and consequently of the subject) which bears a universal connection with the character of the predicate. The pot possesses no such character in common with "all things." The reason moreover is applied in the homogeneous as well as in the heterogeneous ways. We cannot draw a conclusion from a mere homogeneity of the subject with the example in a certain respect. The opposition called "balancing the non-eternal" is therefore unreasonable.

नित्यमनित्यभावादनित्ये नित्यत्वोपपत्तेर्नित्यसमः ॥ ५ । १ । ३५ ॥

नित्यं nityam, eternally ; अनित्यभावात् anitya-bhâvât, from the nature of being non-eternal ; अनित्ये anitye, in the non-eternal ; अनित्यत्वोपपत्तेः anitya-tva-upapatteḥ, from proof of eternality ; नित्यसमः nitya-samaḥ, identical in respect of eternal.

496. If one opposes an argument by attributing eternality to all non-eternal things on the ground of these being eternally non-eternal, the opposition will be called "balancing the eternal."

A certain person, to prove the non-eternality of sound, argues as follows:—

Sound is non-eternal,
because it is a product,
like a pot.

A certain other person offers a futile opposition thus:—You say that sound is non eternal. Does this non-eternality exist in sound always or only sometimes ? If the non-eternality exists *always*, the sound must also be always existent, or, in other words, sound is eternal. If the non-eternality exists only *sometimes*, then too the sound must in the absence of non-eternality be pronounced to be eternal. This sort of opposition is called "balancing the eternal" which counteracts an argument by setting up eternality as a balance against it.

प्रतिषेध्ये नित्यमनित्यभावादनित्ये नित्यत्वोपपत्तेः प्रतिषेधाभावः ॥ ५ । १ । ३६ ॥

प्रतिषेध्ये pratiṣedhye, in what is to be contradicted ; नित्यं nityam, eternally ; अनित्यभावात् anitya-bhâvât, from the nature of being non-eternal ; अनित्ये anitye, in the non-eternal ; नित्यत्वोपपत्तेः nityatva-upapatteḥ, from proof of eternality ; प्रतिषेधाभावः pratiṣedha-abhâvaḥ, absence of contradiction.

497. This is, we say, no opposition because the thing opposed is always non-eternal on account of the eternality of the non-eternal.

The Naiyâyika says :—

By speaking of eternality of the non-eternal you have admitted sound to be *always* non-eternal and cannot now deny its non-eternality. The eternal and non-eternal are incompatible with each other : by admitting that sound is non-eternal you are precluded from asserting that it is also eternal. Hence "balancing the eternal" is not a sound opposition.

प्रयत्नकार्य्यानेकत्वात्कार्य्यसमः ॥ ५ । १ । ३७ ॥

प्रयत्नकार्य्यानेकत्वात् prayatna-kârya-aneka-tvât, from the diversity of the effects of effort ; कार्य्यसमः kârya-samaḥ, identical in respect of effect.

498. If one opposes an argument by showing the diversity of the effect of efforts, the opposition will be called "balancing the effect."

A certain person to prove the non-eternality of sound, argues as follows:—

Sound is non-eternal,

because it is an effect of effort.

A certain other person offers a futile opposition thus :—

The effect of effort is found to be of two kinds, *viz.* (1) the production of something which was previously non-existent, *e. g.* a pot, and (2) the revelation of something already existent, *e.g.* water in a well. Is sound an effect of the first kind or of the second kind ? If sound is an effect of the first kind it will be non-eternal but if it is of the second kind it will be eternal. Owing to this diversity of the effect of effort, it is not possible to conclude that sound is non-eternal. This sort of opposition is called "balancing the effect."

कार्य्यान्यत्वे प्रयत्नाहेतुत्वमनुपलब्धिकारणोपपत्तेः ॥५।१।३८॥

कार्य्यान्यत्वे kârya-anya-tve, in respect of the otherness of the effect; प्रयत्नाहेतुत्वम् prayatna-a-hetu-tvam, effort is not the cause; अनुपलब्धिकारणोपपत्तेः an-upalabdhi-kârana-upapatteh, because of proof of the canse of non-perception.

499. Effort did not give rise to the second kind of effect, because there was no cause of non-perception.

The Naiyâyika answers the opposition called "balancing the effect" as follows :—

We cannot say that sound is revealed by our effort because we are unable to prove that it existed already. That sound did not exist previously is proved by our non-perception of the same at the time. You cannot say that our non-perception was caused by a veil because no veil covered sound. Hence sound is an effect which is not revealed but produced.

प्रतिषेधेऽपि समानो दोषः ॥ ५ । १ । ३९ ॥

प्रतिषेधे pratiṣedhe, in the case of contradiction; अपि api, also; समानः samânaḥ, similar; दोषः doṣaḥ, defect.

500. The same defect, we say, attaches to the opposition too.

A certain person argued:—

Sound is non-eternal,

because it is an effect of effort.

A certain other person opposed it saying that sound would not be non-eternal if "effect" meant a thing revealed.

The Naiyâyika observes that if an argument is to be set aside owing to an ambiguous meaning of the word "effect", why is not the opposition too set aside on the same ground? The reason in the argument is as erratic as that in the opposition. Just as there is no special ground to suppose that the "effect" in the argument signified "a thing produced and not revealed," so also there is no special ground to suppose that the word in the opposition signified "a thing revealed and not produced." Hence the opposition called "balancing the effect" is self-destructive.

सर्व्वत्रैवम् ॥ ५ । १ । ४० ॥

सर्वत्र sarvatra, everywhere ; एवम् evam, similarly.

501. Thus everywhere.

If a special meaning is to be attached to the opposition, the same meaning will have to be attached to the original argument. In this respect there will be an equality of the two sides in the case of all kinds of opposition such as "balancing the homogeneity", etc.

प्रतिषेधविप्रतिषेधे प्रतिषेधदोषवद्दोषः ॥ ५ । १ । ४१ ॥

प्रतिषेधविप्रतिषेधे pratiṣedha-vipratiṣedhe, in respect of the contradiction of a contradiction ; प्रतिषेधदोषवत् pratiṣedha-doṣa-vat, as in the case of defect in contradiction ; दोषः doṣaḥ, defect

502. Defect attaches to the opposition of the opposition just as it attaches to the opposition.

A certain person to prove the non-eternality of sound, argues as follows:—

Sound is non-eternal,
because it is an effect of effort.

A certain other person, seeing that the effect is of diverse kinds, offers an opposition thus :—

Sound is eternal,
because it is an effect of effort.

(Here "effect" may mean "a thing revealed by effort.")

The arguer replies that sound cannot be concluded to be eternal because the reason "effect" is erratic (which may mean "a thing produced by effort").

The opponent rises again to say that sound cannot also be concluded to be non-eternal because the reason "effect" is erratic (which may mean a thing revealed by effort). So the defect which is pointed out in the case of the opposition, may also be pointed out in the case of the opposition of the opposition.

प्रतिषेधं सदोषमभ्युपेत्य प्रतिषेधविप्रतिषेधे समानो दोषप्रसङ्गो मतानुज्ञा ॥ ५ । १ । ४२ ॥

प्रतिषेधं pratiṣedham, contradiction ; सदोषं sadoṣam, with defect, defective ; अभ्युपेत्य abhyupetya, admitting for the sake of argument ; प्रतिषेधविप्रतिषेधे pratiṣedha-vipratiṣedhe, in case of contradiction of a contradiction ; समानः samânaḥ, similar, same ; दोषप्रसंगः doṣa-prasaṅgaḥ, implication of defect ; मतानुज्ञा mata-anujñâ, admission of an opinion.

503. If one admits the defect of his opposition in consequence of his statement that an equal defect attaches to the opposition of the opposition, it will be called "admission of an opinion."

A certain person lays down a proposition which is opposed by a certain other person. The first person, *viz.* the disputant, charges the opposition made by the second person, *viz.* the opponent, with a defect, *e.g*, that the reason is erratic. The opponent instead of rescuing his opposition from the defect with which it has been charged by the disputant, goes on charging the disputant's opposition of the opposition with the same defect. The counter-charge which the opponent brings in this way is interpreted by the disputant to be an admission of the defect pointed out by him. The disputant's reply consisting of this kind of interpretation is called "admission of an opinion."

स्वपक्षलक्षणापेक्षोपपत्त्युपसंहारे हेतुनिर्देशे परपक्षदोषाभ्युपगमात्समानो दोष इति ॥ ५ । १ । ४३ ॥

स्वपक्षलक्षणापेक्षोपपत्त्युपसंहारे svapakṣa-lakṣaṇa-apekṣa-upapatti-upasaṃhâre, in the conclusion by demonstration (in the opposite side) of, instead of removing, the defect in one's own side ; हेतुनिर्देशे hetu-nirdeśe, in the statement of reason ; परपक्षदोषाभ्युपगमात् para-pakṣa-doṣa-abhyupagamât, from admission of the defect of other side ; दोषः doṣaḥ, defect ; इति iti, it is.

504. "Admission of an opinion" also occurs when the disputant instead of employing reasons to rescue his side from the defect with which it has been charged, proceeds to admit the defect in consequence of his statement that the same defect belongs to his opponent's side as well.

Six-winged disputation (Ṣaṭpakṣî kathâ).

Disputant—to prove the non-eternality of sound says:—

Sound is non-eternal,

because it is an effect of effort.

This is the first wing.

Opponent—seeing that the effect is of diverse kinds, offers an opposition thus:—

Sound is eternal,

because it is an effect of effort.

(Here "effect" means a thing which already existed and is now revealed by effort).

This is the second wing.

Disputant—seeing that the reason "effect" is erratic, charges the opposition with a defect thus :—

Sound is *not* eternal,

because it is an effect of effort.

(Here the reason "effect" is erratic meaning (1) either a thing that did not previously exist and is now produced or (2) a thing that already existed and is now revealed by effort).

This is the third wing.

Opponent— finding that the reason "effect," which is erratic, proves neither the eternality nor the non-eternality of sound, brings a counter-charge against the disputant thus :—

Sound is also *not* non-eternal,

because it is an effect of effort.

He alleges that the defect (*viz.* the erraticity of the reason) with which his opposition (*viz.* sound is eternal) is charged, also attaches to the opposition of the opposition made by the disputant (*viz.* sound is *not* eternal or non-eternal).

This is the fourth wing.

Disputant—finding that the counter-charge brought against him amounts to his opponent's admission of self-defect says:—

The opponent by saying that "sound is also not non-eternal" has admitted that it is also not eternal. In other words, the counter-charge has proved the charge, that is, it has indicated that the opponent admits the disputant's opinion.

This is the fifth wing.

Opponent— finding that the disputant instead of rescuing his argument from the counter-charge has taken shelter under his opponent's admission of the charge says:—

The disputant by saying that "sound is also not eternal" has admitted that it is also not non-eternal. In other words, if the counter-charge proves the charge, the reply to the counter-charge proves the counter-charge itself.

This is the sixth wing.

The first, third and fifth wings belong to the disputant while the second, fourth and sixth to the opponent. The sixth wing is a repetition of the fourth while the fifth wing is a repetition of the third. The sixth wing is also a repetition of the meaning of the fifth wing. The third and fourth wings involve the defect of "admission of an opinion." All the wings except the first three are unessential.

The disputation would have come to a fair close at the third wing if the disputant had pointed out that the word "effect" had a special meaning, *viz.*, a thing which did not previously exist but was produced.

The disputant and the opponent instead of stopping at the proper limit has carried on their disputation through six wings beyond which no further wing is possible. After the six-winged disputation has been carried on, it becomes patent that neither the disputant nor the opponent is a fit person to be argued with.

BOOK V.—CHAPTER II.

प्रतिज्ञाहानिः प्रतिज्ञान्तरं प्रतिज्ञाविरोधः प्रतिज्ञासन्न्यासो हेत्वन्तरमर्थान्तरं निरर्थकमविज्ञातार्थमपार्थकमप्राप्तकालं न्यूनमधिकं पुनरुक्तमननुभाषणमज्ञानमप्रतिभा विक्षेपो मतानुज्ञा पर्य्यनुयोज्योपेक्षणं निरनुयोज्यानुयोगोऽपसिद्धान्तो हेत्वाभासाश्च निग्रहस्थानानि ॥ ५ । २ । १ ॥

प्रतिज्ञाहानिः Pratijñâ-hâniḥ, injury to the proposition; प्रतिज्ञान्तरं pratijñâ-antaram, change of proposition; प्रतिज्ञाविरोधः pratijñâ-virodhaḥ, conflict of proposition; प्रतिज्ञासंन्यासः pratijñâ-sannyâsaḥ, abandonment of proposition; हेत्वन्तरं hetu-antaram, change of the reason; अर्थान्तरं artha-antaram, change of topic; निरर्थकं nir-arthakam, meaningless; अविज्ञातार्थं a-vijñâta-artham, unintelligible; अपार्थकं apa-arthakam, senseless; अप्राप्तकालं a-prâpta-kâlam, before-time, disordered, misarranged, न्यूनं nyûnam, deficient; अधिकं adhikam, too much, superfluous, verbose; पुनरुक्तं punar-uktam, repetition; अननुभाषणं an-anubhâṣaṇam, non-reply, silence ; अज्ञानं ; a-jñânam, ignorance; अप्रतिभा a-pratibhâ, want of ready wit; विक्षेपः vikṣepaḥ, evasion, diversion ; मतानुज्ञा, mata-anujñâ, admission of an opinion ; पर्य्यनुयोज्योपेक्षणं paryanuyojya-upekṣaṇam, overlooking the censurable ; निरनुयोज्यानुयोगः niranuyojya-anuyogaḥ, censuring the non-censurable ; अपसिद्धान्तः apa-siddhântaḥ, contrary tenet ; हेत्वाभासाः hetu-âbhâsâḥ. pseudo-marks ; च cha, and ; निग्रहस्थानानि nigraha-sthânâni, grounds of defeat, occasions for rebuke.

505. The occasions for rebuke are the following:—

1. Hurting the proposition, 2. Shifting the proposition, 3. Opposing the proposition, 4. Renouncing the proposition, 5. Shifting the reason, 6. Shifting the topic, 7. The meaningless, 8. The unintelligible, 9. The incoherent, 10. The inopportune, 11. Saying too little, 12. Saying too much, 13. Repetition, 14. Silence, 15. Ignorance, 16. Non-ingenuity, 17. Evasion, 18. Admission of an opinion, 19 Overlooking the censurable, 20. Censuring the non-censurable, 21. Deviating from a tenet, and 22. The semblance of a reason.

The definition of "an occasion for rebuke" has been given in aphorism 1-2-19. "An occasion for rebuke" which is the same as "a ground of defeat", "a place of humiliation" or "a point of disgrace" arises generally in connection with the proposition or any other part of an argument and may implicate any disputant whether he is a discutient, wrangler or caviller.

प्रतिदृष्टान्तधर्म्माभ्यनुज्ञा स्वदृष्टान्ते प्रतिज्ञाहानिः ॥५।२।२॥

प्रतिदृष्टान्तधर्म्माभ्यनुज्ञा pratidṛṣṭânta-dharma-abhyanujñâ, admission of the property of the counter-example ; स्वदृष्टान्ते sva-dṛṣṭânte, in one's own example ; प्रतिज्ञाहानिः pratijñâ-hâniḥ, injury to the proposition.

506. "Hurting the proposition" occurs when one admits in one's own example the character of a counter-example.

A disputant argues as follows:—

Sound is non-eternal,

Because it is cognisable by sense,

Whatever is cognisable by sense is non-eternal as a pot,

Sound is cognisable by sense,

Therefore sound is non-eternal.

A certain other person offers an opposition thus :—

A genus (*e. g.*, potness or pot-type), which is cognisable by sense, is found to be eternal, why cannot then the sound which is also cognisable by sense, be eternal ?

The disputant being thus opposed says :—

Whatever is cognisable by sense is eternal as a pot,

Sound is cognisable by sense,

Therefore sound is eternal.

By thus admitting in his example (pot) the character of a counter-example (genus or type), he has hurt his own proposition (*viz.* sound is non-eternal). A person who hurts his proposition in this way deserves nothing but rebuke.

प्रतिज्ञातार्थप्रतिषेधे धर्म्मविकल्पात्तदर्थनिर्द्देशः प्रतिज्ञान्तरम् ॥ ५ । २ । ३ ॥

प्रतिज्ञातार्थप्रतिषेधे pratijñâta-artha-pratiṣedhe, there being opposition to the object or topic proposed; धर्मविकल्पात् dharma-vikalpât, through a different property; तदर्थनिर्देशः tat-artha-nirdeśaḥ, statement of that object; प्रतिज्ञान्तरम् pratijñâ-antaram, change of proposition.

507. "Shifting the proposition" arises when a proposition being opposed one defends it by importing a new character to one's example and counter-example.

A certain person argues as follows:—

Sound is non-eternal,

because it is cognisable by sense

like a pot.

A certain other person offers an opposition thus:—

Sound is eternal,

because it is cognisable by sense like a genus (or type).

The first person in order to defend himself says that a genus (or type) and a pot are both cognisable by sense, yet one is all-pervasive and the other is not so: hence the sound which is likened to a pot is non-all-pervasively non-eternal.

The defence thus made involves a change of proposition. The proposition originally laid down was:—

Sound is non-eternal,

while the proposition now defended is:

Sound is non-all-pervasively non-eternal.

A person who shifts his proposition in this way is to be rebuked inasmuch as he has not relied upon his original reason and example.

प्रतिज्ञाहेत्वोर्विरोधः प्रतिज्ञाविरोधः ॥ ५ । २ । ४ ॥

प्रतिज्ञाहेत्वोः pratijñâ-hetvoḥ. of the proposition and the reason; विरोधः virodhaḥ, contradiction; प्रतिज्ञाविरोधः pratijñâ-virodhaḥ, conflict of proposition.

508. "Opposing the proposition" occurs when the proposition and its reason are opposed to each other.

Substance is distinct from quality,

because it is perceived to be non-distinct from colour, etc.

In this argument it is to be observed that if substance is distinct from quality, it must also be distinct from colour, etc. which constitute the quality. The reason, *viz.* substance is non-distinct from colour, etc., is opposed to the proposition, *viz.* substance is distinct from quality. A person who thus employs a reason which opposes his proposition is to be rebuked as a fool.

पक्षप्रतिषेधे प्रतिज्ञातार्थापनयनं प्रतिज्ञासन्न्यासः ॥५।२।५॥

पक्षप्रतिषेधे pakṣa-pratiṣedhe, there being opposition to the subject; प्रतिज्ञातार्थापनयनम् pratijñâta-artha apanayanam, removal of the object proposed; प्रतिज्ञासन्न्यासः pratijñâ-sannyâsaḥ, abandonment of the proposition.

509. A proposition being opposed if one disclaims its import, it will be called "renouncing the proposition."

A certain person argues as follows:—

Sound is non-eternal,

because it is cognisable by sense.

A certain other person offers an opposition thus:—

Just as a genus (or type) is cognisable by sense and is not yet non-eternal, so a sound is cognisable by sense and is not yet non-eternal. The first person, as a defence against the opposition, disclaims the meaning of his proposition thus:—

Who says that sound is non-eternal?

This sort of denial of the import of one's own proposition is called "renouncing the proposition" which rightly furnishes an occasion for rebuke.

अविशेषोक्ते हेतौ प्रतिषिद्धे विशेषमिच्छतो हेत्वन्तरम् ॥५।२।६॥

अविशेषोक्ते a-viśeṣa-ukte, stated without particulars, of a general character; हेतौ hetau, reason, mark; प्रतिषिद्धे pratiṣiddhe, being opposed; विशेषं viśeṣam, particular or special character; इच्छतः ichchhataḥ, of one who desires; हेत्वन्तरम hetu-antaram, change of reason.

510. "Shifting the reason" occurs when the reason of a general character being opposed one attaches a special character to it.

A certain person, to prove the non-eternality of sound, argues as follows:—

Sound is non-eternal,

because it is cognisable by sense.

A certain other person says that sound cannot be proved to be non-eternal through the mere reason of its being cognisable by sense, just as a genus (or type) such as pot-ness (or pot-type) is cognisable by sense and is not yet non-eternal.

The first person defends himself by saying that the reason, *viz.* being cognisable by sense, is to be understood as signifying that which comes under a genus (or type) and is as such cognisable by sense. Sound comes under the genus (or type) "soundness" and is at the same time cognisable by sense; but a genus or type such as pot-ness or pot-type does not come under another genus or type (such as pot-ness-ness or pot-type-type) though it is cognisable by sense. Such a defence, which consists in shifting one's reason, rightly furnishes an occasion for rebuke.

प्रकृतादर्थादप्रतिसम्बद्धार्थमर्थान्तरम् ॥ ५ । २ । ७ ॥

प्रकृतात् prakṛitât, real, under consideration; अर्थात् arthât, from the object; अप्रतिसम्बद्धार्थम् a-pratisambaddhârtham, importing an un-correlated, irrelevant object; अर्थान्तरम् artha antaram, change of topic or object.

511. "Shifting the topic" is an argument which setting aside the real topic introduces one which is irrelevant.

A certain person, to prove the eternality of sound, argues as follows:—

Sound is eternal (proposition),

because it is intangible (reason).

Being opposed by a certain other person he attempts, in the absence of any other resource, to defend his position as follows:—

Hetu, which is the Sanskrit equivalent for "reason," is a word derived from the root "hi" with the suffix "tu". A word, as a part of a speech, may be a noun, a verb, a prefix or an indeclinable. A noun is defined as etc. etc.

The defence made in this way furnishes an instance of defeat through non-relevancy. The person who makes it deserves rebuke.

वर्णक्रमनिर्द्देशवन्निरर्थकम् ॥ ५ । २ । ८ ॥

वर्णक्रमनिर्द्देशवत् varṇa-krama-nirdeśa-vat, like the statement of the order of letters (in the alphabet); निरर्थकम् nir-arthakam, meaningless.

512. "The meaningless" is an argument which is based on a non-sensical combination of letters into a series.

A certain person, to prove the eternality of sound, argues as follows:—

Sound is eternal,

because k, c, ṭ, t and p are j, v, g, ḍ and d,

like jh, bh, gh, ḍh and dh.

As the letters k, c, ṭ, etc. convey no meaning, the person who employs them in his argument deserves rebuke.

परिषत्प्रतिवादिभ्यां त्रिरभिहितमप्यविज्ञातमविज्ञातार्थम् ॥ ५ । २ । ९ ॥

परिषत्प्रतिवादिभ्यां pariṣat-prativâdibhyâm, by the assembly and the opponent ; त्रिः triḥ, three times; अभिहितं abhihitam, stated ; अपि api, even; अविज्ञातं a-vijñâtam, not understood ; अविज्ञातार्थं a-vijñâta-artham, unintelligible

513. "The unintelligible" is an argument, which although repeated three times, is understood neither by the audience nor by the opponent.

A certain person being opposed by another person and finding no means of self-defence, attempts to hide his inability in disputation by using words of double entendre or words not in ordinary use or words very quickly uttered which as such are understood neither by his opponent nor by the audience although they are repeated three times. This sort of defence is called "unintelligible" which rightly furnishes an occasion for rebuke.

पौर्वापर्य्यायोगादप्रतिसम्बद्धार्थमपार्थकम् ॥ ५ । २ । १० ॥

पौर्वापर्य्यायोगात् paurvya-âparya-a-yogât, owing to absence of seqnence; अप्रतिसम्बद्धार्थम् a-pratisambaddha-artham, of unconnected import ; अपार्थकम् apa-arthakam, senseless.

514. "The incoherent" is an argument which conveys no connected meaning on account of the words being strung together without any syntactical order.

A certain person being opposed by another person and finding no other means of self-defence, argues as follows:—

Ten pomegranates, six cakes, a bowl, goat's skin and a lump of sweets.

This sort of argument, which consist of a series of unconnected words, is called "the incoherent" which rightly presents on occasion for rebuke.

अवयवविपर्य्यासवचनमप्राप्तकालम् ॥ ५ । २ । ११ ॥

अवयवविपर्य्यासवचनं avayava-viparyâsa-vachanam, statement without the order of the member of an argument ; अप्राप्तकालं a-prâpta-kâlam, disordered.

515. "The inopportune" is an argument the parts of which are mentioned without any order of precedence.

A certain person, to prove that the hill has fire, argues as follows:—

The hill has fire (proposition).

Whatever has smoke has fire, as a kitchen (example).

Because it has smoke (reason).

The hill has fire (conclusion).

The hill has smoke(application).

This sort of argument is called "the inopportune" which rightly presents an occasion for rebuke. Since the meaning of an argument is affected by the order in which its parts are arranged, the person who overlooks the order cannot establish his conclusion and is therefore rebuked.

हीनमन्यतमेनाप्यवयवेन न्यूनम् ॥ ५ । २ । १२ ॥

हीनं hînam, deficient ; अन्यतमेन anya-tamena, by any one ; अपि api, even ; अवयवेन avayavena, member ; न्यूनम् nyûnam, deficient.

516. If an argument lacks even one of its parts, it is called "saying too little."

The following is an argument which contains all its five parts:—

1. The hill has fire (proposition),
2. Because it has smoke (reason),
3. All that has smoke has fire, as a kitchen (example),
4. The hill has smoke (application),
5. Therefore the hill has fire (conclusion).

As all the five parts or members are essential, a person who omits even one of them should be scolded as "saying too little."

हेतूदाहरणाधिकमधिकम् ॥ ५ । २ । १३ ॥

हेतूदाहरणाधिकं hetu-udâharaṇa-adhikam, consisting of more than one reason or example ; अधिकम् adhikam, verbose, redundant.

517. "Saying too much" is an argument which consists of more than one reason or example.

A certain person, to prove that the hill has fire, argues as follows:—

The hill has fire (proposition),
Because it has smoke (reason),
And because it has light (reason),
like a kitchen (example),
and like a furnace (example),

In this argument the second reason and the second example are redundant.

A person, who having promised to argue in the proper way (according to the established usage), employs more than one reason or example is to be rebuked as "saying too much."

शब्दार्थयोः पुनर्वचनं पुनरुक्तमन्यत्रानुवादात् ॥ ५ । २ । १४ ॥

शब्दार्थयोः śabda-arthayoḥ, of the word and the object ; पुनर्वचनं punar-vachanam, restatement ; पुनरुक्त punar-uktam, repetition ; अन्यत्र anyatra, elsewhere ; अनुवादात् anuvâdât, than re-inculcation, anuvâda.

518. "Repetition" is an argument in which (except in the case of reinculcation) the word or the meaning is said over again.

"*Repetition of the word*—Sound is non-eternal,

sound is non-eternal.

Repetition of the meaning—Sound is non-eternal,

echo is perishable, what is heard is impermanent, etc.

A person who unnecessarily commits repetition is to be rebuked as a fool.

Reinculcation has been explained in aphorism 2-1-65.

अर्थादापन्नस्य स्वशब्देन पुनर्व्वचनम् ॥ ५ । २ । १५ ॥

अर्थात् arthât, from context ; आपन्नस्य âpannasya, of what has followed ; स्वशब्देन sva-śabdena, by its own name ; पुनर्वचनं punar-vachanam, restatement.

519. "Repetition" consists also in mentioning a thing by name although the thing has been indicated through presumption.

"A thing possessing the character of a product is non-eternal" —this is a mere repetition of the following:—

"A thing not possessing the character of a product is not non-eternal."

विज्ञातस्य परिषदा त्रिरभिहितस्याप्यप्रत्युच्चारणमननुभाषणम् ॥ ५ । २ । १६ ॥

विज्ञातस्य vijñâtasya, of what has been understood ; परिषदा pariṣadâ, by the assembly; त्रिः triḥ, three times ; अभिहितस्य abhihita- sya, of what has been declared ; अपि. even ; अप्रत्युच्चारणम् a-prati-uchchâraṇam, non-reply; अननुभाषणम् an-anubhâṣaṇam, non-reply.

520. "Silence" is an occasion for rebuke which arises when the opponent makes no reply to a proposition although it has been repeated three times by the disputant within the knowledge of the audience.

How can a disputant carry on his argument if his opponent maintains an attitude of stolid silence? The opponent is therefore to be rebuked.

अविज्ञातञ्चाज्ञानम् ॥ ५ । २ । १७ ॥

अविज्ञातम् a-vijñâtam, the not-understood; च cha, and ; अज्ञानं a-jñânam ignorance.

521. "Ignorance" is the non-understanding of a proposition.

Ignorance is betrayed by the opponent who does not understand a proposition although it has been repeated three times within the knowledge of the audience. How can an opponent refute a proposition the meaning of which he cannot understand ? He is to be rebuked for his ignorance.

उत्तरस्याप्रतिपत्तिरप्रतिभा ॥ ५ । २ । १८ ॥

उत्तरस्य uttarasya, of the answer; अप्रतिपत्तिः a-pratipattiḥ, non-suggestion; अप्रतिभा a-pratibhâ, want of ready wit.

522. "Non-ingenuity" consists in one's inability to hit upon a reply.

A certain person lays down a proposition. If his opponent understands it and yet cannot hit upon a reply, he is to be scolded as wanting in ingenuity.

कार्य्यव्यासङ्गात कथाविच्छेदो विक्षेपः ॥ ५ । २ । १९ ॥

कार्यव्यासङ्गात kârya-vyâsaṅgât, through pretext of other business; कथाविच्छेदः kathâ-vichchhedaḥ, cutting short a discussion ; विक्षेपः vikṣepaḥ, evasion, diversion.

523. "Evasion" arises if one stops an argument on the pretext of going away to attend another business.

A certain person having commenced a disputation in which he finds it impossible to establish his side, stops its further progress by saying that he has to go away on a very urgent business. He who stops the disputation in this way courts defeat and humiliation through evasion.

स्वपक्षदोषाभ्युपगमात् परपक्षदोषप्रसङ्गो मतानुज्ञा ॥ ५ । २ । २० ॥

स्वपक्षदोषाभ्युपगमात् sva-pakṣa-doṣa-abhyupagamât, by admitting defect in one's own side ; परपक्षे para-pakṣe, in the opposite side ; दोषप्रसंगः doṣa-prasaṅgaḥ, attribution of defect ; मतानुज्ञा mata-anujñâ, admission of an opinion.

524. "The admission of an opinion" consists in charging the opposite side with a defect by admitting that the same defect exists in one's own side.

A certain person addressing another person says:—"You are a thief."

The other person replies :—"You too are a thief."

This person, instead of removing the charge brought against him, throws the same charge on the opposite side whereby he admits that the charge against himself is true. This sort of counter-charge or reply is an instance of "admission of an opinion" which brings disgrace on the person who makes it.

निग्रहस्थानप्राप्तस्यानिग्रहः पर्य्यनुयोज्योपेक्षणम् ॥ ५ । २ । २१॥

निग्रहस्थानप्राप्तस्य nigraha-sthâna-prâptasya, of one who has reached the ground of defeat ; अनिग्रहः a-nigrahaḥ, not defeating ; पर्य्यनुयोज्योपेक्षणम् par-yanuyojya-upekṣaṇam, overlooking the censurable.

525. "Overlooking the censurable" consists in not rebuking a person who deserves rebuke.

It is not at all unfair to censure a person who argues in a way which furnishes an occasion for censure. Seeing that the person himself does not confess his short-coming, it is the duty of the audience to pass a vote of censure on him. If the audience failed to do their duty they would earn rebuke for themselves on account of their "over-looking the censurable."

अनिग्रहस्थाने निग्रहस्थानाभियोगो निरनुयोज्यानुयोगः ॥

५ । २ । २२ ॥

अनिग्रहस्थाने a-nigraha-sthâne, in case of non defeat ; निग्रहस्थानाभियोगः nigraha-sthâna-abhiyogaḥ, accusation of defeat ; निरनुयोज्यानुयोगः nir-anu-yojya-anuyogaḥ, censuring the non-censurable.

526. "Censuring the non-censurable" consists in rebuking a person who does not deserve rebuke.

A person brings discredit on himself if he rebukes a person who does not deserve rebuke.

सिद्धान्तमभ्युपेत्यानियमात्कथाप्रसङ्गोऽपसिद्धान्तः ॥ ५ २ ।२३॥

सिद्धान्तं siddhântam, tenet ; अभ्युपेत्य abhyupetya, accepting ; अनियमात a-niyamat, through departure, or wandering ; कथाप्रसंगः kathâ-prasaṅgaḥ, disputation ; अपसिद्धान्तः apa-siddhântaḥ, contrary to tenet.

527. A person who after accepting a tenet departs from it in the course of his disputation, is guilty of "deviating from a tenet."

A certain person promises to carry on his argument in consonance with the Sâṃkhya philosophy which lays down that (1) what is existent never becomes non-existent, and (2) what is non existent never comes into existence, etc. A certain other person opposes him by saying that all human activity would be impossible if the thing now non-existent could not come into existence in the course of time and that no activity would cease if what is existent now could continue for ever. If the first person being thus opposed admits that existence springs from non existence and non-existence from existence, then he will rightly deserve rebuke for his deviation from the accepted tenet.

हेत्वाभासाश्च यथोक्ताः ॥ ५ । २ । २४ ॥

हेत्वाभासाः hetu-âbhâsâḥ, pseudo-marks ; च cha, and ; यथोक्ताः yathâ-uktâḥ, as stated before.

528. "The fallacies of reason" already explained do also furnish occasions for rebuke.

From aphorism 1-2-4 it is evident that the fallacies are mere semblances of a reason. A person who employs them in a disputation does certainly deserve rebuke.

There are infinite occasions for rebuke of which only twenty-two have been enumerated here.

APPENDIX A.

NYÂYA-SÛCHÎ-NIBANDHA

of

VÂCHASPATI MIŚRA

[Based on the text edited by Dr. Gaṅgânâtha Jhâ, M. A., D. Litt., and published in the Chaukhamba Sanskrit Series, Benares.]

The Nyâya-Śâstra contains five books, ten chapters, eighty-four topics, five hundred and twenty-eight aphorisms, one hundred and ninety-six measures, and eight thousand, three hundred and eighty-five syllables.

[Book=adhyâya, Chapter=âhṇika, *lit.* a daily portion, Topic=prakaraṇa, Aphorism=Sûtra, Measure=pada, Syllable=akṣara.]

Adhyâya—I: Âhṇika.—1: Prakaraṇas—7 : Sûtras—41.

1. Statement of the subject matter (viṣaya), purpose (prayojana) and relation (sambandha) of the Śastra—Ss. 1-2.
2. Definition of Pramâṇa (Instrument of Right Cognition)—Ss. 3-8.
3. Definition of Prameya (Object of Right Cognition)—Ss.9-22.
4. Definition of the pre-requisites (pûrva aṅga) of a Nyâya—Ss.23-25.
5. Definition of Siddhânta (Tenet) which is the basis of a Nyâya–Ss.26-31.
6. Definition of Nyâya (Process of Ratiocination or Reasoning) —Ss.32-39.
7. Definition of processes subsidiary (uttara aṅga) to a Nyâya —Ss. 40-41.

Adhyâya—I: Âhṇika-2 : Prakaraṇas-4 : Sûtras-20.

1. Definition of Kathâ (Controversy)—Ss. 1-3.
2. Definition of Hetvâbhâsa (Fallacious Marks of Inference)—Ss.4-9.
3. Definition of Chhala (lit. Fraud, Quibble) —Ss.10-17.
4. Definition of Liṅgadoṣa (General Fault in Marks of Inference) due to incapacity of the arguer (Puruṣa-aśakti)—Ss. 18-20.

Adhyâya—II: Âhnika-1: Prakaranas-9: Sûtras-68.

1. Examination of Saṃśaya (Doubt)—Ss. I-7.
2. Examination of Pramâṇa generally—Ss. 8-20.
3. Examination of Pratyakṣa (Perception)—Ss. 21-32.
4. Examination incidentally of Avayavî (the whole)—Ss. 33-36.
5. Examination of Anumâna (Inference)—Ss. 37-38.
6. Examination (introductory) of the present time—Ss. 39-43.
7. Examination of Upamâna (Analogy)—Ss. 44-48.
8. Examination of Śabda (lit. word, Testimony) generally-Ss. 49-56.
9. Examination of Śabda in particular (the Veda)—Ss. 57-68.

Adhyâya—II: Âhṇika 2: Prakaraṇas-4: Sûtras-69.

1. Examination of the fourfold division of Pramâṇa—Ss. 1-12.
2. Examination of the doctrine of the non-eternality of Śabda—Ss. 13-39.
3. Examination of the doctrine of Śabda-pariṇâma (Transformation of word)—Ss. 40-57.
4. Examination of Śabda-Śakti (Force of Word)—Ss. 58-69.

Adhyâya—III : Âhṇika-1: Prakarnas-9: Sûtras-73.

1. The Soul is over and above the Senses—Ss. 1-3.
2. The Soul is different from the Body—Ss.4-6.
3. Refutation (incidentally) of the doctrine that the Eye is only one —Ss. 7-14.
4. The Manas (Mind) is not the Soul—Ss.—15-17.
5. The Soul is eternal—Ss. 18-26.
6. Examination of the Body—Ss.27-31.
7. Examination of the materiality (bhautika-tva) of the Indriya (Sense)—Ss. 32-51.
8. The Indriya is manifold—Ss. 52-61.
9. Examination of Artha (Sense and Object of Sense)—Ss 62-73.

Adhyâya-III : Âhṇika-2:-Prakaraṇas 7 : Sûtras—72.

1. The Buddhi (Cognition) is not eternal—Ss. 1-9.
2. Introduction of the doctrine of Transiency (ksana-bhaṅga)—Ss. 10-17.
3. The Buddhi is an attribute of the Soul—Ss. 18-41.
4. The Buddhi perishes as soon as produced (utpanna-apavargitva) —Ss. 42-45.

5. The Buddhi is not a quality of the Body—Ss. 46-55.
6. Examination of the Manas—Ss 56-59.
7. The Body is produced by Adṛiṣṭa (Deserts)—Ss. 60-72.

Adhyâya-IV : Âhṇika-1: Prakaraṇas-14: Sûtras–67.

1. Examination of the Faults and Pravṛitti (Activity)—Ss. 1-2.
2. Doṣa (Fault) is threefold—Ss.3-9.
3. Fxamination of Pretya-bhâva (Re-birth)—Ss. 10-13.
4. The Upâdâna (material) cause of the Universe is not the Śûnya (Void)—Ss. 14-18.
5. Îsvara (God) is not the Upâdâna of the Universe—Ss. 19-21.
6. Chance is not the Upâdâna—Ss. 22-24.
7. Refutation of the doctrine that all is non-eternal (Sarva-anitya-tva) —Ss. 25-28.
8. Refutation of the doctrine that all is eternal (Sarva-nitya-tva) —Ss. 29-33.
9. Refutation of the doctrine that all is discrete (Sarva-pṛithak-tva) —Ss. 34-36.
10. Refutation of the doctrine that all is void (Sarva-śûnya-tâ-) —Ss. 37-40.
11. Refutation of the doctrine that the Reality is one or otherwise fixed in number (Saṃkhyâ-ekânta-vâda)—Ss. 41-43.
12. Examination of Phala (Fruit)—Ss. 44-53.
13. Examination of Duḥkha (Pain)—Ss. 54-57.
14. Examination of Apavarga (Release)—Ss. 58-67.

Adhyâya-IV : Âhṇika 2 : Prakaraṇas-6 : Sûtras—51.

1. Production of Tattva-jñâna (Knowledge of Reality)—Ss. 1-3.
2. Incidental examination of the relation of the whole (avayavî) and parts (avayava)—Ss. 4-17.
3. Examinaton of the Partless (niravayava, e. g. Atom)—Ss.18-25.
4. Refutation of the doctrine of the transiency of external objects (bâhya-artha-bhaṅga)—Ss. 26-37.
5. How Tattva-Jñâna is developed—Ss. 38-49.
6. How Tattva-Jñâna is maintained—Ss. 50-51.

Adhyâya-V: Âhṇika-1: Prakaraṇas-17: Sûtras-43.

1. Introduction of Parity of Reasoning (Jâti): (24): Identicals (2) in respect of Resemblance and Difference—Ss. 1-3.
2. Identicals (6) in relation to the Sâdhya (subject) and Dṛiṣṭânta (Example): that is, arising from the diverse properties of the Subject and the Example—Ss. 4-6.
3. Identicals (2) in respect of the extension or non-extension of the Hetu (Mark) to the Sâdhya (subject)—Ss. 7-8.
4. Identicals (2) in respect of regression and counter example—Ss. 9–11.
5. Identical (1) in respect of non-production—Ss. 12-13.
6. Identical (1) in respect of doubt— Ss. 14-15.
7. Identical (1) in respect of the Topic—Ss. 16-17.
8. Identical (1) in respect of non-Mark—Ss. 18-20.
9. Identical (1) in respect of Presumption—Ss. 21-22.
10. Identical (1) in respect of Non-difference—Ss. 23-24,
11. Identical (1) in respect of Demonstration—Ss. 25-26.
12. Identical (1) in respect of Cognition—Ss. 27-28.
13. Identical (1) in respect of Non-Cognition—Ss. 29-31.
14. Identical (1) in respect of the Non-eternal—Ss. 32-34.
15. Identical (1) in respect of the Eternal—Ss. 35-36.
16. Identical (1) in respect of the Effect—Ss. 37-38.
17. Futile Controversy of Six Steps—Ss. 39-43.

Adhyâya V : Âhṇika-2 : Prakaraṇas-7 : Sûtras-24.

1. Enunciation of the five Errors of the opponent depending upon the one or the other of the Proposition and the Mark—Ss. 1-6,
2. The four Errors leading to failure to establish the desired proposition —Ss. 7 10.
3. The three Errors leading to mispresentation of one's own conclusion —Ss. 11-13.
4. The Error of Repetition—Ss. 14-15.
5. The four Errors leading to failure to reply—Ss. 16-19.
6. The three Errors of acquiescence in a defect, failure to attack, and misplaced attack—Ss. 20-22.
7. The two Errors of Inconsistency and Fallacies—Ss. 23-24.

APPENDIX B.

SÛTRAS OMITTED

IN THE SECOND EDITION.

न चैकदेशोपलब्धिरवयविसद्भावात् ॥ २ । १ । ३२ ॥

1. Moreover, the perception is not merely of a part, for there is a whole behind the part.

The perception of a part does not exclude perception of the whole, of which it is a part. If you touch the hand, leg or any other limb of a person, you are said to touch the person. Similarly, if you perceive a part of a thing, you are said to perceive the thing. A part implies the whole, and perception of a part implies perception of the whole.

प्रमाणतोऽनुपलब्धेः ॥ २ । १ । ५३ ॥

2. There is, in the case of verbal testimony, no perception of the connection.

The connection between a sign and the thing signified, which is the basis of inference, is obvious to perception. For instance, the inference that "the hill is fiery, because it is smoky" is based on a certain connection between smoke and fire which is actually perceived in a kitchen or elsewhere. The connection between a word and the objects signified by it, which is the basis of verbal testimony, is not obvious to perception. The word Uttarakuru, for instance, signifies the country of the name, but the connection between the word and the country is not perceived, as the latter lies beyond our observation. Hence, verbal testimony is not inference.

विमर्शहेत्वनुयोगे च विप्रतिपत्तेः संशयः ॥ २ । २ । १३ ॥

3. There is doubt about the nature of sound, because there are conflicting opinions supported by conflicting reasons.

Some say that sound is a quality of ether, and that it is all-pervading, eternal, and capable of being manifested. Others say that sound, like smell, etc., is a quality of the substance in which it abides, and is capable of being manifested. Sound is said by others to be a quality of ether and to be subject to production and destruction, like knowledge. Others again say that sound arises from the concussion of elements, requires no abode, and is subject to production and destruction. Hence, there arises doubt about the true nature of sound.

वर्णत्वाव्यतिरेकाद्वर्णविकाराणामप्रतिषेधः ॥२।२।५०॥

4. There is, according to the objector, no inaptness in the analogy, as the modification of a letter does not relinquish the general notion of letters.

Just as gold is modified into a bracelet without relinquishing the general notion of gold, so the letter *i* undergoes modification as *y* without relinquishing the general notion of letters.

सामान्यवतो धर्म्मयोगो न सामान्यस्य ॥२।२।५१॥

5. A quality belongs, we reply, to a thing possessing a general notion, but not to the general notion itself.

A bracelet is a modification of a ring, inasmuch as both of them are gold which possesses the general notion of goldness. The letter *y* cannot be a modification of the letter *i*, because they have not as their common basis another letter which possesses the general notion of letterness.

अपरिसङ्ख्यानाच्च स्मृतिविषयस्य ॥३।१।१५॥

6. Also because the things remembered are innumerable.

If memory were lodged in things, we could remember innumerable things at a time. But none can remember more things than one at a time. Hence memory must be supposed to be a quality of a separate substance called soul (endowed with a mind).

अव्यभिचाराच्च प्रतीघातो भौतिकधर्म्मः ॥३।१।३८॥

7. The senses are material substances inasmuch as they invariably receive obstruction.

Nothing can offer obstruction to a non-material all-pervading substance. The senses receive obstruction from wall, etc., and are therefore material substances.

नेन्द्रियान्तरार्थानुपलब्धेः ॥३।१।५३ ॥

8. It is, we reply, not so because the objects of other senses are not perceived by touch (skin).

If there had been only one sense, *viz.*, touch (skin), then it could have seen colour, heard sound and so on. But a blind man possessing the sense of touch cannot see colour. Hence it is concluded that senses are many.

त्वगवयवविशेषेण धूमोपलब्धिवत्तदुपलब्धिः ॥३।१।५४॥

9. Perception of various objects of sense is comparable to that of smoke by a special part of touch.

Just ao smoke is perceived by a special part of touch located in the eye, so sound, smell etc., are perceived by special parts of touch specially located.

व्याहतत्वादहेतुः ॥३।१।५५॥

10. This is, according to us, absurd as it involves contradiction.

It has been said that touch is the only sense by the special parts of which special functions are performed. Now it is asked whether the special parts of touch do not partake of the nature of senses. If they do, then the senses are many. If on the other hand they do not partake of the nature of senses, then it is to be admitted that colour, sound, etc., are not cognisable by the senses.

संसर्गाच्चानेकगुणग्रहणम् ॥३।१।६७॥

11. And it is through their commixture, continues the objector, that there is the apprehension of more than one quality.

The objector further says as follows:—

The earth possesses only odour (smell), and if sometimes savour (taste) is also found there it is because the earth is then mixed with water. Similarly if there is odour (smell) in water it is because the earth is mixed with it.

न हेत्वभावात् ॥३।२।१०॥

12. It is, we reply, not so because there is no proof.

The Sâṃkhya says that the variety of knowledge arises from the same intellect appearing to be modified by the various objects which are reflected on it throngh the senses. The various modes which the intellect undergoes, that is, the various kinds of knowledge are not real but only apparent. The Naiyâyikas dispose of this view by saying that there is no proof as to the unreality of the modes, that is, the various kinds of knowledge, inasmuch as they are found to originate and cease in due order in consequence of the contact of senses and their objects and *vice versa*.

प्रातिभवत्तु प्रणिधानाद्यनपेक्षे स्मार्त्ते यौगपद्यप्रसङ्गः ॥३।२।३५॥

13. [It is not true that] there is possibility of simultaneousness in the case of recollections which are independent of the efforts of attention, etc., just as in the case of cogr itions derived from impressions of equal vividness not dependent on stimuli.

Some say that recollections which are not dependent on the efforts of attention, etc., may be simultaneous like several cognitions or acts of knowledge that are produced from impressions of equal vividness without the aid of external stimuli. But this view is untenable because neither the recollections nor the several acts of knowledge are simultaneous. The acts of knowledge, though derived from impressions of equal vividness, will appear in succession according to the amount of attention paid to them, and the recollectons though not dependent on the efforts of attention will appear one after another in proportion to the strength of stimuli that revive them.

कुम्भादिष्वनुपलब्धेरहेतुः ॥३।२।३९।

14. It is unreasonable also on account of the non-perception of knowledge in pots and the like.

In a pot there is activity indicated by the conglomeration of different earthy parts while in sand there is forbearance from activity indicated by the disruption of the parts from one another. Yet there is no knowledge, desire or aversion in a pot or sand. Hence the body is not the seat of knowledge, desire or aversion.

बुद्ध्यवस्थानात प्रत्यक्षत्वे स्मृत्यभावः ॥३।२।४६॥

15. If knowledge were permanent it would always be perceptible so that there would be no recollection,

If there is knowledge it is perceptible and as long as there is perception there is no recollection. Hence on the supposition of knowledge being permanent there would be a total absence of recollection.

उपपन्नश्च तद्वियोगः कर्म्मक्षयोपपत्तेः ॥३।२।७२॥

16. And the separation between the soul and the body is effected by the termination of the deserts,

It is in virtue of its deserts that a soul is joined with a particular body and it is by the exhaustion of the deserts that the separation between the two takes place. The soul cannot be separated from the body until it attains perfect knowledge through the cessation of ignorance and lust.

न करणाकरणयोरारम्भदर्शनात् ॥३।१।७४॥

17. It is not reasonable, because the body is found to be produced in case of both fulfilment and non-fulfilment of its ends.

In the previous aphorism it was stated that the body was produced only to enable the soul to experience objects and to realize its distinction from matter (prakṛiti). In the present aphorism the Naiyâyika points out the worthlessness of the statement by showing that the body is produced irrespective of the fulfilment or non-fulfilment of its ends, that is, it is produced in the case of the soul experiencing objects and realizing its distinction from matter as well as in the case when the soul remains enchained on account of its failure to realize its distinction from matter.

In a certain school of philosphy the desert is supposed to be a quality of the atoms and not of the soul. In virtue of the desert atoms are said to combine together into a body (endowed with a mind) to enable the soul to experience objects, and realize its distinction from matter. This school of philosophy fails to explain why the soul after it has attained emancipation (release) is not again connected with a body inasmuch as the atoms composing the body are never devoid of deserts.

न सद्यः कालान्तरोपभोग्यत्वात् ॥४।१।४५॥

18. The fruit, we reply, is not immediate because it is enjoyable after a lapse of time.

The fruit of maintaining the sacred fire is the attainment of heaven which is not possible until the time of death when the soul departs from our body.

अधिकाराच्च विधानं विद्यान्तरवत् ॥४।१।६१॥

19. An injunction must be appropriate to its occasion just as a topic must be appropriate to the treatise which deals with it.

A treatise on Logic which is to deal with its own special problems cannot be expected to treat of etymology and syntax which form the subject of a separate treatise. A sacred book which professes to deal with the life of a householder can appropriately bestow every encomium on him. A cereain Vedic text extols *karma* by saying that immortality is attained by the force of one's own acts, while another text lays down as a compliment to asceticism that immortality cannot be attained except through renunciation . Some text declares emphatically that it is by the knowledge of Brahman alone that one can attain immortality, there is no other way to it. There are again certain texts which attach an equal importance to study, sacrifice ann charity each of which is to be performed by us at the different stages of our life. Hence a text which aims at extolling the life of a householder can, without creatiag any missapprehension in us, lay down that as soon as we are born we incur three debts which we must go on clearing off until the time of our decay and death.

अनुवादे त्वपुनरुक्तं शब्दाभ्यासादर्थविशेषोपपत्तेः ॥५।२।१५॥

20. In reinculcation there is no repetition in as much as a special meaning is deduced from the word which is repeated.

The hill has fire (proposition),
Because it has smoke (reason),
All that has smoke has fire
as a kitchen (example),
The hill has smoke (application),
Therefore tbe hill has fire (conclusion).

In this argument the "conclusion" is a mere repetition of the "proposition" and yet it serves a special purpose.

APPENDIX C.

Vâtsyâyana's Commentary on the Nyâya-Sûtras of Gotama.

(SUMMARY)

BOOK I: CHAPTER I.

Topic 1 : Subject-matter, purpose and relations : Sûtras *1-2.*

Pramâṇa (Means of Proof) is connected with Artha (Object), because the success of activity (pravṛitti) depends on the establishment of the Artha by means of Pramâṇa. Activity consists in the effort to acquire or to avoid an Artha after its cognition by means of Pramâṇa. Artha is pleasure, cause of pleasure, pain, cause of pain. The knower (pramâtâ), the means of knowledge (pramâṇa), the knowable (prameya) and knowledge (pramiti),—these four terms comprehend artha-Tattva, the truth about the Object. By Tattva (reality) is meant, in the case of an existent thing, the being existent, and, in the case of a non-existent thing, the being non-existent. In other words, an existent something which always appears as existent and in a particular form and is never known in any other form, is called a reality. Similarly in the case of a non-existent thing. But how can a thing which does not exist be known ? The pramâṇa which reveals an existent thing, reveals a non-existent thing as well. Absence of cognition, while the pramâṇas are operative, is the test of non-existence.

The Nyâya-Sûtras groups existent things under sixteen classes (I. i. 1). They constitute its subject-matter : Its purpose is to teach how to know them in their true character. Among these sixteen classes it is the knowledge of the reality of the soul and other knowables (I. i. 9) which is the cause of the attainment of the supreme good (niḥs'reyasa). One attains the supreme good by thoroughly realising the four subjects established in the Nyâya-Sûtras, namely the thing to be avoided (*i.e.*, pain), its causes (*i.e.*, desire and ignorance), absolute avoidance, and the means of such avoidance (*i.e.*, true knowledge) which is to be secured.

It is true that Pramâṇa and Prameya comprise *all* objects. Doubt and the rest (I. i. 1) are included in them. These have been separately mentioned to show that they have received special treatment in the Nyâya-Sûtras. Four Sciences (Vidyâ) have been propounded for the benefit of mankind : Vârttâ, vocation, the science of agriculture, trade, commerce, etc., which produces wealth (artha), supplies the physical needs of man ; Daṇḍanîti, the rule of the rod, polity, controls his passions, desires and emotions and enables him to enjoy the amenities (kâma) of social life ; Trayî, the three Vedas (Rik, Yajus and Sâma), which deals with the sacrifice of Agnihotra, etc., enriches his religious experience (dharma); and Ânvîkṣikî, the science of reflection, critique, which deals with the soul, etc., ministers to his spiritual needs and helps him to attain Release (mokṣa). Nyâya-vidyâ is this fourth science of Ânvîkṣikî. If the Nyâya did not treat of doubt and the rest as its special subjects, it would not be distinguished from a pure science of the self like the Upaniṣads.

Nyâya (reasoning) has no scope where the object either is not perceived or is already ascertained, but only where it is doubted. As has been said, "Ascertainment is the determination of the object by means of opposite views after first impression" (I. i. 41). The order of sequence is: first impression, doubt, opposite views, application of Nyâya (reasoning), determination of the object, ascertainment, knowledge of reality. On this account, Saṃs'aya (Doubt) in the form of "what this may be," which is indeterminate cognition consisting of the mere first impression of an entity, is separately mentioned, though it is included in the class of Prameya (knowable.)

Prayojana (Purpose) is that by which one is prompted to act. It is an object which one desires to secure or desires to reject. Purpose pervades all living beings, all acts and all systems of knowledge. For its promotion does Nyâya proceed.

Nyâya is the investigation of objects by the application of the processes of proposition, etc. (I. i. 32) which are the Pramâṇas (means of knowledge) such as Perception, etc. Inference based on perception and revelation is called Anvîkṣâ, re-view, that is, review of what has been viewed by perception and revelation. The system of knowledge which proceeds by this method, is Ânvîkṣikî, Nyâya-vidyâ, Nyâya-s'âstra. Inference which is contradicted by perception and revelation, is pseudo-nyâya, false reasoning.

Vâda, Jalpa and Vitaṇḍâ are the three forms of discourse or controversy (Kathâ). Vâda and Jalpa have definite ends in view; Vitaṇḍâ has not. Vâda (assertion or discussion) has the ascertainment of the truth as its object. In Jalpa (sophistry) the opponent only seeks personal victory. Vitaṇḍâ (cavil) is merely destructive criticism. If it advances a proposition of its own, it ceases to be itself; if it does not, it becomes a meaningless jargon.

Dṛiṣṭânta (Example) is an object of perception in respect of which the observation of common people and of experts is unobstructed. It is a Prameya. It has been separately mentioned on account of its importance. Both inference and revelation rest upon it: without it neither inference nor revelation would be possible. The application of Nyâya depends upon it. The position taken up by an opponent is assailed on the ground of its contradiction to the Example ; by agreement with it one's own position is established. The Nihilist (nâstika) abandons his nihilism if he admits an Example. If he does not admit one he robs himself of the weapon with which to strike down the opponent. It makes possible to define the Udâharaṇa (instance), the third member of a Nyâya or syllogism (I. i. 36, 37).

When an object is at last known in the form "Such and such exists," it is called a Siddhânta, an established tenet, a conclusion. It is also a Prameya. It has been separately mentioned because Vâda , Jalpa and Vitaṇḍâ find scope only where there exists a diversity of siddhântas or principles of discourse, and not otherwise.

Avayavas (Members), that is, the five beginning with Pratijñâ (Proposition) (I. i. 32), are so called with reference to the concatenation of words considered as a whole, which completes the establishment of the object to be established. In them combine all the Pramâṇas : Pratijñâ (Proposition) (is the enunciation for demonstration to another of the object obtained from) Âgama (revelation, Testimony) ; Hetu (Reason or Mark) is (the vehicle of) Anumâna (Inference) ; Udâharaṇa (Instance) is (an object of) Pratyakṣa (Perception) ; Upanayana (Application) is Upamâna (Comparison) ; Nigamana (Conclusion) shows the convergence of all towards the same object. Such is the Nyâya *par excellence.* Vâda, Jalpa and Vitaṇḍâ proceed by means of it. The ascertainment of the specific character of a reality depends upon it. For this reason, the members have been separately mentioned, though, as forms of Sound, they are included in the general class of the Prameya.

Tarka (Hypothesis) is neither included in the Pramâṇas nor is it an additional Pramâṇa, but is subservient to the Pramâṇas, and as such conduces to tattva-jñâna, knowledge of reality. For instance : Is birth the result of past acts or is it the result of causes other than past acts ? The object being thus unknown, there follows rational doubt or conjecture : if birth is the result of acts, then termination of birth is possible through the termination of the cause ; but if it is the result of causes other than acts, then the termination of the cause being beyond the power of man, the termination of birth is also impossible. Or, if birth is accidental, then as it happens by accident, it will happen again ; the cause of cessation therefore cannot be expected ; hence the termination of birth is not possible. Tarka subserves the Pramâṇas which proceed to establish one out of the alternative suppositions, namely that birth is due to action. It conduces to tattva-jñâna, knowledge of reality, through an analysis of the subject-matter of tattva-jñâna. Tarka which is of such a character, in association with the Pramânas, helps in the establishment as well as in the elimination of the object. For this reason it has been separately mentioned, though it is included in the Prameya.

Nirnaya (Ascertainment) is tattva-jñâna, knowledge of truth. It is the result of the Pramânas. Vâda (discussion) ends with it. For its maintenance are Jalpa and Vitandâ. Tarka (hypothesis) and Nirnaya (ascertainment) help carry on the affairs of the world. For this reason Nirnaya though included in the Prameya, has been separately mentioned.

Vâda is discussion in which different speakers take part, each seeking to make good his own hypothesis, and which ends with the establishment of one or other of the hypotheses. It has been separately mentioned to emphasise its special feature. By the use of it as so defined tattva-jñâna, knowledge of truth, is attained.

Jalpa (sophistry) and Vitandâ (cavil) are varieties of Vâda, and are employed to keep up the effort in the pursuit of truth.

Hetvâbhâsas (Fallacies of Reason) have been mentioned separately from Nigrahasthânas (Occasions for Rebuke,) because they furnish ground of attack in Vâda, while Nigrahasthânas do so in Jalpa and Vitaṇḍâ.

Chhala (Quibble), Jâti (Futility) and Nigrahasthânas have distinctions of their own and are therefore separately mentioned.

Thus is Ânvîkṣikî divided by the topics of the Pramânas, etc. It is the light of all sciences, the way of all actions, the foundation of all pious acts. It is this which has been recited among the four Sciences.

And the tattva-jñâna, knowledge of truth, produced by Ânvîkṣikî for the realisation of the supreme good, should be understood according to the scope of each science. In the present Science of the Soul it means knowledge of the truth about the soul, etc., and the realisation of the supreme good means the attainment of Release.

The supreme good does not arise immediately after the knowledge of the truth about the soul, etc. False knowledge in many forms exists in regard to the prameyas from the soul to release (I. i. 9). *E.g.* the soul does not exist; the not-soul is looked upon as the soul, pain as pleasure, the non-eternal as the eternal, non-release as release, the cause of fear as not the cause of fear, the ugly as the pleasant, what is fit to be avoided as not so; there is no karma (action) nor the fruit of karma; samsâra (stream of births and deaths) is not due to dosa or faults; there is no animal or embodied soul or entity or soul which is to depart and, after departing, to come back; birth has no reason behind it, therefore cessation of births in future comes about by itself, hence existence after departing from life has a beginnig but no end; it has a cause, but karma is not its cause; re-birth does not require a soul, but is brought about by the disjunction and conjunction of the body, the senses and the stream of ideas and sensations; in release we fear there is cessation of all action, in release which means separation from everything much that is good is lost, hence how can an intelligent man like such release which is unconsciousness, the cessation of all experience of pleasure?

From such false knowledge arise attraction for things agreeable and avertion to things disagreeable. Under the influence of attraction and aversion spring up untruthfulness, envy, delusion or attachment, greed, and other faults. The faults incite to acts of vice with the body, speech and mind. Vices p oduce adharma, demerit. Virtues produce dharma, merit. In the text (I. i. 2) pravṛitti, activity, has the sense of its products, merit and demrit. It is the cause of good or evil birth.

Birth is the appearance of the body, the senses and the intellect, or coguition (buddhi) as an aggregate. It is the condition of Pain which is known as disagreeable feeling, hindrance, suffering, burning.

These conditions, namely false knowledge, faults, activity, birth and pain, ever following without interruption, constitute saṃsâra or the wheel of life. Knowledge of truth removes false knowledge. On the removal of false knowledge faults disappear. On the disappearance of faults activity ceases. On the cessation of activity birth does not take place. In the absence of birth there is no pain. In the absence of pain absolute success, *i. e.* release, which is the supreme good, is attained.

Knowlege of truth is the opposite of the false notions mentioned above. And therefore just as food mixed with honey and poison is unacceptable so is also pleasure tainted with pain.

The method of the Nyâya-Sûtras is threefold: enumeration, definition and examination. First is given the division of the subject enumerated, and then the definition of each division. Next is given the subdivision of the subject enumerated and defined.

The subdivisions of Pramâṇa are Pratyakṣa (perception), Anumâna (inference), Upamâna (comparison) and Sabda (word).

Pratyakṣa is the vṛitti (modification) of each sense according to each object appropriate to it. Vṛitti is proximity or knowledge. Whenever there is proximity there is knowledge of reality. The consequence of knowledge is the idea of avoidance or acquisition or indifference.

Anumâna is the knowledge of the object after the observation of the previously known mark.

Upamâna is the knowldge of an object by means of its resemblance to a known object.

Śabda is that by which an object is designated, *i. e.*, made known as such and such.

The four pramâṇas sometimes operate conjointly and sometimes individually according to the nature of the prameya. Thus : the existence of the soul is known from testimony, by inference (I. i. 10), and by perception through a particular conjunction of the internal organ with the soul brought about by the power of meditation of a Yogî. In the case of heaven there can be neither the observation of a mark nor perception. When the rumbling of a cloud is heard, the cloud is not an object of perception or of testimony, but of inference from the sound. In the case of one's own hand there is neither inference nor testimony.

Pramiti, knowledge, which is thus the result of the pramâṇas, ultimately rests on perception. The object of enquiry which is obtained from testimony, is sought to be known by means of the observation of the mark ; that which is inferred from the observation of the mark, is sought to be seen by perception ; and when the object is realised in perception the enquiry ceases.

Topic 2 : Definition of Pramâṇas : Sûtras *3-8.*

Gotama now proceeds to give the definition of each of the four pramâṇas.

Perception is the knowledge which is produced from the contact of the sense with the object. The contact of the soul with the mind and of the mind with the sense is not mentioned, because it is common to cognitions produced by all the pramâṇas. The definition only gives the specific cause of perceptual knowledge. The knowledge of the object produced from the contact of the sense with the object takes the form of "colour", "taste", etc. The words, colour, taste, etc. are the names of the viṣayas or contents of the knowledge. But the name-words have no operation at the time of the production of the knowledge of the object ; they operate only when use has to be made of the knowledge. Hence the knowledge of the object produced from the contact of the sense with the object is independent of words. Again, mirage is also produced from the contact of the sense with the object. But it is not perception, because it is erratic, unreal. Perceptual knowledge must be unerring, real. For the same reason doubt or uncertain knowledge, *e. g.* be that a post or a man, a cloud of smoke or of dust, is not perceptual knowledge. Moreover, the latter must be discreet, specific, particular, and not general such as is produced from the contact of the soul with the mind alone.

The soul, etc. as well as pleasure, etc. are also objects of perception. But their perception is not produced from the contact of the sense with the object.

Manas, the mind, is a sense, but it has been separately mentioned because of its distinctive character. The senses are constituted by the elements, are restricted each to its own province, and possess attributes. The mind, on the other hand, is not constituted by the elements, and is all-extensive and without attribute. Hence it is said that perceptual knowledge of the soul, etc., which is produced from a particular conjunction of the soul and the mind, is not produced from the contact of the sense with the object. Otherwise, the docrtine that the mind is a sense which has been established in the Vais'eṣika-Sûtras, is also admitted in the Nyâya-Sûtras, according to the rule of intepretation that the doctrine of another which is not controverted, is approved.

Inference is the knowledge the antecedents of which are the observation of the connection between the mark and the thing marked, and the observation of the mark (liṅga, sign). Recollection of the mark follows from the observation of the mark and the thing marked as connected. By means of recollection and the observation of the mark an unperceived object is inferred.

Inference of suceession is of three kinds : (1) from cause to effect, (2) from effect to cause, and (3) from change of position, as, *e.g.*, the inference of the movement of the sun from its change of position in the sky. Inference of co-existence is as of the fire by smoke ; that is, when two objects have been previously known as co-existent, the presence of one, though not perceived, is inferred from the presence of the other. Inference also takes place by the method of exhaustion or residue ; *e. g.* Vais'eṣika-Sûtras, II. i. 25. Again, where the connection of the mark and the thing marked is not an object of perception, inference of the thing marked which is unperceived, may yet take place through the resemblance of the mark to some other object *e. g.*, the inference of the soul by means of desire, etc. ; desire, etc. are attributes, attributes reside in substances, the substance in which desire, etc. reside, is the soul.

The sphere of perception is the present ; that of inference is the present, past and future.

Comparison makes an object known through its resemblance to a known object, *e. g.* as the cow so the *bos gavaeus.* Comparison subserves perception. It enables one to know an object designated by a particular name.

Testimony is the direction of an Âpta, *i. e.* of one, be he a seer or a man of culture or a savage, who possesses true knowledge and is truthful. The object of testimony may be of this world or of the other world. The testimony of common people is confined to the things of this world; the testimony of seers embraces things of the other world also. Both kinds of testimony are pramâṇa: the former is based on actual experience; the latter, on inference.

It is by means of these four pramânas and not otherwise, that the affairs of gods, men and lower animals are conducted.

Topic 3 : Definition of Prameya (*knowable*) : Sûtras *9-22.*

The pramânas make known the soul, the body, the senses, object, cognition, the mind, activity, faults, re-birth, the fruit, pain and release. The soul is the seer of all, the experiencer of all, the all-knower, the all-reacher. The body is the field of its experience. The senses are the instruments of its experience. The objects of the senses are the things to be experienced. The experience is cognition. The senses do not extend to all objects. That which embraces all objects is the inner sense, the mind. Activity and faults are the causes which accomplish the soul's experiences of the body, the senses, the objects, cognition, and pleasure. This body is neither its first nor its last. There is no beginning of its past bodies. Its future bodies will end only when release is attained. This is re-birth. The fruit is the action of pleasure and pain with their causes on the soul. Pain is a constant companion of pleasure and enters as an element in its experience. For this reason, and not to ignore the experience of pleasure as an agreeable feeling, pleasure has not been separately mentioned. Release is the negation of all possibility of births and deaths, the total annihilation of all pain. It is the final fruit of a process of self-culture of which the successive stages are withdrawal from the world and concentration upon the self, meditation, thoughtfulness, and dispassion.

There are innumerable prameyas such as substance, attribute, action, genus, species, combination (Vaiśesika-Sûtras, I. i. 4) and their varieties. In the Nyâya-Sûtras twelve prameyas have been specially taught, because knowledge of the truth about them leads to release, while false knowledge about them leads to the stream of births and deaths.

The soul cannot be apprehended through the contact of the senses. It is known from testimony and from inference by the marks of desire, aversion, activity, pleasure, pain and cognitions. Desire, aversion and activity imply recollection of past experiences of pleasure and pain, the power of selection of one particular object out of many as the cause of pleasure or of pain, and the adaptation of activity towards its acquisition or avoidance. They therefore prove the existence of a single entity which witnesses a multitude of objects. Pleasure and pain also persist in memory; the sight of their causes revives their memory. There must be therefore an entity in which pleasure and pain sink into oblivion. Cognition involves doubt and determination. The performer of the two functions must be one and the same.

Some deny the existence of the soul and maintain that there is only a series of conscious states severally corresponding to specific objects. But they also do not admit that the same series re-appears in other bodies. Even so it cannot be said to have influence in the same body at successive periods of time; for the two cases do not materially differ from each other. In the individual body there is only one soul, for one can recollect only what one has seen, and not what has been seen by another, or has not been seen at all. Similarly souls are different in different bodies, for one does not recollect what has been seen by another. Those who deny the existence of the soul fail to explain these phenomena.

The body is the field or vehicle of the soul's experience, because the movement towards the acquisition or avoidance of an object takes place in the body, because the efficiency of the senses varies according to the health or disease of the body, and because the resonance of pleasure and pain appears in the body.

The instruments of experience, *i. e.*, the senses, are the powers of smell, taste, sight, touch and hearing. The elements of the earth, water, fire, air and ether are their respective causes. Smell, taste, sight, touch and sound are respectively the attributes of the elements and the objects of the senses.

Cognition is not, as some hold, the modification of an unconscious or insentient instrument or organ called buddhi, intellect. Consciousness cannot spring from unconsciousness. Buddhi, intellect or reason, is not the medium of cognition. but cognition itself.

Memory, inference, testimony, doubt, ready wit, dream, cognition, conjecture, feeling of pleasure, etc. and desire, etc. are marks of the mind. The senses are not their cause. They must have some other cause. That is the mind. Simultaneous non-production of cognitions even while the senses are in contact with their objects is also the mark of the mind,

Activity is the start or action of the body, speech and mind. In the Sûtra (I. i. 17) the mind is intended by the word "buddhi".

Faults move the knower to activity. They are attraction, aversion and stupidity. Where there is false knowledge there are attraction and aversion. Their existence in others is known from their acts.

Re-birth or transmigration is connection again with the body, the senses, the mind and cognition, whether here or elsewhere. The condition of recurrent births and deaths has no beginning and ceases on the attainment of release.

Fruit is the experience of pleasure or of pain. It is inevitable so long there is connection with the body, the senses, objects and cognition.

The mark of pain is bâdhanâ, *i. e.*, obstruction or hindrance, suffering, burning. The element of pain is present in all things, the body, the senses, the objects, etc. They impede the activity of the soul.

Release is everlasting deliverance from birth which is the source of pain. This is the state which arises when the present birth ends and another birth does not take place. This state continuing unlimited is called Apavarga, release. Abhaya, Ajara, Amṛityupada, Brahmakṣemaprâpti are its other descriptions. Abhaya is fearless: in release there is no longer any fear of saṃsâra. Ajara is undecaying. This disproves the doctrine that Brahman modifies (pariṇâma) as the fabric of the universe of names and forms. If Brahman undergoes modification as a whole, then as a whole it becomes other than it is, and therefore liable to destruction. If, on the other hand, it should modify in part, then being divisible it would be equally liable to destruction. Amṛityupada is the status of non-death or immortality. This is in answer to the Vainâs'ikas who hold that release is the extinction of the mind like the extinction of a lamp. Brahmakṣemaprâpti is the attainment of the bliss of Brahman.

Some think that permanent pleasure, like the largeness of the soul, is manifested in the state of release, and that the absolutely released soul enjoys pleasure as so manifested. But there is no evidence, neither perception, nor inference, nor testimony, that permanent pleasure, like the largeness of the soul, is manifested in the state of release. If manifestation of permanent pleasure takes place at a particular time, then it is a product and therefore requires a cause. If, on the other hand, the manifestation, like pleasure, is ever present, then a soul in bondage will also enjoy it as much as a released soul. If you say that the manifestation of pleasure is a product and that the conjunction of the soul and mind is its cause, then another contributory cause is required. For, in the state of saṃsâra, the conjunction of the soul and mind requires the aid of dharma or acts of virtue to produce the cognition of pleasure. But if in the state of release the conjunction of the soul and mind is an independent cause of the cognition of pleasure, then in the case of the cognition of colour, etc. the senses also will not be needed. If, again, dharma or acts of virtue be the contributory cause, then a cause of dharma is required, because it is a product. If, on the other hand, you say that virtue born of Yogic meditation or trance is the cause, then, as a product, it is liable to destruction, and as such it would negate unlimited enjoyment of pleasure, for, as an effect, the enjoyment will cease with the cessation of its cause. If you say that the manifestation of pleasure is ever present but that the connection of the soul with the body, etc. prevents its experience in the state of saṃsâra, your position would be untenable. The body, etc. have been created to subserve the purpose of the soul's enjoyment. To say that they would obstruct such enjoyment is a contradiction in terms. On the other hand, there is no reason to infer that a soul with ut a body can have any experience. Instructions about release and the activity of the seekers of release do not furnish any such reason. For these are directed not to the attainment of a desired object but to the termination of what is not desired. There is no good which is not interpenetrated with evil. The avoidance of evil therefore necessarily entails the avoidance of good as well. It is impossible to avoid evil separately. If you say that, as a matter of fact, people forsake visible temporary pleasure and long for permanent pleasure, we would rejoin that it would be better to suppose that in the same way after transcending the visible temporary body, senses and cognition, the released soul obtains permanent body, senses and cognition. In this way, the identity of soul in the case of the released will also be accomplished. The eternality of the body, etc. is no more opposed to the pramâṇas and therefore impossible to assume than the eternality of pleasure. When a revealed text predicates everlasting pleasure of a released soul, by pleasure it means non-existence of pain. Instances of such use of the word are plentiful in popular parlance. Should a man strive after release being attracted by the prospect of eternal pleasure, he cannot attain release, for attraction is a bond, and while the bond exists no one can be released. Now, if the soul's attraction for eternal pleasure is abandoned, then on its abandonment attraction for eternal pleasure does not become an obstacle. Such being the case eternal pleasure may accrue to the released soul or may not accrue. But the attainment of release does not stand on the horns of a dilemmaic doubt.

Topic 4 : Definition of the preliminaries of a Nyâya : Sûtras *23-25.*

Doubt is consideration in expectation of a distinction. Expectation

of a distinction is the cognition that one does not find the characteristic which will determine one or another of two or more possible objects as a particular object. It arises (1) from the observation of common properties only appertaining (*a*) to objects of the same class, or (*b*) to objects of the same and different classes, or (2) from contradiction, e. g., the soul exists, the soul does not exist, or (3) from irregularity of perception and non-perception (for example, see text).

Purpose is the object which is determined as fit to be acquired or fit to be avoided. It is the resolution which induces activity for the acquisition or avoidance of such an object.

An Example is an object which is understood by people of insight in the same way as by common people who do not possess intellectual excellence either by nature or by training.

Topic 5 : Definition of Siddhânta : Sûtras *26-31.*

A tenet is the statement of the complete demonstration of an object as of a particular character. It may relate to the subject matter (1) of a system of knowledge or (2) of a topic of discussion or (3) of an admission made with a view to the examination of its special nature.

The senses are the powers of smell, etc., the objects of the senses are smell, etc., the earth, etc. are the elements, objects are known by the pramânas—these are examples of tenets common to all systems of knowledge. Non-existence cannot come into existence, existence cannot pass into non-existence, conscious entities do not change, there are intrinsic differences in the objects of the body, senses and mind as well as in their respective causes—these are peculiar to the Sâṃkhyas, while among the special tenets of the Yogas are : elemental creation is due to the act of the puruṣa, the faults and activity are the causes of acts, conscious entities are endowed with their respective attributes, the non-existent can be brought into existence, what is produced can be destroyed.

The knower is other than the body or the senses, because, *e. g.*, the same object is apprehended by sight and touch (III. i. 1)—this is the example of a leading or governing tenet. For from its establishment follows the establishment of the following : the senses are more than one ; the senses are restricted to their respective objects ; they are known by the apprehension of their own objects, and are the means of the knower's cognition of objects ; substance is other than the attributes of smell, etc., and is the substratum of attributes ; consciousness comprehends all objects.

The following is an example of an admitted tenet : Let it be assumed without examination that sound is a substance. Is it eternal or is it non-eternal? Being a substance it must be either eternal or non-eternal. Let us examine its special character.

Topic 6 : Definition of Nyâya : Sûtras *32-39*.

The avayavas or members are the integral parts of an argument designed to establish a particular object. They are five in number. Some add five more, *viz.* inquiry, doubt, capacity, purpose and removal of doubt. But they are not integral parts of a Nyâya. Inquiry is for the sake of the true knowledge of an object which is yet unknown. True knowledge is for the sake of the acquisition or avoidance of the object or of indifference to it. When one makes such an inquiry another proceeds to demonstrate the object. Inquiry therefore cannot be a part of the argument or demonstration. Similarly, doubt which gives rise to the inquiry, embraces contradictory attributes and therefore cannot be an antecedent or proximate condition of cognition; for only one or the other of two contradictory attributes can be the truth. Capacity is the capacity of the pramâṇas to make the prameya known to the knower, if the prameya is capable of being known at all. It cannot properly be a part of the demonstrative argument. Purpose is the ascertainment of the truth. It is the result of the argument and not its part. Removal of doubt is the censure of the opposite view and its preclusion for the sake of grasping the truth. It is not a part of the argument. Inquiry and the rest help to fix the object to be ascertained; proposition and the other four members help to demonstrate the truth about it.

Proposition is the enunciation of a thing as possessing the attribute which is going to be demonstrated. E. g. Sound is non-eternal.

Reason is the means of the demonstration of the attribute in question through the generic nature of the attribute as shown by its existence in the Example. E. g. because it is a product. A product which is non-eternal, has been seen.

The reason may be negative also. E. g. Sound is non-eternal, because products which are eternal, are the soul and similar substances.

The sâdhya or the thing to be demonstrated may be an attribute, *e.g.* non-eternality of sound, or a thing possessing an attribute, *e.g.* non-eternal sound. In the text (I. i. 36) "Tat" refers to the latter as "dharma," attribute, is separately mentioned. A Dṛistânta, Example, becomes an Udâharana, Instance or reference, when it possesses the attribute as possessing which the thing in question is to be demonstrated, as a necessary consequence of another attribute which it possesses in common with the thing. The instance therefore is the statement of the relation between the two attributes as of that which is to be demonstrated and that which is the means of its demonstration. E. g. The attribute, to be a product, is common to sound and a pot; in the pot the attribute, to be a product, is the cause of the attribute, to be non-eternal; the attribute, to be non-eternal, is to be demonstrated in the case of sound; therefore a pot possessing the attribute of non-eternality which is to be demonstrated in the case of sound as a necessary consequence of its attribute of being a product which it possesses in common with sound, fulfils the function of an Instance in the argument. Similarly an Instance may be of the negative kind. E g. sound is non-eternal, because it is a product; non-products are eternal, such as the soul, etc. Here the soul, etc. are negative Instances.

The force of the Reason and the Instance is very subtle, difficult to understand, to be comprehended only by great scholars.

Application is the statement which brings forward the attribute as such and such or not as such and such which the thing to be demonstrated possesses in common with the Instance. Application is either positive or negat ve according as the Instance or the Reason is positive or negative. E. g. a pot is a product, non-eternal; so is sound a product. The attribute of sound that it is a product is thus brought forward. Similarly, the soul is not a product, eternal; so is not sound. By the negation its attribute of being a product is brought forward (The Instance shows the universal concomitance of the reason and the thing to be demonstrated. Application is the bringing forward of such a reason in the thing to be established.)

Nigamana or conclusion is the bringing together of the Proposition, Reason, Instance and Application. E. g. sound is non-eternal, because it is a product.

In the statement of the argument consisting of the members the pramâṇas appear together and through mutual connection demonstrate the object. Their concurrence is shown thus: The proposition, that sound is non-eternal, comes from Testimony. For, Perception and Inference corroborate it, and he who is not a Ṛiṣi, is not independent of them. Inference is the Reason, because resemblance is discovered in the Instance. The Instance is an object of Perception. Comparison is the Application. Conclusion is the exhibition of the capacity of all of them to demonstrate one single object. Their mutual connection or inter-relation appears thus: The Proposition renders the operation of the reason, etc. possible. The Reason furnishes the means of demonstration; is brought forward in the Instance and the thing to be demonstrated; and by its predication makes the re-statement of the proposition in the Conclusion possible. The

Instance furnishes the resemblance or difference as the means of the demonstration of the thing; and makes Application possible through resemblance to it. Without Application the attribute which is the cause of demonstration cannot be brought forward in the thing, and it cannot in consequence demonstrate the object.. Without Conclusion the proposition, etc., as isolated, cannot operate towards the same end and therefore cannot produce demonstration.

The function of the Proposition is to connect the attribute to be demonstrated with the thing. The function of the Reason is to state that the attribute to be demonstrated, whether it be similar or dissimilar to the Instance, is the cause of demonstration. The function of the Instance is to show that the two attributes are related in the same substratum as the thing to be demonstrated and the means of demonstration. The function of Application is the establishment of the co-existence of the attribute which is the means of demonstration with the attribute which is to be demonstrated. Conclusion serves the purpose to exclude contrary suggestions against the establishment of the relation of that which is to be demonstrated and that which is the means of domonstration between the attributes present in the Instance.

On the clear definition of the Reason and Instance there cannot arise multiplicity of Futility and Occasion for Rebuke (Cf. I. ii. 20) through varieties of opposition by means of resemblance and difference. He who uses Futility offers opposition without determining the inferential relation of the two attributes in the Instance. The inferential relation of the two attributes being grasped as established in the Instance, the attribute which is determined as the means of demonstration, is adopted as the reason, and not mere resemblance nor mere difference.

Topic 7 : Definition of the Accessories of a Nyâya : Sûtras *40—41.*

Tarka, Hypothesis, is cogitation or conjecture, for the sake of knowledge of truth, in respect of an unknown object by the elimination of contrary suppositions. To take the example of the soul : Is it a product or a non-product? This is Vimars'a, contraposition of two opposite attributes. Assent is given to the one or the other according as the reason for such assent is forthcoming. If the soul is a non-product, it will experience the fruit of its action, and will on the eradication of the cause of re-birth attain release ; saṃsâra and release will thus be possible. If it is a product, these will not be possible. For its connection with the body, etc. will not be the result of its action. Neither will there be the experience of the fruit of its own action. In this situation one gives one's assent to the supposition which is based on reason, *i.e.* serves to explain the phenomena of re-birth and release. Cogitation or conjecture (Ûha) in this form is called Tarka, hypothesis. This is not knowledge of the truth which ascertains, determines, makes certain that the soul is such and such and nothing else. It is for the purpose of the knowledge of the truth. It leaves the supposition to which assent is given, to hold the field undisputed; after which knowledge of the truth is produced through the force of the pramâṇas..

Ascertainment is the determination of an object, after doubt, by means of the thesis and the counter-thesis. Here thesis means affirmation; and counter-thesis, negation. In a controversy one of these ultimately must cease and the other must stand. Ascertainment is the determination which will stand. But the .determination of an object cannot be possible by means of thesis and counter-thesis. What really happens is this: The speaker supports the object proposed with reasons and attacks its negation. The opponent contradicts the reasons put forward by the speaker and repels the attack on the negation urged by himself. In the result the reasons and attacks either of the speaker or of the opponent cease. That which remains, whether the thesis or the counter-thesis, is one, and by means of it the object is determined. Such determination is ascertainment.

Vimarsa, contraposition, helps Nyâya by distinguishing two contrary positions, and has reference to contraries residing in the same substratum. But where contradictory attributes of the individuals of a class spring from causes inherent in the individuals, there is not contraposition but collocation. E. g. some substances are active, some are inactive. Again, in the same substratum contradictory attributes may appear at different times. E. g. a substance may be active at one moment and inactive at another moment.

Contraposition is not required in every case of ascertainment. In perception the determination of an object through the contact of the sense and object is ascertainment. Similarly in matters of Sâstra and Discourse there is no room for Contraposition. For Śâstra, *e.g.* by Jyotiṣṭoma sacrifice one attains heaven, there can be no doubt. In Discourse both the speaker and the opponent are sure of their grounds. Contraposition applies only in cases of Examination or investigation.

Book I: Chapter ii.

Topic 8: Definition of Kathâ *(Discourse)*: Sûtras *1—3*.

There are three forms of Discourse, Vâda or discussion (with elders), and Jalpa or sophistry and Vitandâ or cavil (among rivals). Vâda consists in the advancement of the thesis and counter-thesis, *i.e.* contradictory attributes residing in the same substratum; *e.g.* the soul exists, the soul does not exist. Such contradictories as reside in different substrata, *e.g.* the soul is eternal, cognition is non-eternal, do not form thesis and counter-thesis. In Vâda the thesis is maintained by means of the pramâṇas, the counter-thesis is attacked or negatived by showing its absurdity, and *vice versa.* When in the process one is silenced the other is established. There is no room for the Occasion for Rebuke in Vâda, as its place has been assigned to Jalpa (I. ii 2). One form of Occasion for Rebuke, *viz.* the fallacy of reason called the contradictory (I. ii. 6) is permitted in Vâda, as also are "Saying too little" (V. ii. 12) and "Saying too much" (V. ii. 13). In the text (I. ii. 1), "Pramâṇatarka", though included in "Avayava," are separately mentioned to show that the establishment of the thesis only is to be done by pramâṇas, and the negation by tarka. In Vâda the maintenance of the thesis and the negation of the counter-thesis may be done also by the pramâṇas, *e.g.* perception, etc., independently of the five members of a Nyâya. The maintenance of the thesis and the negation of the counter-thesis are equally the functions of Vâda whereas negation is the main function of Jalpa.

As in Vâda the thesis is maintained by means of pramâṇas and the counter-thesis is negatived by means of tarkas, so in Jalpa these two objects are achieved by means of Chhala, Jâti and Nigrahasthâna. These however fulfil a negative function, as is clear from their definitions (I. ii. 10, 18, 19). They therefore do not directly serve to maintain or establish the thesis. But they do so indirectly by lending support to the pramâṇas establishing the thesis, by the negation of the counter-thesis (vide IV. ii. 50) Jalpa thus subserves Vâda.

Vitaṇḍâ, on the other hand, is mere negation. It lends no support to the maintenance either of the thesis or of any counter-thesis. Nor does it seek to establish any thesis of its own. It is not directed to any such end. In this it is distinguished from Jalpa.

Topic 9 : Definition of Fallacy of Reason : Sûtras : *4-9.*

Fallacies of Reason lack the characteristic of a mark of inference in a given case but appear as such a mark as they may be marks of inference in other cases. They fall into five classes. (1) The erratic is not confined to one or the other of two contradictory attributes, *e. g.* where the eternality of sound is to be established, untouchability cannot be the mark of inference, for while a pot which possesses touch is non-eternal, the atoms which also possess touch are eternal. Again, the soul which is without touch is eternal, whereas cognition which is also touchless is non-eternal. (2) The contradictory is the mark which contradicts the very tenet on which it rests. E. g. A modification loses its identity as it cannot be eternal; though it loses its identity, it still exists as it cannot be destroyed. The reason that a modification cannot be eternal is contradicted by the speaker's own tenet that a modification which is losing of identity still exists. For that which loses its identity ceases to exist. Existence and loss of identity are contradictory attributes and cannot abide together. (3) Where the subject matter of the topic is advanced as the reason for the desired inference, the mark is said to be identical with the topic, *e.g.* it is not known whether sound is eternal or non-eternal. Eternality and non-eternality are in this case the contradictory attributes the contraposition of which starts the discussion of the topic. To advance as a reason for the desired inference that sound is eternal or that sound is non-eternal is to stop the discussion altogether and to make the determination of the truth impossible. (4) The mark which itself stands in need of proof equally as the subject is called identical with the subject. (For example see text, I. ii. 8). (5) The time-expired mark: the commentary has been fully given in the text.

Topic 10: Definition of Quibble: Sûtras: *10-17.*

Quibble consists in playing upon (1) words, (2) ideas and (3) metaphors. *E. g.* (1) A quadruped means an animal and not a table. (2) To say that a particular Brâhmaṇa is learned is not to say that learning is an attribate of the genus Brâhmaṇa so that all Brâhmaṇas are learned. (3) The scaffolds cry, means that the men on the scaffolds for execution cry, and not the wooden structures. Between verbal and metaphorical quibbles there is this distinction that while in the former there is supposition of a different sense, in the latter there is negation of the existence of a sense.

Topic 11: Definition of General Faults in Marks of Inference due to incapacity of the speaker: Sûtras: *18-20.*

These are Jâti and Nigrahasthâna. Jâti literally means that which is born. Here it means whatever reply is provoked or called into being by the reason advanced by the opponent. It is applied to negative the opponent's reason through resemblance and difference. Where the reason brings forward the resemblance to the Instance, Jâti opposes the reason by bringing forward the difference from the Instance, and *vice versa.*

Nigrahasthâna is ground of defeat. Examples of Nigrahasthâna are self-contradictory or wrong conclusion, failure to reply, etc.

The varieties of Jâti and Nigrahasthâna are manifold (see I. ii. 20, V. i. 1 and V. ii. 1).

BOOK II : CHAPTER 1.

Topic 12 : Doubt: Sûtras : *1—7.*

Ascertainment has been defined (Sûtra I. i. 41) as the determination, after raising doubts, of an object by means of thesis and counter-thesis. Doubt has been defined in Sûtra I. i. 23. But some doubt the possibility of doubt. Their arguments are stated below:

(1) An attribute belonging to objects of the same class which is either wholly unknown or wholly known cannot cause doubt.

(2) An attribute which is cognised as belonging to two definite objects of the same class cannot cause doubt, because the objects are thereby cognised.

(3) Cognition of a common attribute cannot raise doubt in respect of the object possessing the attribute, as an attribute is different from an object.

(4) Cognition of a common attribute cannot cause doubt because cognition is opposed to doubt.

(5)—(8) The same objections apply *mutatis mutandis* to the case of an attribute belonging to objects of different classes.

(9) Cognition of the attribute of one of two possible objects, *e. g.*, "Be it a man or a post," also cannot cause doubt, because cognition of the attribute means cognition of the object.

(10) Differences of opinion and irregularity of perception and non-perception also cannot be the cause of doubt unless one becomes aware of these differences and of the irregularity, and when one becomes aware of them he has cognition of them and cognition is opposed to doubt.

(11) Those who hold different opinions in respect of an object are certain about their own opinions.

(12) The irregularity of perception and non-perception is also fixed in itself.

(13) If cognition of common attributes be a cause of doubt then doubt will never cease, because even when the objects are determined the common attributes will still belong to them and enter into cognition along with them.

To the above our reply is as follows:

(1) The Sûtra (I. i. 23) does not mean that common attributes themselves are causes of doubt. It means that cognition of common attributes causes doubt. This is clear from the expressions "Apekṣâ", "Upapatti" and

"Dharma". Apekṣâ is need, expectancy, of cognition. Upapatti is existence, the cognition that common attributes are present. Dharma, attribute, is an object and implies the cogniser.

(2) That an attribute is common to two objects of the same class refers to a previous experience when the two objects were cognised. The cognition of the attribute subsequently fails to decide which of the objects is the thing that now stands before the eyes. This decision can be arrived at by the cognition of the attribute which differentiates one of the objects from the other. Hence there is room for doubt.

(3) The Sûtra does not say that the cognition of one object is the cause of doubt in respect of a different object.

(4) It is true that cognition is opposed to doubt. But the cause of doubt is not the cognition of the common attribute but non-cognition *i. e.*, uncertainty, as to the distinctive attribute.

(5)—(8) The same replies apply to the objections in regard to the doubt caused by the cognition of the common attributes of heterogeneous objects.

(9) When an object is cognised as such its specific character is cognised. For this reason, doubt does not arise in respect of it.

(10)—(12). As regards differences of opinion and irregularity of perception and non-perception, their certainty and fixity cannot prevent doubt, because what is wanted to be known is the specific character which will determine which opinion and which perception and non-perception are true. So long as this distinctive attribute is not cognised there must be doubt.

(13) The Sûtra does not say that the cognition of common attributes alone causes doubt. Doubt depends upon the non-cognition of the distinctive attribute. When this is known doubt ceases. Hence perpetual doubt is not entailed.

In every critical examination of an object the thesis and counter-thesis should be thus established first by the removal of objections to them.

Topic 13 : *The* Pramâṇas *in general* : Sûtras : *8-20.*

Some thinkers maintain that Perception, Inference, Comparison and Word are not pramâṇas (sources of knowledge) because it cannot be shown that they exist before, after, or along with, the prameyas (objects of knowledge). If Perception, *e. g.* cognition of smell, etc. by the senses, exists as a pramâṇa before the existence of the smell, etc., then the definition of Perception as cognition produced from the contact of the senses and objects does not hold good. On the other hand, if Perception as a pramâṇa comes after the cognition of the prameya, then it is useless as the prameya has already been otherwise cognised. Lastly, if the pramâṇas co-exist with the prameyas then there would be simultaneity of several cognitions and the inference of the mind by the non-simulateneity of cognitions would be demolished.

To the above objection, we reply as follows :—

The fallacy of the objector's reasoning lies in this that he has distributed the pramâṇas, and has compounded the prameyas, in respect of time. The prameyas (like the pramâṇas) do some come before, some after, and some along with, the pramâṇas. Thus, the sun's rays appear before their effect, the blooming of the lotus ; a lamp which illumines an object in a dark room comes after the object ; where the existence of fire is inferred by the existence of the smoke the cause and object of cognition appear at the same time. There is therefore no hard and fast rule as to the relative position of the pramâṇas and the prameyas in time. Moreover, pramâṇa and prameya are correlative terms as the cause and the object of cognition. Where the pramâṇa follows the prameya the correlation still exists, as a "cook" is always a cook even when he is not actually cooking.

Then, what does the objection establish ? Is it the negation of the existence of the pramâṇas or the knowledge of their non-existence ? It cannot be the former because when you proceed to negate their existence you thereby admit their existence, for what is non-existent cannot be negated. It cannot be the latter, because your very argument becomes a pramâṇa as it makes known the non-existence of the pramâṇas, Perception, etc.

The reason advanced by the objector again can be turned equally against himself. The reason is "non-existence in the past, future and present". The negation cannot precede the thing to be negated, *i. e.* the pramâṇas, because there is then nothing to be negated. If it follows, then in the absence of the negation, the pramâṇas cannot be called the thing to be negated. If it co-exists with the pramâṇas, then the existence of the thing to be negated being admitted the negation becomes useless.

Again, the opponent's reasoning is invalid if he cannot cite a familiar instance (I. i. 32) in support of the reason. If he cites a familiar instance then this being an object of perception, Perception as a pramâṇa is admitted by him and his negation of all pramâṇas falls to the ground. The reason thus becomes what is known as the fallacy of the contradictory reason

(I. ii. 6). Further, we have already shown that in the reasoning of five members all the pramâṇas are combined. The opponent cannot say that the pramâṇas are valid in his reasoning and not in the reasoning of others.

The reason, "non-existence in the past, future and present", advanced by the opponent, does not also stand scrutiny. For pramâṇas do operate subsequently as when the existence of a flute is inferred by its tune.

The pramâṇas are thus established. Pramâṇa and prameya are, however, correlative terms. Whatever is the cause of cognition is pramâṇa ; whatever is the object of cognition is prameya. When the nature, character and strength of a pramâṇa is under examination it is a prameya, just as scales and weights by which things are measured may themselves be objects of measurement. Thus the soul, being the object of cognition, is a prameya (knowable) ; as it is an independent agent in the act of cognition, it is the knower. Cognition, being the cause of apprehension, is pramâṇa ; as an object of apprehension, it is a prameya. Where it is neither pramâṇa nor a prameya it is pramiti (knowledge).

Now, admitting all this, asks the opponent, are the pramâṇas, Perception, etc., established by other pramâṇas or are they independent of any pramâṇa ? Our answer is that to admit the need of other pramâṇas would entail infinite regression which is illogical, while to say that the pramâṇas do not stand in need of establishment would imply that the soul and other prameyas also do not require to be established and that the pramâṇas themselves are futile. Our reply therefore is that just as a lamp which is a cause of perception is itself made known by the contact of the eye which is also a cause of perception, in other words, just as Perception is the pramâṇa of Perception, so the pramâṇas, Perception, etc., are established by themselves mutually. It is not necessary that pramâṇa and prameya should belong to different classes of objects. It is seen that the soul knows itself by itself in such cases as "I feel pleasure, I feel pain." So also is the mind inferred by the mind, non-simultaneity of heterogeneous cognitions being the mark of its inference. Moreover, nothing is known to exist which cannot be cognised by the four pramâṇas. There is therefore no reason to assume other pramâṇas.

Some are of opinion that just as a lamp reveals itself as well an object without the aid of another lamp so the pramâṇas reveal themselves as well as their objects and do not require the aid of other pramâṇas. This view cannot be accepted. For there are objects such as a pot which do not reveal themselves but require pramâṇas. Is there any special reason to account for the difference in the two cases ? If there is no such reason, the example cited leads to no conclusion but stands by itself. If there is such a reason then the example presents a special case and does not establish a general rule.

Topic 14: Of Perception: Sûtras : *21—32.*

Some think that the definition of Perception (I. i. 4) is incomplete as it does not include the contact of the soul and the mind, whereas in the absence of such contact there can be no perception. We also hold that the contact of the soul and the mind is also necessary for the production of perception. Others think that the contact of the sense and the object is the cause of perception because the one precedes the other. In that case space, position, time and ether would also be the cause of perception for they always precede it. But they are not. Let us now explain why the contact of the soul and the mind and the contact of the mind and the sense have not been included in the definition of perception. Cognition is an attribute of the soul and is the mark of its existence (I. i. 10), and non-simultaneity of cognitions has been assigned as the mark of the existence of the mind (I. i. 16). It has thus been mentioned that the contact of the soul and the mind and of the mind and the sense is also a cause of perception. The contact of the soul and the mind is not only a cause of perception but also of inference, comparison and verbal cognition. But the contact of the sense and the object is the specific cause of perception alone. Hence it has been expressly mentioned. Not only is it the specific cause, it is also the dominant cause of perception as evidenced in the case where a loud sound or the like forces itself upon the notice of a man in sleep or absorbed in other things. Moreover, it is by reference to the senses and the objects that cognitions are differentiated as tactual, ocular, olfactory, etc.

When a perception forces itself into the soul during sleep or distraction the contact of the mind with the soul and the sense surely takes place. This contact is not due to the volition and attention of the soul. But in the soul abides another attribute namely adṛiṣṭa, produced by Activity and the Faults,-which accomplishes all things. Directed by adṛiṣṭa the mind comes into contact with the sense. Adṛiṣṭa it is which produces substances, attributes and actions, induces action in the four classes of atoms and in the mind, and produces bodies, senses and objects.

Some argue that Perception is really inference, because in it from the apprehension of a part the whole is cognised. For instance, the eye sees a part of the tree and the cognition of the tree is produced. Let us consider this objection to our doctrine of Perception as a separate pramâṇa. The tree is either a mass of atoms or an organised whole different from the atoms. In the former case neither the part apprehended nor the other part is the tree ; hence there can be no inference from the one to the other. If it is said that from the one part the other part is inferred and then the two parts are integrated producing the cognition of the tree, then the cause of the cognition of the tree is not inference but something else. In the latter case as in the opinion of the opponent the whole is not present in the part apprehended it is not apprehended and even if it is apprehended then there is no occasion for its inference. Moreover, the reason advanced by the opponent, namely apprehension of the part, disproves his case, for at least the part is the object of Perception. Lastly inference is based on Perception, *e.g.* of fire and smoke as connected.

What is then the object other than the part ? Is it a whole or an aggregate of atoms ? By a whole we mean a unity, the product as distinguished from its constituent parts, of which the parts are the substratum and in which the causes of apprehension are present. Every product is such a whole and not a mere aggregare of atoms. Such being the case there is not merely the apprehension of a part only but also of the whole associated with the part. To this the opponent replies by saying that as the whole by its very conception covers all the parts and is not limited to any single part it is impossible that there should be the apprehension of the whole in the apprehension of a part. We reply that partial apprehension is intelligible in the case of the parts which by their nature are disconnected and mutually exclude one another. But in the case of the whole such partial apprehension is impossible because it is an indivisible unity and has no part except its constituents from which it is distinct. By its nature the whole is apprehended as a whole along with the parts which are apprehended and is not apprehended with the parts which are not apprehended.

Topic 15 : Of the Whole (Avayavî): Sûtras : *33—36.*

The doubt as to the existence of the whole as distinct from its constituent parts is not justified. These constituent parts, *viz.*, the atoms, are themselves imperceptible. And if the whole did not exist there would be non-apprehension of " all," that is, substance, attribute, action, genus, species, and combination (vide Vais'eṣika-Sûtra, I. i, 4). But these are actually apprehended, *e. g.* the pot (substance) is dark, one, large, connected with the floor (attributes), shakes (action), exists (genus), is earthen (species) (the attributes inhering in it by combination). The whole therefore exists. The Sûtra (II. i. 35) also supports the existence of the whole by the argument that without there being a whole the parts could not hold together nor could the thing be capable of being pulled, etc. This reasoning may not be convincing. For the holding, pulling, etc. are due to cohesion (saṃgraha, integration). Cohesion is a distinct attribute co-existing with the conjunction of the parts and produced by moistness as in the case of an unburnt pot, and by melting as in the case of the burnt pot. With the whole as their cause these should have been possible in the case of a heap of dust. And where no such whole is produced, as, *e.g.*, when pieces of wood are glued together, even there they should not have held together and been capable of being pulled.

Those who maintain that the object of perception is not the whole but the aggregate of atoms should, on the contrary, be asked : When you apprehend the object as one, what is your idea of unity ? Do you mean by it identity or plurality of objects ? If you say that unity is the identity of the object, then such unity is distinct from the diversity of the atoms, and the whole is thus established. If, on the other hand, you say that the idea that the object is one is in respect of the plurality of atoms constituting the object, then the idea is self-contradictory.

The opponent may rejoin that a plurality can by reason of distance give rise to the idea of unity as in the case of an army or a forest. We reply that this cannot be, for the reason that while diversity of the units composing an army or a forest can be apprehended on nearer approach, the diversity of the individual atoms can never be so apprehended, so that the error as to the apparent unity of an army or a forest cannot arise in regard to an assembly of atoms.

Again, an army or a forest is, on the theory of the opponent, nothing but an aggregate of atoms, and the unity of such aggregates is the very thing which is under examination. The instances cited are therefore themselves in need of proof.

Then, error presupposes correct cognition. It is possible to mistake a post for a man only when one possesse cognition of a real man. Similarly the erroneous idea of unity in respect of an aggregate of atoms presupposes the existence of unity somewhere. It cannot exist in the aggregate for the aggregate is a plurality. It must therefore exist in something distinct from the plural aggregate, *i.e.*, the whole. Hence a pot is not a mere collection of atoms but is a whole, as otherwise it could not be perceived as one.

It may be argued that the idea of unity derived from the apprehension of sound, touch, smell, etc., as one may account for the apprehension of an aggregate of atoms as one. But the argument is not supported by any special reason which would show that the apprehension of a pot as one is erroneous and not correct. Moreover, sound, touch, smell, etc., are also of a composite character like a pot.

Unity and magnitude co-exist. The atoms have no magnitude. Yet a pot constituted by them possesses magnitude. Similarly a pot possesses unity. In respect of magnitude also a pot bears no analogy to sound which is known as minute and large, for sound has no extension which can be delimited like the extension of a pot. Again, the conjunction of two objects which does take place could not be possible were they only aggregates of atoms instead of unities. Conjunction is a distinct attribute and not unreal. It develops a new attribute in the conjoint object ; a flagged staff is neither a staff nor a flag. The cause of the cognition of the staff as thus qualified is conjuction. It is apprehended along with the apprehension of the qualified object. It cannot belong to atoms or collections of atoms as in that case it could not be apprehended.

The existence of natural kinds such as cow-ness, horse-ness, tree-ness, etc. which cannot be ignored, also proves the existence of an object which is present in the aggregotes of atoms aud is yet different from them. These distinct objects are the unitary wholes.

Topic 16 : Of Inference : Sûtras : *37-38.*

Some say that Inference can never be an instrument of true cognition because, e.g., the swelling of a river may be due to obstruction as well as to rain, the carrying off of eggs by ants may be due to disturbance of their nests as well as to imminence of rain and the screaming of the peacock may be imitative as well as real, so that the inference by means of these marks, namely that rain has fallen, that rain will fall and that rain is falling, may be all incorrect. To this we reply that this is not so, that is, that inference as an instrument of right cognition is not invalid, and that the incorrectness of the inference in the cases cited is due not to the defective nature of the process of Inference but is due to the fallacious character of the marks. It is because the man mistakes pseudo-marks for true marks that he falls into error.

Topic 17 : Of the Present Time : Sûtras *39-43.*

We have said that inference operates in respect of matters past, future and present. But the opponent denies the existence of the time present. His argument is that when a falling fruit detached from the stem approaches towards the ground all that can be seen is the distance it has fallen and the distance it has to fall and not any intervening distance which can give the idea of the present that it falls or is falling. We reply that time is manifested not by distance (space) but by action. The past is the time where action has ceased ; the future, where it will take place ; and the present, where action is apprehended in the object. Thus the past and the future depend upon the present. They cannot be a pair of correlated duals like long and short, light and shade, for there is no reason for such correlation; nor is the past or the future itself established otherwise than by reference to the present. Moreover, there is no universal correlation of duals; *e. g.* colour and touch, smell and taste are not correlatives. Further, the past and the future cannot be mutually the cause of each other, for so long as one of them is not established it cannot serve as the cause of the other, and *vice versa.* The truth is that the present is manifested by the existence of the object: substance exists, attribute exists, action exists. He who denies this denies the possibility of Perception, for Perception requires contact of the senses with objects which exist, are present. Inference, etc. depend upon Perception. The denial of the present therefore amounts to a denial of knowledge itself. Again, we have apprehension of the present alone as well as in association with the past and the future. For action may be continuous as in cooking or repeated as in cutting down a tree. In these cases all the three times are associated; e.g. the cooking commenced, the cooking is going on, the cooking will be completed. The object exists, is the instance of the apprehension of the present by itself.

Topic 18: *Of Comparison*: Sûtras: *44-48.*

Comparison (*vide* Sûtra I. i. 6), says the opponent, fails as an instrument of true cognition in any case; for if the resemblance is complete the cognition will be "As a cow so a cow"; if it is incomplete, the cognition will be. "As a bull so a buffalo"; and if it is partial the cognition will be "As one thing so anything else," which are all absurd. To this we reply that Comparison does not proceed on mere resemblance but on the well-known resemblance, that is, on the resemblance which is definitely known to be the means of establishing cognition of an object. Let then Comparison be a form of Inference, rejoins the opponent, as in both cases there is cognition of the unknown by the known. We reply that Comparison is distinguished from Inference in this that in the former it is necessary, while in Inference it is not necessary, to see the object to be known. E. g. the bos gavæus must be seen before it can be known as such by its resemblance to the cow. Moreover, in Comparison the resemblance must be pointed out by one to another. The man who knows both the cow and the bos gavæus points out the resemblance to the man who knows the cow but does not know the bos gavæus. Lastly, the conclusion in Comparison takes the form "as the cow so the bos gavæus" but the conclusion in Inference is not of this form "As the smoke, so the fire."

Topic 19: *Of the Word in general*: Sûtras: *49-56.*

The opponent says that Testimony is not different from Inference, because (1) the meaning which is not known and which is not an object of perception is known by means of the word which is known, as in Inference the unknown is known by means of the known, (2) cognition from Testimony does not, as does cognition from Comparison, differ from cognition from Inference, and (3) there is universal concomitance of the word and its meaning. To this we reply that in Testimony the word by itself is not competent to produce cognition of truth, and that it derives the force to produce such a cognition only from its being spoken by an âpta or truth-knowing benevolent person, as in the case of "heaven," "apsaras," "uttara kurus," "seven islands and seven oceans," "the worlds Bhûḥ, Bhuvah, Svar, etc.," and so on. Inference is not so dependent upon an âpta. This also constitutes the differenee of cognition from Testimony to cognition from Inference. Again, the relation of the word and the meaning is that of the signifier and the significate, and is not natural (dependent on and following from a law of nature). Natural concomitance exists between two objects when both are perceptible to the senses, as in the case of fire and smoke. But objects denoted by words are not perceived by Hearing, and there are objects denoted by words which are not perceptible by any sense. Therefore the supposed natural connection of the word aud meaning cannot be established by any means. It cannot be said that the meaning always accompanies the word, for in that case whenever the words food, fire, and sword are uttered the mouth should be filled with food, burnt with fire and cut with sword. Neither can it be said that the word always accompanies the meaning, for in that case the vocal apparatus should be found near the pot and other objects. It is true there is a uniformity in the relation of the word and the meaning. But this uniformity is due to convention created by the will of man and handed down from generation to generation. This is clear from the fact that the same word conveys different meanings among different races of mankind.

Topic 20 : *Of the* Veda : Sûtras : *57-68.*

Some condemn the Veda on the ground of futility; contradiction and repetition. But where the Vedic injunctions fail of their purpose the fault does not lie with the Veda but with the performer and the performance (in the same way as scientific experiments fail in the hands of novices). The so-called contradictory injunctions have reference to different points of time. The so-called repetition is re-inculcation with a purpose. The statements in the Veda admit of interpretation in the manner of secular statements. They are either : (1) injunctions or (2) exhortations or (3) re-inculcations. E. g. (1) He who desires heaven let him perform the Agnihotra sacrifice ; or let him cook food ; (2) this is the first among the sacrifices, this Jyotiṣṭoma, etc. ; or life, strength, pleasure, etc. are all in the food; (3) he offers Agnihotra, he offers with curd ; or cook, cook. The authoritative character of the Veda rests on its being the declaration of Âptas as in the case of Mantras and Medical Science. Mantras to counteract poisons, ghosts and lightning and medicines to cure diseases are vindicated by results. Some of the Vedic injunctions are similarly vindicated by results. The infallibility of others is inferred from the infallibility of the Âptas who have declared them. The Âptas are persons who have directly known the truth, who are kind to living beings and who are willing to communicate the truth as known by them. In the secular affairs of men also reliance on statements of âptas is seen. Moreover, the same Ṛiṣis who are the seers and speakers of the Veda are also the seers and speakers of Mantras and medicines.

The Vedic words are authoritative because they are significant of truth and not because they are eternal. They are not eternal as in that case all words would be related to all objects at the same time. Non-eternality does not entail loss of significance, for ordinary secular words which are not eternal are yet significant. Secular words cannot be eternal, for in that case the statements of those who are not âptas would not be untrue. It cannot be said that the words of non-âptas are non-eternal, for there is no reason to distinguish them from the words of the âptas. In the case of secular words also their validity depends on convention and not on their eternality. In both cases the authority of the âptas confers authority on their words. The eternality of Vedic words arises from their uninterrupted succession in tradition, study and application in all ages and world-cycles (manvantaras), past and future.

Book II: Chapter ii.

Topic 21 : The Pramâṇas *are not more than four*: Sûtras : *1—12.*

We admit that Tradition (Aitihya), Implication (Arthâpatti), Composition (Sambhava) and Non-existence or Negation (Abhâva) are also means of knowledge; but we do not admit that they are different from the four means enumerated by us, *viz.* Perception, Inference, Comparison and Word. Tradition consists of opinions coming down from generation to generation in uninterrupted succession, the origin of which is lost in oblivion. Implication is cognition following from the sense of what is stated ; e. g., when it is said that without clouds there can be no rain, it follows that with clouds there can be rain. Composition consists in the apprehension of the presence of one object from the apprehension of the presence of another object which never exists without the former ; e. g. the apprehension of the presence of the ounce from the apprehension of the presence of the pound. Non-existence is the negative, the contradictory, as the non-existent of the existent ; e. g., absence of rain in the presence of clouds leads to the cognition of the conjunction of the clouds with high winds.

Tradition is not different from Word or Testimony, as its authority is derived from the same source, *viz.*, its emanating from an Âpta. Implication Composition and Non-existenee are not different from Inference which is cognition of the imperceptible by means of the perceptible. Implication and Non-existence or Negation proceed on the basis of contradiction ; Composition, cognition of the component from the composite, proceeds on the basis of universal concomitance.

Some question the validity of Implication on the ground that even when clouds exist rain does not sometimes fall. In putting forward this objection they mistake for Implication what is not Implication. From the statement that there can be no effect without a cause, it follows that where the cause exists the effect is produced. This is Implication according to the law of contradiction. The failure of the cause to produce the effect on account of the operation of counter-agents is an attribute of the cause, and not the object of cognition by Implication. The object of cognition by Implication is that the production of the effect depends upon the existence of the cause.

Non-existence or Negation is held by some to be not an instrument of cognition on the ground that the object of such cognition does not exist. This is a rash argument. There are innumerable objects of cognition which are apprehended by means of Negation in the form of cognition of non-existence. To take one example : Where from a heap of cloths some of which are marked and the others are not marked, the unmarked ones are taken out, the action of taking them out depends on their cognition and their cognition is produced by the non-existence of any mark. The negation of mark is thus a means of cognition and therefore a pramâṇa ; for a pramâṇa is nothing but a means of cognition. For the purpose of negation it is not necessary that an object should first be produced and then destroyed ; e. g., for cloths to be unmarked, it is not necessary first to put marks on them and then to efface the marks. For the negation of marks in some cloths can be perceived by seeing the presence of marks in other cloths. Negation is correlated to affirmation whether in the same or in a different substratum. Moreover, negation or non-existence is of two kinds, antecedent and consequent. Non-existence prior to production is antecedent non-existence; non-existenee after destruction is consequent non-existence. The absence of marks in cloths which have never been marked is antecedent non-existence of marks in the cloths.

Topic 22 : Sound is not eternal : Sûtras : *13—39*.

Diverse opinions are held as to the duration of Sound. The Mîmâṃsakas assert that Sound is an attribute of Ether, is all-pervading, eternal, and is not produced but manifested. The Sâṃkhyas hold that Sound co-exists with smell, etc., inheres in substances, is existent like smell, etc., and is not produced but manifested. The Vais'eṣikas maintain that Sound is an attribute of Ether and is liable to production and destruction like cognition. The Bauddhas think that Sound is produced from the agitation of the great Elements, is without any support and is liable to production and destruction. These opinions give rise to doubt as to what the truth of the matter may be. The truth is that Sound is non-eternal, because (1) it originates from a cause, (2) is sensible, and (3) is treated as a product. Whatever is caused is non-eternal, i. e., is also destroyed. Conjunction and disjunction of substances are the causes of Sound. They are the causes of its production and not of its manifestation. It is not an object of manifestation because it is apprehended by Hearing. The sense of Hearing is imponderable and therefore cannot go out and reach the place where Sound appears. Sound reaches the sense of Hearing in a series of sounds in the way of waves of water, after the cessation of the Conjunction (e. g. of the axe and the tree in cutting) which produces it. An object which is manifested is apprehended where it is manifested. This is not the case with Sound. The difference in the intensity of Sounds also show that they are not different from other products such as pleasure and pain. It cannot be said that Sound is one and of a uniform character and is manifested by Conjunction the strength of which accounts for the pitch of the Sound as perceived. For this cannot explain the phenomenon of the overpowering of one sound by another, e. g. of the sound of the flute by the sound of the drum. Heterogeneous objects do not overpower one another; e. g. colour does not overpower touch. An object does not overpower itself. Objects of the same class overpower one another; e. g., brighter colours overpower less bright colours. Similarly, when it is seen that the sound of the flute is drowned by the sound of the drum it must be admitted that the two sounds are two separate objects and that they vary in intensity. Intensity is their attribute and is not due to the strength of their causes. Therefore sounds are produced and not that one uniform eternal sound is only manifested.

Moreover, manifestation must take place where the causes of manifestation operate. That being so, as the flute and the drum are operated in different places Sound manifested in the flute cannot be subdued by Sound manifested in the drum. If it is said that difference of place does not matter then the beating of a drum anywhere would drown Sound manifested in all flutes all over the world at the same time. The theory thus is untenable. The phenomena of sound can be explained only on the theory that sounds are produced and that they become perceptible only when they reach the sense of Hearing in waves.

The opponent attacks the three reasons given in support of the non-eternality of sound; (1) the destruction of a pot originates from the disjunction of its causes ; the non-existence of the pot after destruction is eternal, (2) genus which is perceptible is eternal, (3) as we speak of the parts of a tree or a blanket which are non-eternal so we speak of the parts of Ether and the Soul which are eternal. To this we reply; (1) There is a difference between the eternal and the pseudo-eternal. That object is eternal which has come into existence without production (by conjunction or disjunction of parts) and which never loses its self-existence. Non-existence after destruction of an object is not eternal in this sense. Moreover, in the case of sound there is no cause to originate its destruction in the manner of the pot. Therefore the analogy of the pot does not hold good. (2) Sound is non-eternal, not because it is perceptible but because of the manner in which it comes into contact with the sense of Hearing and becomes perceptible. (3) When we speak of the parts of a tree or a blanket we mean their constituents. But Ether and the Soul have no constituent parts. The use of the word parts in regard to them is metaphorical, and conveys the sense that their contact with finite objects does not pervade the whole of them. The conjunction of two fruits does not pervade the whole of them but is confined to parts only. Similarly when we say that an object is in contact with Ether or the Soul we mean that it is not in contact with every part of Ether or the Soul and to convey this meaning we say that it is in contact with a part of Ether or the Soul. As conjunction does not pervade the whole of its substrata, so sound does not pervade the whole of Ether, and cognition, etc. do not pervade the whole of the Soul.

You may ask, Why has not Gotama embodied in an aphorism the tenet that Ether and other eternal substances have no parts? Our reply is that in many topics he has not brought out all the sides ; that is his characteristic. He thinks that in such cases one can ascertain the truth from the tenet of his Śâsrra. The tenet of his Śâstra is, as is well known, Nyâya, that is, many-branched Inference not inconsistent with Perception and Revelation.

Again, how are we to know that an object exists or that an object does not exist? By cognition or non-cognition according to pramâṇa. By this test sound is non-existent before utterance because it is then not cognised and because any obstruction to its cognition is also not cognised.

The reasons given in support of the theory that Sound is eternal are (1) that it is intangible like Ether, (2) that it is capable of being imparted by the teacher to the pupil, (3) that it admits of repetition, and (4) that the cause of its destruction is not perceived. The first reason is fallacious, because the atom which is tangible is eternal, while action which is intangible is non-eternal. As regards the second it is seen that an object of gift is perceptible on its way from the donor to the donee. But sound is not perceptible and therefore does not exist in the interval between the teacher and the pupil. Nevertheless, it may be said, instruction is received by the pupil and from the fact of instruction the existence of Sound in the interval is to be inferred, whereby the gift of Sound from the teacher to the pupil becomes possible. To this we reply that the opponent has yet to establish what constitutes instruction. Is it that Sound residing in the teacher actually moves from him and reaches the pupil, or is it imitation of what is done by the teacher as in the case of a dancing lesson? Such being the case instruction does not remove the doubt as to the validity of instruction as a mark of the possibility of the gift of Sound by the teacher to the pupil. In regard to the third reason, it is argued that as the persistence of colour makes it possible to see it again and again so the persistence of Sound renders possible its utterance times without number. But repetition is possible also in the case of objects which are not persistent, that is, are different at every time they appear. Thus, we say, he danced twice, he eats twice, etc. As regards the fourth reason it is said that the cause of the destruction of non-eternal things, e. g. a clod of earth, is seen; and that if Sound were non-eternal the cause of its destruction would also be perceived; but that such a cause is not perceived; and that therefore Sound is not non-eternal. We reply that if the non-apprehension of the cause of the destruction of Sound implies its non-destruction, the non-apprehension of the cause of its non-hearing also implies its constant hearing. Non-hearing cannot be due to absence of manifesting agents, for we have already shown the impossibility of Sound being an object of manifestation. If then the opponent's theory is reduced to this that the hearing of Sound is without any cause then why should he not admit that the destruction of Sound also is without any cause? We do not say, however, that there can be no cognition of the cause of the destruction of sound. The existence of such cause can be inferred from the fact which we have already established that sounds are produced in a series. The first sound is produced by conjunction and disjunction and gives rise to the second sound which, in its turn, to the third and so on and on till the series is stopped and the last sound is destroyed by some obstruction such as a wall. Each succeeding sound destroys its immediate predecessor. Then, when a bell is rung various sound series of different tones, high and higher, low and lower, are heard. Such diverse differences in tone and timbre cannot co-exist in one eternal permanent Sound. And without them differences in aural cognitions cannot be explained. The cause of the differences in the intensity of sound is the degree of force with which the bell is rung and which is communicated to the sound series produced by it. The existence of such force in the bell cannot be denied. For the ringing of the bell does not produce sound when the hand is placed upon it. This shows that the force is stopped in its action by the conjunction of the hand. It is also perceived by touch that the vibrations set up in the bell by the force of ringing gradually die away. On the other hand, if the non-apprehension of the cause of the destruction of Sound proves its eternality then the manifestation of Sound after its appearance would continue for ever as no cause of its destruction is apprehended.

Sound cannot be an attribute of Ether, says the opponent; because in that case the stopping of the vibrations in the bell by the hand could not cause its destruction. According to him, sound and the vibrations which cause it must reside in the same substratum. We reply that the objection does not apply, because Ether is intangible. The non-cognition of sound in the same substance with colour, taste, smell and touch and the phenomena of sound series show that sound is the attribute of an intangible all-pervading substance, i. e. Ether. Sound exhibits a twofold difference: a bell, e. g., produces different varieties of sound and in each variety there is a difference of pitch. These differences could not be possible if sound were an attribute of the same substance with colour, etc.; as in that case like colour, etc., it would be of one unalterable character.

Topic 23 : Of the Modification of Sound : Sûtras *40-51.*

Sound is either Varṇa, articulate, letter, or Dhvani, inarticulate, noise. In regard to sound as letter, when *Dadhi* and *Atra*, for instance, become *Dadhyatra*, what does happen? Modification or substitution? Is *i* modified as *y* or is replaced by *y*? We say that *i* is replaced by *y*. Our reasons are as follows: (1) When one object. *e.g.*, a piece of gold, modifies into another object, *e.g.*, a ring, some attributes disappear, other attributes appear : while the same material subsists in the modification ; but this is not the case where *i* gives place to *y*. (2) The effort required in the utterance of *i* is different from the effort required in the utterance of *y*. (3) Where *y* comes in the place of *i* and where *y* stands by itself as in *yatate*, and where *i* gives place to *y* and where *i* stands by itself as in *idam*, the effort required in the utterance of the *y* in the two cases does not differ, and the effort required in the utterance of the *i* in the two cases also does not differ. (4) The modification of *i* into *y* is not cognised as the modification of milk into curd is perceived. (5) The theory of modification of letters is not necessary for the purpose of the rules of grammar. (6) One letter is not the product of another. They are all independently produced. (7) Modification can be either transformation, *i.e.*, change of form or production. But neither is possible in the case of letters. (8) Where *bhu* takes the place of *as*, *vach* of *bru*, you do not say modification takes place. Similarly not modification but substitution takes place in the case of single letters. (9) In the case of modification the bulk of the modification varies accordfng to the bulk of the original ; but whether *i* is long or short makes no difference in *y*. The opponent rejoins that modifications are sometimes greater than the original as in the case of a tree from an acorn and sometimes equal to the original as in the case of a ring from a piece of gold and sometimes less than the original as in the case of yarns from cotton. To this we reply first that mere example unsupported by any reason, homogeneous or heterogenous, cannot establish a proposition ; otherwise a horse would be a modification of a bullock, both being beasts of burden. In the second place, when we refer to the bulk of the original and the modification we intend to say that a modification follows its original in essentials so that if the originals differ the modifications also must differ. But in the case in question *y* does not follow its original, *i.e.*, it does not become long or short according as it takes the place of *i* long or short. It is therefore not a modification of *i*. It cannot be said that the base *i* is not affected by its attributes of longness and shortness and that *y* follows the base. For what happens in the modification of a base, *e.g.*, gold or clay, is that its original form is destroyed and a new form is produced. But in the case in question there is no evidence that *i* is destroyed and *y* is produced from the disintegrated *i*. (10) When *Dadhyatra* is disjoined *i* returns to its orignal form, but curd never returns to milk ; therefore *y* is not a modification of *i*. It is true that a ring can be reduced to a piece of gold again. But the analogy does not hold good here. For gold remains constant ; it becomes a ring by giving up and taking up some attributes. A similar change does not take place in the case of *i* and *y*. It cannot be said that letter-ness remains constant in *i* and *y* ; for *i* and *y* cannot be attributes of the general attribute letter-ness.

(11) Again, the letters are either eternal or non-eternal. If they are eternal, they cannot undergo modification. If they are non-eternal, then one is destroyed before another takes its place. To this it may be replied by the opponent that there are eternal things which vary in their attributes ; *e.g.*, the atoms are imperceptible while the letters are perceptible ; therefore while the atoms do not undergo modification letters may. The argument is invalid. The reason advanced, namely difference of attributes, is a contradictory reason, it contradicts the supposed eternal character of letters. Modification and eternality are contradictory terms. On the other hand, it cannot be said that as the hearing of the letters is possible though they are destroyed at the third moment after their production, so their modification also may be possible. For a mere example cannot establish a proposition. The reason must be stated. If the hearing of the letters be the reason, then we say that the universal concomitance of the hearing of the letters and of the modifications of the letters is yet to be established. The fallacy of the opponent's argument is sâdharmya-sama (V. i. 2).

(12) A further reason why *y* cannot be a modification of *i* is that sometimes we find *i* in the place of *y* as in *Vyadh* becoming *vidhyati*.

The expression "mcdif.caiton of letter" used by grammarians does not mean that one letter is transformed into, or produced by, another letter. It means the substitution of one letter in place of another. It appears in six different forms : (*a*) change of attribute, as when the grave takes the place of the acute accent ; (*b*) suppression, as when *bhu* takes the place of *as* ; (*c*) decrease, as when the long is replaced by the short ; (*d*) increase, as when the short is replaced by the long or the prolated ; (*e*) curtailment, as when *stah* comes in the place of *as* ; and (*f*) coalescence, as when the base or the affix is augmented. These are all instances of substitution.

The result of the above examination is to show that sound is non-eternal. Sound does not remain constant under change of forms nor survives in its product. It is produced at one moment, exists at the second moment and is destroyed at the third moment by the sound to which it gives rise or by the obstruction which it meets.

Topic 24 : Of the Force of Words : Sûtras : *58-69.*

Gotama now proceeds to determine the force of words on which depend the validity of Word as pramâṇa. A word consists of letters ending in an affix. Affixes are nominal or verbal. Prefixes and indeclinables have their nominal affixes elided (Paṇini, II. iv. 28). Words lead to the cognition of objects. It is therefore necessary to determine the nature or force of words. Let us take the word, cow, for example. The Word is used to denote an individual, a form and a genus. The doubt therefore arises as to whether it denotes any one or all of these objects. One party says that the word denotes the indivdiual, because individuals which differ from one another and possess attributes, and not the genus which is unproduced, undifferentiated and devoid of form, parts and atributes, admit of (*a*) specification, this cow, that cow, etc. ; (*b*) collection, a herd of cows ; (*c*) gift, he gives cows to the learned ; (*d*) possession, the Brâhmaṇa's cow ; (*d*) enumeration, ten cows ; (*e*) growth, the cow grows ; (*f*) emaciation, the cow grows lean ; (*g*) colour, white cow ; (*h*) association, the good of the cow ; and (*i*) propagation, the cow produces a calf. To this we reply that the above uses of the word cow are rendered possible only because the objects indicated are endowed with the genus cow-ness. The use of the word cow in respect of the individual is metaphorical, as in such cases as when we say, he is a Shakespeare, he dwells on the lake, he is weaving a mat (when the mat is yet non-existent), etc., etc.

Some think that the form is the denotation of the word ; because form consists in the configuration of parts which endures, and because without the cognition of the forms we cannot distinguish a cow from a horse. This is not correct, because mere form has no connection with the genus. It is the substance cow which is connected with the genus. When we say, wash the cow, bring the cow, we mean the substance in which the genus cow-ness is present, and not a wooden cow though it possesses the appearance (individual) and form of a cow. Neither can the genus alone be the denotation of the word ; for there can be no cognition of the genus without the cognition of the individual and form.

The truth is that the individual, form and genus are all the denotation of the word. There is no fixed rule of the relation as principal and secondary among them. The force of the word is the same in regard to each of them. When specification is intended, the individual becomes principal, genus and form become secondary ; when specification is not intended, the genus becomes principal, the individual and form become secondary.

The individual is that which is manifested. It is perceptible by the senses. Every subtance is not manifested to the senses. The individual is that substance which is produced by the conjunction of parts and which is the substratum, as far as may be, of specific attributes such as smell, taste, colour, touch, gravity, density, fluidity, impetus, and finite magnitude.

The form is that by which the genus and the marks of the genus are made known. It consists in the enduring or fixed configuration of the parts of the entities, cow, etc., and of the parts of those parts.

The genus is that which produces similar cognition in respect of different substrata. By reason of it individual objects are not differentiated from one another. It is the cause of the assimilation of objects. It is a minor Sâmânya or genus when it establishes non-difference of some objects among themselves and their difference from some other objects.

Book III: Chapter I.

Topic 25 : The Senses are not the Soul : Sûtras : *1—3*.

There are two kinds of predication : (1) a part is predicated of a whole of which it is a part, *e.g.* the tree stands by the roots ; (2) one thing is predicated of a different thing, *e.g.* he cuts with the axe. What is the nature of the predication in such cases as " A man sees with the eye, knows with the mind, discriminates with the intellect, feels pleasure and pain with the body " ? Are the eye, the mind, the intellect and the body predicated as parts of a whole of which they are the parts, or of something different from them ? Thus arises the doubt as to whether the soul is indentical with the organism of the body, the senses, the mind, the intellect and the feelings, or distinct from it ? The truth is that it is distinct from the organism of the body, etc. Because the same object is apprehended by the different senses. That agent which apprehends the same object by means of the different senses and assimilates or integrates the mutually independent intuitions of the different senses, is a different object. It is the soul. The senses cannot effect the assimilation, because one sense cannot perform the function of another sense. Nor can the organism, because, being an aggregate, it lacks the unity of apperception (anuvyavasâya, I see *and* touch). It is true that objects are allotted to the senses ; so that in the absence of a sense its object cannot be apprehended. *E.g.* the blind cannot see, the deaf cannot hear. But this does not show that each sense is a conscious entity and that the supposition of another conscious entity is superfluous. For the apprehension or non-apprehension of objects according to the efficiency or inefficiency of the senses will be the same whether the senses are themselves regarded as the conscious agents or as the instruments of a conscious agent. On the contrary, the very fact that the senses are limited in their respective functions proves the existence of the soul, as conscious, all-knowing, the receiver of the contents of all the senses, unaffected by the distribution of objects among the senses. The following instances of the operations of the conscious agent will show that its recognition as a distinct entity cannot be avoided. (i) He who sees colour, infers (recalls) taste and smell previously perceived. He who perceives smell infers colour and taste. And so in the case of the other senses also. Again, after seeing colour one smells the flavour, and after smelling flavour one sees colour. This assimilated apprehension of the objects of all the senses without any fixed order of succession must take place in the same site and cannot have any other agent but the soul. (ii) It also assimilates the various intuitions of perception, inference, testimony and doubt, embracing manifold objects and having it as their cause, and assimilating knows, as illustrated in its comprehending the contents of a book, treating of all sensible objects. Thus, hearing letters uttered one after another, it integrates them as words and sentences and assimilates them with meaning which is not to be grasped by the ear; then, cognising the fixed relation of words and meanings, it apprehends quite a number of objects belonging to more than one sense, which cannot be apprehended by the senses severally. This absence of limitation of the objects to be known in the case of the all-knower, which meets us at every step, cannot be circumvented, by attributing consciousness to the senses.

Topic 26 : The Body is not the Soul : Sûtras *4*—6.

In the Sûtra III. i. 4 the word "Body" stands for the living being in the shape of the organism of the body, the senses, cognitions and feelings. Now, the scriptures declare that killing is a sin and that sin accrues to the agent. (Even those Bauddhas who deny the existence of a soul admits the existence of virtue and vice). But if there were no soul other than the organism of the body, senses, cognitions and feelings, then the declaration of the scriptures would be meaningless and virtue and vice would be impossible. For, the organism undergoes change at every moment and is nothing but a series of changes one taking the place of another at every moment. It would follow that the organism to which the sin of killing would accrue would be different from the organism which would kill. Again, if re-birth be possible of such an organism it would not be due to past acts, so that there would be no law of 'karma' and study and practices for the sake of release would be futile. It may be argued that in the case of the kiiling of an organism endowed with a soul there would also be no sin, for the reason that the soul is eternal and cannot be killed. But the argument does not hold good, because we do not say that killing is the destruction of an eternal entity. By killing we mean the destruction, or the causing the anaesthesia, disease, inefficiency, disturbance of the interconnections or the disorganisation of the body which is the field of the experience of pleasure and pain, and also of the senses which are the instruments of the apprehension of their respective objects. Or the Sûtra (III. i. 6) may mean that killing is the disturbance or disorganisation of the association of the soul with the organism of the body, senses and cognitons by virtue of which association only the soul is the agent in the expericnce of pleasure and pain, and without which it can have no experience. It does not mean the distruction of the soul as an eternal entity.

Topic 27 : The sense of sight is not one : Sûtras *7—14.*

What is seen with the right eye is recognised as having been seen with the left eye. Such recognition also is a mark of the existence of the soul. But the opponent urges that here at any rate a soul is not needed to account for the phenomena, because the sense of sight is really one and appears as dual owing to its operating on either side of the nasal bone. The objection is futile. When one eye is destroyed the other does not suffer destruction along with it. Of course, a tree remains a tree even after a branch is cut off. But the analogy does not apply here. For a tree is an aggregate of parts each of which is an aggregate by itself. So that the destruction of a part does not entail the destruction of the other parts. But the eye is supposed to be a unity. Or, " Dṛiṣṭânta-virodha " in the Sûtra (III. i. 11) may mean that the supposition is contrary to experience. For, in the skull there are two sockets for the eyes. Again, when one eyeball is pressed the apprehension of the object by the two eyes becomes different, and on the removal of the pressure the apprehension by the two eyes becomes similar.

(*a*) *Association of ideas.*

The mouth waters on seeing or smelling an orange; this is due to the recollection of the taste. And this shows that consciousness is not in the sense, for what is seen by one is not recollected by another. To this the opponent replies by alleging that recollection is caused by the receipt (the object recollected) and that this, and not the soul, causes the action in the mouth at the sight or smell of an orange. But recollection must be an attribute of the soul, and as such prove the existence of the soul. On the supposition of the senses being conscious there would be either no recollection or there would be no order of recollection. For the senses are diverse agents and on the supposition there is nothing to assimilate or co-ordinate their experiences ; hence there would be no recollection. Or every sense would recollect the experience of every other sense ; which is contrary to experience : one does not remember what is seen by another. It follows that there must be a different agent capable of apprehending diverse objects ; and that is the soul. The affairs of living beings depend on memory. The watering of the mouth as the mark of the existence of the soul is a mere instance.

Then our opponent argues that memory does not infer the soul, because the cause of recollection is impression and its content the object recollected and not the soul in either case. But he has not exactly determined the content of memory. Let us see what it really is. The statement which indicates the content of memory takes one or another of the following forms ; (a) I knew that object ; (b) I have known that object ; (c) that object has been known by me ; and (d) I had knowledge in respect of this object. In each of these statements not merely the object, but the object previously known associated with the knower and the knowledge forms the content of memory ; in other words, every act of recollection comprehends the agent, the act and the object of cognition. This is in regard to an object which is not before the senses. In regard to an object which is before the senses, i. e. in the case of recognition, three cognitions are assimilated, proceeding from the one and the same agent and not from diverse agents nor from no agent. Thus, in the statement, I see now what I have seen before, the previous seeing and the consciousness of seeing are two cognitions, while the present seeing is the third cognition. These cognitions combine to connect a single object with a single agent. Thus this content of memory, the soul, which the opponent leaves undetermined, but which is present in memory and is clearly known, is sought to be negated by the reason that the object remembered is the content of memory.

Memory is not mere memory nor is the object remembered its only content. The assimilation of experiences which takes place in an act of memory cannot be possible without something to which all objects are equally accessible, as in the case of assimilation in an act of cognition. A single knower within whose purview are all objects assimilates its own cognitions as I shall know that object, I know that object, I knew that object, and, desiring to know, and not knowing for a long time, feels certain at last that it knew the object. Similarly it assimilates memory drawing its contents from the time future, present and past, operating with the desire to remember. Were the entity merely a series of impressions (or ideas), as impressions (and ideas) disappear as they arise at every moment, not a single impression (or idea) would be left which could be aware of any cognition and act of memory in association with all the three times. And without such awareness there can be no assimilation of cognition and memory in the form of "I (know or remember)", "(This cognition or re-collection is) Mine", as it is not possible in the case of cognition and memory in different bodies. It follows, therefore, that there does exist a single entity penetrating all objects which unites and maintains the unity of the series of cognitions and the series of memories, and which does not establish such unity of its cognitions and memories with that of another on account of the absence of its operation in the latter's body.

Topic 28 : The Mind is not the Soul: Sûtras *: 15-17.*

But, urges the opponent, the functions attributed to the soul may all be possible for the mind. We reply that the opponent is quarrelling about names and not about the reality. The instruments of knowledge such as the eye, nose, touch, must belong to a knower. So also does the thinker penetrating all objects possess an instrument of thinking in the form of the internal organ competent to reach all objects. That being so, the opponent errs in calling the knower the mind and not the soul, and not allowing the mind to be called the mind, though admitting that it is the instrument of thought. On the other hand, if he denies that the thinker possesses an instrument of thought which can reach all objects, then the knower can very well do without the instruments of knowledge, and the opposition will thereby entail the disappearance of all the senses as well. The distinction between sense-experience and thought-experience is not unfounded. Each sense is limited to its special object and cannot go beyond that limit. None of the senses can reach that other class of objects which include pleasure, etc. For the cognition of pleasure, etc. a different instrument is needed. It is known by its mark of non-simultaneity of cognitions, due to its coming into contact with the external senses one at a time.

Topic 29 : The Soul is eternal : Sûtras *: 18-26.*

Some entities are eternal, some are non-eternal. Is the soul which is established as distinct from the organism of the body, senses, mind and cognitions, eternal or non-eternal ? The answer is that the very reasons which prove the existence of the soul throughout the stages of infancy, childhood, youth and old age, also prove its existence after its separation from the body, etc. For, an infant to whom the things of the world are yet unknown feels joy, fear and grief. This is rendered possible by memory, and not otherwise, and memory depends upon past experience, and this depends upon past life and nothing else. The somatic resonance of the infant in the presence of the causes of joy, fear and grief cannot be explained on the analogy of the opening and closing of a lotus ; for in the case of a full grown man it is found that his changes of countenance due to joy, fear and grief are not automatic like the opening and closing of a lotus. There is therefore no reason why these should be so in the case of an infant. Moreover, the changes in a lotus are known to be due to a definite cause, namely the action of heat, cold, rain and season, and are not quite automatic. Similarly the changes of joy, etc. must be due to a definite cause, and that cause cannot be anything but the continuity of memory. Again, the new-born baby's instinctive desire for the mother's milk shows the habit of taking food and this habit necessarily implies a previous body in which the soul has experienced hunger and its satisfaction with food. This instinctive desire for food bears no analogy to the attraction of the iron towards a magnet. For the approach of the iron towards a magnet has also a definite cause; otherwise pebbles, etc., would also be drawn towards a magnet. But the cause is not apparent to the eye and has to be inferred both as regards its nature and its limitation. The inference must be made from the action itself. Thus iron approaches only a magnet, and only at a certain distance. Similarly only an infant moves for food only and when in the mother's arms. Is the cause of such movement past habit or something else? It is seen that memory of past experience causes adults to approach food for the satisfaction of hunger. The same must be the cause also in the case of the infant.

Then a man is born possessing Attraction, and the source of Attraction is the after-thought of the contents of previous experience which can be possible only in a previous body. The soul, remembering the objects experienced in a previous body, becomes attracted to those objects. Attraction thus links together two successive births and it is not possible to point to a beginning of its connection with the body.

But how do you know that the recollectlon of past experience gives rise to Attraction in a new-born baby, and that it is not produced in the same way as are the properties of a substance (e.g., jar) along with the substance itself from the same cause? The soul and its attraction are not produced simultaneously like a pot and its properties, because Attraction, etc. are due to saṃkalpa, imagination, thought. It is seen that Attraction is produced by the thought of living beings enjoying objects; the thought springs from the memory of past experiences. Hence it is inferred that the Attraction which the baby feels is also caused by the memory of past experiences. Attraction could be produced like the property of a pot were the soul a product and were the cause of Attraction something other than the memory of past experiences. But neither of these is the case. Should it be supposed that adṛṣṭa, *i.e.*, merit and demerit, is the cause of Attraction, even then connection with a previous body cannot be denied; for the production of adṛiṣṭa must have taken place in the previous life and not in this.

The truth is that Attraction for an object arises from the entire occupation of the mind with that object, and this is nothing but habitual experience of the object which determines modes of thinking in future. Attraction differs according to the sphere of birth which is determined by karma or adṛiṣṭa, and the new-born entity derives its name from the sphere of its birth.

Topic 30 : The Body is of the Earth, earthy : Sûtras : *27-31.*

It has been demonstrated that the soul's connection with the body is without beginning and that the body in which it experiences pleasure and pain is due to its own karma. It is to be investigated whether the body possesses a single character like the sense of smell, etc., or a diverse character. Doubt arises in this respect owing to the differences of opinion on the subject. The truth is that the human body is constituted by the element of Earth alone, because the distinctive attribute of Earth, namely smell, is observed in it. At the same time it is not denied that the other elements conjoin with Earth as conditions in the production of the human body. Similarly all the elements conjoin to produce aqueous, igneous, aerial and etherial bodies in different worlds to serve the particular purposes of the souls. There is also scriptural authority for the view that the human body is constituted by Earth alone, e.g., "Let thy eye go to the sun...let thy body go to the Earth" (Ṛigveda, X. xvi. 3); "I make the sun thy eye ...I make the Earth thy body" (Satapatha Brâhmaṇa, XVII. viii. 4-6.) In the one the product resolves into its quiescent original; in the other the product is derived from the original.

Topic 31 : The Senses are constituted by the Elements : Sûtras : *32-51.*

To take the case of the eye (Sight): Colour is perceived when the pupil of the eye is unimpaired, and is not perceived when it is impaired. The pupil is a material body. On the other hand, the pupil itself does not come into contact with the object when its colour is perceived. At the same time there must be some contact as otherwise perception of colour cannot be possible. The eye therefore must be immaterial in the sense of not being constituted by the manifested or visible elements, and must be all-pervading. In this state of uncertainty one argues that the senses must be immaterial and all-pervading because they apprehend objects of widely divergent dimensions from the acorn to the Himalaya mountain. To this the reply is that the preception of objects of different dimensions by the eye is due to different contacts of ocular rays with the objects. Such contact is essential in ocular perception as is proved by the fact there is no perception where there is an obstruction. It is no argument against the existence of ocular rays that they are not perceived. For perception is not the sole test of existence. Inference by the mark of obstruction preventing contact proves their existence, as it does in the case of the other side of the moon and the lower portion of the earth. The rule of perception varies in its application according to the nature of substances and attributes. E. g., water vapour hanging in the air is not perceived but its cool touch is felt ; heat rays are not perceived, but their warmth is experienced. Similarly Fire exists in various conditions. In the solar rays both colour and touch are developed and so they are perceived. In the rays of light from a lamp colour is developed and touch is undeveloped ; these too are perceptible. Fire in hot water possesses developed touch and undeveloped colour ; hence it is imperceptible. In the ocular fire both colour and touch are undeveloped ; hence it is imperceptible. The development or accession of intensity of colour is one of the conditions of the perception of colour.

This peculiarity of the ocular rays arises from the nature of the senses. Like the multi-form aggregations of all substances the organisation of the senses is brought about by merit and demerit to subserve the purpose of the soul which consists in the cognition of objects and the experience of pleasure and pain.

Some thinkers argue as follows : The resilience of the sense of sight on meeting an obstruction is an attribute of a material substance. For this is the case with all material substances in all circumstances. On the other hand, the penetration of glass, mica, etc., by the ocular rays shows that they are non-material. So the point remains doubtful. We say that this is not so, for the reason given is erratic. For such penetration is also seen in the case of the light of a lamp which illumines objects beyond glass, etc., and of heat which cooks grains in a vessel.

Non-perception again may be due to overpowering, as in the case of a meteor which is not seen when the sun shines. In the case of ocular rays there is such a special cause of their non-perception, namely, as already stated, want of development or intensity. That the ocular rays lack in intensity also appears from the fact that the eye cannot apprehend objects without the aid of external light. The ocular rays are not overpowered, for overpowering can take place only when the thing overpowered has been developed. The ocular rays are not perceived even at night in all cases.

That such rays exist appears from the observation of these rays in the eyes of prowlers by night, e. g., cat, tiger, etc. There is no generic difference between the eyes of these animals and of men, because the sight in both cases is impeded by obstructions.

The perception of objects behind a plate of glass or mica or a thin stratum of cloud offers no argument against the proposition that the contact of the senses with the objects is the cause of cognition. For in these cases there is really no obstruction, but actual contact is established through the glass, etc. The sun's rays also cause burning through a crystal. In all such cases the interspaces among the components of the intervening substances provide a passage whereby direct contact is established between the rays and the objects on which they operate.

But why cannot a wall, e. g., offer such a passage? Because a wall is not constituted in the same way as glass is. How do you know this? This is known from the nature of the things as revealed by their effects. The ocular rays reflected from the smooth surface of the mirror makes one's own face perceptible. This clarity of the mirror is its nature. Similarly a wall does not reflect light rays. This is its nature. Thus experience shows that glass, etc., offers no obstruction, while a wall, etc., do, to the passage of light rays. And no arbitrary limitations can be imposed upon facts established by perception and inference. For these pramâṇas reveal reality as it is. Objects as they really are, in their own nature, in their own character, are established by the pramâṇas. These must be accepted as such and must not be modified at random. Obstruction is inferred in the case of a wall by the fact of the non-perception of objects behind it. Non-obstruction is inferred in the case of glass, etc. by the fact of perception of objects behind them.

Topic 32 : The Senses are manifold : Sûtras *: 52-61.*

Some say that, though the senses are located in different parts of the body, they are in reality only one, as the skin is present in every such location. It is true that even inspite of the presence of the skin a blind man does not see. But the skin is differentiated in its power in different parts of the body and that is the reason why the blind do not see, because blindness means loss of the particular power in the particular part of the skin. This argument of the opponent is self-destructive. For it amounts to an admission of the difference of the senses. Moreover, not only the skin but the elements of Earth, etc., constitute the site of the senses Touch cannot be the one and universal sense, as in that case colour, touch, taste, etc. would all be perceived simultaneously, which is not the case. In the perception of colour Touch cannot establish contact between itself and an object screened from view, and perception without contact of sense and object is impossible. The objects of sense again are more than one, and the senses have to perform more than one function. The sense of touch cannot serve the purpose of the sense of sight and *vice versa*. So also in the case of the other senses. Sensible objects being five, the senses also must be five in number. Moreover, they produce five different kinds of cognition, are located in five different sites, have five different operations, possess five different shapes and have five different origins. Sight operates by going out of the eyes and reaching its objects. Sound reaches Hearing in waves. The other senses operate when the objects come into contact with them by the movement of the body. Smell, Taste and Touch are limited in shape to their sites. Sight residing in the pupils of the eyes goes out to pervade objects. Hearing is nothing else than Ether and is all-pervading. It is inferred by the perception of sound. It does not reveal all sounds because it is limited by its site acccording to the merit and demerit of the soul. The origins of the senses are the five elements respectively, as they severally make manifest and apprehend the specific attributes of the five elements. They are not modifications of the unmanifest matter (avyakta.)

Topic 33 : The Objects of the Senses : Sûtras : *62-73*.

Smell, Taste, Colour and Touch are the attributes of Earth ; Taste, Colour and Touch, of Water ; Colour and Touch, of Fire ; Touch, of Air ; and Sound, of Ether. The opposite view is that the elements possess only one attribute each and that other attributes are perceived in them owing to their interpenetration by other elements. The interpenetration, it is also said, is not mutual among all the elements but of the preceding by the succeeding in the order of their mention as Earth, Water, Fire, Air and Ether. This view is not correct. For, as a matter of fact, bodies formed of Earth and Water are perceptible to the eye ; they must therefore possess colour. Moreover, interpenetration must affect both the element interpenetrated and that interpenetrating. But colour is not perceived in Air though it is said to interpenetrate Fire. The theory of interpenetration therefore has to be rejected.

What is the explanation then of the fact that the senses constituted by the elements do not apprehend all the attributes of their respective elements? The explanation is that the senses become dominant in respect of that attribute which is prominent in their respective elements. This limitation of the scope of the senses is due to the saṃskâra, i.e., tendency or potency which is the resultant of karma (appetency) of the soul which they serve, just as the things of the world, e.g., poison, herbs, gems, etc., serve specific purposes of man according to his karma, and every single thing does not serve all his purposes.

The senses are also limited in their scope in this that they are themselves insensible in respect of their own attributes. Sight, for instance, cannot see its own colour. Smell cannot smell its own smell. This is because in perception the instrument must be endowed with the same attribute as the object, and when its own attribute is to be the object of its apprehension, the condition of perception is not present. In other words, an attribute cannot apprehend itself :—a sense does not apprehend its own attribute because of the absence of the auxiliary attribute. The perception of sound by Hearing is an exception which tests the rule. Hearing is composed of Ether. In the perception of sound it is independent of the possession of the attribute of sound as an auxiliary. That Hearing is composed of Ether is known as follows : The soul is the hearer. Mind cannot be the instrument of hearing ; as in that case there would be no deafness as mind is not liable to destruction. Earth, Water, Fire and Air are not known to have the capacity to produce Hearing. Ether therefore is the constituent of Hearing.

Book III : Chapter ii.

Topic 34 : Cognition is not eternal : Sûtras *1-9.*

It is a matter of common experience that cognitions appear and disappear. Their non-eternality is quite manifest, and is taken for granted in N.-S., I. i. 16. The topic is concerned with the refutation of the speculation of the Sâṃkhyas that Buddhi is eternal. In support of the view they argue that unless Buddhi, cognition, were eternal, re-cognition would not be possible. To this the reply is that the reason given is not valid, because it has yet to be proved that re-cognition is done by Buddhi, and not by the soul, as we hold. We maintain that cognition, perception, apprehension, awareness, intuition, understanding is an attribute of the soul. If you hold that consciousness belong to the instrument you have to explain the nature of the conscious soul. If you admit that cognition is by the Buddhi, the inner instrument, you should explain what nature, what attribute, what reality is left to the conscious soul, what use it makes of cognition residing in Buddhi. If you say that the soul makes conscious and Buddhi knows, then where is the difference ? To make conscious, to know, to perceive and to apprehend convey the same meaning. If, on the other hand, you admit that Buddhi makes known and the soul knows, we agree. Buddhi is then the instrument of cognition, the mind. The mind is eternal, but recognition of objects is not the reason for its eternality. For then the eyes too would be eternal, for one recognises with the left eye what is seen with the right eye. Recognition belongs to the knower and not to the instrument of knowledge.

The Sâṃkhyas also hold that Buddhi is eternal and that modifications in the form of cognitions emanate from it according to objects and that the modifications are in essence not different from the original. This view again is not correct. For in that case all objects would be perceived at the same time, which is not the case. Again, if Buddhi and its modifications were identical then the disappearance of the modification would entail the disappearance of Buddhi also. This shows that Buddhi and its modifications are not identical in essence. Further, they are different and modifications arise in the mind one after another which account for the fact that the objects of all the senses are not apprehended all at once. Also when the mind is attached to one object there can be no cognition of another object. This shows that the mind is not all-pervading and moves from one object to another. Our view is that the inner instrument, the mind, is eternal but not all-pervading ; that the mind is one while its cognitive modifications are manifold ; and that this could not be possible were the modifications identical with the mind in essence. The soul therefore knows and not the mind. The mind's attachment to one object really means its contact with one sense. The attachment or occupation is really of the soul. There is no force in the argument that the modification like the mind with which it is identical is really one but looks as many in the same way as does a crystal look diverse in the proximity of different colours in succession, so that simultaneous cognitions of all objects need not necessarily be entailed. For the diversity in the case of the crystal is only apparent while the diversity of cognitions is real, as it is a fact of experience that cognitions appear and disappear one after another.

Topic 35 : The transiency of the things of the world : Sûtras : *10-17.*

The Sâṃkhya who maintains that the crystal remaining constant undergoes modifications is opposed by the Nihilist who urges that nothing in the world is permanent, that everything is in a flux, and that the crystal is a new crystal at every successive moment, as is found in the case of the human body which decays, throws off refuse and grows again by assimilating food. We have to point out that the proposition is too wide and is supported neither by perception nor by inference, and that we can give our assent to it in accordance with our observation of nature. Growth and decay in recurrence are seen in the human body. These are not seen in stones and crystals. We also demur to the speculation of the thorough-going Nihilist that a new entity is produced at every moment out of the ashes of the old, for the reason that the causes of such wholesale production and destruction are not apprehended. The destruction of milk and the production of curd furnishes no analogy. For the destruction of milk is seen and the cause of its destruction is inferred. The production of curd is seen and its cause is inferred. In the case of the crystal no such production or destruction is seen, and there is no occasion for the inference of any cause.

Some (Sâṃkhyas) say in reply to the Nihilist that milk is not destroyed but only transforms into a different character, or merely develops different properties. To them we say that the constituents of milk disintegrate and redintegrate as curd, whereby the destruction of milk is inferred. What we deny is that there is a total destruction of milk and that curd is entirely a new product and that there is no cause for such destruction and production. Seeing that in some cases the cause of destruction is apprehended and that in some it is not apprehended it cannot be admitted that all is a flux.

Topic 35 : Cognition is an attribute of the Soul : Sûtras : *18-41.*

Cognition is either present when it is called intuition, or past when it is called recollection. The intuition of the red colour of a rose, for instance, survives in memory even after the destruction of the eye and the rose. It therefore belongs not to the object nor to the sense but to the knower. The knower, again, is not the mind, but the soul. For the mind is only an instrument under the control of the soul. It is the inner instrument which brings about the cognition of pleasure and pain and recollection. If cognition be its attribute then it would cease to be an instrument. Its existence as an instrument is inferred by the non-simultaneity of cognitions. If you distinguish between the mind and the inner instrument, then what we call the soul you call the mind, and what we call the mind you call the inner instrument. Your difference with us is about names only. Or the Sûtra (III. ii. 19) may mean that whereas simultaneous cognitions of diverse objects by the mind is impossible, the Yogins by their power of Yoga bring about simultaneous cognitions in several bodies with all the senses created by them for the purpose to exhaust their karma, and that this shows that cognitions do not belong to the mind but to the soul. It may be objected that cognitions cannot belong to the soul because as the soul is all-pervading and eternal, (i) simultaneous cognitions of all objects and (ii) the eternality of cognitions will be thereby entailed. Our reply to the first is that the cause of the production of cognition is not merely the contact of the senses with the objects but also the contact of the senses with the mind, and that as mind is atomic simultaneous cognitions of all objects is impossible. To the last we reply that every embodied soul knows within itself that cognition is non-eternal ; and that like one sound by another a preceding cognition is destroyed by a succeeding one.

But then impressions produced by cognitions are the causes of recollection, and these, according to you, says an objector, abide in the soul ; the contact of the soul and the mind which is equally a cause of recollection, also exists ; how is it that all the memories of the soul from the beginning of time are not revived at one and the same moment ? Some meet the objection with the reply that the mind serially comes into contact with the different parts of the soul on which cognitions have left their impress and that for this reason all memories are not revived simultaneously. The reply is not correct. For the mind can never come into contact with the soul as transcending the body, (the soul being a universal and eternal substance, it pervades the body and also transcends it), because the function of the mind is confined within the body. The life of an embodied soul consists in its conjunction with the mind together with a vehicle of the experience (body) necessitated by past karma which is in fruition. That the mind without a body is incapable of subserving the purpose of soul appears from the fact that the contact of the mind and the soul generates the double effort of support and direction, and that if the mind operated outside the body the body would drop down by graviry for want of support.

The swift movement of the mind will not solve the difficulty, for there are memories which take a considerable length of time to revive them through a series of intermediate stages which for long keep the mind engaged. Moreover, conjunction of the soul and mind independently of the body is not the cause of recollection. The body is the field of the soul's experience. If without it the mere conjunction of the mind with the soul could produce cognition, pleasure, etc., then the body would be perfectly useless.

Some of us point out that the contact of the mind and the soul outside the body cannot be established either by the direction of the soul, or by chance, or by the mind's being the knower. For the direction of the soul implies that the soul already knows the object of memory to which it directs the mind ; and if the memory is already revived there is no need for any contact of the mind. All memories are not revived by chance, i. e. all of a sudden ; some take mental effort for a long time to revive them. Nor is the mind the knower. But this, we say, is only a partial view of the matter. For cognitions do take place and there must be particular conjunction of the soul and the mind, as when a thorn suddenly pricks the foot of a man and pain is felt by him when his mind was engaged elsewhere, e. g. a beautiful scenery. As this particular conjunction is due to adṛiṣṭa, conjunction may be similarly produced by adṛiṣṭa serially in the case of non-simultaneous revival of all memories. The true reply, however, to the explanation offered, namely that the mind serially comes into contact with parts of the soul, is as given, that is, that the mind must operate within the body and not outside it.

The contact of the soul and the mind and the impressions are not the sole causes of recollections. These depend also on attention and cognition of signs (vide Sûtra III. ii. 41). Recollections do not occur simultaneously because their causes do not occur simultaneously. Even in cases of flashes of memory recollection is not independent of attention, etc. What happens in such cases is that the mind is occupied with several objects and one of them engages attention and revives a memory without our being aware of the cause of such revival. The mind is associated with the soul in the body for a specific purpose determined by adṛiṣṭa. Its dimension is atomic. It can come into contact with one impression at a time. Hence there can be no simultaneity of recollections.

Some hold the view that while cognition is an attribute of the soul, desire, aversion, volition, pleasure and pain are the attributes of the inner instrument, i. e. the mind. This view is not correct. For we find that these refer to one and the same agent and substratum as cognition. It is the knower which resolves to put forth effort for the acquisition of pleasure and the avoidance of pain. Therefore, these must also be the attributes of the soul.

The Materialist twists the above argument to his advantage. Says he : You argue that acquisition and avoidance proceed from desire and aversion and that desire and aversion are attributes of consciousness. But atoms are acted upon by attraction and repulsion. They must then possess desire and aversion and therefore be conscious. To this we reply that uniformity in the one and want of uniformity in the other distinguish the two cases. Gravity, e. g., is a property of all material substances ; it adheres to them in all circumstances. But while activity is found in atoms it is absent from such things as a pot. The activity which is found in material bodies such as an axe, or in the atoms, is caused by the will of the knower or by his karma under the will of the All-Knower. A second objection to the materialistic view is that as each atom would be endowed with consciousness, there would be a plurality of knowers in a single product, which is not warranted by any reason. Moreover, the reasons previously given for the existence of the soul and its eternality completely refute the theory that consciousness belongs to material substances.

To sum up : Consciousness does not belong to the mind or for the matter of that to the senses or the elements ; for the reasons already adduced commencing with Sûtra I. i. 10, "Desire, aversion, volition, pleasure and pain are the marks of the Soul", and also on account of their existing for the sake of another, and also in virtue of the moral law. They exist for the sake of another whose volition incites them to activity. Then, on the supposition that consciousness belongs to the elements, senses and the mind, all of which disintegrate at death, the consequences of their activity would befall the soul at or as rebirth, which is contrary to the moral law. Hence by proof by exhaustion consciousness must be the attribute of the soul. Moreover, the reasons already given in support of this have been vindicated by the refutation of the arguments against them. Or the word "Upapatti" in the Sûtra (III. ii. 41) means rebirth, and furnishes an additional reason in support of the view that consciousness belongs to the soul. A series of cognitions without a soul cannot account for rebirth. It can offer no explanation of saṃsâra and release. If the world were a congeries of series of conscious states there could be no harmony, no co-ordination, no organisation in society and the conduct of the affairs of the world would be impossible. Within the man also there would be the same chaos and confusion, and recollection would be an impossibility, because one state could not remember what was experienced by an antecedent state. Therefore the soul which knows also recollects. Its nature is to know. Every one is aware of the unity of the cognitions "I shall know", "I know," "I knew."

Topic 37 : Cognition is momentary : Sûtras : *42-45.*

Cognition lasts but an instant, as it is action. Its continuity is only apparent as in the case of the motion of an arrow shot from a bow which is really a series of instantaneous motions. So long as the pot, e. g., is present before the eyes there is cognition ; as soon as it is removed the cognition ceases. The duration of cognition is made up of cognitions arising every moment. On the other hand, the persistence of cognition will mean perpetual perception, and recollection will be rendered unnecessary; for the cause of recollection is not cognition but the impression left by cognition. It is a misconception to hold that cognition which disappears as soon as it is produced can give us only the apprehension of the genus and not of the individual, as in the case of a flash of lightning. In the flash of lightning you can see that a thing is a man but cannot determine his individual characteristics. Similar would be the case were cognition instantaneous. The objection is groundless. For the character of the cognition depends upon the causes which give rise to it. Where the cause of the cognition is fleeting the apprehension is indeterminate, general; where it is not fleeting the apprehension is determinate, detailed. For cognition is the apprehension of an object, whether indeterminate or determinate. The various characteristics of an object, generic and specific, provide cognition with its manifold contents. In respect of each such content the cognition is self-complete and determinate. It is merely a convention to speak of the cognition of the generic aspects of an object as indeterminate and of the cognition of its specific aspects as determinate. The instantaneity of cognition in no way affects perception even when the object is also momentary. E. g. in a lamp the flame consists of a series of radiant energies emitted by the lamp. Each such radiation is an object of cognition and the series of such cognitions gives us the perception of the flame of the lamp.

Topic 38 : Consciousness is not in the Body : Sûtras : *46-55.*

The colour and other attributes of the body co-exist with the body. But a dead body does not possess consciousness. It cannot be compared to momentum, for momentum depends upon definite causes and no such causes of consciousness are found present or absent in the body. The cause of consciousness in the body can be neither in the body as in that case death would make no difference, nor in another substance as in that case there would be no reason why it should not produce consciousness in stones and stocks, nor in both as in that case there would be no reason why consciousness should be produced in the body and not in other things of the same class with it. The disappearance of consciousness from the body at death cannot also be compared to the destruction of the dark colour of earth by baking, for baking does not merely destroy black colour but also produces red colour, while no such new production in the body is found at death, but the total cessation of consciousness. Moreover, baking produces red colour in earth because the materials for such colour exist in the earth. But in the body are not found agencies destructive of consciousness. Further, consciousness pervades every particle of the body and on the theory in question there would be innumerable conscious entities in a single body : so that pleasure, pain and cognition would be entirely localised in the part affected and would not affect any other part, which is contrary to experience. Our statement that consciousness pervades every part of the body of course excludes the hair, nails, etc. For they do not constitute the body which extends upto the skin only. The body is defined as the seat of the senses, the field of the activity of the soul and the mind, and of the experience of pleasure, pain, cognition. Moreover, the attributes of the body are either imperceptible as, e.g., gravity, or perceptible as, e.g., colour ; but consciousness is neither imperceptible because one is aware of it nor sensible because it is apprehended by the mind. It follows that consciousness is not an attribute of the body. And this conclusion further confirms the previous conclusion that cognition does not belong to the mind, the senses and the body but to the soul.

Topic 39 : Of the Mind : Sûtras : *56-59.*

In the organism of the mind, senses, cognitions and the body there is only one mind. The unity of the mind is inferred from the non-simultaneity of cognitions of several objects through the different senses. When we observe the different movements of an individual we seem to have several cognitions at one and the same time. But this is due to the swiftness of the cognitions and of the movements of the mind. Every one is aware within oneself that cognitions arise in sequence according to the serial operation of the senses in respect of their objects. Recollections also appear in sequence. This shows that succession and not simultaneity is the truth. That swiftness of cognitions and of the movements of the mind obliterates, as it were, their succession is best illustrated when we at a glance grasp the meaning of a sentence which involves the hearing of each letter as uttered, their formation into words, the recollection of the meanings of the words, their syntactical connection, etc. And the same reason, namely non-simultaneity of cognitions, also establishes that the mind is atomic.

Topic 40 : Adṛiṣṭa is the cause of the Body : Sûtras : *60-72.*

Karma, i.e. the activity or the start made by speech, cognition and the body, produces as its fruit merit and demerit which abide in the soul. Moved by these and not independently the elements produce the body. Dwelling in the body the soul regards the body as itself. Being attached to the body and out of the craving for enjoyment in it the soul cognises objects and creates saṃskâras or appetencies in the form of merit and demerit which lead to rebirth where again the same sequence of cause and effect is repeated, and so on. This succession of events can be possible only on the explanation that the elements are moved for the production of the body under the influence of karma to subserve the ends of the soul. It is seen that a man, to serve his purposes, makes conveyances and the like from suitable materials. The Atheist says that in making a statue sand, stone, colouring and other materials are used as they exist in nature without reference to any karma and that so the case may be with the production of the body from the elements. We reply that it is yet to be established that sand, stone, etc. exist in nature by themselves without reference to any karma and not to serve the ends of the soul. Moreover, a statue is not produced from seeds whereas the body is. This involves three karmas, viz. of the soul experiencing life in the womb and of the parents enjoying the fruit in the shape of a son. Further, food taken by the mother nourishes and develops the embryo till birth through various processes of assimilation. It is thus clear that the action of the materials in forming and developing the body is dependent upon karma. The operation of karma is also manifest from the fact that every approach of the parents does not become fruitful.

Not only is karma the cause of the production of the body; it is also the cause of the conjunction of a particular body with a particular soul. The body is a highly intricate mechanism and cannot as such be brought about by the fortuitous concourse of atoms. Similarly the bodies of no two men are exactly the same. This perplexing diverṣity of outfit in the form of the body can be explained only by karma, namely that every man has his own destiny to fulfil and that he gets the body which he merits.

The causality of karma in the production of the body also accounts for the soul's disjunction from the body on the exhaustion of karma, through the removal of delusion by true knowledge. Thus the seed of future birth is not produced and karma in fruition is exhausted by experience. Were the elements, on the other hand, which are indestructible, independent causes of the production of the body, there would be no release.

The Sâṃkhyas hold that the soul's non-experience of Prakṛiti or Matter is the cause of the production of the body in and through which the soul is to experience Prakṛiti, and that when the experience is accomplished the soul regains final separation from the body. On this theory a released soul also may again be connected with the body. For if experience is necessary for the soul when it had no body experience may be necessary also after its separation from the body. It cannot be argued that separation from the body takes place after the purpose of the soul's experience of Prakṛiti has been accomplished and that therefore there is no reason for its being again connected with the body. For the experience of a single soul fulfils the purpose of the experience of Pakṛiti, and Pakṛiti which has performed before one soul has its object accomplished; yet we find that the production of bodies is uninterrupted. The production of the body is therefore not from non-karma and for the purpose of the soul's experience of Prakṛiti. It is due to karma and for the experience of the fruit of karma.

Others maintain that the soul's experience is not of Pakṛiti but of the fruits of karma and that this is brought about by adṛiṣṭa inhering in atoms. This attribute of the atoms is a cause of activity. Impelled by it the atoms come together and form the body. The mind then enters the body. In the body so formed and possessed by the mind the soul cognises objects. But in this view also bodies can be produced even for a released soul because the attribute of adṛiṣṭa appertaining to the atoms is indestructible.

Others again opine that the mind by its own adṛiṣṭa enters the body. In that case also there can be no separation of the mind from the body. For to what will this separation be due? On our theory karma in fruition in the present body is exhausted by experience and separation from the body takes place. The adṛiṣṭa of the mind, on the other hand, cannot be the cause of both birth and death.

Further, if the elements as such could produce the body then the body once produced would, in the absence of any cause of destruction, continue for ever. If death were due to chance then there would not be so much diversity in the manner of death as is seen.

Some think that as the dark colour of the atom is destroyed for ever by the application of heat and red colour is produced in its place, so on the theory of the production of the body by adṛiṣṭa the body will not be produced again in the state of release. This view is altogethe unsupported by any reason. No familiar instance is cited. Neither perception nor inference is advanced.

Or "Akṛita—abhyâgama—prasaṅga," in the Sûtra (III-ii-72) means that the doctrine that the production of the body is not due to karma will entail that the experience of pleasure and pain is without any cause. This is contrary to perception, inference and scriptural texts. This would mean that acts are neither good nor bad and that the acts of men are not responsible for their experience of pleasure and pain. This is the false view of perverted minds.

BOOK IV : CHAPTER i.

Topic 41 : Activity and Faults : Sûtras *1—2.*

Activity (I. i. 17) and Faults (I. i. 18) have already been explained. They have been examined in the examination of the body, etc. from which spring merits and demerits. The Faults, like cognition, are attributes of the soul. They are the causes of saṃsâra or transmigration, because they are the causes of activity and re-birth. As saṃsâra is without beginning, they also proceed without beginning. They cease to be when false knowledge is destroyed by knowledge of the truth.

Topic 42 : Faults fall into three groups : Sûtras : *3—9.*

There are three collections of Faults : (1) Attraction consisting of lust, greed, craving, longing and covetousness ; (2) Aversion consisting of anger, envy, jealousy, hatred and implacability ; (3) Delusion consisting of false knowledge, doubt, pride and carelessness. Attachment is the mark of Attraction ; want of forbearance, of Aversion ; and misapprehension, of Delusion. Every man is aware of their existence within himself. The fact that they are all liable to be destroyed by knowledge of the truth does not show that they do not fall into distinct classes. For the colours of the earth such as blue, etc. are distinct colours, though they can be all destroyed by the application of heat. The colours again are quite distinct though they have a common source, *viz.* fire. Similarly, the Faults are quite distinct from one another, though false knowledge is their common origin.

Among the Faults Delusion is the worst. For a man who is free from it is not influenced by the other two. Misapprehension runs through Attraction and Aversion also. Delusiou therefore is their cause. And it is thus that they disappear on the removal of Delusion by knowledge of the truth.

Topic 43 : Pretyabhâva *(Transmigration) :* Sûtras : *10—13.*

Birth is not production ; death is not destruction. The eternity of the soul makes pretyabhâva possible. The eternal soul forsakes the former body and takes up another body. Both these processes constitute pretyabhâva. To say that the production and destruction of entities conspetitute pretyabhâva is to deny the moral law according to which one experiences the consequences of one's own acts. While the doctrine of total annihilation would render the teachings of the Ṛiṣis meaningless.

How, from causes of what character, are bodies, etc. produced? A body is not produced from another body. A pot is not produced from another pot. All is not the cause of all. Like produces like. A pot is produced from potsherds of the like material. This is the testimony of perception which is the highest evidence. On the strength of this experience it can be inferred that the causes of the gross elements of earth, etc. are the most subtle supersensible eternal substances possessing colour and other attributes found in the gross elements. The existence of such substances is thus revealed The inference is from the known to the unknown.

The gross elements which are produced from the most subtle eternal elements furnish the materials for the production of the body, senses and objects with which the soul becomes associated after leaving its previous body. This is the truth. The views of sectarians will be next considered.

Topic 44 : The Void is not the cause of the World: Sûtras : *14-18.*

Some say that the sprout comes into existence by destroying the seed, i.e., that from the non-existence of the seed is the existence of the sprout. This is not correct. For if the sprout is the cause of the destruction of the seed then it must have existence before the seed is destroyed, and in that case it cannot be said to come into existence from the destruction of the seed. It is true that causal predication is made in respect of objects past and future; e.g., a lost article causes sorrow; a son yet to be born causes pleasure. But such predication rests on mere sequence. So also when the sprout which is yet to appear is said to be the cause of the destruction of the seed the predication of causality merely states a sequence, and not a true causal relation, namely that the sprout is produced from the destroyed seed, i.e., that existence springs from non-existence. The truth is that the parts of a structure disintegrate and redintegrate into another structure, and that bodies are produced from such redintegration and not from non-existence or void. The relation of antecedent and consequent between these two processes is not denied.

Topic 45 : Îs'vara *(God) is not the material cause of the World :* Sûtras *19-21.*

Some say that the void may not be the material cause of the world but that Brahman is the material cause of the fabric of names and forms; because it is seen that the destiny of man does not depend upon the efforts of man alone but also on the dispensation of God also. This view is not correct. For Brahman cannot be conceived otherwise than as a soul. Îs'vara is a soul which is all-doing, all-knowing, all-embracing. Aṇimâ (power to become smaller than even an atom), etc. are

His eight excellences. He acts by mere will (and not by physical means) and disposes the merits and demerits appertaining to each soul and the elements of earth, etc. to activity. He is thus absolutely free in the work of creation. He is like a friend; He is the father of created beings. These attributes cannot be possible in Him without the possession of cognition. Therefore He cannot be anything but a soul. So also declares the Śruti: "The seer, the cogniser, the all-knower, the Lord." He cannot be comprehended by perception, inference and revelation. He can be indicated only by the analogy of our own souls.

Topic 46 : The World is not the Result of Chance : Sûtras *: 22-24.*

Some say that like the sharpness of thorns, streaks of colour in rock minerals and the smoothness of the stone, the production of the body, etc. is from material causes without the intervention of an efficient cause. This view does not differ from the view that the creation of the body, etc. is not the result of the action of man, which has been refuted in III. ii. 60-72.

Topic 47 : All is not non-eternal : Sûtras *: 25-28.*

Some say that all things are non-eternal as production and destruction are their nature. Some oppose this tenet by asserting that the alleged non-eternality must itself be eternal and thus will furnish an opposition to the non-eternality of all things (including non-eternality.) But non-eternality cannot be eternal; like fire destroying itself along with the fuel, it ceases to be along with the destruction of all things. The true reply to the tenet of the non-eternality of all things is that there can be no denial of what is really eternal. What is eternal and what is non-eternal is to be settled by the test of cognition. Things which are found by means of the pramâṇas to be liable to production and destruction must be regarded as non-eternal, while things which are not found to be so liable must be regarded as eternal. The eternals thus determined are the most subtle elements, ether, time, space, soul, mind, their attributes, genus, species, combination.

Topic 48 : All is not eternal : Sûtras *: 29-33.*

Some say that as all things are nothing but the five elements and as the five elements are eternal, all things must, therefore, be eternal. This tenet is negatived by our actual cognition of the production and destruction of things. The mere resemblance of things to the elements in respect of their attributes is not a true mark of the inference of their eternality. For there are reasons also to account for their difference in regard to duration. The resemblance in respect of attributes only shows that the elements are the material causes of the things. On the other hand, there is actual cognition of production, and of the cause of production, of things. This cognition proves their non-eternality. The activity of man who seeks to produce what is pleasant and to destroy what is painful, also presupposes that all things are not eternal. It is further well-known that composite substances undergo production and destruction. Again, sound, action, cognition, pleasure, pain, desire, aversion, and volition are neither included among the elements nor possess their attributes. It cannot be said that the cognition of production is as unreal as cognition in a dream ; for the same can be said about the cognition of the elements. Moreover, there is this fundamental difference between eternal and non-eternal things that the former are beyond the reach of the senses and are not subject to production and destruction. (Thus is the Sâṃkhya view refuted. The view of those who believe in autogenesis is next considered.)

It is said that production and destruction are mere changes of attribute and not of substance which is constant, and so eternal ; in other words, that there are really not production and destruction but only development and envelopment. But this view of the persistence of entities at all times fails to provide any means of differentiation as to (1) development and envelopment, (2) the attribute developed and the one enveloped, (3) the moments of development and envelopment, (4) the particular attribute developed and enveloped and another, (5) the past and the future. Hence the view must be rejected.

Topic 49 : All is not discrete : Sûtras : *34-36.*

Some say that an entity as a single unity does not exist, because the names by which entitles are denoted connote a plurality ; *e. g.* a "Jar" is the name of a bundle of attributes such as colour, taste, touch and smell, and of parts such as bottom, sides, neck, etc. But this is not right ; for attributes are different from substance and parts are different from the whole, as already explained (see II. i. 33-36.) Moreover, names do not change ; for instance, we say, "The jar I saw I touch, the jar I touched I see". Then, mere collocations of atoms are imperceptible, because atoms are so. That which is perceived in a collocation of atoms is a single entity. Again, the admission of a collocation whether of atoms or of attributes or of parts is the admission of a unity.

Topic 50 : All is not void : Sûtras : *37-40.*

Some say that all is non-existence, because existence and non-existence appear in every entity ; *e. g.* in a cow there is presence of cow-ness and there is absence of horse-ness and everything else. The argument involves a twofold contradiction. (i) "All" is definable, as it means more than one and without exception ; while "non-existence" is not definable, as it is the negation of existence. (2) If all is non-existence then one thing, *e. g.* cowness, cannot be the negation of another thing *e. g.* horseness. Then, all entities have existence by their own nature ; a cow is existent as a cow. There is no cognition of a cow as non-existence. When it is said that a cow is non-existent in the form of a horse and it is not said that a cow is non-existent in the form of a cow, it is admitted that a cow as a cow is existent. The statement that a cow is not a horse is a denial of their identity and not of the cow as an entity.

The opponent rejoins that what is called the nature or character of an entity has merely a relative existence like length and shortness. To this the reply is that relativity depends upon an absolute standard. If both the terms long and short are relative then they destroy each other. These terms, again, do not apply to atoms or objects of equal size. If relativity were a fact as asserted, then surely some difference would have appeared in them. What relativity really implies is that when two objects are seen together it enables us to see the excess of the one over the other.

Topic 51 : Reality is not numerically fixed : Sûtras : *41-43.*

Some say that (1) all is one, being equally existent, (2) all is dual, being eternal and non-eternal, (3) all is a triad, being the cogniser, the means of cognition, and the cognisable, (4) all is a quartet, being the knower, the means of knowing, the knowable, and knowledge ; and so forth. This is not correct, because of impossibility of proof. For if the matter to be proved and the reason for it are diverse then the number asserted is exceeded ; if not, then in the absence of any reason there can be no proof. It is no answer to say that a part of the matter to be proved will furnish the reason for the proof. For in unity there can be no part. So in the case of duality, etc. These views deny the diversity of objects formed in special characters, and are thus opposed to perception, inference and testimony, and therefore false. The truth is that objects are classified according to their resemblances and diversified according to their differences.

Totic 52 : Phala (*Fruit*) *:* Sûtras : *44-53.*

It is seen that when a man cooks his food, he gets the fruit of his labour immediately, while when he sows seed he gets the harvest after a lapse of time. Therefore when it is said that heaven is the fruit of the performance of *agnihotra* sacrifice, the doubt arises as to whether the fruit will be obtained immediately or after a lapse of time. We know that heaven is not obtained immediately. On the other hand, we do not see how it can be obtained afterward, for the activity in the shape of the performance of the sacrifice must have ceased to operate long ago. To this the reply is that activity produces Saṃskâra (potency) in the form of merit and demerit, which in co-operation with other conditions produces the fruit at another time, in the same way as water poured at the root of a tree causes through intermediate agencies the appearance of flowers and fruits. It is true that in the case of the tree, the action and the result both appear in the same body, *i.e.*, the tree, while in the case of the sacrifice, the action is performed in one body and the fruit is enjoyed in another body. But bodies are merely the fields, the performer-enjoyer is the soul. The soul performs the action, the merit resides in the soul, the fruit in the form of happiness accrues to the soul. Where the fruit of action is declared to be a son, a wife, cattle, wealth, etc., these are only the symbols and sources of happiness which is the real fruit.

Topic 53 : Duḥkha (*Pain*) : Sûtras : *54-57*.

Pain has been enumerated after Fruit (in I. i. 9, and defined in I. i. 21. Pleasure has been neither enumerated nor defined.) The omission however does not imply a total denial of pleasure ; for such denial is impossible seeing that all beings bear testimony to the existence of pleasure. The teaching that pleasure is to be regarded as denoted by the word pain is given, for the purpose of the avoidance of pain, to one who, on account of the experience of the stream of births and deaths, has become indifferent and desires to avoid pain. For all beings, all the worlds, all re-births are, through the co-existence of pain, penetrated with bâdhanâ or impediment or hinderance or obstruction which is the characteristic of pain. In the text (IV. i. 54) "Birth" means that which is born, namely the body, senses and cognition. The impediment is of various grades. It is the greatest in the case of those who are in hell ; middling, of the lower animals ; least, of men ; less, of the celestial beings and of dispassionate men. Thus seeing that impediment in some degree or other exists in all the worlds the teachers apply the definition of pain to pleasure as well as to its means, namely the body, senses, cognition. Hereby attraction towards the worlds ceases, thirst for them is cut off, release is obtained from all pain. It is like the avoidance of the pain of death by one who throws away milk mixed with poison.

Pleasure no doubt appears in the intervals of pain. But the longing for and pursuit of pleasure and the attendant evils such as non-fulfilment of desire, its partial fulfilment, fulfilment with risks, etc., produce various mental suffering, and consequently even at the moment of pleasure the impediment to the freedom of the soul continues. It is for this reason that "birth" is declared as pain, and not on account of the non-existence of pleasure. Again, there is no pleasure in the attainment and enjoyment of which pain in some form or other is not experienced. Moreover, "birth", infirmity, disease, contact with disagreeable things, separation from agreeable things, non-fulfilment of desire are the necessary conditions and inevitable consequeuces of the pursuit of pleasure. But a man with whom pleasure is the supreme good regards these also as grades of pleasure and thus never gets free from transmigration. For the awakening of such a man also "birth" is declared as pain. The expression " Birth is pain " (in IV. i. 54) however does not mean that the body, senses and cognition are by their own nature pain, but that they like pleasure are so being interpenetrated with impediment.

Topic 54 : Apavarga (*Release*) *:* Sûtras *58-67.*

Some say that the attainment of release is impossibie on account of (1) the chain of debts, (2) the chain of perversions, and (3) the chain of activity. The repayment of debts is enjoined as follows : "A Brâhmaṇa, as he is born, is born encumbered with three debts : by celibacy and study he repays the debt to the Ṛiṣis ; by performing sacrifices, to the deities ; and by begetting progeny, to the Pitṛis" (Śatapatha Brâhmaṇa. 1-7-2-1). As regards sacrifices it is further laid down : "These sacrifices agnihotra, darṣ'a and purṇamâsa shall be performed until death or infirmity intervenes. Either by infirmity or by death is one freed from the obligation to perform." So no time is left for the pursuit of release. (Perversions are false knowledge, egotism, attraction, aversion and love of life. Yoga-Sûtra, II. 3). These cling to one from life to life. Again, from birth till death the activity of the speech, mind and body never leaves a man for a moment. Therefore the attainment of release as described in I. i. 2 is not established.

To the above the reply is as follows : (1) In the text of the Śatapatha Brâhmaṇa the word "debts" is used not in its primary but in a secondary sense. For primarily a debt and its repayment must be *inter vivos.* That condition is not present in the case under consideration. The secondary application of the word is for the sake of condemnation and commendation. Like a debtor who does not repay his debts a man who does not perform acts deserves condemnation ; and like a debtor who repays his debts a man who performs acts deserves commendation. Again, the expression " as he is born " is also used in a secondary sense. For surely an infant has neither the desire for the fruit of, nor the capacity to perform, all those acts, sacrifice, etc. Similarly the declaration about performance of acts till infirmity or death should be rationally interpreted. For if it is taken literally it becomes superfluous, for infirmity and death necessarily put a stop to all performance. The declaration really means that performance should be continued till the desire is satisfied with the attainment of fruit. The word "Jarâ" which the objector has explained as infirmity really means the fourth stage of life, the stage of renunciation. For it is then that a man having, after realising the futility of all worldly objects, renounced the desire for worlds, wealth and progeny, is freed from the obligation to perform acts. "Jarâ" cannot mean infirmity or inability here, for in the case of men who are not themselves able to perform acts, a proxy is allowed such as a disciple whose service is required by the gift of learning.

Again, the text in question is a re-inculcation (and not an original injunction, as there is no word in it to express an injunction). It can be interpreted either as a re-inclucation or as one pleases. The former interpretation is the more rational. The sense therefore is that a householder has no option but to perform prescribed acts as a debtor has no option but to repay debts. The performances which accomplish the fruit, and not the fruit, are the subject of a man's effort. Injunctions lay down the means which is to be brought into operation and the fruit which is to be produced. "Jâyamâna", as he is born, therefore refers to him whom these concern, namely the householder. This is not to deny the other stages of life, namely the student, the renunciate and the recluse. For every Śâstra is confined to its own subject matter. These Brâhmaṇa texts are concerned with the duties of householders only.

Ṛiks (sacred verses) and Brâhmaṇas (sacred prose texts) declare release (for all stages of life). Thus there are the Ṛiks: (a) Ṛiṣis, begetting progeny and desiring wealth, entered death by reason of acts; other Ṛiṣis, discriminative, attained immortality beyond the reach of acts.

(b) Neither by act nor by progeny nor by wealth but by renunciation some attained immortality; beyond heaven (i. e. outside the reign of Avidyâ), hidden in the cave (i. e. beyond the reach of ordinary pramâṇas), that which shines, the yatis (recluses) enter.

(c) Know I this Person, great, of the splendour of the sun, beyond darkness; by knowing Him one crosses over death; there is no other path for the journey.

There are also the Brâhmaṇas: (a) There are three supports of Dharma, sacrifice, study and gift. The first is penance; the second is the celibate-student residing in the university or college of the preceptor; the third is such a student who spends his life in the college. All of them go to the regions of the virtuous. He who is steady in Brahman attains immortality. (Chhândogya Upaniṣad, II. xxiii. 1).

(b) Desiring this world only the renunciates take to renunciation. (Bṛihat Âraṇyaka Upaniṣad, IV. iv. 22).

(c) Now tney declare that man is in essence desire. As he desires so he resolves; as he resolves so he acts; as he acts so he becomes.

Thus declaring that transmigration is the result of acts, the texts teach what is good: Desiring, when he becomes non-desiring, desire-free, desire-less, self-desiring, desire-fulfilled, his prâṇas (vital forces) do not go out, they are withdrawn into the soul even here. Being truly Brahman, he attains Brahman. (Bṛihat Âraṇyaka Upaniṣad, IV. iv. 5, 6).

Therefore it is unreasonable to say that the chain of debts prevents release. The text, Those four paths leading to deities, (Taittirîya Saṃhitâ, V. vii. 23), again, shows that there are four, and not one, stages of life.

The text about the performance of agnihotra, dars'a and pûrṇamâsa applies only to those who desire the fruit. For the Veda enjoins the closing of sacrifices and renunciation. Thus, "Having fulfilled the prâjâpatya sacrifice, having offered all his possessions in it, transplanting the fires in the soul, let a Brâhmaṇa walk away from the world". This shows that the removal of the sacrificial fires is enjoined for those who have risen above the desire for progeny, wealth and worlds and have ceased to desire the fruit of sacrifices. So declare the Brâhmaṇa texts; e. g. Resolving to take to another order of life Yâjñavalkya addressed Maitreyî thus: I wish, O dear one, to go away from this place; let me reconcile you to Kâtyâyanî. O Maitreyî, you have received initiation from me. That much, O dear one, is immortality. So saying Yâjṇavalkya went away.

The performance of acts till infirmity and death could not be intended for all without distinction. For such acts end with the collection of the sacrificial vessels at death which can be possible in the case of householders only. Had that been the intention there would have been no declaration of rising above desires as in the text: It so happened in days of yore that Brâhmaṇas, versed in the sacred lore and learned, did not desire progeny; (they thought) what should we do with progeny? we for whom the soul is the whole world. They, rising above the desires for progeny, wealth and worlds, led the life of mendicants. (Bṛihat Âraṇyaka Upaniṣad, III. v. 1). For such men acts ending with the collection of the sacrificial vessels cannot be possible. Moreover, the fruit does not incite all men to activity to the same extent

The order of the householder is not the only order of life. Itihâsas, Purâṇas and Dharmas'âstras declare four orders of life. These as well as the sacred verses and Brâhmaṇa texts are authoritative in regard to their respective subject matters, like the senses. Sacrifice is the subject matter of the sacred verses and Brâhmaṇa texts; the character of men, of Itihâsas and Purâṇas; and social conduct, of the Dharmas'âstras. If Dharmas'âstras had no authority, chaos would ensue through non-regulation of the conduct of men. The authority of Itihâsas and Purâṇas has been declared by the Brâhmaṇa text: Atharvâṅgirasa declared the Itihâsa and Purâṇa; they constitute the fifth of the Vedas (Chhândogya Upaniṣad, III. iv. 2).

(2) The chain of perversions also can offer no obstacle to the attainment of release. For as in the case of a man in deep sleep, when he dreams no dreams, the chain of attraction and the chain of pleasure and pain are snapped, so also in the state of release. And this the knowers of Brahman instance as the condition of the released soul.

(3) In the case of a man whose perversions have suffered decay, the activity does not tend to re-birth at the end of the previous birth. Such re-birth is caused by adṛṣṭa, *i.e.* merit and demerit abiding in the soul. Absence of re-birth at the end of the previous birth is release. This does not entail the futility of acts. For what is declared is that re-birth does not take place at the end of the previous birth, and not that the experience of the consequences of acts is denied. In such a case all previous acts reach fruition in the last birth.

An objection is raised by some who say that the stream of perversions is natural and without beginning and therefore impossible of being cut short. It is no answer to this objection that just as antecedent non-existence (which is without beginning) of an entity is terminated by the entity when produced, so the natural stream of perversions is not eternal. Neither is the objection met by the argument that just as the natural dark colour of the atom from before time is terminated by the application of fire, even so is the stream of perversions. For eternality and non-eternality are attributes of positive entities only; their application to non-entities is only metaphorical. There is also no reason for the conclusion that the dark colour of the atom is without beginning. Nor is there any reason for the proposition that what is not in need of production is non-eternal.

The true answer to the objection is as follows: Subconscious will is the efficient cause of the perversions, attraction, etc. They are due to acts and to themselves mutually. Attraction, aversion and delusion arise from subconsciously produced wrong notions of things as attractive, repulsive and delusive. Acts produce the bodies of living beings and in them the perversions of attraction, aversion and delusion according to a fixed rule. For it is actually seen that attraction is dominant in some bodies, and delusion in some others. Their production is also reciprocal. The deluded man is attracted; the deluded man is angered; the attracted man is deluded; the angered man is deluded. Now, the production of the false notions of things ceases through knowledge of the truth and owing to the non-production of their cause there follows the absolute non-production of attraction, etc. There is again no special force in the statement that the stream of perversions is without beginning. For all these entities, the body, etc., associated with the soul, come down in sequence without beginning. There is nothing which was not produced before and has been produced for the first time, except knowledge of the truth. Such being the case it is not premised by us that what is not liable to production is capable of destruction. As regards acts which produce the bodies of living beings in diverse classes of animal life, they do not become the efficient cause of the production of attraction, etc., after the destruction of false notions of things is brought about by the knowledge of the truth about them. They continue, however, to be productive of pleasure and pain, for in producing them they are independent of false notions.

Book IV : Chapter ii.

Topic 55 : Production of knowledge of Truth : Sûtras *1—3.*

Now, false knowledge is not mere non-production of true knowledge. It is not a negative but a positive thing. It is delusion. The object the false knowledge of which is the seed of saṃṣâra or succession of births and deaths, is to be known in its essence. False knowledge consists in the apprehension of the not-soul as the soul, in the delusion, the ahamkâra (I—manufacture) in the form " I am (this)". Ahaṃkâra is the vision of one who sees the not-soul as " I am (this)". The objects of ahaṃkâra are the body, senses, mind, feelings and cognitions. When a man feels convinced about this assemblage of objects, the body, etc., as " I am (this) ", as his very self, their destruction he regards as the destruction of himself, and being overcome with the desire for their non-destruction, adopts them again and again, and so adopting them, strives for birth and death ; and as no separation from them takes place, he is never absolutely released from pain. He who sees all this as pain, the vehicle of pain, and pleasure tinged with pain, knows pain thoroughly, and pain so known decays for want of adoption or acceptance, like food mixed with poison. Similarly he sees the faults and action as causes of pain. So he abandons the faults. The faults having decayed, activity does not tend to re-birth (IV. i. 63). Thus the man discriminates (1) that re-birth, fruit and pain are the things to be known, (2) that action and faults are to be avoided, (3) that release is to be attained, and (4) that knowledge of truth is the means of its attainment.

Having thus divided the knowables as those which are wrongly identified with the soul, those to be known, those to be abandoned and those to be attained, when the man devotes himself to them, constantly turns them over in thought and influences them with thought, there appears to him perfect vision, awareness of the things as they are, knowledge of truth. The knowables from the body to pain (I. i. 9) are due to faults because they are the objects of false knowledge. True knowledge about them prevents ahaṃkára or their identification with the soul. And so through knowledge of truth, on the successive removal of pain, birth, etc. (I. i. 2), release is obtained. This is a resume of the teachings of all Śâstras and is not a new teaching.

The objects of the senses are the objects of desire. They are colour, etc. When they are wrongly conceived they cause the operation of attraction, aversion and delusion. So meditation for the sake of true knowledge should be first concentrated on them. After wrong notions about them have ceased then thought should be focussed on the body, etc. which are more nearly connected with the soul so as to remove ahamkára in respect of them. Thus the man who is dispassionate to objects external as well as internal, is called released.

The cause of the faults is the conceit which regards objects as wholes and pays no attention to their parts. For instance, when a man is attracted to a woman, and a woman is attracted to a man, they are attracted by the particular parts of the body such as the teeth, lips, eyes, nose, or by some special features in them, Such attention increases the passion for each other. The faults which it entails are to be abandoned. Attention should be directed to the impure aspects of the body such as the hair, flesh, blood, bones, sinews, etc. By this means the attraction of passion is destroyed. Thus everything presents a twofold aspect, good and bad. It should be regarded as bad. Food mixed with poison is considered as poison.

Topic 56 : Relation of the Whole and Parts : Sûtras *4–17*.

There can be no doubt about the existence of the whole over and above the parts (see II. i. 33 *et seq.*) To this the following objections are urged : (1) Each single part cannot exist in the entire whole owing to the difference of their size and as that would entail the exclusion of the other parts. (2) It cannot occupy a portion of the whole because the whole as conceived has no such portions. (3) The whole cannot reside in each single part as their sizes are different and as that would entail that a substance is constituted by a single component. (4) It cannot reside in a portion of a part because parts have no portions. (5) It is not known to exist away from the parts. (6) It cannot be an attribute of the parts for the reasons stated before.

To this the reply is : The doubt is not justified ; for the whole being a single entity, the distinction of entire and parts is inapplicable to it. When it is said that the whole resides in the parts what is meant is that the whole covers the parts, *i. e.* it makes possible for the parts to combine to form a single entity. So that parts may have independent existence, but there can be no whole unless there were parts. Therefore in the case of a person who seeks the supreme good what is prohibited is the conceit which regards objects as wholes, and not that the existence of wholes is denied. Just as false notions in respect of colour, etc. is prohibited, and not that colour, etc. are denied.

Again, single atoms are not perceptible. They cannot be therefore perceptible in mass. Yet bodies constituted by atoms are perceptible. What makes them perceptible is the existence of wholes over and above the parts. The something perceptible in the collocation of atoms is the whole. To say that there is no perception of the whole in the parts is suicidal ; for in the last analysis only the atoms are left and they are not object of perception ; so that the required object of perception, *i. e.* parts, is reduced to something imperceptible. On the other hand, the argument cannot be pushed to the extreme conclusion denying the total existence of all things. For atoms cannot be so negated. They are the least indivisible parts of bodies.

Topic 57 : The Partless : Sûtras *18--25.*

Nothing exists, rejoins the pessimist ; the wholes are reduced to partless atoms, but partless eternal atoms are an impossibility, because the ether must pervade them both inside ahd outside in which case they cannot be partless, or, if the ether does not so pervade them, then the ether cannot be all-pervading as is claimed for it. To this the reply is that the terms inside and outside can be applied only to a body composed of parts and are inapplicable to the atoms themselves which are partless. As regards the ether it cannot but be all-pervading. For nothing ponderable or corporeal exists which is not in conjunction with the ether. A sound produced spreads over the ether. Conjunctions with minds, atoms, and their effects also spread over the ether. The characteristics of the ether are that it is nowhere parted and re-united like water by a passing boat, and that nowhere does it offer resistance to moving bodies. This shows that it is partless and intangible.

Then an atom cannot be a product ; for if it is a product its constitutents must be more minute and in that case it will not be an atom. As partless it is eternal. A product is non-eternal, not because of the pervasion of the ether but because of the disintegration of the parts. The pessimist rejoins that the atoms cannot be partless, for the reason that they possess a definite shape (spherical) and also enter into conjunctions among themselves. The objection to this rejoinder is that it will lead to infinite regression which is illogical, and will also eliminate gravity and diversity of dimensions and entail equality of dimension between the whole and the part as a consequence of infinity of parts in each part and part of a part.

Topic 58 : External objects are not transient : Sûtras *26–37.*

(The Buddhist addresses the Naiyâyika thus :) You defend the existence of external objects on the ground of our cognitions of those objects. But they are false cognitions. For instance, the cognition of a piece of cloth is a figment of the imagination. Because when a cloth is dissected only the yarns are left, and no cloth is found. Similarly in all cases. (The Naiyâyika replies :) This argument involves a self-contradiction. If an analysis of things by reason is possible then the non-cognition of the real nature of the things is impossible. The product is not perceived separately from its causes because it subsists in them. Where the causes are imperceptible analysis of their products by reason surely causes their distinct apprehension ; as in the case of the atoms. Moreover, analysis by reason is the same as cognition by means of the pramâṇas. The pramâṇas establish the existence of external objects. On the other hand, there can be no proof of the proposition that all is non-existent. For if there is any proof then "all" which includes proof is not non-existence. If there is no proof the proposition is not established. It cannot be said that there is no existence, but only a conceit, of pramâṇas and prameyas as in the case of objects seen in a dream, hallucination, mirage, etc. For there is no reason to support the supposition. In the first place, there is no reason to believe that objects seen in a dream are unreal. On the contrary, there are reasons to show that they are real. Diversity of dream cognitions must be due to different causes. In the second place, if it is said that dream cognitions are unreal because they disappear on waking then it is admitted that apprehension and non-apprehension are respectively the marks of inference of the existence of things existent and non-existent. Objects of dream are no more unreal than objects of recollection and imagination. All these objects are based on reality previously apprehended. After waking, by comparison with waking cognitions, dreams are found to be unreal. So that the experiences of the waking consciousness form the real basis of dream cognitions.

Thus there are objects and wrong cognitions of objects. Wrong cognitions of objects are destroyed through true knowledge as the conceit of the cognition of objects in dreams disappears on waking. Similarly the sun's rays opposed by the radiation of heat from the earth quiver and are mistaken for water. On nearer view the wrong cognition is removed. So everywhere what is destroyed is the wrong cognition, and not the object. No man has ever at any place a wrong cognition which is not without a real cause. Moreover, there is a duality of cognition in each of the cases cited : the magician, the waking man and the man near by know the phenomena of the magic, dream and mirage as unreal, while the spectators, the sleeping man and the man at a distance know them as real. These diverse cognitions could not be possible if all things were non-existent.

(As to the Nihilist) : wrong cognition itself cannot be negated ; for its cause and its existence are apprehended. Every man is aware of wrong cognition and of its cause. Wrong cognition therefore has existence. Wrong cognition embraces a twofold object, reality and appearance, *e. g.* the pillar and man, where a pillar is mistaken for a man. It arises from the perception of the common attributes of two similar things. Where, on the other hand, all objects are of a uniform character devoid of name and reality (as with the opponent), there can be no possibility of wrong cognition. In the case of smell and other prameyas, the cognitions of which are said to be wrong, the cognitions are certainly true cognitions, because they do not embrace the duality of reality and appearance. Therefore it is unreasonable to hold that the cognitions of pramâṇas and prameyas are wrong.

Topic 59 : Development of True Knowledge : Sûtras *38-49.*

When the mind is withdrawn from the senses and is held steadfast by the retentive effort, its conjunction with the soul takes place (as in the state of deep sleep). When this conjunction of the mind with the soul is associated with the desire to know the truth (which is not the case in deep sleep), cognitions in respect of the objects of the senses are not produced. From the habitual cultivation of this state does cognition of truth arise. There are objects however which by their intensity or by their nature force themselves upon consciousness even in this state of the mind ; *e. g.* thunderclap, hunger, thirst, heat, cold, diseases, etc. Nevertheless the habit of Yoga or concentration or communion is possible as the result of excellence of virtue or merit which is the cause of true knowledge, accumulated by practice preformed in previous lives. For the purpose of avoiding distractions instruction has been given for the practice of Yoga in forests, caves and river beds. The virtue born of the practice of Yoga accompanies a man even in another life. In the fullness of its accumulation as the cause of true knowledge, and there being the contemplation of Samâdhi or the repose of the mind in the soul, true knowledge is produced. Even in ordinary affairs a man is heard to say : "I did not see, my mind was elsewhere."

In the state of release objects, however intense, cannot force themselves on the soul. For they can produce cognitions only throngh conjunction with the senses. And the necessary condition of the production of cognitions is the body brought into existence under the influence of past acts, as the seat of effort, senses and objects. Release is the non-existence, through the non-existence of merit and demerit, of the body and senses as the seat of the condition of the production of cognitions. It follows therefore that release is deliverance from all pain. Because in the state of release the seed of all pain, the vehicle of all pain, is destroyed.

For the attainment of release reclamation of the soul is to be accomplished by means of Yama and Niyama and of the practices enjoined by the rules of self-culture. Yama (non-violence, veracity, non-covetousness, study and non-accumulation of wealth) is enjoined for all men. Niyama (cleanliness of body and mind, contentment, penance, sacred study and contemplation of God) is enjoined for special classes. Reclamation of the soul means decrease of demerit and increase of merit. Rules of self-culture are to be known from the treatises on Yoga. The practices therein taught are Tapas (penance), Prâṇâyâma (control of breath), Pratyâhâra (withdrawal of the mind), Dhyâna (contemplation) and Dhâraṇâ (fixity of contemplation). The practice of meditation in respect of the objects of the senses is for the sake of the destruction of attraction and aversion. The means is the adoption of the conduct of the Yogins.

The other means are the study and practice of the science of the soul, *i. e.* Ânvîkṣikî, the spiritual science. Practice consists in constant study, hearing and judging. For the maturity of the wisdom so acquired, in the form of removal of doubt and awakening to unknown objects, in other words, for the confirmation of what has been ascertained by oneself as the truth, converse should be held with those who are versed in the lore, whether they be disciples, preceptors, or fellow students, who are eager to attain the supreme good, provided they are not jealous. If it is considered that the advancement of a counter-thesis to the thesis propounded by them may not be welcome to them, attempt need not be made to establish one's own thesis. One should merely express the desire to know the truth and be willing to receive wisdom. In this way one should engage in converse with them and correcst one's own view as well as the conflicting views of extreme thinkers.

Topic 60 : Maintenance of True Knowledge : Sûtras *50-60.*

Like the cover of thorns for the safety of the sprouting seed, sophism and cavil may be employed for the safety of the search for the truth, by those who are not yet free from faults and who have not yet attained true knowledge, against those who launch an attack out of zeal for their own views. And a counter-attack may be made upon those who offer insult from pride of learning, for their subjugation and not out of the desire to know the truth. This permission is only for the sake of maintaining the knowledge acquired and not for the sake of gain, worship or reputation.

Book V. Chapter I.

Topic 61. Examination of Jâtis *by resemblance and difference:* Sûtras *1—3.*

Jâtis are reasons urged in opposition to the reason advanced in support of a demonstration. They are of twenty-four kinds. They do not succeed in refuting the opposition. Their common function is to equate or to reduce the opponent's reason to the same class with themselves. This they do in twenty-four different ways and from these they derive their respective definitions. Thus, (1) to oppose resemblance to resemblance as the reason: The soul possesses action, because it possesses volition or adṛiṣṭa (merit and demerit) which is the cause of action, in the same way as does a pebble possess action as it is shot from a catapult which is a cause of action. This demonstration by means of resemblance is opposed by the following equally based on resemblance. The soul does not possess action, because it is all-pervading, in the same way as the sky, being all-pervading, does not possess action. And no special reason exists to determine the validity of the one as against the other conclusion. In the absence of such a reason the opposition counteracts the demonstration. (2) To oppose difference to (*a*) resemblance and (*b*) difference: (*a*) The pebble shot from a catapult is finite but the soul is not finite, therefore the soul does not possess action like the pebble. (*b*) The sky is inactive because it does not possess the cause of activity; but the soul possess the cause of activity, therefore it is not inactive. The reply to these antinomies of reason is that the thesis or the counter-thesis is established in the same way as a particular animal is established to be a cow through its possession of cowness. Antinomies arise where the demonstration is based on mere resemblance or mere difference, and not on the possession of a distinctive attribute or character. An animal is established as a cow, not merely through its resemblance to another animal possessing dewlap, etc., but through such resemblance and the possession of the particular or distinctive genus, *viz.*, cowness. Similarly mere dissimilarity to a horse does not establish a cow, but dissimilarity of characteristic attribute. Antinomies arise from fallacies of reason.

Topic 62: Six Jâtis *relative to the* Sâdhya *and* Dṛiṣṭânta : Sûtras *4-6.*

These arise from confusion of the diverse attributes of the sâdhya (the thing to be established) and the dṛiṣṭânta (example). (1) If the soul is active like a pebble, it is also touchable like the pebble, on the other hand, if it is not touchable, it cannot be active. (2) The pebble which is active is not all-pervading; therefore the soul which is active like the pebble, must also be not all-pervading. (3) The activity of the pebble is certain, therefore the activity of the soul is equally certain. (4) The activity of the soul is uncertain, being yet to be demonstrated, therefore the activity of the pebble is equally uncertain. (5) Objects possessing the cause of action are some heavy, *e. g.*, the pebble, and some light, *e. g.* air; therefore objects possessing the cause of action are some active, *e.g.*, the pebble and some inactive, *e. g.*, the soul. (6) If, as is the pebble so is the soul, then as is the soul so is also the pebble.

The reply to the above is that what is established cannot be repudiated and that comparison through resemblance in parts is established as in the case: as the cow so the *bos gavæus*, where their difference in many respects is no reason against the inference. Similarly where the inferential attribute is found in the dṛiṣṭânta in universal relation with the attribute to be established, the difference between the sâdhya and the dṛiṣṭânta in other respects cannot hinder the inference. As regards the assumption of uncertainty in the dṛiṣṭânta and certainty in the sâdhya, (3), (4) and (6) above, no such confusion is possible, because a dṛiṣṭânta for the purpose of demonstration is that object in respect of which there is unanimity of opinion amongst men both trained and untrained.

Topic 63. Extension or Non-extension of the Hetu *to the* Sâdhya. Sûtras *7—8.*

The opposition to the demonstration takes this form: The inferential mark and the attribute to be established either co-exist or do not co-exist in the sâdhya or subject. If they co-exist then nothing else remains to be demonstrated. If they do not co-exist, then there can be no demonstration; for a lamp cannot illumine an object with which it does not co-exist in the same place. To this the reply is that the co-existence or non-co-existence of the two attributes is not a material factor in the production of an effect. For it is seen that a pot is produced when the agent, instruments and the ground come into contact with the lump of clay, while suffering may be caused to a man by means of supernatural powers directed from a distance.

Topic 64. Regression and Counter-example: Sûtras *9—11.*

The opposition is to the effect that the example itself requires demonstration and that an equally suggestive counter-example exists. To this the reply is: (1) Those who wish to see, bring a lamp for the illumination of the object to be seen, while the lamp itself is seen without another lamp.

Similarly an example is an already known object and serves the purpose of making known what is yet unknown. It is useless to establish its cause. (2) If the counter-example can cause an inference why not an example? The absence of any special character is common to both.

Topic 65. Non-production : Sûtras *12—13*.

The opposition is to the effect that sound, *e. g.*, is said to be non-eternal because it comes after effort, but that prior to its production when sound is not produced the character of coming after effort which is the cause of non-eternality, does not exist, and that therefore sound is eternal and cannot be produced. To this the reply is that when sound becomes sound it is produced and in being produced comes after effort and that thus the cause of its non-eternality is obtained.

Topic 66. Doubt : Sûtras *14—15*.

The opposition is to the effect that there is resemblance of sound, e. g. to the eternal, namely potness, both being cognisable by the senses, and also to the non-eternal, namely pot, the character of coming after an effort appertaining to both, and that therefore it is doubtful whether sound be eternal or non-eternal. To this the reply is that where doubt arises from the, cognition of resemblance without the cognition of difference the doubt ceases on the cognition of difference, e. g., the cognition of coming after effort; that where doubt arises from the cognition of both resemblance and difference the doubt can never cease; and that mere resemblance can never be an eternal source of doubt.

Topic 67 : Prakaraṇa (*Topic*) : Sûtras : *16—17*.

Here the opposition moves within the topic and does not advance any outside reason for or against the thesis or counterthesis which constitutes the topic. Thus, sound is non-eternal because it comes after effort, like a pot; and sound is eternal because it resembles potness which is eternal, both being perceptible to the senses. It is required to determine which of these two views represents the truth. To say that sound resembles the non-eternal because it comes after effort is futile. It leaves the counter-thesis unimpared. For both proceed upon resemblance. The truth is that the thesis and counter-thesis arise not from resemblance but from absence of true knowledge. As soon as truth is determined the topic comes to an end.

Topic 68 : Hetu (*Reason, Mark*) *:* Sûtras : *18—20*.

The opposition is to the effect that the Mark is no Mark, because, if it exists before or after the sâdhya (subject), it can have no operation, and if it exists along with the sâdhya there is no knowing which is the sâdhya and which the Mark. To this the reply is that the same argument would apply to the opponent's denial of the Mark. The truth is that it is a matter of common experience that the production of what is to be produced and the knowledge of what is to be known do follow from causes. The opposition based on the points of time is futile.

Topic 69: Arthâpatti (*Presumption*): Sûtras: *21—22*.

The opposition is that the argument that sound is non-eternal by reason of its resemblance to non-eternal objects, namely in coming after effort, implies that sound is eternal by reason of its resemblance to eternal objects, namely in being touchless. To this the reply is that the argument by presumption would apply equally against the opponent, that the presumptive argument does not determine the truth, and that mere divergence of nature is no ground for presumption, e. g., the fact that pebbles which are solid fall to the ground, does not imply that water which is liquid does not fall to the ground.

Topic 70: Non-difference: Sûtras: *23—24*.

The opposition is to the effect that if the resemblance of sound and the pot in respect of their coming after effort leads to their resemblance in being non-eternal, then the resemblance of all objects in respect of their being existent leads to their resemblance in other respects. To this the reply is that the "other respects" should be defined. If the expression means non-eternality, then the non-eternality of sound which is the thesis is admitted by the opponent. The truth is that existence is the highest genus and there is no other common attribute possessed by all existent objects. The Vainâs'ikas (Nihilists) no doubt maintain that like existence non-eternality also is a common attribute of all objects. Their thesis then should be: All entities are non-eternal, because they are existent. The thesis is so wide that no instance can be found for the demonstration. And a Reason or Mark without an instance does not exist. A part of the sâdhya (all entities) cannot be the instance, because the character of a sâdhya is that it is yet to be established. Moreover, if the sâdhya is to furnish the instance it will furnish instances both eternal and non-eternal whereby the object of the nihilist will be defeated.

Topic 71 : Demonstration: Sûtras: *25-26*.

The opposition is to the effect that as in the case of sound, e. g., the cause of its non-eternality is demonstrable, so is also the cause of its eternality, *viz.* absence of touch. To this the reply is that if the opposition is valid the non-eternality of sound is admitted, and that if the argument is not valid the opposition also falls to the ground.

Topic 72 : Cognition: Sûtras: *27-28*.

The opposition is that the cognition of sound does not depend only on the cause which is specified, *viz.* its coming after effort, but that there is cognition of sound also when the branches of trees are broken by high winds (without the effort of man). To this the reply is " coming after effort " is the statement of a cause and not of *the* cause of sound, and that as to be a product is the mark of non-eternality, the opposition does not rebut the demonstration. The existence of sound bears no analogy to the existence of underground water, for example. The latter exists but is not perceived because of some obstruction. But no such obstruction to perception exists in the case of sound. Therefore it cannot be said to exist unperceived. Hence sound is not an instance of the manifestation of an existent object but of the production of a non-existent object.

Topic 73 : *Non-cognition* : Sutras *29-31*.

The opposition is to the effect that in the case of sound the non-cognition of the obstruction to its perception is itself as such incapable of cognition, and that the non-cognition of its non-cognition proves the existence of such obstruction, and that therefore it does not follow that obstructions do not prevent the cognition of sound (prior to its manifestation). In other words, non-cognition which is urged against the existence of obstruction equally applies to the non-cognition of obstruction.

To this the reply is that cognition is of the nature of apprehension, while non-cognition is of the nature of non-apprehension, and that the object of cognition is something that exists, while the object of non-cognition is something that does not exist. Therefore when cognition does not apprehend, come into contact with, any obstruction in the case of sound it follws that such obstruction does not exist. Cognition or non-cognition is not its own object ; the object is something different. Otherwise non-cognition will destroy itself ; and leave obstruction and its cognition unaffected. Moreover, every body is aware of diverse forms of cognition within himself. So that a man becomes aware of the non-cognition of obstruction to the preception of sound in the same way as when he feels that his doubt remains or that his doubt is removed.

Topic 74 : *Non-eternal* : Sûtras : *32-34*.

The opposition is that as sound is said to be non-eternal by reason of its resemblance to a pot, so for the same reason all entities would be non-eternal. To this the reply is that the opposition destroys itself, because if all entities are to be non-eternal owing to their resemblance to a pot, then the opposition will be equally futile as the thesis which it seeks to refute (i. e. non-etenality of sound), owing to its resemblance to the thesis in being presented in the form of an argument of five members. Moreover, mere difference does not constitute the inferential mark. The mark of inference is that particular form of resemblance or difference which is universally known to be the means of the establishment of the proposed attribute in the sàdhya.

Topic 75 : the Eternal : Sûtras : *35-36.*

The opposition is that the non-eternality of sound is itself either eternal or non-eternal and that in the former case sound also must be eternal and that in the latter case the supposed non-eternality of sound will some time cease and sound will be eternal. To this the reply is that the allegation that the non-eternality of sound is eternal is an admission of its non-eternality which is sought to be opposed. Moreover, by the non-eternality of sound is meant that sound which has been produced, ceases to exist after destruction, and not that non-eternality is a positive quality inhereing in sound. In such a case of non-existence due to destruction as the non-eternality of sound the question does not arise as to whether the non-eternality is eternal or non-eternal. Eternality and non-eternality again are contradictory attributes and cannot be predicated together of the same thing at the same time.

Topic 76 : the Effect : Sûtras : *37-38.*

The opposition is to the effect that the reason, "coming after effort", does not necessarily infer the production of something which had no existence before, e. g. a pot, but that it may also infer the effect as manifestation by the removal of obstruction, so that sound, though an effect, being manifested, may yet be eternal. To this the reply is that where manifestation is effected by the removal of obstruction the obstruction is known, but that in the case of sound there is cognition of no such obstruction the removal of which by effort causes its manifestation. It follows that sound is non-eternal.

Topic 77 : Futile Controversy of Six Steps : Sûtras : *39-43.*

(Where the opposition employs a futile reason and the speaker meets it with a proper reply the controversy ends in the determination of the truth as shown in the Sûtras 1 to 38. But where the speaker also employs a futile reason to meet a futile reason the controversy drifts into six steps and ends in confusion). The six steps have been exhibited in the text.

Book V : Chapter ii.

Topic 78 : Errors of the Proposition and the Mark : Sutras : *1-6.*

They are five in number :

(1) Admission of the attribute of the counter-example in one's own example which is the means of the establishment of one's proposition.

(2) Substitution for one's own proposition a different proposition suggested by the reason put forward by the opponent.

(3) Contradiction between the proposition and the reason.

(4) Abandonment of the proposition on opposition.

For examples of the above see pages 208-210.

(5) Qualification of the Mark, on opposition. E. g.: The speaker sets out with the proposition that all manifested objects must have a common origin, and advances the reason that magnitude is their common attribute. The opponent urges that magnitude is seen in things not having the same origin as well as in things having the same origin. Upon this the speaker qualifies his reason and re-states it as that all manifested things, while endowed with the same nature of causing pleasure, pain and delusion, possess magnitude. He thus changes the reason and admits that the reason previously advanced was not sufficient to establish the proposition. And as regards the reason subsequently put forward, it fails of its purpose in the absence of an Example; for an Example must be of a different class and his own reason, all things etc. precludes the possibility of any such example being found; while, if it is found, it must be something having a different origin and thereby hurt his proposition.

Topic 79 : Errors of Failure to Establish the Proposition : Sutras : *7—10.*

The number of such errors is four:

(1) Irrelevancy, (2) absence of sense, (3) obscurity, and (4) incoherence. For examples see pages 211-213.

Topic 80 : Errors of Misstatement of one's argument : Sûtras : *11—13.*

There are three of such errors:

(1) Absence of order among the members of the Nyâya.

(2) Absence of one or more of the members of the Nyâya.

(3) Redundancy of Reasons or Examples.

For examples see pages 213-214.

Topic 81 : Error of Repetition : Sutras : *14—15.*

Repetition should be distinguished from re-inculcation (see II. i. 65). Repetition also includes express mention of what appears clear by implication. For examples see page 215.

Topic 82 : Errors of Non-reply : Sûtras : *16—19.*

Their number is four:

(1) Failure to re-state the counter-thesis, so as to demolish it.

(2) Ignorance of the meaning of the counter-thesis, which cannot therefore be demolished.

(3) Want of ready wit, which naturally courts defeat.

(4) Evasion on some pretext.

Topic 83 : Errors of Weakness and Confusion : Sutras : *20—22.*

They are:

(1) Admission of the opponent's view and turning it against him.

(2) Overlooking the censurable in the opposition.

(3) Censuring the non-censurable in the opposition.

Topic 84 : Errors of Inconsistency and Fallacies of Reason : Sûtras : *23—24.*

These are:

(1) Deviation from tenet, i. e., random discourse at variance with the subject proposed. For example see the text.

(2) Fallacies of reason are, as described, grounds of defeat, and not on any other account. By their very nature they furnish occasions for rebuke.

APPENDIX D.

Alphabetical Index to the Sutras.

—*—

अ.

PAGE

अणुश्यामतानित्यत्ववदेतत्-
स्यात् ... iii 2 71 132
अणुश्यामतानित्यत्ववद्वा iv 1 66 156
अत्यन्तप्रायैकदेशसाधर्म्या-
दुपमानासिद्धिः ii 1 44 46
अथ तत्पूर्वकं त्रिविधमनुमानं
पूर्ववच्छेषवत्सामान्यतो
दृष्टं च ... i 1 5 4
अध्यापनादप्रतिषेधः ii 2 27 64
अनर्थापत्तावर्थापत्त्यभि-
मानात् ... ii 2 4 57
अनवस्थाकारित्वादनवस्थानु-
पपत्तेश्चाप्रतिषेधः iv 2 25 164
अनवस्थायित्वे च वर्णोप-
लब्धिवत्तद्विकारोपपत्तिः ii 2 52 72
अनिग्रहस्थाने निग्रहस्थाना-
भियोगो निरनुयोज्यानु-
योगः ... v 2 22 217
अनित्यत्वग्रहाद्बुद्धेर्बुद्ध्यन्त-
राद्विनाशः शब्दवत् iii 2 24 113
अनिमित्ततो भावोत्पत्तिः
कण्टकतैक्ष्ण्यादिदर्श-
नात् ... iv 1 22 139
अनिमित्तनिमित्तत्वान्नानिमि-
त्ततः ... iv 1 23 139
अनियमे नियमान्नानियमः ii 2 55 74
अनुक्तस्यार्थापत्तेः पक्षहानेरुप-
पत्तिरनुक्तत्वादनैकान्ति-
कत्वाच्चार्थापत्तेः v 1 22 192

PAGE

अनुपलम्भात्मकत्वादनुप-
लब्धेरहेतुः ii 2 21 63
अनुपलम्भात्मकत्वादनुप-
लब्धेरहेतुः v 1 30 197
अनुपलम्भादप्यनुपलब्धि-
सद्भावान्नावरणानुप-
पत्तिरनुपलम्भात् ii 2 20 62
अनुवादोपपत्तेश्च ... ii 1 60 52
अनेकद्रव्यसमवायाद्रूपवि-
शेषाच्चरूपोपलब्धिः iii 1 38 92
अनैकान्तिकः सव्यभिचारः i 2 5 21
अन्तर्बहिश्च कार्यद्रव्यस्य
कारणान्तरवचनादकार्ये
तदभावः ... iv 2 20 162
अन्यदन्यस्मादनन्यत्वादन-
न्यदित्यन्यताभावः ii 2 31 65
अपरीक्षिताभ्युपगमात् तद्वि-
शेषपरीक्षणमभ्युपगम-
सिद्धान्तः ... i 1 31 13
अपवर्गेऽप्येवं प्रसङ्गः iv 2 43 171
अप्तेजोवायूनां पूर्वं पूर्वम-
पोह्याकाशस्योत्तरः iii 1 63 100
अप्रतीघातात्सन्निकर्षोप-
पत्तिः ... iii 1 47 95
अप्रत्यभिज्ञानं च विषयान्त-
रव्यासङ्गात् ... iii 2 7 107
अप्रत्यभिज्ञाने च विनाशप्र-
सङ्गः ... iii 2 5 106
अप्राप्य ग्रहणं काचाभ्रपटल-
स्फटिकान्तरितोपलब्धेः
... ... iii 1 45 94

				PAGE
अभावाद्भावोत्पत्तिर्नानुपमृद्य-प्रादुर्भावात् ...	iv	1	14	136
अभिव्यक्तौ चाभिभवात्	iii	1	43	94
अभ्यासात् ...	ii	2	29	65
अभ्युपेत्य कालभेदे दोषवच-नात् ...	ii	1	59	1
अयसोऽयस्कान्ताभिगमन-वत्तदुपसर्पणम्	iii	1	22	87
अरण्यगुहापुलिनादिषु यो-गाभ्यासोपदेशः	iv	2	42	170
अर्थादापन्नस्य स्वशब्देन पुन-र्वचनम् ...	v	2	15	215
अर्थापत्तितः प्रतिपक्षसिद्धे-रर्थापत्तिसमः	v	1	21	192
अर्थापत्तिरप्रमाणमनैकान्ति-कत्वात् ...	ii	2	3	56
अलातचक्रदर्शनवत्तदुपलब्धि-राशुसंचारात्	iii	2	58	128
अवयवनाशेऽप्यवयव्युप लब्धेरहेतुः	iii	1	10	83
अवयवविपर्यासवचनमप्राप्र-कालम् ...	v	2	11	213
अवयवान्तराभावेऽप्यवृत्ते-रहेतुः ...	iv	2	12	160
अवयवावयविप्रसङ्गश्चैवमा-प्रलयात्	iv	2	15	161
अविज्ञाततत्त्वेऽर्थे कारणोप-पत्तितस्तत्त्वज्ञानार्थमूह-स्तर्कः ...	i	1	40	17
अविज्ञातं चाज्ञानम्	v	2	17	216
अविशेषाभिहितेऽर्थे वक्तु-रभिप्रायादर्थान्तरकल्पना वाक्छलम् ...	i	2	12	24
अविशेषे वा किंचित्साधर्म्यादे-कच्छलप्रसङ्गः ...	i	2	17	26
अविशेषोक्ते हेतौ प्रतिषिद्धे विशेषमिच्छतो हेत्वन्तरम्	v	2	6	210
अव्यक्तग्रहणमनवस्थायित्वा-द्विद्युत्संपाते रूपाव्यक्त-ग्रहणवत् ...	iii	2	43	122
अव्यवस्थात्मनि व्यवस्थि-तत्वाच्चाव्य वस्थायाः	ii	1	4	30
अव्यूहाविष्टम्भविभुत्वानि चाकाशधर्माः	iv	2	22	162
अश्रवणकारणानुपलब्धेः सततश्रवणप्रसङ्गः	ii	2	34	66
असत्यर्थे नाभाव इति चेद् नान्यलक्षणोपपत्तेः	ii	2	9	58
अस्पर्शत्वात् ...	ii	2	22	63
अस्पर्शत्वादप्रतिषेधः	ii	2	38	67
आ.				
आकाशव्यतिभेदात्तदनुपपत्तिः	iv	2	18	162
आकाशासर्वगतत्वं वा	iv	2	19	162
आकृतिर्जातिलिङ्गाख्या	ii	2	68	78
आकृतिस्तदपेक्षत्वात् सत्त्व-व्यवस्थानसिद्धेः	ii	2	63	77
आत्मनित्यत्वे प्रेत्यभावसिद्धिः	iv	1	10	135
आत्मप्रेरणयदृच्छाज्ञताभिश्च न संयोगविशेषः	iii	2	31	116
आत्मशरीरेन्द्रियार्थबुद्धिमनः प्रवृत्तिदोषप्रेत्यभावफल दुःखापवर्गास्तु प्रमेयम्	i	1	9	5
आदर्शोदकयोः प्रसादस्वाभा-व्याद्रूपोपलब्धिवत्तदुप-लब्धिः ...	iii	1	50	96
आदित्यरश्मेः स्फटिकान्त-रितेऽपि दाह्येऽविघातात्	iii	1	48	95

PAGE

आदिमत्त्वादैन्द्रियकत्वात्कृत-
कवदुपचाराच्च ii 2 13 59
आप्तोपदेशः शब्दः i 1 7 5
आप्तोपदेशसामर्थ्याच्छब्दा-
दर्थसंप्रत्ययः ... ii 1 52 48
आश्रयव्यतिरेकाद्वृक्षफलोत्प-
त्तिवदित्यहेतुः iv 1 50 149

इ.

इच्छाद्वेषप्रयत्नसुखदुःख-
ज्ञानान्यात्मनो लिङ्ग-
मिति ... i 1 10 6
इन्द्रियान्तरविकारात् iii 1 12 83
इन्द्रियार्थपञ्चत्वात् iii 1 56 98
इन्द्रियार्थसन्निकर्षोत्पन्नं
ज्ञानमव्यपदेश्यमव्य-
भिचारि व्यवसायात्मकं
प्रत्यक्षम् ... i 1 4 3
इन्द्रियैर्मनसः सन्निकर्षाभा-
वात्तदनुत्पत्तिः iii 2 21 112

ई.

ईश्वरः कारणं पुरुषकर्माफल्य-
दर्शनात् ... iv 1 19 138

उ.

उत्तरस्याप्रतिपत्तिरप्रतिभा v 2 18 216
उत्पादव्ययदर्शनात् iv 1 48 149
उदाहरणसाधर्म्यात्साध्य-
साधनं हेतुः ... i 1 34 14
उदाहरणापेक्षस्तथेत्यु-
पसंहारो न तथेति वा
साध्यस्योपनयः i 1 38 16
उपपत्तिकारणाभ्यनुज्ञानाद-
प्रतिषेधः ... v 1 26 195
उपलब्धेरद्विप्रवृत्तित्वात् ii 1 50 48

PAGE

उपलभ्यमाने चानुपलब्धे-
रसत्वादनपदेशः ii 2 35 66
उभयकारणोपपत्तेरुपपत्ति-
समः ... v 1 25 195
उभयसाधर्म्यात् प्रक्रिया-
प्रसिद्धेः प्रकरणसमः v 1 16 189
उभयो पक्षयोरन्यतरस्या-
ध्यापनादप्रतिषेधः ii 2 28 64

ऋ.

ऋणक्लेशप्रवृत्त्यनुबन्धादप
वर्गाभावः ... iv 1 58 152

ए

एकधर्मोपपत्तेरविशेषे
सर्वाविशेषप्रसङ्गात्सद्भा-
वोपपत्तेरविशेषसमः v 1 23 193
एकविनाशे द्वितीयाविनाशा-
न्नैकत्वम् ... iii 1 9 83
एकस्मिन् भेदाभावात्भेद-
शब्दप्रयोगानुपपत्तेरप्रश्नः
... iv 2 11 160
एकैकश्येनोत्तरोत्तरगुण-
सद्भावादुत्तराणां तदनु-
पलब्धिः ... iii 1 65 101
एतेनानियमः प्रत्युक्तः iii 2 67 30

ऐ.

ऐन्द्रियकत्वाद्रूपादीनाम-
प्रतिषेधः ... iii 2 55 127

क.

कर्मकारितश्चेन्द्रियाणां व्यूहः
पुरुषार्थतन्त्रः ... iii 1 39 92
कर्माकाशसाधर्म्यात्सं-
शयः ... iii 2 1 105
कर्मानवस्थायिग्रहणात् iii 2 42 122

PAGE

कारणद्रव्यस्य प्रदेशशब्दे-
नाभिधानान्नित्येष्व-
प्यव्यभिचार इति ii 2 17 61
कारणान्तरादपि तद्धर्मो-
पपत्तेरप्रतिषेधः v 1 28 196
कार्यव्यासङ्गात्कथाविच्छे-
दो विक्षेपः ... v 2 19 216
कार्यान्यत्वे प्रयत्नाहेतुत्व-
मनुपलब्धिकारणो-
पपत्तेः ... v 1 38 202
कालात्ययापदिष्टः काला-
तीतः ... i 2 9 23
कालान्तरेणानिष्पत्तिर्हेतु-
विनाशात् ... iv 1 45 148
किञ्चित्साधर्म्यादुपसंहार-
सिद्धेर्वैधर्म्यादप्रति-
षेधः ... v 1 5 180
कुड्यान्तरितानुपलब्धेर-
प्रतिषधः ... iii 1 46 94
कृतताकर्तव्यतोपपत्तेस्तू-
भयथा ग्रहणम् ii 1 43 46
कृत्स्नैकदेशावृत्तित्वादवयवा-
नामवयव्यभावः iv 2 7 159
कृष्णसारे सत्युपलम्भाद्
व्यतिरिच्य चोपलम्भात्
संशयः ... iii 1 32 90
केशसमूहे तैमिरिकोपलब्धि-
वत्तदुपलब्धिः ... iv 2 13 160
क्रमनिर्देशादप्रतिषेधः iv 1 18 137
क्रमवृत्तित्वादयुगपद्ग्रह
णम् ... iii 2 6 107
क्वचित्तद्धर्मानुपपत्तेः
क्वचिच्चोपपत्तेः
प्रतिषेधभावः v 1 24 194

PAGE

क्वचिन्निवृत्तिदर्शनादनिवृत्ति-
दर्शनाच्च क्वचिदने-
कान्तः ... ii 1 20 37
क्वचिद्विनाशकारणानुपलब्धेः
क्वचिच्चोपलब्धेर-
नेकान्तः ... iii 2 17 111
क्षीरविनाशे कारणानुपल-
ब्धिवद्दध्युत्पत्तिः iii 2 13 109
क्षुदादिभिः प्रवर्तनाच्च iv 2 40 170

ग.

गन्धक्लेदपाकव्यूहावकाश-
दानेभ्यः पाञ्चभौति-
कम् ... iii 1 30 89
गन्धत्वाद्यव्यतिरेकाद्गन्धा-
दीनामप्रतिषेधः iii 1 58 98
गन्धरसरूपस्पर्शशब्दानां
स्पर्शपर्यन्ताः पृथिव्याः iii 1 62 100
गन्धरसरूपस्पर्शशब्दाः
पृथिव्यादिगुणास्त-
दर्थाः ... i 1 14 7
गुणान्तरापत्त्युपमर्दह्रास-
वृद्धिलेशश्लेषेभ्यस्तु
विकारोपपत्तेर्वर्णवि-
काराः .... ii 2 57 74
गोत्वाद्गोसिद्धिवत्त-
त्सिद्धिः ... v 1 3 176

घ.

घटादिनिष्पत्तिदर्शनात्पीडने
चाभिचारादप्रतिषेधः v 1 8 183
घ्राणरसनचक्षुस्त्वक्श्रोत्राणी-
न्द्रियाणि भूतेभ्यः i 1 12 6

च.

चेष्टेन्द्रियार्थाश्रयः शरीरम् i 1 11 6

PAGE

ज.

जातिविशेषे चानियमात् ii 1 56 50
ज्ञस्येच्छाद्वेषनिमित्तत्वा-
दारम्भनिवृत्त्योः iii 2 34 117
ज्ञातुर्ज्ञानसाधनोपपत्तेः
संज्ञाभेदमात्रम् iii 1 16 85
ज्ञानग्रहणाभ्यासस्तद्विद्यैश्च
सह संवादः iv 2 47 172
ज्ञानलिङ्गत्वादात्मनो
नानवरोधः ... ii 1 24 39
ज्ञानविकल्पानां च भावाभाव-
संवेदनादध्यात्मम् v 1 31 198
ज्ञानसमवेतात्मप्रदेशसन्निक-
र्षान्मनसः स्मृत्युत्पत्तेर्न
युगपदुत्पत्तिः ... iii 2 25 114
ज्ञानायौगपद्यादेकं मनः iii 2 56 127

त.

तत्कारितत्वादहेतुः iv 1 21 138
तत्त्रिविधं वाक्छलं सामा-
न्यच्छलमुपचारच्छलं-
चेति ... i 2 11 24
तत्त्रैराश्यं रागद्वेषमोहार्थान्तर-
भावात् ... iv 1 3 133
तत्त्वप्रधानभेदाच्च मिथ्याबुद्धे-
र्द्वैविध्योपपत्तिः iv 2 37 169
तत्त्वभाक्तयोर्नानात्वविभागाद-
व्यभिचारः ... ii 2 15 61
तत्त्वाध्यवसायसंरक्षणार्थं
जल्पवितण्डे बीजप्ररोह-
संरक्षणार्थं कण्टकशाखावर-
णवत् ... iv 2 50 173
तत्प्रामाण्ये वा न सर्वप्रमाण-
विप्रतिषेधः ... ii 1 14 34

PAGE

तत्प्रामाण्ये वा नार्थापत्त्य-
प्रामाण्यम् ... ii 2 6 57
तत्सम्बन्धात् फलनिष्पत्ते-
स्तेषु फलवदुपचारः iv 1 53 150
तत्सिद्धेरलक्षितेष्वहेतुः ii 2 10 59
तथात्यंतसंशयस्तद्धर्मसात-
त्योपपत्तेः ... ii 1 5 30
तथा दोषाः ... iv 1 2 133
तथा भावादुत्पन्नस्य
कारणोपपत्तेर्न कारण-
प्रतिषेधः ... v 1 13 187
तथा वैधर्म्यात् ... i 1 35 15
तथाऽहारस्य ... iii 2 64 129
तथेत्युपसंहारादुपमान-
सिद्धेर्नाविशेषः ii 1 48 47
तदत्यन्तविमोक्षोऽपवर्गः i 1 22 9
तददृष्टकारितमिति चेत्पुनस्त-
त्प्रसङ्गोऽपवर्गे iii 2 68 131
तदनित्यत्वमग्नेर्दाह्यं विनाश्या-
नुविनाशवत् iv 1 27 140
तदनुपलब्धेरनुपलम्भादभाव-
सिद्धौ तद्विपरीतोपपत्तेर-
नुपलब्धिसमः v 1 29 197
तदनुपलब्धेरनुपलम्भादा-
वरणोपपत्तिः ii 2 19 62
तदनुपलब्धेरहेतुः iii 1 35 91
तदन्तरालानुपलब्धेरहेतुः ii 2 26 64
तदप्रामाण्यमनृतव्याघात-
पुनरुक्तदोषेभ्यः ii 1 57 50
तदभावश्चापवर्गे ... iv 2 45 171
तदभावः सात्मकप्रदाहेऽपि
तन्नित्यत्वात् iii 1 5 81
तदभावे नास्त्यनन्यता-
तयोरितरेतरापेक्ष-
सिद्धेः ii 2 32 66

PAGE

तदयौगपद्यलिङ्गत्वान्न मनसः ... ii 1 25 39
तदर्थं यमनियमाभ्यामात्मसंस्कारो योगाच्चाध्यात्मविध्युपायैः . . iv 2 46 171
तदर्थे व्यक्त्याकृतिजातिसन्निधावुपचारात्संशयः ... ii 2 59 75
तदसंशयः पूर्वहेतुप्रसिद्धत्वात् ... iv 2 5 158
तदात्मगुणत्वेऽपि तुल्यम् ... iii 2 20 112
तदात्मगुणसद्भावादप्रतिषेधः ... iii 1 14 84
तदाश्रयत्वादपृथग्ग्रहणम् iv 2 28 166
तदुपलब्धिरितरेतरद्रव्यगुणवैधर्म्यात् ... iii 1 73 103
तद्विकल्पाज्जातिनिग्रहस्थानबहुत्वम् ... i 2 20 28
तद्विनिवृत्तेर्वा प्रमाणसिद्धिवत्प्रमेयसिद्धिः ii 1 18 36
तद्विपर्ययाद्वा विपरीतम् i 1 37 15
तद्व्यवस्थानं तु भूयस्त्वात् ... iii 1 69 102
तद्व्यवस्थानादेवात्मसद्भावादप्रतिषेधः iii 1 3 80
तन्त्राधिकरणाभ्युपगमसंस्थितिः सिद्धान्तः ... i 1 26 11
तन्निमित्तं त्ववयव्यभिमानः ... iv 2 3 157
तयोरप्यभावो वर्तमानाभावे तदपेक्षत्वात् ... ii 1 40 45
तल्लक्षणावरोधादप्रतिषेधः iv 1 31 141
तल्लिङ्गत्वादिच्छाद्वेषयोः पार्थिवाद्येष्वप्रतिषेधः iii 2 35 118

PAGE

तं शिष्यगुरुसब्रह्मचारिविशिष्टश्रेयोर्थिभिरनसूयुभिरभ्युपेयात् iv 2 48 172
ताभ्यां विगृह्य कथनम् iv 2 51 173
तेनैव तस्याग्रहणाच्च iii 1 71 103
ते विभक्त्यन्ताः पदम् ii 2 58 75
तेषां मोहः पापीयान्नामूढस्येतरोत्पत्तेः iv 1 6 134
तेषु चावृत्तेरवयव्यभावः iv 2 8 159
तैश्चापदेशो ज्ञानविशेषाणाम् ... ii 1 28 40
त्रैकाल्याप्रतिषेधश्च शब्दादातोद्यसिद्धिवत्तत्सिद्धेः ii 1 15 35
त्रैकाल्यासिद्धेः प्रतिषेधानुपपत्तिः ... ii 1 12 34
त्रैकाल्यासिद्धेर्हेतोरहेतुसमः ... v 1 18 190
त्वक्पर्यन्तत्वाच्छरीरस्य केशनखादिष्वप्रसङ्गः ... iii 2 52 126
त्वगव्यतिरेकात् iii 1 53 97

द.

दर्शनस्पर्शनाभ्यामेकार्थग्रहणात् ... iii 1 1 80
दिग्देशकालाकाशेष्वप्येवं प्रसङ्गः ... ii 1 23 39
दुःखजन्मप्रवृत्तिदोषमिथ्याज्ञानानामुत्तरोत्तरापाये तदनन्तराभावादपवर्गः i 1 2 2
दुःखविकल्पे सुखाभिमानाच्च ... iv 1 57 152
दृष्टानुमितानां नियोगप्रतिषेधानुपपत्तिः iii 1 51 96
दृष्टान्तविरोधादप्रतिषेधः iii 1 11 83

PAGE

दृष्टान्तस्य कारणानपदेशात् प्रत्यवस्थानाच्च प्रतिदृष्टान्तेन प्रसङ्गप्रतिदृष्टान्तसमौ … v 1 9 184
दृष्टान्ते च साध्यसाधनभावेन धर्मस्य हेतुत्वात्तस्य चोभयथाभावान्नाविशेषः … v 1 34 199
दोषनिमित्तं रूपादयो विषयाः सङ्कल्पाकृताः … iv 2 2 157
दोषनिमित्तानां तत्त्वज्ञानादहङ्कारनिवृत्तिः iv 2 1 157
द्रव्यगुणधर्मभेदाच्चोपलब्धिनियमः … iii 1 37 91
द्रव्यविकारे वैषम्यवद् वर्णविकारविकल्पः ii 2 45 70
द्रव्ये स्वगुणपरगुणोपलब्धेः संशयः … iii 2 46 123
द्विविधस्यापि हेतोरभावादसाधनं दृष्टान्तः ii 2 43 70

ध.

धर्मविकल्पनिर्देशेऽर्थसद्भावप्रतिषेध उपचारच्छलम् … i 2 14 25
धारणाकर्षणोपपत्तेश्च ii 1 35 43

न.

न कर्मकर्तृसाधनवैगुण्यात् … ii 1 58 51
न कर्मानित्यत्वात् ii 2 23 63
न कारणावयवभावात् iv 1 42 146
न कार्याश्रयकर्तृवधात् iii 1 6 81
न केशनखादिष्वनुपलब्धेः … iii 2 51 125

PAGE

नक्तंचरनयनरश्मिदर्शनाच्च … iii 1 44 94
न क्लेशसन्ततेः स्वाभाविकत्वात् … iv 1 64 155
न गत्यभावात् … iii 2 8 107
न घटाद् घटानिष्पत्तेः iv 1 12 136
न घटाभावसामान्यनित्यत्वान्नित्येष्वप्यनित्यवदुपचाराच्च … ii 2 44 60
न चतुष्ट्वमैतिह्यार्थापत्तिसंभवाभावप्रामाण्यात् … ii 2 1 55
न चावयव्यवयवाः … iv 2 10 159
न तदनवस्थानात् ii 2 61 76
न तदर्थबहुत्वात् iii 1 57 98
न तदर्थान्तरभावात् i 2 16 26
न तदाशुगतित्वान्मनसः iii 2 29 115
न तद्विकाराणां सुवर्णभावाव्यतिरेकात् ii 2 49 71
न दोषलक्षणावरोधान्मोहस्य … iv 1 8 135
न निष्पन्नावश्यंभावित्वात् … iv 2 44 171
न पयसः परिणामगुणान्तरप्रादुर्भावात् iii 2 15 110
न पाकजगुणान्तरोत्पत्तेः … iii 2 48 124
न पार्थिवाप्ययोः प्रत्यक्षत्वात् … iii 1 67 101
न पुत्रपशुस्त्रीपरिच्छद हिरण्यान्नादिफलनिर्देशात् iv 1 52 150
न पुरुषकर्माभावे फलानिष्पत्तेः … iv 1 20 138
न प्रत्यक्षेण यावत्तावदप्युपलम्भात् ii 1 32 42

				PAGE
न प्रदीपप्रकाशवत्त-				
त्सिद्धेः ...	ii	1	19	36
न प्रलयोऽणुसद्भावात्	iv	2	16	162
न प्रवृत्तिः प्रतिसन्धानाय				
हीनक्लेशस्य	iv	1	63	155
न बुद्धिलक्षणाधिष्ठानगत्या-				
कृतिजातिपञ्चत्वेभ्यः	iii	1	60	99
न युगपदग्रहणात्	iii	2	4	106
न युगपदनेकक्रियोप-				
लब्धेः ...	iii	2	57	127
न युगपदर्थानुपलब्धेः	iii	1	54	97
न रात्रावप्यनुपलब्धेः	iii	1	41	93
न रूपादीनामितरेतर-				
वैधर्म्यात् ...	iii	2	54	126
न लक्षणावस्थितापेक्षा-				
सिद्धेः ...	ii	2	11	59
न विकारधर्मानुपपत्तेः	ii	2	46	70
न विनष्टेभ्योऽनिष्पत्तेः	iv	1	17	137
न विषयव्यवस्थानात्	iii	1	2	80
न व्यवस्थानुपपत्तेः	iv	1	33	142
न शब्दगुणोपलब्धेः	iii	1	72	103
न सर्वगुणानुपलब्धेः	iii	1	64	100
न सङ्कल्पनिमित्तत्वाच्च				
रागादीनाम्	iv	1	67	156
न सङ्कल्पनिमित्तत्वाद्रा-				
गादीनाम्	iii	1	26	88
न साध्यसमत्वात्	iii	2	62	129
न सामयिकत्वाच्छब्दार्थ				
सम्प्रत्ययस्य	ii	1	55	50
न सुखस्यान्तराल-				
निष्पत्तेः ...	iv	1	55	151
न स्मरणकालानियमात्	iii	2	30	416
न स्मृतेः स्मर्तव्यविषय-				
त्वात् ...	iii	1	13	84

				PAGE
न स्वभावसिद्धिरापेक्षि-				
कत्वात् ...	iv	1	39	145
न स्वभावसिद्धिर्भावानाम्	iv	1	38	145
न हेतुतः कार्यसिद्धेस्त्रै-				
काल्यासिद्धिः	v	1	19	191
नाकृताभ्यागमप्रसङ्गात्	iii	2	72	132
नाकृतिव्यक्त्यपेक्षत्वाज्जात्य-				
भिव्यक्तेः ...	ii	2	65	78
नाणुनित्यत्वात् ...	ii	2	24	63
नातीतानागतयोरितरेतरा-				
पेक्षासिद्धिः	ii	1	41	45
नातीतानागतयोः कारकशब्द-				
प्रयोगात् ...	iv	1	16	137
नातुल्यप्रकृतीनां विकार-				
विकल्पात्	ii	2	44	70
नात्मप्रतिपत्तिहेतूनां मनसि				
सम्भवात्	iii	1	15	84
नात्ममनसोः सन्निकर्षाभावे				
प्रत्यक्षोत्पत्तिः	ii	1	22	38
नानित्यतानित्यत्वात्	iv	1	26	140
नानुमीयमानस्य प्रत्यक्षतो-				
ऽनुपलब्धिरभावहेतुः	iii	1	36	91
नानुवादपुनरुक्तयोर्विशेषः				
शब्दाभ्यासोपपत्तेः	ii	1	66	54
नानेकलक्षणैरेकभाव-				
निष्पत्तेः ...	iv	1	35	143
नान्तःशरीरवृत्तित्वान्म-				
नसः ...	iii	2	26	114
नान्यत्र प्रवृत्त्यभावात्	iii	1	23	87
नान्यत्वेऽप्यभ्यासस्योप-				
चारात् ...	ii	2	30	65
नाप्रत्यक्षे गवये प्रमाणार्थ-				
मुपमानस्य पश्यामः	ii	1	47	47
नाभावप्रामाण्यं प्रमेया-				
सिद्धेः ...	ii	2	7	58

PAGE

नार्थविशेषप्राबल्यात् ii 1 30 41
नार्थविशेषप्राबल्यात् iv 2 39 170
नासन्न सन्न सदसत्
सदसतोर्वैधर्म्यात् iv 1 47 148
निग्रहस्थानप्राप्तस्यानिग्रहः
पर्यनुयोज्योपेक्षणम् v 2 21 217
नित्यत्वप्रसङ्गश्च प्रायणा-
नुपपत्तेः ... iii 2 70 131
नित्यत्वे विकारादनित्यत्वे
चानवस्थानात् ii 2 50 72
नित्यमनित्यभावादनित्ये
नित्यत्वोपपत्तेर्नित्य-
समः ... v 1 35 200
नित्यस्याप्रत्याख्यानं यथोपल-
ब्धिव्यवस्थानात् iv 1 28 141
नित्यानामतीन्द्रियत्वा-
त्तद्धर्मविकल्पाच्च
वर्णविकाराणाम-
प्रतिषेधः ... ii 2 51 72
निमित्तनैमित्तिकोपपत्तेश्च
तुल्यजातीयानाम-
प्रतिषेधः ... iv 1 9 135
निमित्तनैमित्तिकभावाद-
र्थान्तरभावो दोषेभ्यः iv 1 7 134
निमित्तानिमित्तयोरर्थान्त-
रभावादप्रतिषेधः iv 1 24 I39
नियमानियमौ तु तद्विशे-
षकौ ... iii 2 37 118
नियमश्च निरनुमानः iii 1 17 85
नियमहेत्वभावाद्यथादर्शन-
मभ्यनुज्ञा ... iii 2 11 108
नियमानियमविरोधादनियमे
नियमाच्चाप्रतिषेधः ii 2 56 74
निरवयवत्वादहेतुः iv 1 43 147

PAGE

निर्दिष्टकारणाभावेऽप्युपल-
म्भादुपलब्धिसमः v 1 27 196
निःश्वासोच्छ्वासोपलब्धे-
श्चातुर्भौतिकम् iii 1 29 89
नेतरेतरधर्मप्रसङ्गात् iii 1 49 95
नेन्द्रियार्थयोस्तद्विनाशेऽपि
ज्ञानावस्थानात् iii 2 18 111
नैकदेशत्राससादृश्येभ्यो
ऽर्थान्तरभावात् ii 1 38 44
नैकप्रत्यनीकभावात् iv 1 4 133
नैकस्मिन्नासास्थिव्यवहिते
द्वित्वाभिमानात् iii 1 8 82
नोत्पत्तिकारणानपदे-
शात् ... iii 2 22 113
नोत्पत्तितत्कारणोपलब्धेः iv 1 32 142
नोत्पत्तिनिमित्तत्वान्माता-
पित्रोः ... iii 2 63 129
नोत्पत्तिविनाशकारणो-
पलब्धेः ... iii 2 12 109
नोत्पत्तिविनाशकारणो-
पलब्धेः ... iv 1 30 141
नोष्णशीतवर्षकालनिमित्त-
त्वात्पञ्चात्मकविका-
राणाम् ... iii 1 20 86
न्यूनसमाधिकोपलब्धेर्विका-
राणामहेतुः ... ii 2 42 69

प.

पक्षप्रतिषेधे प्रतिज्ञातार्था-
पनयनं प्रतिज्ञासंन्यासः v 2 5 210
पद्मादिषु प्रबोधसंमीलन-
विकारवत्तद्विकारः iii 1 19 86
परश्वादावारम्भनिवृत्ति-
दर्शनात् ... iii 2 36 118
परं वा त्रुटेः ... iv 2 17 162

PAGE

परिशेषाद्यथोक्तहेतू-
पपत्तेश्च ... iii 2 39 119
परिषत्प्रतिवादिभ्यां
त्रिरभिहितमप्यविज्ञातम-
विज्ञातार्थम् v 2 9 212
पश्चात्सिद्धौ न प्रमाणेभ्यः
प्रमेयसिद्धिः ii 1 10 33
पाणिनिमित्तप्रश्लेषाच्छब्दाभावे
नानुपलब्धिः ii 2 36 67
पात्रचयान्तानुपपत्तेश्च
फलाभावः iv 1 61 153
पार्थिवं गुणान्तरो-
पलब्धेः ... iii 1 27 88
पार्थिवाप्यतैजसं
तद्गुणोपलब्धेः iii 1 28 89
पुनरुत्पत्तिः प्रेत्यभावः i 1 19 9
पूरणप्रदाहपाटनानु-
पलब्धेश्च सम्बन्धा-
भावः ... ii 1 53 49
पूर्वकृतफलानुबन्धात्त-
दुत्पत्तिः ... iii 2 60 128
पूर्वकृतफलानुबन्धात्त-
दुत्पत्तिः ... iv 2 41 170
पूर्वपूर्वगुणोत्कर्षात्तत्तत्प्रधा-
नम् ... iii 1 68 102
पूर्वंहि प्रमाणसिद्धौ नेन्द्रि-
यार्थसन्निकर्षात् प्रत्य-
क्षोत्पत्तिः ... ii 1 9 32
पूर्वाभ्यस्तस्मृत्यनुबन्धाज्जा-
तस्यहर्षभयशोकसम्प्रति-
पत्तेः ... iii 1 18 86
पृथक्चावयवेभ्यो ऽवृत्तेः iv 2 9 159
पृथिव्यापस्तेजो वायुराकाश-
मितिभूतानि i 1 13 7

PAGE

पौर्वापर्यायोगादप्रतिसम्ब-
द्धार्थमपार्थकम् v 2 10 21?
प्रकृतादर्थादप्रतिसम्बद्धार्थ-
मर्थान्तरम् v 2 7 211
प्रकृतिविवृद्धौ विकारवि-
वृद्धेः ... ii 2 41 69
प्रकृत्यनियमाद्वर्णविकारा-
णाम् ... ii 2 54 73
प्रणिधाननिबन्धाभ्यास-
लिङ्गलक्षणसादृश्य-
परिग्रहाश्रयाश्रितस-
म्बन्धानन्तर्यवियोगै-
ककार्यविरोधातिशय-
प्राप्तिव्यवधानसुखदुःखे-
च्छाद्वेषभयार्थित्वक्रिया-
रागधर्माधर्मनिमित्ते-
भ्यः ... iii 2 41 120
प्रणिधानलिङ्गादिज्ञानाना-
मयुगपद्भावादयुगपत्स्म-
रणम् ... iii 2 33 117
प्रतिज्ञाहेतूदाहरणोपनय-
निगमनान्य-वयवाः i 1 32 13
प्रतिज्ञातार्थप्रतिषेधे धर्मविक-
ल्पात्तदर्थनिर्देशः प्रतिज्ञा-
न्तरम् ... v 2 3 208
प्रतिज्ञाहानिः प्रतिज्ञान्तरं
प्रतिज्ञाविरोधः प्रतिज्ञा-
संन्यासोहेत्वन्तरमर्थान्तरं
निरर्थकमविज्ञातार्थमपा-
र्थकमप्राप्तकालं न्यूनम-
धिकं पुन रुक्तमननुभाष-
णमज्ञानमप्रतिभाविक्षेपो
मतानुज्ञा पर्यनुयोज्योपे-

				PAGE
प्रवर्तनालक्षणा दोषाः	i	1	18	8
प्रवृत्तिदोषजनितो ऽर्थः फलम् ...	i	1	20	9
प्रवृत्तिर्यथोक्ता ...	iv	1	1	133
प्रवृत्तिर्वाग्बुद्धिशरीरारम्भ इति ...	i	1	17	8
प्रसिद्धसाधर्म्यात्साध्यसाधनमुपमानम्	i	1	6	4
प्रसिद्धसाधर्म्यादुपमानसिद्धेर्यथोक्त दोषानुपपत्तिः	ii	1	45	46
प्रागुत्पत्तेरभावानित्यत्ववत्स्वाभाविकेऽप्यनित्यत्वम् ...	iv	1	65	155
प्रागुच्चारणादनुपलब्धेरावरणाद्यनुपलब्धेश्च	ii	2	18	62
प्रागुत्पत्तेरभावोपपत्तेश्च	ii	2	12	59
प्रागुत्पत्तेः कारणाभावादनुत्पत्तिसमः	v	1	12	186
प्राङ्निष्पत्तेर्वृक्षफलवत्तत्स्यात् ...	iv	1	46	148
प्राप्तौ चानियमात्	iii	2	65	130
प्राप्य साध्यमप्राप्य वा हेतोः प्राप्त्या ऽविशिष्टत्वादप्राप्त्या ऽसाधकत्वाच्च प्राप्त्यप्राप्तिसमौ	v	1	7	182
प्रीतेरात्माश्रयत्वादप्रतिषेधः	iv	1	51	150
प्रेत्याहाराभ्यासकृतात्स्तन्याभिलाषात्	iii	1	27	87
ब				
बाधनानिवृत्तेर्वेदयतः पर्येषणदोषादप्रतिषेधः	iv	1	56	151
बाधनालक्षणं दुःखमिति	i	1	21	9
बाह्यप्रकाशानुग्रहाद् विषयोपलब्धेरनभिव्यक्तितो ऽनुपलब्धिः	iv	1	42	93
बुद्धिरुपलब्धिर्ज्ञानमित्यनर्थान्तरम् ...	i	1	15	7
बुद्धिसिद्धन्तु तदसत्	iv	1	49	149
बुद्धेश्चैवं निमित्तसद्भावोपलम्भात्	iv	2	36	169
बुद्ध्या विवेचनात्तु भावानां याथात्म्यानुपलब्धिस्तन्त्वपकर्षणे पटसद्भावानुपलब्धिवत्तदनुपलब्धिः ...	iv	2	26	165
भ				
भूतगुणविशेषोपलब्धेस्तादात्म्यम् ...	iii	1	61	100
भूतेभ्यो मूर्त्युपादानवत्तदुपादानम् ...	iii	2	61	128
म				
मध्यन्दिनोल्काप्रकाशानुपलब्धिवत्तदनुपलब्धिः	iii	1	40	92
मनःकर्मनिमित्तत्वाच्च संयोगानुच्छेदः	iii	2	69	131
मन्त्रायुर्वेदप्रामाण्यवच्च तत्प्रामाण्यमाप्त प्रामाण्यात् ...	ii	1	68	54
महदणुग्रहणात् ...	iii	1	33	90
मायागन्धर्वनगरमृगतृष्णिकावद्वा ...	iv	2	32	167
मिथ्योपलब्धिविनाशस्तत्त्वज्ञानात्स्वप्न विषयाभिमानप्रणाशवत्प्रतिबोधे ...	iv	2	35	168

PAGE

मूर्तिमतां च संस्थानोपपत्ते-
रवयवसद्भावः iv 2 23 164

य.

यत्र संशयस्तत्रैवमुत्तरोत्तर-
प्रसंगः ... ii 1 7 32
यत्सिद्धावन्यप्रकरणसिद्धिः
सोऽधिकरण सिद्धा-
न्तः .... i 1 30 12
यथोक्तहेतुत्वाच्चाणु iii 2 59 128
यथोक्तहेतुत्वात्पारतन्त्र्याद-
कृताभ्यागमाच्च न
मनसः ... iii 2 38 119
यथोक्ताध्यवसायादेव तद्वि-
शेषापेक्षात्संशये नासं-
शयो नात्यन्तसंशयो वा ii 1 6 30
यथोक्तोपपन्नच्छलजातिनिग्र-
हस्थानसाधनोपालम्भो-
जल्पः ... i 2 2 20
यमर्थमधिकृत्य प्रवर्तते
तत्प्रयोजनम् i 1 24 11
यस्मात् प्रकरणचिन्ता स
निर्णयार्थमपदिष्टः प्रक-
रणसमः ... i 2 7 22
यावच्छरीरभावित्वाद्रू-
पादीनाम् .. iii 2 47 124
याशब्दसमूहत्यागपरिग्रह-
संख्यावृद्ध्युपचयवर्ण-
समासानुबन्धानां व्यक्ता-
वुपचाराद्व्यक्तिः ii 2 60 75
युगपज्ज्ञानानुत्पत्तिर्मनसो
लिङ्गम् ... i 1 16 7
युगपज्ज्ञेयानुपलब्धेश्च न
मनसः ... iii 2 19 112

PAGE

युगपदसिद्धौ प्रत्यर्थनियत-
त्वात् क्रमवृत्तित्वाभावो
बुद्धीनाम् ... ii 1 11 33

र.

रश्म्यर्थसन्निकर्षविशेषा-
त्तद्ग्रहणम् ... iii 1 34 91
रोधोपघातसादृश्येभ्यो
व्यभिचारादनुमानम-
प्रमाणम् ... ii 1 37 43

ल.

लक्षणव्यवस्थानादेवाप्रति-
षेधः ... iv 1 36 144
लक्षितेष्वलक्षणलक्षितत्वा-
दलक्षितानां तत्प्रमेय-
सिद्धेः ... ii 2 8 58
लिङ्गतो ग्रहणान्नानुपल-
ब्धिः ... iii 2 14 110
लौकिकपरीक्षकाणां यस्मि-
न्नर्थे बुद्धिसाम्यं स
दृष्टान्तः ... i 1 25 11

व.

वचनविघातोऽर्थविकल्पोप-
पत्त्या छलम् i 2 10 23
वर्णक्रमनिर्देशवन्निरर्थकम् v 2 8 212
वर्तमानाभावः पततः पतित-
पतितव्य कालोपपत्तेः ii 1 39 44
वर्तमानाभावे सर्वाग्रहणं
प्रत्यक्षानुपपत्तेः ii 1 42 45
वाक्छलमेवोपचारच्छलं
तदविशेषात् i 2 15 25
वाक्यविभागस्य चार्थग्रह-
णात् ii 1 61 52
विकारधर्मित्वे नित्यत्वाभा-
वात् कालान्तरे विका-
रोपपत्तेश्चाप्रतिषेधः ii 2 53 73

PAGE

विकारप्राप्तानामपुनरावृत्तेः ii 2 47 71
विकारादेशोपदेशात्संशयः ii 2 40 69
विज्ञातस्य परिषदा त्रिरभिहितस्याप्यप्रत्युच्चारणमननुभाषणम् ... v 2 16 215
विद्याविद्याद्वैविध्यात् संशयः ... iv 2 4 158
विधिर्विधायकः ... ii 1 63 52
विधिविहितस्यानुवचनमनुवादः ... ii 1 65 53
विध्यर्थवादानुवादवचनविनियोगात् ... ii 1 62 52
विनाशकारणानुपलब्धेश्चावस्थानेतन्नित्यत्वप्रसङ्गः ii 2 37 67
विनाशकारणानुपलब्धेश्चावस्थाने तन्नित्यत्वप्रसङ्गः ... iii 2 23 113
विनाशकारणानुपलब्धेश्च ii 2 33 66
विप्रतिपत्तिरप्रतिपत्तिश्च निग्रहस्थानम् i 2 19 27
विप्रतिपत्तौ च संप्रतिपत्तेः ii 1 3 30
विप्रतिपत्त्यव्यवस्थाध्यवसायाच्च ... ii 1 2 29
विप्रतिषेधाच्च न त्वगेका iii 1 55 97
विभक्त्यन्तरोपपत्तेश्च समासे ... ii 2 39 68
विमृश्य पक्षप्रतिपक्षाभ्यामर्थावधारणं निर्णयः i 1 41 17
विविधबाधनायोगाद्दुःखमेव जन्मोत्पत्तिः iv 1 54 151
विषयत्वाव्यतिरेकादेकत्वम् ... iii 1 59 98
विषयप्रत्यभिज्ञानात् iii 1 2 105
विरुद्धं ह्यपरं परेण ... iii 1 66 101

PAGE

वीतरागजन्मादर्शनात् iii 1 24 88
वृत्त्यनुपपत्तेरपि तर्हि न संशयः ... iv 2 6 158
व्यक्ताद्‍घटनिष्पत्तेरप्रतिषेधः ... iv 1 13 136
व्यक्ताद्व्यक्तानां प्रत्यक्षप्रामाण्यात् ... iv 1 11 135
व्यक्तिर्गुणविशेषाश्रयो मूर्तिः ... ii 2 67 78
व्यक्त्याकृतिजातयस्तु पदार्थः ... ii 2 66 78
व्यक्त्याकृतियुक्तेऽप्यप्रसङ्गात् प्रोक्षणादीनां मृद्गवके जातिः ii 2 64 77
व्यभिचारादहेतुः iv 1 5 134
व्याघातादप्रयोगः iv 1 15 139
व्यासक्तमनसः पादव्यथनेन संयोगविशेषेण समानम् ... iii 2 32 117
व्याहतत्वादयुक्तम् iv 1 40 145
व्याहतत्वादहेतुः ii 1 29 41
iv 2 27 165
व्यूहान्तराद्द्रव्यान्तरोत्पत्तिदर्शनं पूर्वद्रव्यनिवृत्तेरनुमानात् ... iii 2 16 110

श.

शब्दऐतिह्यार्थान्तरभावादनुमानेऽर्थापत्तिसम्भवाभावानर्थान्तरभावाच्चाप्रतिषेधः ... ii 2 2 55
शब्दसंयोगविभवाच्चसर्वगतम् ... iv 2 21 163
शब्दार्थयोः पुनर्वचनं पुनरुक्तमन्यत्रानुवादात् v 2 14 214

PAGE

शब्दार्थव्यवस्थानादप्रति-
षेधः ... ii 1 54 50
शब्दोऽनुमानमर्थस्यानुप-
लब्धेरनुमेयत्वात् ii 1 49 48
शरीरगुणवैधर्म्यात् iii 2 53 126
शरीरदाहे पातकाभावात् iii 1 4 81
शरीरव्यापित्वात् iii 2 50 125
शरीरोत्पत्तिनिमित्तवत्संयो-
गोत्पत्ति निमित्तं कर्म iii 2 66 130
शीघ्रतरगमनोपदेशवदभ्या-
सान्नाविशेषः ii 1 67 54
श्रुतिप्रामाण्याच्च ... iii 1 31 89

स.

सगुणद्रव्योत्पत्तिवत्त-
दुत्पत्तिः ... iii 1 25 88
सगुणानामिन्द्रियभावात् iii 1 70 1 3
सद्यः कालान्तरे च निष्पत्तेः
संशयः ... iv 1 44 147
स द्विविधो दृष्टादृष्टार्थ-
त्वात् ... i 1 8 5
स प्रतिपक्षस्थापनाहीनो
वितण्डा ... i 2 3 20
समाधिविशेषाभ्यासात् iv 2 38 169
समानतन्त्रसिद्धः पर-
तन्त्रासिद्धः प्रति-
तन्त्रसिद्धान्तः i 1 29 12
समानप्रसवात्मिका जातिः ii 2 69 79
समानानेकधर्माध्यवसाया-
दन्यतरधर्माध्यवसाया-
द्वा न संशयः ii 1 1 29
समानानेकधर्मोपपत्तेर्विप्रति-
पत्तेरुपलब्ध्यनुपलब्ध्य-
व्यवस्थाश्च विशेषापेक्षो-
विमर्शः संशयः i 1 23 10

PAGE

समारोपणादात्मन्यप्रति-
षेधः ... iv 1 60 153
सर्वतन्त्रप्रतितन्त्राधिकरणा-
भ्युपगमसंस्थित्यर्थान्त-
रभावात् ... i 1 27 11
सर्वतन्त्राविरुद्धस्तन्त्रे
ऽधिकृतोऽर्थः सर्वतन्त्र-
सिद्धान्तः ... i 1 28 12
सर्वत्रैवम् ... v 1 40 203
सर्वं नित्यं पञ्चभूतनित्य-
त्वात् ... iv 1 29 141
सर्वं पृथग्भावलक्षणपृथ-
क्त्वात् ... iv 1 34 142
सर्वप्रमाणप्रतिषेधाच्च प्रति-
षेधानुपपत्तिः ii 1 13 34
सर्वमनित्यमुत्पत्तिविनाश-
धर्मकत्वात् ... iv 1 5 140
सर्वमभावो भावेष्वितरेत-
राभावसिद्धेः iv 1 37 144
सर्वाग्रहणमवयव्यसिद्धेः ii 1 34 42
सव्यदृष्टस्येतरेण प्रत्यभि-
ज्ञानात् ... iii 1 7 82
सव्यभिचारविरुद्धप्रकर-
णसमसाध्यसमकाला-
हेत्वाभासाः ... i 2 4 21
सहचरणस्थानतादर्थ्यवृत्त-
मानधारणसामीप्ययोग-
साधनाधिपत्येभ्यो ब्राह्म-
णमञ्चकटराजसक्तुचन्द-
नगङ्गाशाटकान्नपुरुषेष्व-
तद्भावेऽपि तदुपचारः ii 2 62 76
संख्यैकान्तासिद्धिः कारणा-
नुपपत्त्युपपत्तिभ्याम् iv 1 41 146
सन्तानानुमानविशेषणात् ii 2 16 61

PAGE
सम्प्रदानात् ... ii 2 25 64
सम्बन्धाच्च ... ii 1 51 48
सम्भवतोऽर्थस्यातिसामान्य-
योगादसम्भूतार्थकल्पना
सामान्यच्छलम् i 2 13 24
संयोगोपपत्तेश्च ... iv 2 24 164
साधर्म्यवैधर्म्याभ्यामुपसंहारे
तद्धर्म विपर्ययोपपत्तेः-
साधर्म्यवैधर्म्यसमौ v 1 2 174
साधर्म्यवैधर्म्याभ्यां प्रत्यव-
स्थानं जातिः ... i 2 18 26
साधर्म्यवैधर्म्योत्कर्षापकर्षव-
र्ण्यावर्ण्यविकल्पसाध्य-
प्राप्त्यप्राप्तिप्रसङ्गदृष्टा-
न्तानुत्पत्तिसंशयप्रकरण-
हेत्वर्थापत्त्यविशेषोपपत्त्यु-
पलब्ध्यनुपलब्धिनित्या-
नित्यकार्यसमाः v 1 1 174
साधर्म्यात्तुल्यधर्मोपपत्तेः
सर्वानित्यत्व प्रसंगाद-
नित्यसमः ... v 1 32 198
साधर्म्यात्संशये न संशयो वैध-
र्म्यादुभयथा वा संशये-
ऽत्यन्तसंशयप्रसङ्गोनि-
त्यत्वानभ्युपगमाच्च
सामान्यस्याप्रतिषेधः v 1 15 188
साधर्म्यादसिद्धेः प्रतिषेधा-
सिद्धिः प्रतिषेध्यसाध-
र्म्याच्च ... v 1 33 199
साध्यत्वादवयविनि संदेहः ii 1 33 42
साध्यत्वादहेतुः ... iii 2 27 115
साध्यदृष्टान्तयोर्धर्मविकल्पा-
दुभयसाध्यत्वाच्चोत्क-

PAGE
र्षापकर्षवर्ण्यावर्ण्यवि-
कल्पसाध्यसमाः v 1 4 176
साध्यनिर्देशः प्रतिज्ञा i 1 33 14
साध्यसमत्वादहेतुः iii 2 3 105
साध्यसाधर्म्यात्तद्धर्मभावी
दृष्टान्त उदाहरणम् i 1 36 15
साध्यातिदेशाच्च दृष्टान्तो-
पपत्तेः ... v 1 6 181
साध्याविशिष्टः साध्यत्वात्सा-
ध्यसमः ... i 2 8 22
सामान्यदृष्टान्तयोरैन्द्रियक-
त्वे समाने नित्यानित्य
साधर्म्यात्संशयसमः v 1 14 187
सिद्धान्तमभ्युपेत्य तद्विरोधी-
विरुद्धः ... i 2 6 21
सिद्धान्तमभ्युपेत्यानियमात्
कथाप्रसंगो ऽपसिद्धा
न्तः ... v 2 23 218
सुप्तव्यासक्तमनसां चेन्द्रिया-
र्थयोः संनिकर्षनिमित्त-
त्वात् ... ii 1 27 40
सुवर्णादीनां पुनरापत्तेरहेतुः ii 2 48 71
सुषुप्तस्य स्वप्नादर्शने क्लेशा-
भाववदपवर्गः iv 1 62 154
सेनावनवद्ग्रहणमिति चेन्ना-
तीन्द्रियत्वादणूनाम् ii 1 36 43
स्तुतिर्निन्दा परकृतिः पुराकल्प
इत्यर्थवादः ... ii 1 64 53
स्थानान्यत्वे नानात्वादवय
विनानास्थानत्वाच्च-
संशयः ... iii 1 52 96
स्फटिकान्यत्वाभिमानवत्त-
दन्यत्वाभिमानः iii 2 9 108

PAGE

स्फटिके ऽप्यपरापरोत्पत्तेः-
क्षणिकत्वाद् व्यक्तीनाम-
हेतुः ... iii 2 10 108
स्मरणं त्वात्मनो ज्ञस्वाभा-
व्यात् ... iii 2 40 120
स्मरतः शरीरधारणोपपत्तेर-
प्रतिषेधः ... iii 2 28 115
स्मृतिसंकल्पवच्च स्वप्न-
विषयाभिमानः iv 2 34 168
स्वपक्षदोषाभ्युपगमात्परपक्षे
दोषप्रसंगो मतानुज्ञा v 2 20 216
स्वपक्षलक्षणापेक्षोपपत्त्युपसंहारे
हेतुनिर्देशे परपक्षदोषाभ्यु-
पगमात्समानो दोष
इति ... v 1 43 204

PAGE

स्वप्नविषयाभिमानवदयं
प्रमाणप्रमेयाभिमानः iv 2 31 167
स्वविषयानतिक्रमेणेन्द्रियस्य
पटुमन्दभावाद्विषयग्रह-
णस्य तथाभावो नविषये
प्रवृत्तिः ... iv 2 14 161

ह.

हीनमन्यतमेनाप्यवयवेन
न्यूनम् ... v 2 12 213
हेतूदाहरणाधिकमधिकम् v 2 13 214
हेतूपादानात्प्रतिषेद्धव्या-
भ्यनुज्ञा ... iii 2 44 123
हेत्वपदेशात्प्रतिज्ञायाः पुनर्व-
चनं निगमनम् i 1 39 17
हेत्वभावदसिद्धिः iv 2 33 167
हेत्वाभासाश्च यथोक्ताः v 2 24 218

APPENDIX E.

Word Index to the Nyâya Sûtras.

—*—

अ

अकार्ये iv. 2. 20.
अकृत iii. 2. 72.
अकृताभ्यागमात् iii. 2. 38.
अग्ने: iv. 1. 27.
अग्रहणं ii. 1. 42., iii. 2. 6.
अग्रहणात् iii. 1. 71., iii. 2. 4.
अज्ञानं v. 2. 1., v. 2. 17.
अणु ii. 2. 24., iii. 1. 33., iii. 2. 59., iii. 2. 71., iv. 1. 66., iv. 2. 16.
अणूनाम् ii. 1. 36.
अतद्भावे ii. 2. 62.
अत्यन्त i. 1. 22., ii. 1. 5., ii. 1. 6., ii. 1. 44., v. 1. 15.
अत्यन्तसंशय: ii. 1. 5., v. 1. 15.
अत्यय i. 2. 9.
अतिदेशात् v. 1. 6.
अतिशय iii. 2. 41.
अतिसामान्य i. 2. 13.
अतिसामान्ययोगात् i. 2. 13.
अतीत ii. 1. 41., iv. 1. 16.
अतीन्द्रियत्वात् ii. 1. 36., ii. 2. 51.
अतुल्यप्रकृतीनां ii. 2. 44.
अथ i. 1. 5,
अदर्शनात् iii. 1. 24.
अदर्शने iv. 1. 62.
अदृष्टार्थत्वात् i. 1. 8.
अद्विप्रवृत्तित्वात् ii. 1. 50.
अधर्म iii. 2. 41.
अधिकं v. 2. 1., v. 2. 13.
अधिकरण i. 1. 26., i. 1. 27., i, 1. 30.
अधिकृत्य i. 1. 24.
अधिकृत: i. 1. 28.
अधिगम: i. 1. 1.
अधिष्ठान iii. 1. 60.
अध्यवसाय iv. 2. 50.
अध्यवसायात् ii. 1. 1., ii. 1. 2., ii. 1.6.
अध्यात्म iv. 2. 46.
अध्यात्मम् v. 1. 31.
अध्यापनात् ii. 2. 28.
अनतिक्रमेण iv. 2. 14.
अनन्यता ii. 2. 32.
अनन्यत्वात् ii. 2. 31.
अननुभाषणं v. 2. 1.
अनपदेश: ii. 2. 35.
अनपदेशात् iii. 2. 22,, v. 1. 9.
अनभिव्यक्तित: iii. 1. 42.

अनभ्युपगमात् v. 1. 15.
अनर्थ i. 1. 15.
अनर्थान्तरम् i. 1. 15.
अनर्थापत्तौ ii. 2. 4.
अनवरोधः ii. 1. 24.
अनवस्था iv. 2. 25.
अनवस्थानात् ii. 2. 50., ii. 2. 61.
अनवस्थायि iii. 2. 42.
अनवस्थायित्वात् iii. 2. 43.
अनवस्थायित्वे ii. 2. 52.
अनसूयिभिः iv. 2. 48.
अनागतयोः ii. 1. 41., iv. 1. 16.
अनिग्रहः v. 2. 21.
अनिग्रहस्थाने v. 2. 22.
अनित्य v. 1. 1., v 1. 15.
अनित्यं iv. 1. 25.
अनित्यत्व iii. 2. 25., v. 1. 32.
अनित्यत्वं iv. 1. 27., iv. 1. 65.
अनित्यता iv. 1 26.
अनित्यत्वात् ii. 2. 23
अनित्यभावात् v. 1. 35, v. 1. 35
अनित्ये v. 1. 35., v. 1. 36.
अनित्यत्वे ii. 2. 50.
अनित्यवत् ii. 2. 14., iv. 1. 66.
अनित्यसमः v. 1. 32.
अनिमित्त iv. 1. 23.
अनिमित्ततः iv. 1. 22., iv. 1. 23.
अनिमित्तयोः iv. 1. 23.
अनियम ii. 2. 56.
अनियमः ii. 2. 55., iii. 2. 67.
अनियमात् ii. 1. 54., iii. 2. 30., iii. 2. 65., v. 2. 23.
अनियमे ii. 2. 55.
अनियमौ iii. 2. 37.
अनिवृत्ति ii. 1. 20.
अनिवृत्तेः iv. 1. 56.
अनिष्पत्तिः iv. 1. 45.
अनिष्पत्तेः iv. 1. 12. iv. 1. 17., iv. 1. 20.
अनुक्तत्वात् v. 1. 22.
अनुग्रहात् iii. 1. 42.
अनुच्छेदः iii. 2. 69.
अनुत्पत्ति v. 1. 1.
अनुत्पत्तिः i. 1. 16., iii. 2. 21.
अनुपपत्ति ii. 2. 20., iv. 1. 41., iv. 2. 30.
अनुपपत्तिः ii. 1. 45., iii. 1. 51. iv. 2. 18. v. 1. 17.
अनुपपत्तेः ii. 1. 42., ii. 2. 46., iii. 2. 70., iv. 1. 33., iv. 1. 61. iv 2. 6., iv. 2. 11., iv. 2. 25. v. 1. 20., v. 1. 24.
अनुपलंभ ii. 2. 21., v. 1. 30.
अनुपलंभात् ii. 2. 20., v. 1. 29.
अनुपलब्धि i. 1. 23., ii. 2. 20., v. 1. 38.
अनुपलब्धिः ii. 2. 36., iii. 1. 36., iii. 1. 40., iii. 1. 65., iii. 2. 14. iv. 2. 26.
अनुपलब्धिवत् iii. 1. 40., iv. 2. 26.
अनुपलब्धिसमः v. 1. 29.
अनुपलब्धेः ii. 1. 49., ii. 1. 53., ii. 2. 19., ii. 2. 21., ii. 2. 26., ii. 2. 34., ii. 2. 35., ii. 2. 37, iii. 1. 41., iii. 1. 64., iii. 2.

17., iii. 2. 19., iii. 2. 23. v. 1. 29. v. 1. 30.
अनुपमृद्य iv. 1. 14.
अनुवचनम् ii. 1. 65.
अनुबन्धात् iii. 1. 18., iv. 1, 58., iv. 2. 41.
अनुबन्धानां ii. 2. 60.
अनुभाषणं v. 2. 16.
अनुमान i. 1. 3.
अनुमानं i. 1. 5., ii. 1, 31., ii. 1. 37, ii. 1. 49., ii. 2. 16., iii. 2. 16.
अनुमाने ii. 2. 2.
अनुमितानां iii. 1. 51.
अनुमीयमानस्य iii. 1. 36.
अनुमेयत्वात् ii. 1. 49.
अनुयोगः v. 2. 1., v. 2. 22.
अनुविनाशवत् iv. 1. 27.
अनुवाद ii. 1. 60., ii. 1. 62., ii. 1. 66.
अनुवादः ii. 1. 65., iv. 1. 59.
अनुवादात् v. 2. 14.
अनेक i. 1. 23. ii. 1. 1., iii. 1. 38., iv. 1. 35.
अनेकत्वात् v. 1. 37.
अनेकधर्म ii. 1. 1.
अनेकान्तः ii. 1.20., iii. 2. 17.
अनैकान्तिकः i. 2. 5.
अनैकान्तिकत्वात् ii. 2. 3., ii. 2. 5., v. 1. 22.
अनृत ii. 1. 57.
अन्तः iii. 2. 26.
अन्तर i. 1. 2, i. 2. 16., ii. 2. 39. iii. 1. 12, iii. 2. 48., iv. 2. 12., iv. 2. 20.
अन्तरम् i. 1. 15., v. 2. 1., v. 2. 3, v. 2. 6.
अन्तरभावात् ii. 2. 2, iv. 1. 24.
अन्तरविकारात् iii. 1. 12.
अन्तरात् v. 1. 28.
अन्तराल ii. 2. 26, iv. 1. 55,
अन्तरित iii. 1. 45, iii. 1. 46,
अन्तरे iv. 1. 44.
अन्यतमेन v. 2. 12.
अन्यतर ii. 1. 1.
अन्यतरधर्म ii. 1. 1.
अन्यतरस्य ii. 2. 28.
अन्यता ii, 2, 31.
अन्यत्व iii. 2. 9.
अन्यत्वे ii. 2. 30., v. 1. 38,
अन्यत्र iii. 1. 23, v. 2. 14.
अन्यप्रकरण i. 1. 30
अन्यस्मात् ii. 2. 31.
अन्यलक्षण ii. 2. 9.
अन्यत् ii. 2. 31.
अप् iii. 1. 63.
अपकर्ष v. 1. 1., v. 1. 4.
अपकर्षणे iv. 2. 26.
अप्तेजोवायूनां iii. 1. 63.
अपदिष्टः i. 2. 7, i. 2. 9.
अपदेशः ii. 1. 28.
अपदेशात् i. 1. 39.
अपनयन v. 2. 5.
अपरम्परेण iii. 1. 66.
अपरापर iii. 2. 10.
अपरीक्षित i. 1. 31.
अपवर्ग iv. 1. 58.

अपवर्गः i. 1. 2., i. 1. 22., iv. 1. 62.
अपवर्गाः i. 1. 9.
अपवर्गे iii. 2. 68 , iv. 2. 43., iv. 2. 45.
अपसिद्धान्तः v. 2. 1. v. 2. 23.
अपायात् i. 1 2.
अपाये i. 1. ?.
अपार्थं v. ?. 1.
अपार्थकम् v. 2. 10.
अपि ii. 1. 23., ii. 1. 32., ii. 1. 40., ii. 2. 14., ii. 2. 17., ii. 2. 20. ii. 2. 30., ii. 2, 62., ii. 2. 64., iii. 1. 5. iii. 1. 10., iii. 1. 41. iii., 1. 48., iii. 2. 10., iii. 2. 18 , iii. 2. 20., iv. 1.65., iv. 2. 6., iv. 2. 12., iv. 2. 43., iv. 2. 49., v. 1, 27., v. 1. 28., v. 1. 39., v. 2. 9., v. 2. 12., v. 2. 16.
अपुनर् ii 2. 47.
अपेक्ष v. 1. 43.
अपेक्षः i. 1. 23., i. 1. 38.
अपेक्षत्वात् ii. 1. 40., ii. 2. 65.
अपेक्षसिद्धे : ii. 2. 3?.
अपेक्षा ii. 1. 41., ii. 2. 11.
अपेक्षात् ii. 1. 6.
अपृथक् iv. 2. 28.
अपोह्य iii 1. 63.
अप्रतिषेध ii. 1. 15., ii. 1. 54., ii. 2. 2., ii. 2. 27., ii. 2. 38., ii. 2. 51 , ii 2. 53., ii. 2. 56., iii. 1. 3., iii. 1. 11., iii. 1. 14., iii. 1. 46., iii. 2. 28., iii. 2, 35., iii. 2. 49., iii. 2. 55., iv. 1. 13., iv. 1.18. iv. 1. 24., iv. 1. 31., iv. 1. 51., iv. 1. 36., iv. 1. 66., iv., 2. 25., v. 1. 8., v. 1. 15., v. 1. 20., v. 1. 26.,
अप्रतिघातात् iii. 1. 47.
अप्रतिपत्तिः i. 2. 19., v. 2. 18.
अप्रतिभा v. 2. 1.. v. 2. 18.
अप्रतिसंबद्धार्थं v. 2. 7., v. 2. 10.
अप्रत्यक्ष ii. 1. 46.
अप्रत्यक्षसिद्धे : ii. 1. 46.
अप्रत्यक्षे ii 1. 47.
अप्रत्यभिज्ञानं iii. 2. 7.
अप्रत्यभिज्ञाने iii. 2. 5.
अप्रत्याख्यानं iv. 1. 28.
अप्रमाणम् ii. 1. 37., ii. 2. 3.
अप्रयोगः iv. 1. 15.
अप्रश्नः iv. 2. 11.
अप्रसंगः iii. 2. 52.
अप्रसंगात् ii. 2. 64.
अप्राप्ति v. 1. 1.
अप्राप्तिसमौ v. 1. 7.
अप्राप्तकालं v. 2. 1., v. ?. 11.
अप्राप्य iii. 1. 45 . v. 1. 7.
अप्रामाण्यं ii. 1. 8., ii. 1. 57., ii. ?. 5.
अभाव ii. 2 1., ii 2. 9., iv. 1. 37., iv. 1. 65., v. 1. 29., v. 1. 31.
अभावः ii. 1. 11., ii. 1. 39., ii. 1. 40., ii. 1. 53 , ii. 2. 31.. iv. 1. 58. iv. 2. 7., iv. 2. 8, iv. 2. 14., iv. 2. 20., iv. 2. 45., v. 1. 24., v. 1. 36.
अभावप्रामाण्यं ii. 2. 7.
अभावहेतुः iii. 1. 36.
अभावात् ii. 2. 53 , iii. 1. 4., iii. 1. 23 , iii. 2. 8, iii. 2. 11.,

iv. 1. 14., iv 1. 62., iv. 2. 11., iv. 2. 33., v. 1. 12. v. 1. 13., v. 1. 34.
अभावे ii. 1. 40., ii. 1. 42., ii. 2, 32, iv. 1. 20., iv. 2. 12., v. 1. 27.
अभावोपपत्तेः ii. 2. 12,
अभिगमनवत् iii. 1 22.
अभिचारात् v. 1 8.
अभिधानात् ii. 2. 17.
अभिप्रायात् i. 2. 12.
अभिभवात् iii. 1. 43.
अभिमानः iii. 2. 9., iv. 2. 3., iv. 2. 31., iv. 2. 34.
अभिमानवत् iii. 2. 9., iv. 2. 31.
अभिमानात् iv. 1. 57.
अभियेाग v. 2. 22.
अभिव्यक्त iii. 2. 45.
अभिव्यक्तेः ii. 2. 65.
अभिव्यक्तौ iii. 1. 43.
अभिलाषात् iii. 1. 21.
अभिहितं v. 2. 9.
अभिहितस्य v. 2. 16.
अभिहिते i. 2. 12.
अभ्यनुज्ञा iii. 2. 11., iii. 2. 44. v. 2. 2.
अभ्यनुज्ञानात् v. 1. 26.
अभ्यागम iii. 2. 72.
अभ्यास ii. 1. 66., iii. 2. 41., iv 2. 47.
अभ्यासकृतात् iii. 1, 21.
अभ्यासस्य ii. 2. 30,
अभ्यासात् ii. 1. 67., ii. 2. 29., iv. 2. 38.
अभ्युपगम i. 1. 26., i. 1. 27.
अभ्युपगमसिद्धान्तः i. 1. 31.
अभ्युपगमात् i. 1. 31., v. 1. 43., v. 2. 20.
अभ्युपेत्य i. 2. 6., ii. 1. 59., v. 1. 42. v. 2. 23.
अभ्युपेयात् iv. 2. 48.
अमूढस्य iv. 1. 6.
अयं iv. 2. 31
अयसः iii. 1. 22.
अयस्कान्तः iii. 1. 22.
अयुक्तम् iv. 1. 40.
अयुगपत् iii. 2. 6., iii. 2. 33.
अयोगात् v. 2. 10.
अयौगपद्य ii. 1. 25.
अयौगपद्यात् iii. 2 56.
अर्चिः iii. 2. 45.
अर्थ i. 1. 4.. i. 1. 28., i. 1. 41., i. 2. 10., i. 2. 14., i. 2. 16., iv. 2 . 29., iv. 2. 39., v. 2. 3., v. 2. 5.,
अर्थं i. 1. 24., i. 1. 40., i. 2. 7., ii. 1. 47., iv. 2. 46., iv. 2. 49., v. 2. 9.
अर्थः i. 1. 20.
अर्थकल्पना i. 2. 13.
अर्थग्रहणात् ii. 1. 61.
अर्थयोः v. 2. 14.
अर्थवादः ii. 1. 64.
अर्थविशेष ii. 1. 30.
अर्थसंप्रत्ययः ii. 1. 52
अर्थसंनिकर्ष iii. 1. 32.
अर्थस्य i. 2. 13., ii. 1. 49.
अर्थाः i. 1. 14.
अर्थात् v. 2. 7., v. 2. 15.

अर्थान्तर i. 1. 27., i. 2. 12.. i. 2. 16., ii. 1. 38., iv. 1. 3., iv. 1. 7 , iv. 1. 24.
अर्थान्तरं v. 2. 1., v. 2. 7.
अर्थान्तरकल्पना i. 2. 12.
अर्थान्तराभावात् i. 2. 16., ii. 1. 38.
अर्थानुपलब्धेः iii. 1. 54.
अर्थापत्त्यप्रामाण्यं ii. 2. 6.
अर्थापत्त्यभिमानात् ii. 2. 4.
अर्थापत्ति ii. 2. 2.. v. i. 1.
अर्थापत्तिः ii. 2. 3.
अर्थापत्तितः v. 1. 21·
अर्थापत्तिसमः v. 1. 21.
अर्थापत्तेः v. 1. 22.
अर्थित्व iii. 2. 41.
अर्थित्वे iv. 2. 49
अर्थिभिः iv. 2. 48.
अर्थे i. 1, 25., i. 1. 40.. i 2. 12.
अरण्य iv. 2. 42.
अलक्षण ii. 2, 8.
अलक्षितानां ii. 2. 8.
अलक्षितेषु ii. 2. 10.
अवकाश iii. 1. 30.
अवधारणं i. 1. 41.
अवयव i, 1. 1., i. 1. 32., i. 2. 1., iii. 1. 10., iv. 1. 42., iv. 2. 12., iv. 2. 15., iv. 2. 23., v. 2, 11.
अवयवनाशे iii. 1. 10.
अवयवानां iv. 2. 7.
अवयवाः i. 1. 32., iv. 2. 10.
अवयवि iv. 2. 15.
अवयविनि ii. 1. 33.
अवयवी ii. 1, 34., iii. 1. 10., iv. 2. 3 , iv. 2. 7., iv. 2. 8., iv. 2. 10.
अवयवेन v. 2. 12.
अवयवेभ्यः iv. 2. 9.
अवरोधात् iv. 1. 8., iv. 1. 31.
अवर्ण्य v. 1. 1., v. 1. 4.
अवश्यं iv. 2. 44.
अवस्थानात् iii. 2. 18.
अवस्थाने ii. 2. 37., iii. 2. 23.
अवस्थित ii, 2. 11.
अविज्ञात i. 1. 40., v. 2. 9.
अविज्ञातं v. 2. 9., v. 2. 17
अविज्ञाततत्त्व i. 1. 40.
अविज्ञातार्थं v. 2. 1.
अविघातात् iii. 1. 48.
अविद्या iv 2. 4.
अविरुद्धः i. 1. 28.
अविशिष्ट i. 2. 8.
अविशिष्टत्वात् v. 1. 7.
अविशेषः i. 2. 12., v. 1. 7., v. 1 34.
अविशेष ii. 1. 45., ii. 1. 68., v. 1. 23., v. 2. 6.
अविशेषसमः v. 1. 23·
अविशेषात् i. 2. 15.
अविशेषे i. 2. 17. v. 1. 23.
अविषये iv. 2. 14.
अविष्टंभ iv. 2. 22.
अवृत्तित्वात् iv. 2. 7.
अवृत्तेः iv, 2. 8., iv. 2. 9., iv. 2. 12.
अव्यतिरेकात् ii. 2. 49., iii. 1. 53. iii. 1. 53., iii. 1. 59.

अव्यपदेश्यं i. 1. 4.
अव्यभिचारः ii. 2. 15, ii. 2. 17.
अव्यभिचारि i. 1. 4.
अव्यवस्था ii. i. 2., ii. 1. 4.
अव्यवस्थाया: ii. 1. 4.
अव्यवस्थात्मनि ii. 1. 4.
अव्यूह iv. 2. 22.
अश्रवण ii. 2. 34.
असत् iv. 1. 49.
असत्यर्थं ii. 2. 9.
असद् iv. 1. 47.
असमग्र ii. 1. 21.
असंभूत i. 2. 13.
असंशयः ii. 1. 6, iv. 2. 5.
अस्ति ii. 2. 32.
अस्पर्शत्वात् ii. 2. 22., ii. 2. 38.
असाधकत्वात् v. 1. 7.
असिद्धिः ii. 1. 41., ii. 1. 44., iv. 1. 41., iv. 2. 33, v. 1. 19., v. 1. 33.
असिद्धेः ii. 1. 8., ii. 1. 12., ii. 1. 34. ii. 2. 7., ii. 2. 11., v. 1. 18., v. 1. 33.
अहेतुः ii. 1. 29., ii. 2. 10., ii. 2. 21., ii. 2. 26., ii. 2. 42., ii. 2. 48., iii. 1. 10., iii. 1. 35. iii. 2. 3., iii. 2. 10., iii. 2. 27., iv. 1. 5., iv. 1. 21., iv. 1 43., iv. 1. 50., iv. 2. 12., iv. 2. 27., v. 1. 11., v. 1. 30.
अहेतुसमः v. 1. 18.
अहंकार iv. 2. 1.

आ.

आकर्षण ii. 1. 35.
आफल्यदर्शनात् iv. 1. 19.
आकाशस्य iii. 1. 63.
आकाश iii. 2. 1., iv. 2. 18., iv. 2. 19., iv. 2. 22.
आकाशम् i. 1. 13.
आकाशेषु ii. 1. 23.
आकृति ii. 2. 59., ii. 2. 64., ii. 2. 65., ii. 2. 66.
आकृतिः ii. 2. 63, ii. 2. 68.
आतोद्य ii. 1. 15.
आत्म i. 1. 9., iii. 2. 31., iv. 1. 10.
आत्मक त्वात् v. 1. 30.
आत्मकं i. 1. 4.
आत्मगुण iii. 1. 14.
आत्मगुणत्वे iii. 2. 20.
आत्मनि ii. 1. 4., iv. 1. 60.
आत्मनो iii. 2. 40.
अत्मनः i. 1. 10., ii. 1. 24.
आत्मप्रतिपत्ति iii. 1. 15.
आत्ममनसः ii. 1. 22.
आत्मसद्भावात् iii. 1. 3.
आत्मसंस्कार iv. 2. 46.
आत्मा iv. 1. 51.
आदर्श iii. 1. 50.
आदि i. 1. 14., ii. 2. 18., iii. 1. 58., iv. 1. 22., iv. 1. 52.
आदित्यरश्मेः iii. 1. 48.
आदिमत्वात् ii. 2. 13.
आदिषु iii. 2. 51., iii. 2. 52., iv. 2. 42.
आदीनां ii. 1. 8., iii. 2, 47., iii. 2. 54., iii. 2. 55.
आदेश ii. 2. 40.
आद्येषु iii. 2. 35.
आधिपत्येभ्यः ii. 2. 62.

आनन्तर्य्य iii. 2. 41.

आप: i. 1. 13.

आपत्ति ii. 2. 1.

आपत्ते: ii. 2. 48.

आपन्नस्य v, 2. 15.

आपेक्षिकत्वात् iv. 1. 39.

आप्त i. 1. 7., ii. 1. 52., ii. 1. 68.

आप्रलयात् iv. 2. 15.

आप्तप्रामाण्यात् ii. 1. 68.

आयुर्वेद ii. 1. 68.

आरंभ i. 1. 17., iii. 2. 34., iii. 2. 36.,

आवरण ii. 2. 19., ii. 2. 20.,

आवृत्ते: ii. 2. 47.

आशु iii. 2. 29., iii. 2. 58.

आश्रय iii. 2. 41., iv. 1. 50.

आश्रय: i. 1. 11.

आश्रयत्वात् iv, 1, 51., iv. 2. 28.

आश्रित iii. 2. 43.

आपन्न v. 2. 15.

आहारस्य iii. 2. 64.

आहार iii. 1. 21.

इ.

इच्छत: v. 2. 6.

इच्छा i. 1. 10., iii. 2. 3.4, iii. 2. 35., iii. 2. 41.,

इतर iv. 1. 6.

इतरेण iii. 1. 7.

इतरेतर ii. 1. 41., ii. 2. 32., iii. 1. 49., iii. 1. 73., iii. 2. 54., iv. 1. 37.

इति i. 1 10., i. 1. 13., i. 1. 15., i. 1. 17., i. 1. 21. i. 1. 38., i. 2. 11., ii. 1. 36., ii. 1. 48., ii. 1. 64., ii. 2. 9., ii. 2, 17., ii. 2. 31., iv. 1. 50., v. 1. 43.

इन्द्रिय i. 1. 4., iii. 1. 12.

इन्द्रियभावात् iii. 1. 70.

इन्द्रियस्य iv. 2. 14.

इन्द्रियाणां iii. 1. 39.

इन्द्रियाणि i. 1. 12.

इन्द्रियान्तर iii. 1. 12.

इन्द्रियार्थ i. 1. 4., i. 1. 9., i. 1. 11., ii. 1. 9., iii. 1. 56.

इन्द्रियार्थयो: ii. 1. 26., iii. 2. 18.

इन्द्रियै: iii. 2. 21.

ई.

ईश्वर: iv. 1. 19.

उ.

उक्त i. 2. 2., ii. 1. 6., ii. 1. 45., ii. 1. 57., iii. 2. 38., iii. 2. 39., iii. 2. 59.

उक्तम् v. 2. 1., y. 2. 14.,

उक्तयो: ii. 1. 66.

उक्ता iv. 1. 1.

उक्ता: v. 2. 24.

उक्ते v. 2. 6.

उच्चारणात् ii. 2. 18.

उत्कर्ष v. 1. 1., v. 1. 4.

उत्कर्षात् iii. 1. 68.

उत्तर i. 1. 2., ii. 1. 7.

उत्तर: iii. 1. 63.

उत्तरप्रसंग: ii. 1. 7.

उत्तरस्य v. 2. 18.

उत्तरापाये i. 1. 2.
उत्तरोत्तर ii. 1. 7., iii. 1. 65.
उत्तरोत्तराणां iii. 1. 65.
उत्पत्ति iii. 2. 12. iii. 2. 13., iii. 2. 16., iii. 2. 63., iii. 2. 66., iv. 1. 30., iv. 1. 32., v. 1. 1.
उत्पत्तिः i. 1. 19., ii. 1. 9., ii. 1. 22., iii. 1. 25., iii. 2. 25. iii. 2. 60., iv. 1. 14, iv. 1. 22., iv. 1. 54., iv. 2. 41.,
उत्पत्तिवत् iii. 1. 25., iv. 1. 50.
उत्पत्तेः ii. 2. 12., iii. 2. 10., iii. 2. 25., iii. 2. 48., iv. 1. 6, iv. 1. 65., v. 1. 12.
उत्पन्न i. 1. 4.
उत्पन्नस्य v. 1. 13.
उत्पाद् iv. 1. 48.
उदकयोः iii. 1. 50.
उदाहरण i. 1. 32., i. 1. 34., i. 1. 38., v. 2. 13.
उदाहरणं i. 1. 36.
उपघात ii. 1. 37.
उपचय ii. 2. 60.
उपचार i. 2. 11. i. 2. 14, i. 2. 15.
उपचारः ii. 2. 62. iv. 1. 53.
उपचारात् ii. 2. 13., ii. 2. 14., ii. 2. 30., ii. 2. 60.
उपदेश ii. 1. 52.
उपदेशः i. 1. 7., iv. 2. 42.
उपदेशवत् ii. 1. 67.
उपदेशात् ii. 2. 40.
उपनय i. 1. 32.
उपनयः i. 1. 38.
उपपत्त्या i. 2. 10.
उपपत्ति v. 1. 25., v. 1. 43.
उपपत्तिः ii. 2. 19, iv. 2. 37., v. 1. 22.
उपपत्तितः i. 1. 40.
उपपत्तिसमः v. 1. 25.
उपपत्तेः i. 1. 23., ii. 1. 5., ii. 1. 21, ii. 1. 35., ii. 1. 39., ii. 1. 43., ii. 1. 60., ii. 1. 66., ii. 2. 9, ii. 2. 39., iii. 1. 16., iii. 2. 28., iii. 2. 39., iii. 2. 70., iv. 1. 9., iv. 1. 59., iv 2. 24., v. 1. 6., v. 1 13., v. 1. 17., v. 1. 23., v. 1. 24., v. 1. 25., v. 1. 28., v. 1. 29., v. 1. 32., v. 1. 35., v. 1. 36., v. 1. 38.
उपपन्नः i. 2. 1., i. 2. 2.
उपपत्तिभ्यां iv. 1. 41., iv. 2. 30.
उपमर्द ii. 2. 57.
उपमान i. 1. 3., ii. 1. 44., ii. 1. 45., ii. 1. 48.
उपमानं i. 1. 6.
उपमानशब्दाः i. 1. 3.
उपमानस्य ii. 1. 47.
उपमानासिद्धिः ii. 1. 44.
उपलब्धि i. 1. 23., iv. 1. 28., iv. 2. 35., v. 1. 1.
उपलब्धिः i. 1. 15., iii. 1. 73., iii. 2. 58., iv. 2. 13.
उपलब्धिनियमः iii. 1. 37.
उपलब्धिवत् ii. 2. 52., iii. 1. 50., iii. 2. 13.,
उपलब्धिसमः v. 1. 27.
उपलब्धेः ii. 1. 31., ii. 1. 50., ii. 2. 42., iii. 1. 10., iii. 1. 28., iii. 1. 45., iii. 1. 61., iii. 1. 72., iii. 2.

12, iii. 2. 46., iii. 2. 57., iv. 1. 30., iv. 1. 32.
उपलभ्यमाने ii. 2. 35.
उपलंभात् ii. 1. 3.2, iii. 1. 32., iv. 2. 36., v. 1. 27.
उपसर्पणम् iii. 1. 22.
उपसंहार v. 1. 5.
उपसंहारः i. 1. 38.
उपसंहारात् ii. 1. 48.
उपसंहारे v. 1. 2., v. 1. 43.
उपादानम् iii. 2. 61.
उपादानवत् iii. 2. 61.
उपादानात् iii. 2. 44.
उपायैः iv. 2. 46.
उपालंभः i. 2. 1., i. . 2.
उपेक्षणं v. 2. 1., v. 2. 21.
उभय v. 1. 4., v. 1. 16., v. 1. 25.
उभयथा ii. 1. 43., v. 1. 15., v. 1. 34.
उभयोः ii. 2. 29.
उल्काप्रकाश iii. 1. 40.
उष्ण iii. 1. 20.

ऊ.

ऊहः i. 1. 40.

ऋ.

ऋण iv. 1. 58.

ए.

एक i. 2. 17., iii. 1. 9. iii. 2. 41, iii. 2. 57. iv. 1. 4., v. 1. 23.
एकत्वं iii. 1. 9., iii. 1. 59.
एकदेश ii. 1. 31., ii. 1. 38., ii. 1. 44., iv. 2. 7.
एकदेशग्रहणात् ii. 1. 31.
एकभाव iv. 1. 35.
एकविनाशे iii. 1. 9.
एकस्मिन् iii. 1. 8., iv. 2. 11.
एका iii. 1. 55.
एकान्त iv. 1. 41.
एकार्थग्रहणात् iii. 1. 1.
एकैकस्य iii. 1. 65.
एकं iii. 2. 56.
एतत् iii. 2. 71.
एतेन iii. 2. 67.
एत्र ii. 1. 6., iii. 1. 3., iii. 1. 71., iv. 1. 36., iv. 1. 54.
एवं ii 1. 7., ii. 1. 23., iv. 2. 15., iv. 2. 36., iv. 2. 43., v. 1. 40.

ऐ.

ऐतिह्य ii. 2. 2.
ऐन्द्रियकत्वात् ii. 2. 13., iii. 2. 55.
ऐन्द्रियकत्वे v. 1. 14.

क.

कट ii. 2. 62.
कंटक iv. 1. 22., iv. 2. 50.
कथा v. 2. 19., v. 2. 23.
कर्तृ ii. 1. 58.
कर्तृबधात् iii. 1. 6.
कर्म ii. 1. 58., ii. 2. 23., iii. 2. 1., iii. 2. 42., iii. 2. 69., iv. 1. 19., iv. 1. 20.
कर्मकारितः iii. 1. 39.
कल्पना i. 2. 12.
काच iii. 1. 45.
कारक iv. 1. 16.
कारण i. 1. 40., ii. 2. 17., ii. 2. 33., ii. 2. 34., iii. 2. 13., iii. 2. 17., iii. 2. 22., iii. 2. 23., iv. 1. 19., iv. 1. 0., iv. 1. 32., iv. 1. 41., iv. 1. 42., iv. 2. 20., v. 1. 12.,

v. 1. 12., v. 1. 25., v. 1. 26., v. 1. 27., v. 1. 28., v. 1. 38.

कारितत्वात् iv. 1. 21.
कारितं iii. 2. 68.
कारित्व iv. 2. 25.

कार्य iii. 2. 41., iv. 2. 20., v. 1. 37., v. 1. 38., v. 2. 19.

कार्यसमः v. 1. 37.
कार्यसमाः v. 1. 1.
कार्याश्रय iii. 1. 6.

काल i. 2. 9., ii. 1. 23., ii. 1. 39., iii. 2. 30., iv. 1. 44

कालभेदे ii. 1. 59.
कालातीतः i. .9.
कालान्तर iv. 1. 45.
कालान्तरे iv. 1. 44.
कालान्तरेण iv. 1. 45.
किंचित् i. 2. 17., v. 1. 5.
कुड्य iii. 1. 45.
कुड्यान्तरित iii. 1. 46.
कृतकवत् ii. 2. 13.
कृतता ii. 1. 43.
कृत्स्न iv. 2. 7.
कृष्णसारे iii. 1. 32.
केश iii. 2. 51., iii. 2. 52., iv. 2. 13.
क्रम iv. 1. 18., v. 2. 8.
क्रमवृत्तित्व ii. 1. 11.
क्रमवृत्तित्वात् iii. 2. 6.
क्रिया iii. 2. 41., iii. 2. 57.

क्लेश iv. 1. 58., iv. 1. 62., iv. 1. 64.
क्लेशस्य iv. 1. 63.
क्वचित् ii. 1. 20. iii. 2. 17., v. 1. 24.
क्षणिकत्वात् iii. 2. 10.
क्षीर iii. 2. 13.
क्षुधादिभिः iv. 2. 40.

ग.

गंगा ii. 2. 62.
गतम् iv. 2. 21.
गति iii. 1. 60., iii. 2. 8.
गतित्वात् iii. 2. 29.
गन्ध i. 1. 14., iii. 1. 62.
गन्धत्व iii. 1. 58.
गन्धर्व iv. 2. 32.
गन्धादीनां iii. 1. 58.
गमन ii. 1. 67.
गवये ii. 1. 47.

गुण ii. 2. 67, iii. 1. 61. iii 1. 64, iii. 1 65., iii. 1. 72, iii. 1. 73, iii 2 48., iii. 2 46, iii. 2. 53, iv. 1. 9.

गुणाः i. 1. 14
गुणान्तर iii. 1. 27., iii 2. 15.
गुणान्तरापत्ति ii 2. 57.
गुहा iv. 2. 42
गोत्वात् v. 1. 3.
गोसिद्धिवत् v. 1. 3.
ग्रहण iii. 2. 45., iv. 2. 47.
ग्रहणं ii 1 42, iii. 1. 43., iii. 2. 43, iv. 2. 28.

ग्रहणवत् iii. 2. 43., iii. 2. 45.
ग्रहणस्य iv. 2. 14.
ग्रहणात् iii. 1. 33., iii. 2. 14., iii. 2. 42.
ग्रहात् iii. 2. 24.

घ

घट iv. 1. 12., iv. 1. 13.
घटात् iv. 1. 12.

घटाभाव ii 2. 14.

घ्राण i. 1. 12.

च

च i. 1. 5., i. 1. 23., i. 2. 11., i 2. 19., ii. 1. 2., ii. 1. 3., ii. 1. 4., ii. 1 15., ii. 1. 16., ii. 1. 26., ii. 1. 27., ii. 1. 28, ii 1. 35., ii. 1. 51, ii. 1. 53., ii. 1. 56, ii. 1 60., ii. 1. 61., ii. 1. 68, ii. 2 2, ii. 2 5, ii. 2. 12, ii. 2. 13, ii. 2. 14, ii. 2. 33., ii. 2 35., ii. 2. 37., ii. 2 39., ii 2 50., ii. 2. 51., ii. 2 52., ii 2. 53., ii. 2. 56., iii. 1. 17., iii 1. 31., iii 1. 32., iii. 1. 37., iii. 1. 39, iii. 1. 43, iii. 1. 44. iii. 1. 52 iii. 1. 55., iii. 1. 71, iii. 2. 5. iii. 2 7., iii. 2. 13., iii. 2, 19., iii. 2. 2[illegible]., iii. 2 31., iii. 2. 38., iii. 2. 39., iii. 2. 9, iii. 2. 65., iii. 2. 69., iv. 1. 9., iv. 1. 44., iv. 1. 57., iv. 1. 61., iv. 1. 67. iv. 2. 8., iv. 2. 9., iv. 2. 10., iv. 2 15., iv. 2. 20, iv. 2. 21., iv. 2. 22., iv. 2. 23., iv. 2. 24., iv. 2. 25, iv. 2. 29., iv. 2. 34., iv. 2. 36., iv. 2 37., iv. 2. 40., iv. 2. 45. iv 2. 46., iv. 2. 47, v. 1. 4., v. 1 6., v. 1 7., v. 1. 8, v. 1. 9., v. 1. 11., v, 1. 15., v. 1. 22., v. 1. 31., v. 1. 33., v. 1. 34. v. 2. 1., v. 2. 17., v. 2. 25.

चक्र iii. 2. 58

चक्षुः i. 1. 12.

चतुष्ट्वम् ii. 2. 1.

चन्दन ii. 2. 62.

चरण ii. 2. 62.

चिन्ता i 2. 7.

चेत् ii. 2. 9., ii. 1. 36, iii 2. 68.

चेतन ii. 2 9.

चेष्टा i. 1. 1 .

छ

छल i. 1. 1., i. 2. 2., i. 2 17.

छलं i. 2. 10, i. 2. 11., i. 2. 12., i. 2. 13. i. 2. 14., i. 2. 15.

ज

जन्म i. 1. 2., iii. 1. 24., iv. 1. 54.

जन्मादर्शनात् iii. 1. 24.

जनितः i. 1. 20.

जल्प i. 1. 1., iv. 2. 50.

जल्पः i. 2. 2.

जातयः ii. 2. 66.

जातस्य iii 1. 18.

जाति i 1. 1., i. 2. 2., i. 2. 20., ii 2. 59, ii. 2. 68., iii. 1 62

जातिः i 2. 18, ii. 2. 64, ii. 2. 69.

जातिविशेषे ii. 1. 5 .

जातिलिंगाख्या ii. 2. 68

ज्ञस्य iii. 2. 34.

ज्ञातुः iii. 1. 16.

ज्ञान i 1. 16, ii. 1. 23., ii. 1. 28., iii. 1. 16., iii. 2. 18., iii. 2. 25., iii. 2. 56., iv. 2. 47, v. 1. 31.

ज्ञानं i. 1. 4., i. 1. 15.

ज्ञानानां i. 1. 2., iii. 2. 33.

ज्ञानानि i. 1. 10.
ज्ञेय iii. 2. 19.

त.

तत् i. 1. 2., i. 1. 5., i. 1. 14., i. 1. 22., i. 1. 24., i. 1. 31., i. 1. 36., i, 1. 37., i. 2. 6., i. 2. 11., i. 2. 15., i. 2. 16., i. 2. 20., ii. 1. 6., ii. 1. 14., ii. 1. 15., ii. 1. 18, ii. 1. 19., ii. 1. 25., ii. 1. 40., ii. 1. 57., ii. 1. 68., ii 2. 6, ii. 2. 10., ii. 2. 19., ii. 2. 26., ii. 2. 32., ii. 2. 37., ii. 2. 49., ii. 2. 52., ii. 2. 62., iii. 1. 3., iii. 1 5., iii. 1. 22. iii. 1. 65. iii. 1. 68., iii. 1. 69, iii. 1. 73., iii. 2. 9., iii, 2. 18. iii. 2. 20., iii. 2. 21., iii. 2. 23., iii. 2. 2)., iii. 2. :5., iii. 2. 37., iii. 2. 45., iii. 2. 58., iii. 2. 60., iii. 2. 61. iii, 2. 68., iv. 1. 3., iv. 1. 21., iv. 1. 27., iv. 1. 31., iv. 1. 32., iv. 1. 46., iv. 1. 49., iv. 1. 53., iv. 2. 3., iv. 2. 5., iv. 2. 13., iv. 2. 18, iv. 2 20., iv. 2. 26. iv. 2. 41., iv. 2. 45., iv. 2. 46., v, 1. 2., v. 1. 3., v. 1. 10., v. 1. 29., v. 2. 3.

तत्पूर्वकं i. 1. 5.
तत्प्रमेयसिद्धेः ii. 2. 8.
तत्र ii. 1. 7.
तत्त्व iv. 2. 37., iv. 2. 50.
तत्त्वज्ञान i. 1. 4).
तत्त्वज्ञानात् i. 1. 1., iv. 2. 1., iv. 2. 35.
तत्त्वभाक्तयोः ii. 2. 15.
तत्त्वे i. 1. 40.
तत्सिद्धेः ii. 1. 19.
तथा i. 1. 35., I. 1. 38., ii. 1. 5., ii. 1. 48., iii. 2. 64, iv. 1. 2., iv. 2. 14. v. 1. 13.
तदनुपलब्धि iii. 1. 40.
तदनुपलब्धे: iii. 1. 3).
तदपेक्षत्वात् ii. 2. 63.
तदभाव; iii. 1. 5.
तदर्थबहुत्वात् iii. 1. 57.
तदर्थाः i. 1. 14.
तदर्थे ii. 2. 59.
तद्ग्रहणम् iii. 1 34.
तद्विकारः iii. 1. 19.
तद्विधेः iv. 2. 47.
तदुपचारः ii. 2. 6 .
तदुपपत्तिः iii. 2. 13.
तदुपलब्धिः iii. 1. 70.
तं iv. 2. 48.
तंतु iv. 2. 26.
तंत्र i. 1. 26., i. 1. 27., i. 1, 28., i. 1. 29., iii. 1. 39.
तंत्रे i. 1. 28.
तयोः ii. 1. 40., ii. 2. 32.
तर्क i. 1. 1., i. 2. 1.
तर्कः i. 1. 40.
तर्हि iv. 2. 6.
तस्य iii. 1. 71., v, 1. 34.
तादर्थ्य ii. 2. 62.
तादात्म्यम् iii. 1. 61.
तावत् ii. 1. 32.
तु i. 1. 9., ii. 2. 66., iii. 1. 69., iii. 2. 37., iii. 2. 40., iv. 1. 49., iv. 2. 3., iv. 2. 26.,

तुला ii. 1. 16.
तुलाप्राभाण्यवत् ii. 1. 16.
तुल्यजातीयानां iv. 1. 9.
तुल्यधर्म v. 1. 32.
तुल्यं iii. 2. 20.
ते ii. 2. 58.
तेजो iii. 1. 63.
तेजः i. 1. 13.
तेन iii. 1. 71.
तेषां iv. 1. 6.
तेषु iv. 1. 53., iv. 2. 8.
तैः ii. 1. 28.
तैक्ष्ण्य iv. 1. 22.
तैमिरिक iv. 2. 13.
त्वक् i. 1. 12., iii. 1. 53., iii. 2. 52.
त्याग ii. 2. 60
त्रास ii. 1. 38.
त्रिः v. 2. 9., v. 2. 16.
त्रिविधम् i. 1. 5., i. 2. 11.
त्रुटेः iv. 2. 7.
त्रैकाल्य ii. 1. 8., ii. 1. 12., ii. 1. 15., v. 1. 18., v. 1. 19.
त्रैराश्यं iv. 1. 3.

द

दर्शनं iii. 2. 11., iii. 2. 16.
दर्शनवत् iii. 2. 58.
दर्शनस्पर्शनाभ्यां iii. 1. 1.
दर्शनात् iii. 1. 44., iii. 2. 36., iv. 1. 22., iv. 1. 48., v. 1. 8.
दाहे iii. 1. 4.
दाह्यं iv. 1. 27.
दाह्ये iii. 1. 48.
दुःख i. 1. 2., i. 1. 9., i. 1. 10., iii. 2. 41., iv. 1. 57.
दुःखं. i 1. 21., iv. 1. 54.
दृष्ट i. 1. 8., iii. 1. 51.,
दृष्टं i. 1. 5.
दृष्टान्त i 1. 1., i. 1. 36., iii. 1. 11., v. 1. 6.
दृष्टान्तः i. 1. 25., v. 1. 11.
दृष्टान्तयोः v. 1. 4., v. 1. 14.
दृष्टान्तविरोधात् iii. 1. 11.
दृष्टान्तस्य v. 1. 9.
दृष्टान्ते v. 1. 34.
देश ii. 1. 23.
दोष i. 1. 2., i. 1. 9., i. 1. 20., ii. 1. 45., ii. 1. 59., iv. 1. 8., iv. 2. 1., iv. 2. 2., v. 1. 42., v. 1. 43., v. 2. 20.
दोषः v. 1. 39., v. 1. 41.
दोषवचनात् ii. 1. 59.
दोषवत् v. 1. 41.
दोषात् iv. 1. 57.
दोषाः i. 1. 18., iv. 1. 2.
दोषेभ्यः ii. 1. 57. iv. 1. 7.,
द्रव्य iii. 1. 25., iii. 1. 73., iii. 2. 16.
द्रव्यविकारे ii. 2. 45.
द्रव्यस्य ii. 2. 17., iv. 2. 20.
द्रव्यसमवायात् iii. 1. 38.
द्रव्यान्तर iii. 2. 16.
द्रव्ये iii. 2. 46.
द्वित्वाभिमानात् iii. 1. 8.
द्वितीयाविनाशात् iii. 1. 9.
द्विविधः i. 1. 8.
द्वेष i. 1. 10., iii. 2. 34., iii. 2. 41., iv. 1. 3.
द्वेषयोः iii. 2. 35.

ध.

धर्म i. 1. 23., i. 1. 36., i. 2. 14., ii. 1. 1., ii. 2. 46., ii. 2. 51., iii. 2. 41., v. 1. 2., v. 1. 4., v. 1. 3., v. 1. 24., v. 2. 2., v. 2. 3.

धर्माः iv. 2. 22.

धर्मकत्वात् iv. 1. 25.

धर्मप्रसंगात् iii. 1. 49.

धर्मभावी i. 1. 36.

धर्मस्य v. 1. 44.

धर्मित्वे ii. 2. 53.

धर्मोपपत्तेः i. 1. 23.

धारण ii. 1. 35., ii. 2. 62.

न.

न i. 1. 38., i. 2. 16., ii. 1. 1., ii. 1. 6., ii. 1. 9., ii. 1. 10., ii. 1. 14., ii. 1. 19., ii. 1. 22., ii. 1. 24., ii. 1. 25., ii. 1. 30., ii. 1. 32., ii. 1. 36., ii. 1. 38., ii. 1. 41., ii. 1. 47., ii. 1. 48., ii. 1. 55., ii. 1. 58., ii. 1. 66., ii. 1. 67., ii. 2. 6., ii. 2. 7., ii. 2. 9., ii. 2. 11., ii. 2. 14., ii. 2. 23., ii. 2. 24., ii. 2. 30., ii. 2. 32., ii. 2. 36., ii. 2. 44., ii. 2. 46., ii. 2. 49., ii. 2. 55., ii. 2. 61., ii. 2. 65., iii. 1. 2., iii. 1. 6., iii. 1. 8., iii. 1. 13., iii. 1. 15., iii. 1. 20., iii. 1. 23., iii. 1. 26., iii. 1. 36., iii. 1. 41., iii. 1. 49., iii. 1. 54., iii. 1. 55., iii. 1. 57., iii. 1. 60., iii. 1. 64., iii. 1. 67., iii. 1. 72., iii. 2. 4., iii. 2. 8., iii. 2. 12., iii. 2. 14., iii. 2. 15., iii. 2. 18., iii. 2. 19., iii. 2. 22., iii. 2. 25., iii. 2. 26., iii. 2. 29., iii. 2. 30., iii. 2. 31., iii. 2. 38., iii. 2. 48., iii. 2. 54., iii. 2. 57., iii. 2. 62., iii. 2. 63., iii. 2. 72., iv. 1. 4., iv. 1. 6., iv. 1. 8., iv. 1. 12., iv. 1. 16., iv. 1. 17., iv. 1. 20., iv. 1. 23., iv. 1. 26., iv. 1. 30., iv. 1. 32., iv. 1. 33., iv. 1. 35., iv. 1. 38., iv. 1. 39., iv. 1. 42., iv. 1. 47., iv. 1. 52., iv. 1. 55., iv. 1. 63., iv. 1. 64., iv. 1. 67., iv. 2. 6., iv. 2. 10., iv. 2. 14., iv. 2. 16., iv. 2. 39., iv. 2. 44., v. 1. 11., v. 1. 13., v. 1. 15., v. 1. 19., v. 1. 34.

नक्तंचर iii. 1. 44.

नख iii. 2. 51., iii. 2. 52.

नगर iv. 2. 32.

नयन iii. 1. 44.

नाना ii. 2. 15.

नानात्वात् iii. 1. 52.

नाशे iii. 1. 10.

निगमनं i. 1. 39.

निगमनानि i. 1. 32.

निग्रह i. 1. 1., i. 2. 2., i. 2. 19., i. 2. 20., v. 2. 1.

निग्रहस्थान v. 2. 21. v. 2. 22.

निग्रहस्थानम् i. 2. 19.

नित्य v. 1. 1., v. 1. 14.

नित्यं iv. 1. 29., v. 1. 35., v. 1. 36.

नित्यत्व ii. 2. 37., ii. 2. 53., iii. 2. 23., iii. 2. 70., v. 1. 15., v. 1. 35., v. 1. 36.

नित्यत्वात् ii. 2. 14., ii. 2. 24., iii. 1. 5., iv. 1. 29.,

नित्यत्वे ii. 2. 50., iv. 1. 10.

नित्यस्य iv. 1. 28.

नित्यसमः v. 1. 35.
नित्यानां ii. 2. 51.
नित्येषु ii. 2. 14., ii. 2. 17.
निन्दा ii. 1. 64., iv. 1. 59.
निबन्ध iii. 2. 41.
निमित्त ii. 2. 36., iv. 1. 7., iv. 1. 9., iv. 1. 24., iv. 2. 36.
निमित्तं iii. 2. 66., iv. 2. ?., iv. 2. 3.
निमित्तवत् iii. 2. 66.
निमित्तत्वात् ii. 1. 26., ii. 1. 27., iii. 1. 20., iii. 1. 26., iii. 2. 34., iii. 2. 63., iii. 2. 69., iv, 1. 23. iv. 1. 67.
निमित्तानां iv. 2. 1.
निमित्तेभ्यः iii. 2. 41.
नियतत्वात् ii. 1. 11.
नियम ii. 2. 56., iii. 2. 37., iv. 2. 46.
नियमः iii. 1. 17.
नियमात् ii. 2. 55., ii. 2. 56.
नियमहेतु iii. 2. 11.
नियोग iii. 1. 51.
निरर्थकं v. 2. 1., v. 2. 8.
निरनुमानः iii. 1. 17.
निरनुयोज्य v. 2. 22.
निरवयवत्वात् iv. 1. 43.
निर्णय i. 1. 1., i. 2. 7.
निर्णयः i. 1. 41.
निर्दिष्ट v. 1. 27.
निर्देशः v. 2. 3.
निर्देशवत् v. 2. 8.
निर्देशात् iv. 1. 18., iv. 1. 52.
निर्देशे i. 2. 14., v. 1. 43.
निवृत्ति iii 2. 36.
निवृत्तिः iv. ?. 1., v. 1. 10.
निवृत्तिवत् v. 1. 10.
निवृत्तेः iii. 2. 16.
निवृत्त्योः iii. 2. 34.
निःश्रेयस i. 1. 1.
निष्पत्ति v. 1. 8.
निष्पत्तेः iv. 1. 13., iv. 1. 35., iv. 1. 44., iv, 1. 46., iv. 1. 53., iv. 1. 55.
निष्पन्न iv. 2. 44.
नैमित्तिक iv. 1. 7., iv. 1. 9.
न्यून ii. 2. 42.
न्यूनं v. 2. 1., v. 2. 12.

प.

पक्ष i. 1. 41., i. 2. 1., v. 2. 5.
पक्षप्रतिपक्षाभ्यां i. 1. 41.
पक्षयोः ii. 2. 28.
पक्षहानेः v. 1. 22.
पंच i. 2. 1.
पंचत्वात् iii. 1. 56.
पंचत्वेभ्यः iii. 1. 60.
पंचभूत iv. 1. 29.
पंचात्मक iii. 1. 20.
पट iv. 2. 26.
पटल iii. 1. 45.
पटु iv. 2 14.
पततः ii. 1. 39.
पतितव्य ii. 1. 39.
पदार्थः ii. 2. 66.
पदं ii. 2. 58.
पद्मादिषु iii. 1. 19.
पर i. 1. 29.
परकृतिः ii. 1. 64.
परगुण iii. 2. 46.
परतंत्र i. 1. 29.

परतंत्रसिद्धः i. 1. 29.
परपक्ष v. 1. 43., v. 2. 21.
परश्वादिषु iii. 2. 38.
परं iv. 2. 17.
पर्यनुयोज्य v. 2. 1., v. 2. 22.
पर्यन्तत्वात् iii. 2. 56.
पर्येषण iv. 1. 57.
परिग्रह ii. 2. 62., iii. 2. 44.
परिग्रहः i. 2. 1.
परिच्छद iv. 1. 53.
परिणाम iii. 2. 16.
परिशेषात् iii. 2. 42.
परिषत् v. 2. 9.
परिषदा v. 2. 17.
परीक्षकाणां i. 1. 25.
परीक्षणम् i. 1. 31.
पश्चात् ii. 1. 10.
पश्याम ii. 1. 47.
पशु iv. 1. 53.
पाकज iii. 2. 52.
पाकजानां iii. 2. 53.
पातक iii. 1. 4.
पातकाभावात् iii. 1. 4.
पाद iii. 2. 32.
पाटन ii. 1. 53.
पाणि ii. 2. 36.
पापीयान् iv. 1. 6.
पारतन्त्र्यात् iii. 2. 38.
पार्थिव iii. 2. 35.
पार्थिवं iii. 1. 27.
पार्थिवाप्ययोः iii. 1. 67.
पीडने v. 1. 8.
पुत्र iv. 1. 52.
पुनः i. 1. 19., ii. 1. 57., ii. 1. 66., iii. 2. 68., v. 2. 1., v. 2. 14., v. 2. 15.
पुनर् i. 1. 39., ii. 2. 48.
पुनरुक्तयोः ii. 1. 66.
पुराकल्प ii. 1. 64.
पुरुष iv. 1. 19., iv. 1. 20.
पुरुषार्थतन्त्रः iii. 1. 39.
पुरुषेषु ii. 2. 62.
पूरण ii. 1. 53.
पूर्व ii. 1. 9., iii. 1. 63., iii. 1. 68., iii. 2. 16.
पूर्वकं i. 1. 5.
पूर्वकृत iii. 2. 60., iv. 2. 41.
पूर्वगुण iii. 1. 68.
पूर्ववत् i. 1. 5.
पूर्वहेतुः iv. 2. 5.
पूर्वाभ्यस्त iii. 1. 18.
पृथक् iv. 1. 34., iv. 2. 9.
पृथक्त्वात् iv. 1. 34.
पृथिवी i. 1. 13., i. 1. 14.
पृथिव्याः iii. 1. 62.
पौर्वापर्य v. 2. 10.
प्रकरण i. 1. 30., i. 2. 4., i. 2. 7., v. 1. 1.
प्रकरणसम i. 2. 4.
प्रकरणसमः i. 2. 7., v. 1. 16.
प्रकरणसिद्धेः v. 1. 17.
प्रकाशसिद्धिवत् ii. 1. 19.
प्रकृतात् v. 2. 7.
प्रकृति ii. 2. 41., ii. 2. 54.
प्रक्रिया v. 1. 16.
प्रज्ञातस्य v. 1. 34.
प्रणिधान iii. 2. 33., iii. 2. 41.

प्रत्यक्ष i. 1. 3., ii. 1. 8., ii. 1. 9., ii. 1. 21., ii. 1. 22., ii. 1. 26., ii. 1. 42 , iv. 1. 11.
प्रत्यक्षम् i. 1. 4., ii. 1. 31.
प्रत्यक्षतः iii. 1. 36.
प्रत्यक्षत्वात् iii. 1. 67.
प्रत्यक्षेण ii. 1. 32., ii. 1. 46.
प्रत्यनीक iv. 1. 4.
प्रत्यभिज्ञानात् iii. 1. 7., iii. 2. 2.
प्रत्यर्थ ii. 1. 11.
प्रत्यवस्थानं i. 2. 18.
प्रत्यवस्थानात् v. 1. 9.
प्रत्युक्तः iii. 2. 67.
प्रतिज्ञा i. 1. 32., i. 1. 33., v. 2. 1 , v. 2. 2., v. 2. 4., v. 2. 5.
प्रतिज्ञान्तरम् v. 2. 3.
प्रतिज्ञातार्थं v. 2. 3., v. 2. 5.
प्रतिज्ञाय i. 1. 39.
प्रतितन्त्र i. 1. 27.
प्रतितन्त्रसिद्धान्तः i. 1. 29.
प्रतिदृष्टान्त v. 1. 1., v. 1. 11., v, 2. 2.
प्रतिदृष्टान्तसमौ v. 1. 9.
प्रतिदृष्टान्तेन v. 1. 9.
प्रतिद्वन्द्वि iii. 2. 49.
प्रतिपक्ष i. 2. 1., i. 2. 3., iv. 2. 49., v. 1. 17., v. 1. 21.
प्रतिपक्षात् v. 1. 17.
प्रतिपक्षाभ्यां i. 1. 41.
प्रतिपत्तेः iv. 2. 29.
प्रतिबोधे iv. 2. 35.
प्रतिवादिभ्यां v. 2. 9.
प्रतिषिद्धे v. 2. 6.
प्रतिषेध i. 2. 14., ii. 1. 12., ii. 1. 13., ii. 2. 5., iii. 1. 51., v. 1. 17., v. 1. 20., v. 1. 24., v. 1. 33., v. 1. 36., v. 1. 41., v. 1. 42.
प्रतिषेधे v. 1. 39., v. 2. 3., v. 2. 5.
प्रतिषेधं v. 1. 42.
प्रतिषेधः ii. 1. 14., iv. 1. 9., v. 1. 13.
प्रतिषेद्धव्य iii. 2. 44., v. 1. 20.
प्रतिषेध्य v. 1. 33.
प्रतिषेध्ये v. 1. 36.
प्रतिसन्धानाय iv. 1. 63.
प्रदाह ii. 1. 53.
प्रदाहे iii. 1. 5.
प्रदीप ii. 1. 19., iii. 2. 45., v. 1. 10.
प्रदेश ii. 2. 17., iii. 2. 25.
प्रधान iv. 1. 59., iv. 2. 37.
प्रधानं iii. 1. 68.
प्रबोध iii. 1. 19.
प्रमाण i. 1. 1., i. 2. 1., ii. 1. 9., ii. 1. 14., ii. 1. 17., ii. 1. 18 , ii. 1. 47., iv. 2. 30., iv. 2. 31.
प्रमाणतः ii. 1. 17., iv. 2. 29.
प्रमाणसिद्धौ ii. 1. 9.
प्रमाणान्तर ii. 1. 17.
प्रमाणानां ii. 1. 17.
प्रमाणानि i. 1. 3.
प्रमाणार्थं ii. 1. 47.
प्रमाणेभ्यः ii. 1. 10.
प्रमेय i. 1. 1., ii. 1. 10., ii. 2. 7., iv. 2. 31.
प्रमेयम् i. 1. 9.
प्रमेया ii. 1. 16.
प्रमेयासिद्धेः ii. 2. 7.
प्रयत्न i. 1. 10., v. 1. 37., v. 1. 38.
प्रयोग iv. 2. 11.
प्रयोगात् iv. 1. 16.
प्रयोजन i. 1. 1., iv. 2. 49.

प्रयोजनं i. 1. 24.
प्रवर्त्तते i. 1. 24.
प्रवर्तना i. 1. 18.
प्रवर्तनात् iv. 2. 40.
प्रवृत्ति i. 1. 2., i. 1. 9., i. 1. 20., iii. 1. 23., iv. 1. 58.
प्रवृत्तिः i. 1. 17., iv. 1. 1., iv. 1. 63., iv. 2. 14.
प्ररोह iv. 2. 50.
प्रलयः iv. 2. 16.
प्रशंसा iv. 1. 59.
प्रश्लेषात् ii. 2. 36.
प्रसवात्मिका ii. 2. 69.
प्रसाद iii. 1. 50.
प्रसिद्ध i. 1. 6 , ii. 1. 45.
प्रसिद्धत्वात् iv. 2. 5.
प्रसङ्ग v. 1. 1., v. 1. 9.
प्रसङ्गात् iii. 1. 49., iii. 2. 72., v. 1. 23., v. 1. 32.
प्रसङ्गः i. 2. 17., ii. 1. 7., ii. 1. 17., ii. 1. 23., ii. 2. 34., ii. 2. 37., iii. 2. 5., iii. 2. 23., iii. 2. 52., iii. 2. 68., iii. 2. 70., iv. 2. 15., iv. 2. 43., v. 1. 42., v. 2. 20., v. 2. 23.
प्राक् ii. 2. 12., ii. 2. 18., iv. 1. 46., iv. 1. 65., v. 1. 12.
प्रादुर्भावात् iii. 2. 15., iv. 1. 14.
प्राप्य v. 1. 7.
प्राप्त्या v. 1. 7.
प्राप्तानां ii. 2. 47.
प्राप्ति iii. 2. 41., v. 1. 1., v. 1. 7.
प्राप्तौ iii. 2. 65.
प्राबल्यात् iv. 2. 39.
प्रामाण्यवत् ii. 1. 16., ii. 1. 68.
प्रामाण्यात् ii. 2. 1., iv. 1. 11.
प्रामाण्ये ii. 1. 14., ii. 2. 6.
प्रामाण्यं ii. 1. 68.
प्राय ii. 1. 44.
प्रायण iii. 2. 70.
प्राबल्यात् ii. 1. 29.
प्रीतेः iv. 1. 57.
प्रेत्य i. 1. 9., iii. 1. 21., iv. 1. 10.
प्रेत्यभावः i. 1. 19.
प्रेरण iii. 2. 31.
प्रोक्षणादीनां ii. 2. 64.

फ.

फल i. 1. 9., iii. 2. 60., iv. 1. 20., iv. 1. 44., iv. 1. 50. iv. 1. 52., iv. 1. 53., iv. 2. 41.
फलम् i. 1. 20.
फलवत् iv. 1. 46., iv. 1. 53.

ब.

बधात् iii. 1. 6.
बहिः iv. 2. 20.
बहुत्वम् i. 2. 20.
बाधना i. 1. 21., iv. 1. 54., iv. 1. 56.
बाह्यप्रकाश iii. 1. 42.
बुद्धि i. 1. 9., i. 1. 17., i. 1. 25., iii. 1. 60., iii. 2. 24., iv. 1. 49.
बुद्धिः i. 1. 15.
बुद्धिसाम्यं i. 1. 25.
बुद्धीनाम् ii. 1. 11.
बुद्धेः iii. 2. 24., iv. 2. 36. , iv. 2. 37.
बुद्ध्यन्तरात् iii. 2. 24.
ब्राह्मण ii. 2. 62.

भ.

भय iii. 1. 18., iii. 2. 41.
भाव i. 1. 9., ii. 2. 49., iv. 1. 10., iv. 1. 14., iv. 1. 22., iv. 1. 34., v. 1. 31.

भाव: iv. 1. 7.
भावात् i. 1. 27., i. 2. 16., ii. 1. 38., iv. 1. 3., iv. 1. 4., iv. 1. 7., iv. 1. 24., iv. 1. 42., v. 1. 34.
भावानां iv. 1. 38., iv. 2. 26.
भावित्वात् iii. 2. 47., iv. 2. 44.
भावी i. 1. 36.
भावेन v. 1. 34.
भावेषु iv. 1. 37.
भूतगुण iii. 1. 61.
भूतेभ्य: i. 1. 12., iii. 2. 61.
भूयस्त्वात् iii. 1. 69.
भेद iv. 2. 11.
भेदमात्रं iii. 1. 16.
भेदात् iv. 2. 37.

म.

मतानुज्ञा v. 1. 42., v. 2. 1., v. 2. 20.
मध्यन्दिन iii. 1. 40.
मन: i. 1. 9., iii. 2. 56., iii. 2. 69.
मनस: i. 1. 16., ii. 1. 25., iii. 2. 19., iii. 2. 21., iii. 2. 25., iii. 2. 26., iii. 2. 29., iii. 2. 32., iii. 2. 38.
मन्दभावात् iv. 2. 14.
मनसां ii. 1. 27.
मनसि iii. 1. 15.
महत् iii 1. 33.
महदणु iii. 1. 33.
मातापित्रो: iii. 2. 63.
माया iv. 2. 32.
मिथ्या i. 1. 2., iv. 2. 35., iv. 2. 37.
मिथ्याज्ञानानां i. 1. 2.
मूर्त्ति iii. 2. 61.
मूर्त्ति: ii. 2. 67.
मूर्त्तिमतां iv. 2. 23.
मृगतृष्णिकावत् iv. 2. 32.
मृद्गवके ii. 2. 64.
मोह iv. 1. 3.
मोह: iv. 1. 6.
मोहस्य iv. 1. 8.
मंत्र ii. 1. 68.

य.

यत् i. 1. 30., iii. 2. 31.
यत्र ii. 1. 7.
यथा i 2. 2., ii. 1. 6., ii. 1. 45., iii. 2. 11., iii. 2. 38., iii. 2. 39., iii. 2. 59., iv. 1. 1., iv. 1. 28., v. 2. 24.
यम iv. 2. 46.
यस्मात् i. 2. 7.
यस्मिन् i. 1. 25.
या ii. 2. 60.
याथात्म्य iv. 2. 26.
यावत् ii. 1. 32., iii. 2. 47.
युक्त ii. 2. 64.
युगपत् i. 1. 16., ii. 1. 11., iii. 1. 54., iii. 2. 4., iii. 2. 19., iii 2. 25., iii. 2. 57.
योगसाधन ii. 2. 62.
योगात् i. 2. 13., iv 1. 54., iv. 2. 46.
योगाभ्यास iv. 2. 42.
यौगपद्य ii. 1. 25., iii. 2. 56.

र.

रश्मि iii. 1 34.
रश्मिदर्शनात् iii. 1. 44.
रस i. 1. 14., iii. 1. 62.
रसन i. 1. 12.
राग iii. 2. 41., iv. 1. 3.
रागादीनां iii. 1. 26., iv 1. 67.
राज ii. 2. 62.

रात्रौ iii. 1. 41.
रूप i. 1. 14., iii. 1. 62., iii. 2. 47., iii. 2. 54., iii. 2. 55.
रूपविशेषात् iii. 1. 38.
रूपाद्य: iv. 2. 2.
रूपोपलब्धि iii. 1. 38.
रूपोपलब्धिवत् iii. 1. 50.
रोध ii. 1. 37.

ल.

लक्षण ii. 1. 21., ii. 2. 11., iii. 1. 60., iii. 2. 41., iv. 1. 8., iv. 1. 31., iv. 1. 34., iv. 1. 36., v. 1. 43.,
लक्षणं i. 1. 21.
लक्षणै: iv. 1. 35.
लक्षितेषु ii. 2. 8.
लक्षितत्वात् ii. 2. 8.
लिङ्ग iii. 2. 35.
लिङ्गं i. 1. 10., i. 1. 16.
लिङ्गत: iii. 2. 14.
लिङ्गत्वात् ii. 1. 24., ii. 1. 25., iii. 2. 35.
लिङ्गादि iii. 2. 33.
लेश ii. 2. 57.
लौकिक i. 1. 25.

व.

वस्तु: i. 2. 12.
वचन i. 2. 10., ii. 1. 62.
वचनं i. 1. 39., ii. 1. 26., v. 2. 11., v. 2. 14., v. 2. 15.
वचनात् ii. 1. 21., ii. 1. 59., iv. 2. 20.
वनवत् ii. 1. 36.
वर्ण ii. 2. 45., ii. 2. 51., ii. 2. 52., ii. 2. 54., ii. 2. 57., ii. 2. 60., v. 2. 8.
वर्णविकार ii. 2. 45.
वर्णविकार: ii. 2. 57.
वर्णविकाराणां ii. 2. 51., ii. 2. 54.
वर्ण्य v. 1. 1., v. 1. 4.
वर्तमान ii. 1. 39., ii. 1. 40., ii. 1. 42.
वर्षकाल iii. 1. 20.
वा i. 1. 37., i. 1. 38., i. 2. 17., ii. 1, 1., ii. 1. 6., ii. 1. 14., ii. 1. 18., ii. 2. 6., iv. 1. 66., iv. 2. 17., iv. 2. 19., iv. 2. 32., iv. 2. 49., v. 1. 7., v. 1. 15.
वाक् i. 1. 17., i. 2. 11., i. 2. 12.
वाक्छलं i. 2. 11., i. 2. 12.
वाक्य ii. 1. 61.
वाद i. 1. 1.
वाद: i. 2. 1.
वायु: i. 1. 13.
वायूनां iii. 1. 63.
विकल्प i. 2. 10., i. 2. 14., v. 1. 1., v. 1. 4.
विकल्प: ii. 2. 45.
विकल्पात् i. 2. 20., ii. 2. 44., ii. 2. 51., v. 1. 4., v. 2. 3.
विकल्पानां v. 1. 31.
विकल्पे iv. 1. 57.
विकार ii. 2. 40., ii. 2. 41., ii. 2. 44., ii. 2. 45., ii. 2. 46., ii. 2. 47., ii. 2. 53.
विकारवत् iii. 1. 20.
विकारात् ii. 2. 50., iii. 1. 12.
विकाराणां ii. 2. 42., ii. 2. 49., ii. 2. 51., ii. 2. 54., iii. 1. 20.
विकारोपपत्ते: ii. 2. 53., ii. 2. 57.
विक्षेप: v. 2. 1., v. 2. 19.
विघात: i. 2. 10.
विज्ञातस्य v. 2. 16.
वितंडा i. 1. 1., i. 2. 3.

वितंडे iv. 2. 50.
विद्या iv. 2. 4.
विद्युत् iii. 2. 43.
विधायकः ii. 1. 63.
विधि ii. 1. 63., ii. 1. 65., iv. 2. 46.
विध्यर्थवाद ii. 1. 62.
विनष्टेभ्यः iv. 1. 17.
विनाश iii. 2. 5., iii. 2. 12., iii. 2. 17., iii. 2. 23., iv. 1. 25., iv. 1. 30.
विनाशः iii. 2. 24., iv. 2. 25.
विनाशकारण ii. 2. 33., ii. 2. 37., iii. 2. 12., iv. 1. 30.
विनाश्य iv. 1. 27.
विनाशात् iv. 1. 45.
विनाशे iii. 2. 13., iii. 2. 18.
विनियोगात् ii. 1. 62.
विनिवृत्तेः ii. 1. 18.
विपरीत v. 1. 29.
विपरीतम् i. 1. 37.
विपर्यय v. 1. 2.
विपर्ययात् i. 1. 37.
विपर्य्यास v. 2. 11.
विप्रतिपत्ति ii. 1. 2.
विप्रतिपत्तिः i. 2. 19.
विप्रतिपत्तेः i. 1. 23.
विप्रतिपत्तौ ii. 1. 3.
विप्रतिषेधात् iii. 1. 55.
विप्रतिषेधे v. 1. 41., v. 1, 42.
विभक्ति ii. 2. 39.
विभवात् iv. 2. 21.
विभागात् ii. 2. 15.
विभागस्य ii. 1. 61.
विभुत्वानि iv. 2. 22.
विमर्शः i. 1. 23.
विमृश्य i. 1. 41.
विमोक्षः i. 1. 22.
वियोग iii. 2. 41.
विरुद्ध i. 2. 4.
विरुद्धः i. 2. 1., i. 2. 6.
विरोध iii. 2. 41.
विरोधः v. 2. 1., v. 2. 4.
विरोधात् ii. 2. 56., iii. 1. 11.
विरोधी i. 2. 6.
विविध iv. 1. 54.
विवृद्धेः ii. 2. 41.
विवृद्धौ ii. 2. 41.
विवेचनात् iv. 2. 26.
विशिष्ट iv. 2. 48.
विशेष i. 1. 23., i. 1. 31., ii. 1. 56., iii. 1. 61., iv. 2. 38., iv. 2. 39.
विशेषं v. 2. 6.
विशेषः ii. 1. 66., iii. 2. 31.
विशेषकौ iii. 2. 37.
विशेषणात् ii. 2. 16.
विशेषपरीक्षणं i. 1. 31.
विशेषात् iii. 1. 34.
विशेषाणां ii. 1. 28.
विशेषेण iii. 1. 54., iii. 2. 32.
विष्ठं iii. 1. 66.
विषय iii. 1. 2., iii. 2. 2., iv. 2. 14., iv. 2. 31., iv. 2. 34., iv. 2. 35.
विषयत्व iii. 1. 59.
विषवत्वात् iii. 1. 13.
विषयाः iv. 2. 2.
विषयान्तर iii. 2. 7.
विषयोपलब्धेः iii. 1. 42.
विहितस्य ii. 1. 65.
वीज iv. 2. 50.
वीतराग iii. 1. 24.

बुद्ध्या iv. 2. 26.
वृक्ष iv. 1. 46., iv. 1. 50.
वृत्ति iv. 2. 6.
वृद्धि ii. 2. 57.; ii. 2. 60.
वेदयतः iv. 1. 56.
वैगुण्यात् ii. 1. 58.
वैधर्म्य i. 2. 18., v. 1. 1., v. 1. 2.
वैधर्म्यात् i. 1. 35 , iii. 1. 73., iii. 2. 53., iii. 2. 54., iv. 1. 47 , v. 1. 5., v. 1. 15.
वैषम्यवत् ii. 2. 45.
व्यक्तात् iv. 1. 11., iv. 1. 13.
व्यक्तानां iv. 1. 11.
व्यक्ति ii. 2. 59., ii. 2. 64., ii. 2. 65., ii. 2. 66.
व्यक्तिः ii. 2. 60., ii. 2. 67.
व्यक्तीनां iii. 2. 10.
व्यक्तौ ii. 2. 60.
व्यतिभेदात् iv. 2. 18.
व्यतिरिच्य iii. 1. 32.
व्यतिरेकात् iv. 1. 50.
व्यथनेन iii. 2. 32.
व्यभिचारात् ii. 1. 37., iv. 1. 5.
व्यय iv. 1. 48.
व्यवधान iii. 2. 41.
व्यवस्थातः i. 1. 23.
व्यवस्थान ii. 2. 63.
व्यवस्थानं iii. 1. 69.
व्यवस्थानात् ii. 1. 54., iii. 1. 2., iii. 1. 3., iv. 1. 28., iv. 1. 36.
व्यवस्थिततत्वात् ii. 1. 4.
व्यवसाय i. 1. 4.
व्यवसायात्मकं i. 1. 4.
व्यवहिते iii. 1. 8.
व्याघात ii. 1. 57.
व्याघातात् iv. 1. 15.
व्यापित्वात् iii. 2. 50.
व्यासक्त ii. 1. 27., iii. 2. 32.
व्यासक्तमनसः iii. 2. 32.
व्यासङ्गात् iii. 2. 7., v. 2. 19.
व्याहतत्वात् ii. 1. 29., iv. 1. 40., iv. 2. 27.
व्यूहः iii. 1. 30., iii. 1. 39.
व्यूहान्तरात् iii. 2. 16.

श.

शक्तु ii. 2. 62.
शब्द ii. 1. 54., ii. 1. 66., ii. 2. 60., iii. 1. 72., iv. 1. 16., iv. 1. 59., iv. 2. 11., iv. 2. 21., v. 2. 14., v. 2. 15.
शब्दः i. 1. 7., ii. 2. 2., ii. 1. 49.
शब्दवत् iii. 2. 24.
शब्दाः i. 1. 3., 1. 1. 14.
शब्दात् ii. 1. 15., ii. 1. 52.
शब्दानां iii. 1. 62.
शब्दाभावे ii. 2. 36.
शब्दार्थ ii. 1. 54., ii. 1. 55.
शब्देन ii. 2. 17., iv. 1. 59., v. 2. 15.
शरीर i. 1. 9., i. 1. 17., iii. 2. 26., iii. 2. 47., iii. 2. 50., iii. 2. 53., iii. 2. 66.
शरीरम् i. 1. 11.
शरीरदाहे iii. 1. 4.
शरीरधारण iii. 2. 28.
शरीरवृत्तित्वात् iii. 2. 26.
शरीरस्थ iii. 2. 52.
शाखा iv. 2. 50.

शिष्य iv. 2. 48.
शीघ्रतर ii. 1. 67.
शीत iii. 1. 20.
शेषवत् i. 1. 5.
शोक iii. 1. 18,
श्यामता iii. 2. 71., iv. 1. 66.
श्रवण ii. 2. 34.
श्रुति iii. 1. 31.
श्रोत्राणि i. 1. 12.
श्लेषेभ्यः ii. 2. 57.

स.

संकल्प iii. 1. 26., iv. 1. 67.
संकल्पकृताः iv. 2. 2.
संकल्पवत् iv. 2. 34.
संख्या ii. 2. 60., iv. 1. 41.
सगुण iii. 1. 25.
सगुणानां iii. 1. 70.
संचारात् iii. 2. 58.
संज्ञा iii. 1. 16.
संज्ञाभेदमात्रं iii. 1. 16.
सतत ii. 2. 34.
सति iii. 1. 32.
सत्त्व ii. 2. 63.
सदोषं v. 1. 42.
सद् iv. 1. 47.
सद्भाव i. 2. 14., iv. 2. 26., iv. 2. 36., v. 1. 23.
सद्भाववत् ii. 2. 20.
सद्भावात् iii. 1. 14., iii. 1. 65., iv. 2. 16.
सद्भावः iv. 2. 23.
सद्यः iv. 1. 44.
सन्तति iii. 2. 45.
सन्ततेः iv. 1. 64.
सन्तान ii. 2. 16.
सन्देहः ii. 1. 33.
संन्यासः v. 2. 1., v. 2. 5.
सन्निकर्ष i. 1. 4., ii. 1. 27., iii. 2. 21.
सन्निकर्षस्य ii. 1. 26.
सन्निकर्षात् ii. 1. 9., iii. 2. 25.
सन्निकर्षाभावे ii. 1. 22.
सन्निधौ ii. 2. 59.
संप्रत्ययः ii. 1. 52.
संप्रतिपत्तेः iii. 1. 18.
सब्रह्मचारि iv. 2. 48.
सम्बन्ध ii. 1. 53., iii. 2. 41.
संबन्धात् ii. 1. 51., iv. 1. 53.
संभव ii. 2. 1., ii. 2. 2.
संभवतः i. 2. 13.
समवेत iii. 2. 25.
समाधि iv. 2. 38.
समान i. 1. 23., i. 1. 29., ii. 1. 1.
समाने v. 1. 14.
समानम् iii. 2. 32.
समानः v. 1. 39., v. 1. 42., v. 1. 43.
समारोपणात् iv. 1. 60.
समास ii. 2. 60.
समासे ii. 2. 39.
सम्पाते iii. 2. 43.
सम्प्रत्ययस्य ii. 1. 55.
सम्प्रतिपत्तेः ii. 1. 3.
सम्प्रदानात् ii. 2. 25.
समूह ii. 2. 60.
समूहे iv. 2. 13.
संयोग iii. 2. 31., iii. 2. 32., iii. 2. 66., iii. 2. 69., iv. 2. 21., iv. 2. 24.
सर्व i. 1. 27., i. 1. 28., ii. 1. 14., ii. 1. 42., iv. 2. 21., v. 1. 23., v. 1. 32.

सर्वगुण iii. 1. 64.
सर्वगतत्वं iv. 2. 19.
सर्वतंत्र i. 1. 27., i. 1. 28.
सर्वत्र v. 1. 40.
सर्वाग्रहणं ii. 1. 34.
सर्वं iv. 1. 25., iv. 1. 29., iv. 1. 34., iv. 1. 37.
संरक्षणार्थं iv. 2. 50.
सव्यभिचार: i. 2. 4., i. 2. 5.
सव्यदृष्टस्य iii. 1. 7.
संवाद: iv. 2. 47.
संवेदनात् v. 1. 31.
संशय i. 1. 1., v. 1. 1.
संशयसम: v. 1. 14.
संशये ii. 1. 6., v. 1. 15.
संशय: i. 1. 23., ii. 1. 1., ii. 1. 5., ii. 1. 6., ii. 1. 7., ii. 2. 40., ii. 2. 59., iii. 1. 32., iii. 1. 51., iii. 2. 1., iii. 2. 46., iv. 1. 44., iv. 2. 4., iv. 2. 6., v. 1. 15.
संस्थान iv. 2. 23.
संस्थिति i. 1. 26., i. 1. 27.
सह ii. 2. 62., iv. 2. 47.
सादृश्य iii. 2. 41.
सादृश्येभ्य: ii. 1. 37., ii. 1. 38.
साधन i. 2. 1., i. 2. 2., ii. 1. 58., iii. 1. 16., v. 1. 34.
साधनं i. 1. 6., i. 1. 34.
साधर्म्य i. 2. 18., v. 1. 1., v. 1. 2.
साधर्म्यात् i. 1. 6., i. 1. 34., i. 2. 17., ii. 1. 44., ii. 1. 45., iii. 2. 1., v. 1. 5., v. 1. 14., v. 1. 15., v. 1. 16., v. 1. 32., v. 1. 33.
साध्य i. 1. 6., i. 1. 36., i. 2. 4., i. 2. 8., v. 1. 1., v. 1. 4., v. 1. 6., v. 1. 7., v. 1. 19., v. 1. 34
साध्यत्वात् i. 2. 8., ii. 1. 33., iii. 2. 27., v. 1. 4.
साध्यस्य i. 1. 38.
साध्यसम i. 2. 4., i. 2. 8.
साध्यसमत्वात् iii. 2. 3., iii. 2. 62.
साध्यसमा: v. 1. 4.
साध्यसाधनं i. 1. 6., i. 1. 34.
सामर्थ्यात् ii. 1. 52.
सामयिकत्वात् ii. 1. 55.
साम्यं i. 1. 25.
सामान्य i. 2. 11., ii. 2. 14., v. 1. 14.
सामान्यच्छलम् i. 2. 11., i. 2. 13.
सामान्यत: i. 1. 5.
सामान्यस्य v. 1. 15.
सामीप्य ii. 2. 62.
सिद्ध: i. 1. 29.
सिद्धं iv. 1. 49.
सिद्धान्त i. 1. 1., i. 2. 1.
सिद्धान्तं i. 2. 6., v. 2. 23.
सिद्धान्त: i. 1. 26., i. 1. 28., i. 1. 29., i. 1. 30.
सिद्धि ii. 1. 17.
सिद्धि: i. 1. 30., iv. 1. 10., iv. 1. 39., v. 1. 3.
सिद्धिप्रसङ्ग: ii. 1. 17.
सिद्धिवत् ii. 1. 15., ii. 1. 18.
सिद्धे: ii. 1. 15., ii. 1. 17., ii. 1. 19., ii. 1. 45., ii. 1. 46., ii. 1. 48., ii. 2. 10., ii. 2. 63., iii. 2. 49., iv. 1. 37., iv. 1. 38., v. 1. 5., v. 1. 16., v. 1. 19., v. 1. 21.
सिद्धौ i. 1. 30., ii. 1. 9., ii. 1. 10., ii. 1. 11., v. 1. 29.

सुख i. 1. 10., iii. 2. 41., iv. 1. 57.
सुखस्य iv. 1. 55.
सुप्त ii. 1. 27.
सुवर्ण ii. 2. 49.
सुवर्णादीनां ii. 2. 48.
सुषुप्तस्य iv. 1. 62.
सेना ii. 1. 36.
सेनावनवत् ii. 1. 36.
स्तन्य iii. 1. 21.
स्त्री iv. 1. 52.
स्तुतिः ii. 1. 64.
स्थान i. 2. 2., i. 2. 20., ii. 2. 62.
स्थानान्यत्वे iii. 1. 52.
स्थानानां i. 1. 1.
स्थानानि v. 2. 1.
स्थापना i. 2. 3.
स्पर्श i. 1. 14., iii. 1. 62.
स्पर्शपर्य्यन्ताः iii. 1. 62.
स्फटिक iii. 1. 45., iii. 2. 9.
स्फटिकान्तरे iii. 1. 48.
स्फटिके iii. 2. 10.
स्मरण iii. 2. 30.
स्मरणं iii. 2. 33. iii. 2. 40.
स्मरतः iii. 2. 28.
स्मर्तव्य iii. 1. 13.
स्मृति iii. 1. 18., iii. 2. 25., iv. 2. 34.
स्मृतेः iii. 1. 13.
स्व iii. 2. 46., v. 2. 15.
स्वपक्ष v. 1. 43., v. 2. 20.
स्वप्न iv. 1. 62., iv. 2. 31., iv. 2. 34., iv. 2. 35.
स्वभाव iv. 1. 38., iv. 1. 39.
स्वविषय iv. 2. 14.
स्वाभाविकत्वात् iv. 1. 64.
स्वाभाविके iv. 1. 65.
स्वाभाव्यात् iii. 1. 50., iii. 2. 40.

ह.

हर्ष iii. 1. 18.
हानिः v. 2. 1., v. 2. 2.
हि ii. 1. 9., iii. 1. 66.
हिरण्य iv. 1. 52.
हीन iv. 1. 63.
हीनं iv. 2. 49., v. 2. 12.
हीनः i. 2. 3.
हेतु i. 1. 32., i. 1. 39., iii. 2. 11., iii. 2. 39., iii. 2. 44., iv. 1. 45., iv. 2. 33, v. 1. 1., v. 1. 43., v. 2. 1., v. 2. 6., v. 2. 13.
हेतुः i. 1. 34.
हेतुत्वम् v. 1. 38.
हेतुत्वे v. 1. 11.
हेतुतः v. 1. 19.
हेतुत्वात् iii. 2. 38., iii. 2. 59., v. 1. 34.
हेतूनां iii. 1. 15.
हेतोः v. 1. 7., v. 1. 18.
हेतौ v. 2. 6.
हेत्वभावात् iii. 2. 11.
हेत्वाभास i. 1. 1.
हेत्वाभासाः i. 2. 4., v. 2. 1., v. 2. 24.
हेत्वोः iii. 2. 4.
ह्रास ii. 2. 57.

APPENDIX F.

Index of Words in English.

A

	Page.
Abhâva ...	3, 144
Abode ...	13
Abode of particular qualities	78
Absence	138, 171
Absence of link ...	109
Absence of perception ...	63
Absolute rule ...	109
Abstinence ...	172
Absurd ...	108
Absurdities ...	112
Absurdity ...	17
Acceptance ...	12
Act ...	11, 51
Action	6, 8, 43, 52, 63, 105, 121
Activities ...	152
Activity	2, 6, 8, 9, 118, 133, 155
Act of knowledge ...	146
Acts	138, 139
Acuteness ...	161
Acuteness or dullness of apprehension ...	161
Admission of an opinion	204, 207, 217
Adultery ...	8
Advantage ...	52
Affection	2, 9, 121, 133, 156
Affirmative ...	15, 16
Affirmative application ...	16
Affirmative example ...	15
Affix ...	75
Âgama ...	3
Agent of knowledge ...	146
Aggregates ...	143
Air	12, 100
Airy ...	89
Aitihya ...	3
Akṛitâbhyâgama ...	135
All-pervading	26, 90, 164
Alteration ...	51
Alteration of time ...	51
Alternating character ...	177
Alternative ...	24
Analogy	23, 140, 148, 150.
Annihilation ...	2, 161
Ant hill ...	109
Antecedent	59, 156
Anumâna ...	3
Apavarga ...	155
A posteriori ...	4, 45
Apparently ...	100
Apparent modification ...	75
Appearance ...	169
Appearances ...	144
Appearance of difference ...	108
Application ...	13, 16
Apprehension	7, 91, 122, 158, 161
A priori ...	4
A priori inference ...	45
Approach ...	87
Aprâpta-kâla ...	23
Arbitrariness ...	116
Arbuda ...	129
Argument	60, 64, 66, 182, 186
Argumentation ...	1

	Page.
Arguments	27, 84, 120, 158
Arrogance	... 154
Arthâpatti	... 3
Artificial	... 60, 62
Ârya	... 5
Ârya Deva	143, 149
Âryas	... 50
Ascertainment	... 1, 18
Âḍhaka	... 55
Asleep	... 154
Assumption	... 24
Assent	... 109
Assertion	... 5
Association	77, 152
Association of troubles	... 154
Assumption	... 111
Atom	63, 128, 132, 156, 162
Atomic dimension	... 119
Atomic mind	... 112
Atomic substance	... 8, 39
Atoms	21, 162
Attack	... 20
Attainment of supreme felicity	1
Attendants	... 150
Attention	117, 121
Audience	... 31
Auditory	... 27, 99
Auditory perception	... 27, 41
Augmentation	... 75
Authority	11, 20, 90
Authors	... 54
Avayava	... 1
Aversion	3, 6, 9, 118, 133
Awaking	168
Awanting	... 150

B

	Page.
Balancing the addition	174, 177
Balancing the alternative	174, 177
Balancing the co-presence	174, 182
Balancing the counter-example	... 174, 184
Balancing the controversy	174, 189
Balancing the demonstration	174, 195
Balancing the doubt	174, 188
Balancing the effect	174, 201
Balancing the eternal	... 200
Balancing the eternality	... 174
Balancing the heterogeneity	174, 175
Balancing the homogeneity	174, 175
Balancing the infinite regression	... 174, 184
Balancing the mutual absence	... 174, 182
Balancing the non-difference	174, 193
Balancing the non-eternality	174, 198
Balancing the non-perception	174, 197
Balancing the non-produced	174, 186
Balancing the non-reason	174, 190
Balancing the perception	174, 196
Balancing the presumption	174, 192
Balancing the questionable	174, 177
Balancing the reciprocity	174, 177
Balancing the subtraction	174, 177
Balancing the unquestionable	174, 177
Bauddhas	... 3
Beginning	... 60
Beginningless	... 155
Bhâttas	... 3
Birth	2, 9, 151
Blackness	... 156
Blame	... 53, 153
Blanket	... 24
Block-head	... 27
Bodily actions	... 8
Body	6, 8, 81, 89, 125, 126, 171
Bone	... 82
Bos gavaeus	... 5, 47
Bragging	... 20

Page

Brâhmaṇa 4, 25, 76
Breast ... 87
Buddhi ... 7
Buddhist 20, 30, 108
Buddhist Sanskrit and Pali Literature ... 154
Bulk ... 69
Burning ... 49

C

Capacity 14, 105
Carelessness ... 139
Carping ... 20
Chârvâkas ... 3
Categories ... 1, 32
Cattle ... 150
Cause 4, 30, 129, 138, 141, 157
Cause and effect ... 134
Cause of destruction 111, 113
Cause of growth and decay ... 109
Cause of in-audition ... 66
Cause of production 129, 139
Causes of faults ... 157
Cave ... 170
Cavil 1, 19, 20, 73
Caviller ... 20
Censuring the non-censurable 207, 217
Cessation ... 131
Cessation of ogotism ... 157
Cessation of recognition ... 106
Cessation of the intellect ... 106
Channels ... 13
Character 10, 14, 16, 17, 30, 71, 92, 96, 99, 120, 126, 140, 169,
Characterised ... 102
Character of an object ... 99
Character of a modification ... 71
Character of perception ... 141
Character of transparency ... 96
Charaka ... 53

Page

Change ... 110
Chhala ... 1
Circle of fire brand ... 128
City of the celestial quiristers ... 167
Classification of Vedic speech... 52
Clay ... 184
Clay statue ... 129
Co-abide ... 68
Cognisable ... 110
Cognised ... 60
Cognitions 33, 34, 114, 127
Collection of parts... ... 164
Colour 7, 12, 23, 40, 76, 92, 100, 122, 125, 126, 157
Combustibles ... 140
Command ... 54
Common ... 29
"Commonly seen" ... 4, 45
Comparison ...3, 4, 5, 33, 46, 47
Common properties .. 29
Compendious expression ... 47
Complete destruction ... 2
Compound ... 76
Compassion ... 8
Conceit 82, 108, 152
Conceit of difference ... 108
Conceit of duality ... 82
Conceit of pleasure ... 152
Concept ... 168
Concept of means ... 167
Conception 79, 157
Concentration ... 139
Conclusion 13, 17, 21, 85, 111, 180
Concomitant ... 14
Conditions ... 14
Conduct ... 25
Confirmation ... 17
Conflicting ... 29
Conflicting judgment ... 10

	Page
Conflicting testimony	... 29
Confutation	1, 17, 46
Conjointly	... 29
Conjunction	8, 38, 77, 114, 116, 117, 130, 131, 151, 163
Connection	3, 27, 48, 49, 50
Connoted	... 186
Consciousness	... 7, 19
Consequence	93, 100
Constant audition	... 66
Constituents	... 163
Contact	3, 33, 40, 91, 94, 107
Context	... 121
Continuity	... 30
Contingency	106, 113
Contradiction	... 51
Contradictory	21, 22, 74
Contradictory reason	... 22
Contrary	...17, 30
Controversy	174, 189
Convention	... 50
Conviction	... 30
Co-presence	... 182
Corresponding element	... 102
Corresponding substrata	... 104
Corruption	... 154
Countenance	... 86
Counter argument	... 68
Counter example	184, 186
Course	... 2
Covetousness	... 8
Cow	... 4
Cowhood	... 176
Critical examination	... 1
Crystal	94, 96, 108, 109
Curd	... 109
Cuticle	... 126
D	
Deaths	... 9
Debt to Gods	... 152
Debt to progenitors	... 152
Debt to sages	... 152
Debts	... 152
Decay	105, 109
Declaration	.. 4
Deeds	119, 128
Defect	... 51
Defence	... 20
Defilement	...2, 154
Definite form	... 78
Definition	.. 2, 32
Deliverance	... 9
Demarcate	... 118
Demerits	92, 155
Demonstration	... 195
Denial	141, 169
Depravity	... 155
Desert	130, 131, 132
Design	... 77
Desire	6, 87, 88, 117
Desire and aversion	... 121
Destruction	2, 61, 73, 83, 110, 111, 113, 131, 136, 138, 141, 149
Determinate	... 3, 4
Determination	... 18
Deva-ṛina	... 152
Deviating from a tenet	207, 218
Devotion	... 8
Dharma Śâstra	... 153
Dialogue	... 19
Diminutiion	... 75
Dimness	... 161
Direct	... 26
Direction	... 39
Disappearance	... 132
Disconnection	... 27
Disciples	... 172
Discussion	1, 13, 19, 172

	Page
Disjoined	... 111
Disputant	27, 30, 31
Disputation	... 19
Dissimilarity	... 26
Dissolution	... 90
Distinct	... 136
Distress	152, 154
Distribution	... 144
Divisible	... 133
Doctrine	20, 164
Dogma	...12, 13
Doubt	1, 10, 29, 30, 42, 69, 75, 147, 154, 158, 188, 189
Dream	154, 167, 168
Dṛṣṭânta	... 1
Drum	...23, 35
Duality	... 82
Dullness	... 161
Durable	... 23
Duration	... 116
Dust	... 3
Duties	... 172
Dvyaṇuka	... 162

E

Ear	7, 103
Earth	... 7, 12
Earthenware	... 77
Earthy	89, 102
Effect	4, 134, 201
Efforts of attention	... 117
Egotism	... 157
Element	7, 12, 100, 102, 129
Emancipation	131, 132
Endless doubt	... 31
Entity	37, 77, 136, 137, 139, 143, 145
Entreaty	... 121
Enunciation	... 2, 32
Epithet	... 3, 16
Equal to the question	... 22

	Page
Erratic	21, 134
Essence and appearance	... 169
Established tenet	... 1, 11
Establishment	... 146
Eternal	10, 13, 17, 21, 60, 63, 65, 67, 72, 81, 88, 113, 131, 135, 140, 141, 163, 195, 201
Eternalness	... 73
Eternality	16, 22, 189
Eternity	... 12
Ether	7, 12, 27, 39, 68, 100, 162
Ethereal	... 89
Evasion	207, 216
Evidence	136, 166
Examination	2, 13, 32
Example	10, 16, 17, 175, 177, 180
Excess	... 121
Excitement	... 84
Exclusion	... 120
Exercise	... 121
Existence	...63, 80, 134, 158
Existent	... 148
Extension	... 62
Expanding	... 86
Experience	... 5
Expert	... 5, 11
Expression	... 137
Expressive of action	... 137
External light	... 94
External objects	... 170
Eye	... 7
Eye ball	... 90
Eye knowledge	... 40

F

Factitious	... 163
Fallacies	... 21
Fallacies of a reason	21, 218
Fallacious argument	... 182
Fallacy	... 2

	Page
False apprehension	... 168
False knowledge	... 169
Familiar instance	... 1
Fault	... 6
Faults	2, 9, 134, 157
Fear	86, 121
Felicity	... 1, 2
Fences	... 173
Fiery	...13, 89
Figuratively	... 76
Filling	... 49
Five	... 10
Fire brand	... 128
Fineness	... 102
Fire sacrifice	... 52
Five elements	... 141
Five objects	... 98
Five senses	... 98
Fixation	... 76
Fixed character	... 96
Fixed connection	... 50
Fixed relation	... 80
Fixity	... 74
Fixity of number	... 146
Food	49, 150
Forbearance	... 118
Forbearance of activity	... 118
Forest	...4, 170
Forester	... 4
Form	75, 78, 79, 99
Formation	... 171
Fortuitous effects	... 139
Fruit	6, 9, 17, 119, 128, 138, 139, 147, 170
Fruit of previous deeds	... 128
Function	77, 97, 115
Futile	... 27
Futilities	20, 28, 174
Futility	2, 26, 180
Future	45, 137

G

	Page
Ganges	... 76
General notion	... 37
Generality	... 6, 43
Genus	25, 60, 75, 78, 79, 211
Gesture	... 6
Glass ...	... 94
God ...	... 138
Gold ...	71, 150
Good ...	... 157
Greed ...	... 154
Grief ...	... 86
Ground	... 113
Growth	... 109
Gustatory	... 99
Gustatory perception	... 41

H

	Page
Habitual	... 170
Hatchet	... 49
Hair ...	... 125
Happiness	... 150
Horse sacrifices	... 5
Hatred	... 154
Heat ...	... 86
Heterogeneous	... 15
Heterogeneous example	15, 175
Heterogeneity	... 189
Hetvâbhâsa	...2, 21
Hîna-kles'a	... 155
Hunger	... 170
Homogeneity	188, 189, 199
Homogeneous	... 15
Homogeneous example	... 175
Homogeneous things	... 135
Hurting the proposition	... 207
Hypothesis	... 11
Hypothetical	... 12
Hypothecial dogma	... 12
Hypothetical reasoning	... 1

Page.

I

Ideas ... 88
Identical 100, 106
Ignorance 27, 207, 216
Illumination ...37, 185
Illusion ... 37
Imagination ... 168
Immediate subsequency ... 121
Immolation ... 77
Impelling ... 115
Impermanent ... 72
Implication ... 11
Implied dogma ... 13
Impossibility 25, 158, 162
Impropriety ... 160
Inactive ... 26
Inadmissible ... 153
Inanimate ... 25, 86
Inaudition ... 66
Incapacity ... 119
Inconsistency ... 137
Incoherent 207, 213
Incompatible ... 64
Incongruous ... 148
Inconsistent ... 137
Indifference ... 14
Indirect ... 26
Indeterminate ... 4
Individual 75, 76, 78, 108
Individuality ... 77
Indivisibility ... 164
Indivisibility of atoms ... 164
Inequality ... 130
Inexperience ... 131
Inference 3, 4, 33, 36, 42, 44, 85, 91
Infinite regression ...174. 184
Injunction ... 52, 96
Inopportune ... 213

Page.

Inquiry ... 14
Instance 1, 11, 15
Instructive assertion ... 5
Instrument ... 85
Instrument of knowledge ... 85
Intangible 21, 63, 68
Intellect 6, 7, 9, 105, 106, 107
Intelligence ... 6
Internal perception ... 198
Interpenetrated... ... 101
Interrelation ... 134
Interrelation of cause and effect 134
Interval .. 64, 151
Intervention ... 121
Intimate relation ... 6, 43
Intimately ... 92
Invalid ... 57
Invariable ... 14
Investigator ... 11
Investigation ... 18
Invisibility ... 94
Iron ... 87
Ironball ... 14
Irregularity 29, 30, 118
Irregularity of perception ... 10
Itihâsa ... 153

J

Jalpa ... 2
Jar 23, 60, 136
Jâti ... 2
Jijñâsâ ... 14
Jnâna ... 7
Judgment ... 10
Jugglery 167, 169
Jyosiṣṭoma ... 53

K

Kalala ... 130
Kandara ... 130
Karma ... 103

Page.

Kathâ ... 19
Kileso ... 154
Killing ... 8
Kitchen ... 11, 13
Kles'a ... 154
Knave ... 27
Knower 85, 120
Knowledge 1, 2, 3, 4, 8, 13, 32, 39, 46, 85, 99, 106, 111, 113, 114, 120, 122, 126, 157, 170, 171
Knowledge ot truth ... 170
Kṛitahâni ... 135

L

Lalitavistara Sûtra ... 167
Lamp 23, 37, 123, 185
Laṅkâvatâra Sûtra ... 165
Light 7, 12, 93, 94
Likeness ... 121
Link ... 109
Letter ... 72, 73
Loadstone ... 87
Locomotion ... 29
Lotus ... 86

M

Mâdhyamika Buddhist philosophy ... 149
Mâdyamika Sûtra 145, 167
Magnitude ... 92
Mahâyâna works ... 167
Mâṃsa-pes'i ... 129
Malice ... 8
Manifestation 23, 78, 94, 136, 138
Mark 8, 58, 110, 121, 143, 144
Mat ... 76
Material 51, 69, 90, 99
Material substance ... 90
Matter 5, 7, 118
Maturation ... 125
Mâyâ ... 169

Page.

Meaningless 207, 212
Means of knowledge ... 146
Means of right knowledge ...1, 3, 35
Measure ... 77
Medical Science ... 54
Meditation ... 170
Members ... 1, 13
Membrane ... 94
Memory ...86, 121
Merit 139, 155
Merit and demerit ... 121
Metaphor ... 24, 25
Metaphorically ... 25
Meteor ... 93
Mica ... 94
Milk ... 109
Mimâṃ-sakas ... 12
Mind 8, 13, 38, 85, 114, 116
Mirage ...10, 167
Mirror ... 96
Misapprehension 2, 139. 156
Mistimed ... 21, 23
Mistimed reason ... 23
Mleccha ... 5, 50
Modification 70, 71, 72, 75
Modification and substitute ... 69
Momentary 108, 123
Motion ...23, 107
Magical power ... 112
Multiplicity ... 28
Mutual absence 174, 182
Mutual difference ... 126

N

Nâgârjuna 143, 149
Nails ... 125
Naiyâyika 3, 30, 102, 106, 118
Natural ... 155
Natural connection ... 49
Natural quality ... 124

Page.

Nature ... 1, 7, 98
Navakambala 24
Necessity 173
Negative 15
Negative application ... 16
Newborn 87, 88
Night 94
Nigraha-sthâna 2, 23
Nirṇaya 2
Nirvikalpaka 4
No-cause ... 139, 140
Non-difference 47, 193
Non-distinction 200
Non-distinguished ... 182
Non-erratic ... 3
Non-entity 136, 137, 144
Non-eternal 10, 13, 14, 15, 16, 21, 62, 63, 114, 140, 156, 188, 200, 201
Non-eternalness ... 140
Non-eternality ... 16, 198
Non-existence 3, 55, 56, 59, 60, 91, 156, 158, 197
Non-existent ...144, 148
Non-ingenuity ...207, 216
Non-material ... 90
Non-perception 29, 30, 42, 62, 63, 110, 197 202
Non-produced ... 186
Non-production ... 112
Non-reality ... 166
Non-simultaneous ... 107
Non-simultaneousness ...117, 127
Non-simultaneousness of cognitions ... 127
Non-simultaneity ... 39
Non-transparent ... 96
Nose ... 7, 82

Page.

Nyâya Sûtra 3, 13, 23

O

Object 3, 7, 10, 33, 40, 84, 97, 98, 103, 105, 107, 111, 170,
Objection ... 46
Object of knowledge ...146, 167
Object of right knowledge ... 1
Objects of sense .. 7, 98, 99
Obscurity ... 94
Observance ... 172
Observation ... 139
Obstruction .. 95, 155
Obviousness 92, 93, 94
Occasion for rebuke 2, 27, 207
Occurrence ... 109
Odour ... 98, 100
Olfactory ... 99
Olfactory perception ... 41
Omnipresence ... 163
One ... 160
Operation 82, 84, 117
Operations of stimuli ... 117
Operations of the Soul ... 82
Operator ... 51
Opponent 19, 27, 30
Oppression of persons by spells 184
Opportunity ... 153
Opposing the proposition ...207, 209
Opposition 24, 64, 80, 121, 142, 180
Organ of vision ... 82
Origination ... 105
"Other" ... 65
Otherness .. 65
Overlooking the censurable...207, 217

P

Pâda ... 130

	Page.
Pain	2, 6, 9, 151
Paradise	... 52
Part	42, 157, 158, 159
Partially	... 159
Partially eternal	... 61
Partial similarity	... 46
Particularity	. 6, 43
Parts	158, 159, 161
Parts in an atom	... 164
Past	... 45, 137
Paurâṇikas	... 3
Perception	3, 4, 5, 7, 10, 29, 32, 33, 37, 38, 39, 40, 41, 42, 55, 72, 90, 91, 96, 102, 136, 166, 196, 197
Perception of sound	... 104
Perfect tranquillity	... 2
Perishable	... 65
Permanency	... 105
Persistent	.. 67, 105
Permanent intellect	... 106
Person	... 151
Persuasion	... 52, 53
Pervades	... 125
Philosophy	.. 10
Physician	... 5
Pitṛi ṛiṇa	... 152
Pleasure	...6, 9, 151
Pleasure and pain	... 121
Ploughing	... 147
Possession	96, 100, 118, 121, 170
Pot	... 22, 120
Prâbhâkaras	... 3
Practice	... 87
Practicable	... 170
Praise	... 53, 153
Prakṛiti	... 7, 131
Pramâṇa	... 1
Prameya	... 1
Pratyakṣa	... 3, 7, 94
Prayojana	... 1, 14
Preceptors	... 172
Predicable	... 187
Predicate	...182, 191
Predominance	...102, 170
Predominant quality	... 103
Prescription	... 53
Present time	... 44
Presumption	3, 55, 56, 57, 192, 193
Previous life	... 87, 88
Pride	... 154
Primordial matter	... 7, 90
Principle	... 120
Principle of injunction	... 52
Probability	... 3, 55
Processes	... 99
Produced	136, 147, 148
Product	... 27
Production	59, 112, 129, 130, 136, 138, 139, 141, 142, 148, 156, 184
Prohibition	... 96, 135
Promiscuously	... 148
Pronunciation	... 62
Proof	... 22, 106
Propagation	... 76
Proper	... 164
Properties	10, 29, 31
Property	15, 186
Proposition	11, 13, 14, 15, 16, 17, 19, 21, 22, 207, 209, 210
Purâṇa	... 153
Purifying	... 172
Purpose	1, 11, 14, 92
Puruṣa	... 7, 117

Page.

Q

Qualities 6, 7, 13, 68, 88, 89, 92, 101, 124, 127, 139
Qualities of earth ... 89
Quality 6, 43, 75, 84, 100, 124
Quality of soul ... 112
Quality of sound ... 103
Question ... 10
Questioning ... 14
Quibble 2, 20, 24, 25

R

Radish ... 10
Rain ... 86
Rapt in mind ... 117
Ray 91, 93, 94, 95
Reality ...161, 166
Really eternal ... 61
Reason 13, 14, 15, 16, 17, 106, 115, 146, 168, 182, 190
Reasoning ... 1
Rebirth .. 9, 155
Rebuke 2, 20, 23, 27, 28
Receipt ... 121
Receptacle ... 150
Receptacle of happiness ... 150
Reception ... 170
Recognition 10, 29, 31, 105, 106, 107
Recognition of objects ... 105
Recollection 40, 114, 115, 116, 120
Recklessness ... 154
Reductio ad absurdum ... 1, 45
Reflection ... 7
Refuge 160, 166
Refuge and refugee ... 121
Refutation ... 142
Regressus ad infinitum ... 164
Regularity ... 30, 118

Page.

Regulation ...141, 142
Reinculcation 52, 53, 54, 215
Relation ... 135
Relation of refuge and refugee 121
Release 2, 6, 9, 81, 152, 153, 172
Reliable ... 54
Reliable person ... 5, 49
Reliability ... 54
Reliance ... 48
Remembrance ... 84, 168
Renouncing the proposition ...207, 210
Repelled ... 163
Repetition 53, 65, 207, 215
Residence ...159, 160
Right knowledge 1, 3, 19, 35, 36, 55
Ṛiṣi ... 5, 50
Ṛiṣi ṛiṇa ... 152
River ... 43
Rumour ... 3, 55

S

Śabda ... 3
Sacred books ... 8
Sacrifice ... 51, 152
Sâdhya ... 46
Śakya prâpti ... 14
Samâdhirâja Sûtra ... 167
Sambhava ... 3
Sameness ... 66
Sâṅkhya Philosophy ... 7
Sâṅkhyas 3, 12, 105, 117
Saṃs'aya ... 1, 14
Saṃs'aya vyudâsa ... 14
Saṃskâra ... 103
Sarvajit sacrifice ... 53
Satisfaction ... 11
Ṣatpakṣî kathâ ... 204
Savikalpaka ... 4
Savour ... 100

Page.

Saying too little ...207, 214
Saying too much ...207, 214
Scaffolds ... 25, 76
Scepticism ... 8
School ... 12
Screened ... 94
Scriptures 18, 19, 20, 90
Search of truth ... 173
Season ... 86
Seat of knowledge ... 119
Secondary meaning ... 153
Sacred fire ... 150
Seeds ... 173
Self-existent ... 145
Sense 4, 7, 12, 40, 60, 82, 84, 85, 90, 92, 97, 98, 90, 100, 102, 103, 107, 111, 161
Sense organ 8, 9, 13, 112
Sense perception ... 45
Sentiments ... 6, 9
Separately ... 29
Separation 9, 121, 113
Series ... 9
Series of reasons ... 185
Several marks ... 143
Shadow ... 22
Shamelessness ... 154
Shifting the proposition ...207, 209
Sidfting the reason ...207, 211
Shifting the topic .. 207, 211
Siddhânta ... 1
Significate ... 191
Sight ... 80
Sign ...121, 191
Silence ...207, 215
Similarity 4, 26, 43, 46
Simultaneous ... 33, 117

Page.

Simultaneous cognitions ... 112
Simultaneously 97, 106, 112
Simultaneous production ... 114
Sin ... 81
Single entity ... 143
Single thing ... 133
Śiraḥ ... 130
Site of operations of the soul 82
Sites ...6, 82, 91
Sixteen categories .. 1
Six-winged disputation ...204, 206
Skin ... 7
Sloth ... 154
Smell ...7, 12, 86
Smoke ... 4, 11
Smoky ... 13
Solution ... 22
Son ... 150
Soul 6, 8, 15, 38, 39, 80, 81, 82, 84, 85, 86, 88, 113, 116, 117, 118, 120, 135, 150, 153, 172
Soul is receptacle of happiness ... 150
Sound 7, 35, 60, 62, 63, 64, 65, 66, 67, 68, 100, 103, 104, 114, 130, 131, 163
Space ... 39
Speech ... 52
Special qualities ... 89 100.
Special practice of meditation 170
Spell ... 34, 184
Spiritual injunction ... 172
Splitting ... 49
Statements ...129, 204
State of formation ... 171
Statue of stone ... 129
Stealing ... 8

Page.

Step ... 138
Study ... 172
Stupidity 3, 9, 133, 134, 135 154,
Subject 180, 181, 187, 193, 194
Subject in dispute ... 106
Subservient ... 92
Substance 6, 43, 70, 90, 92, 124
Substitute ... 69
Substrata ... 104
Substratum ... 68
Succession 33, 107, 128
Successive annihilation ... 2
Summer ... 4
Summum bonum ... 172
Sun ... 4, 95
Supersensuous ... 91
Supreme felicity ... 1, 3
Supremacy ... 77
Sustain ... 115
Sustenance ... 77
Syllogism ... 13

T

Tactual ... 99
Tactual perception ... 41
Taking ... 76
Tallness ... 10
Tangibility ... 64
Tank ... 10
Tarka ... 1
Taste ... 7
Tautology 51, 52, 54
Teaching ... 64
Technicalities ... 6
Tenet ... 1, 13
Term ... 24, 26
Testimony 3, 5, 10, 29
" That " ... 76
Thing ... 94, 111

Page.

Thing denoted ... 186
Thorn ... 139
Thoughts 165
Time ... 39
Tongue ... 7
Touch 7, 80, 97, 126
Touching ... 13
Total absence ... 93
Totally ... 159
Tranquillity ... 2
Transcend ... 161
Transitory 105, 122, 123
Transmigration 3, 9, 13, 135
Transparency ... 96
Transparent consciousness ... 7
Treatise on knowledge ... 172
Tree ... 148
Trick ... 85
Troubles 152, 154, 155
True knowledge ... 2
True nature ... 1, 157
Trusted to the soul ... 153
Tryasareṇu ... 162
Twilight ... 10, 29
Type ... 211

U

Umpire ... 31
Unassailable ... 73
Unattended ... 138
Uncertainty 56, 57, 111
Uncommon properties ... 29
Undemonstrable ... 132
Understanding ... 149
Uneasiness ... 9
Unenvious persons ... 172
Uniformity ... 50
Unintelligible ...207, 212
Uninterrupted course ... 2

	Page.
Union	... 23, 26
Universal	... 27
Universality	... 163
Universal uniformity	... 50
Unlimited dimensions	... 164
Unmarked	... 58
Unnameable	... 3
Unobviousness	... 93
Unperceived	... 47
Unproved	... 22
Unreasonable	145, 150, 160, 186
Unsaid	... 193
Unsaid conclusion	... 193
Untenable	... 113
Untruth	... 51
Upakles'a	... 154
Upalabdhi	... 7
Upamâna	... 3
Uttara Kurus	... 49

V

Vacuum	... 68
Vâda	... 1
Vais'eṣikas	... 3
Vais'eṣika Philosophy	... 5
Valid	55, 106, 147
Validity	... 35
Vanquisher	... 29
Vapour	... 14
Varieties	... 68
Variety	... ,60
Vâtsyâyana	2, 3, 23, 35
Veda	51, 52, 54
Vedântin	... 3
Verbal	... 3
Verbal testimony	3, 5, 33, 49
Verbal trick	... 85
Vicinity	... 77
Veil	... 62
Vision	... 82
Visual	... 99
Visual perception	... 102
Vitaṇḍâ	... 1
Vocal actions	... 8
Voice	... 8
Volition	... 6

W

Warning	... 53
Water	4, 7, 10, 12, 96, 101
Watery	... 89, 102
Waxing	... 76
Web	... 165
Whole	42, 157, 158, 159, 160, 161
" Within "	... 163
Wife	... 150
" Without "	... 163
Word	5, 49, 50, 75, 76
World	... 2
Wrangler	... 20
Wrangling	1, 19, 20, 173

Y

Yoga institute	... 172
Yogâchâra Buddhist philosphy	165
Yogî	... 112
" Yava "	... 50

Z

Zeal for truth	... 173